CW00725128

The
HIDDEN INNS
of the
HEART OF ENGLAND

including
Derbyshire, Leicestershire, Lincolnshire,
Northamptonshire, Nottinghamshire,
Rutland, Staffordshire and Warwickshire

Edited by
Barbara Vesey

© Travel Publishing Ltd.

Published by:
Travel Publishing Ltd
7a Apollo House, Calleva Park
Aldermaston, Berks, RG7 8TN
ISBN 1-902-00751-4
© Travel Publishing Ltd

First Published: *2001*

Regional Titles in the Hidden Inns Series:

Central & Southern Scotland	Heart of England
Southeast England	South of England
Wales	Welsh Borders
West Country	Yorkshire

Regional Titles in the Hidden Places Series:

Cambridgeshire & Lincolnshire	Chilterns
Cornwall	Derbyshire
Devon	Dorset, Hants & Isle of Wight
East Anglia	Gloucestershire & Wiltshire
Heart of England	Hereford, Worcs & Shropshire
Highlands & Islands	Kent
Lake District & Cumbria	Lancashire and Cheshire
Lincolnshire	Northumberland & Durham
Somerset	Sussex
Thames Valley	Yorkshire

National Titles in the Hidden Places Series:

England	Ireland
Scotland	Wales

Printing by: Ashford Colour Press, Gosport

Maps by: © MAPS IN MINUTES ™ 2001 © Crown Copyright, Ordnance Survey 2001

Line Drawings: Sarah Bird

Editor: Barbara Vesey

Cover Design: Lines & Words, Aldermaston

Cover Photographs: Wheatsheaf Inn, Woodhouse Eaves, Leicestershire; The Blue Ball, Braunston, Rutland; The Windmill, Badby, Northamptonshire

FOREWORD

The *Hidden Inns* series originates from the enthusiastic suggestions of readers of the popular *Hidden Places* guides. They want to be directed to traditional inns "off the beaten track" with atmosphere and character which are so much a part of our British heritage. But they also want information on the many places of interest and activities to be found in the vicinity of the inn.

The inns or pubs reviewed in the *Hidden Inns* may have been coaching inns but have invariably been a part of the history of the village or town in which they are located. All the inns included in this guide serve food and drink and many offer the visitor overnight accommodation. A full page is devoted to each inn which contains a line drawing of the inn, full name, address and telephone number, directions on how to get there, a full description of the inn and its facilities and a wide range of useful information such as opening hours, food served, accommodation provided, credit cards taken and details of entertainment. *Hidden Inns* guides however are not simply pub guides. They provide the reader with helpful information on the many places of interest to visit and activities to pursue in the area in which the inn is based. This ensures that your visit to the area will not only allow you to enjoy the atmosphere of the inn but also to take in the beautiful countryside which surrounds it.

The *Hidden Inns* guides have been expertly designed for ease of use. *The Hidden Inns of the Heart of England* is divided into 10 regionally based chapters, each of which is laid out in the same way. To identify your preferred geographical region refer to the contents page overleaf. To find a pub or inn simply use the index and locator map at the beginning of each chapter which refers you, via a page number reference, to a full page dedicated to the specific establishment. To find a place of interest again use the index and locator map found at the beginning of each chapter which will guide you to a descriptive summary of the area followed by details of each place of interest.

We do hope that you will get plenty of enjoyment from visiting the inns and places of interest contained in this guide. We are always interested in what our readers think of the inns or places covered (or not covered) in our guides so please do not hesitate to write to us using the form at the back of the book. This is a vital way of helping us ensure that we maintain a high standard of entry and that we are providing the right sort of information for our readers. Finally if you are planning to visit any other corner of the British Isles we would like to refer you to the list of Hidden Inns and Hidden Places guides to be found at the rear of the book.

Travel Publishing

Locator Map

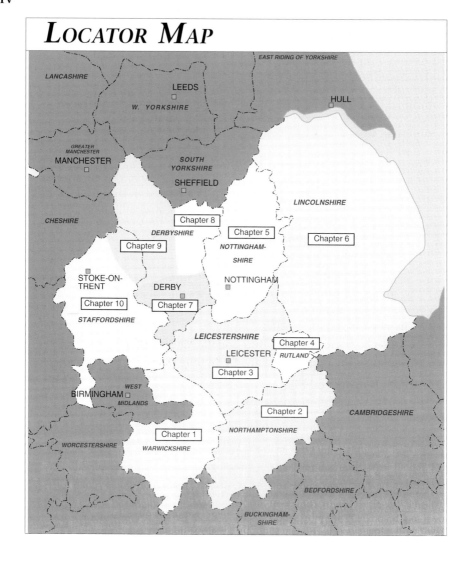

CONTENTS

1 Warwickshire

PLACES OF INTEREST:

Arbury Hall 3
Arrow 3
Bedworth 4
Charlecote 4
Compton Verney 5
Coughton 5
Dunchurch 6
Farnborough 6
Fenny Compton 6
Ilmington 7
Kenilworth 7
Kingsbury 8
Lapworth 8

Long Compton 8
Nuneaton 8
Royal Leamington Spa 9
Rugby 9
Ryton-on-Dunsmore 10
Stratford-upon-Avon 11
Upper Tysoe 13
Upton House 13
Warmington 13
Warwick 13
Wellesbourne 15
Wootton Wawen 16

PUBS AND INNS:

The Bear, Long Lawford 17

The Bell Inn, Welford-on-Avon 18

The Boat Inn, Newbold-on-Avon 19

The Boot Inn, Ansley Village 20

The Bridge, Napton 21

The Cock Horse Inn, Rowington 22

The Fox and Dogs, Warton 23

The Gaydon Inn, Gaydon 24

The Great Western, Southam 25

The Queens Head, Newton Regis 26

The Royal Oak, Whatcote 27

The Stags Head, Offchurch 28

The Hidden Inns of the Heart of England

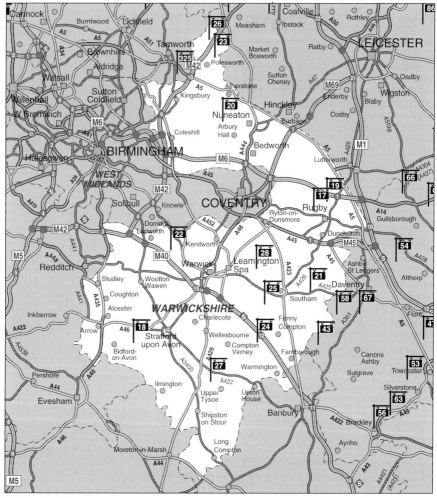

© MAPS IN MINUTES ™ 2001   © Crown Copyright, Ordnance Survey 2001

17 The Bear, Long Lawford		**23** The Fox and Dogs, Warton
18 The Bell Inn, Welford-on-Avon		**24** The Gaydon Inn, Gaydon
19 The Boat Inn, Newbold-on-Avon		**25** The Great Western, Southam
20 The Boot Inn, Ansley Village		**26** The Queens Head, Newton Regis
21 The Bridge, Napton		**27** The Royal Oak, Whatcote
22 The Cock Horse Inn, Rowington		**28** The Stags Head, Offchurch

Please note all references refer to page numbers

Warwickshire

Warwickshire is home to some outstanding country parks, woodland and waterways. The Oxford and Union Canals run through it, as do the Rivers Leam, Avon and Swift, all affording a wealth of boating and watersports facilities as well as some very peaceful and attractive walks along the towpaths and riverbanks. The county is also rich in history, having seen the hatching and foiling of the Gunpowder Plot in 1605, and some of the greatest battles of the English Civil War. The region also boasts many fine museums. A rich vein of medieval and Tudor history runs through the heart of Warwickshire. The romantic ruins of Kenilworth Castle, the grandeur of Warwick Castle and the elegance of Leamington Spa set the tone for this most delightful part of the county.

While Stratford will be the obvious focal point for most visitors to southern Warwickshire, the region boasts any number of lovely villages well off the beaton tourist track. Southern Warwickshire's waterways form an important and extensive part of the 2,000 miles of Britain's inland network. Quite apart from from the outstanding cultural and historic treasures in Stratford itself, there are many delights around the extremem southern edge of the county, which skirts the Cotswold Scarp and is dotted with the distinctive ochre-coloured ironstone cottages indigenous to this part of the world. The 'Heart of England Way' runs south from the remains of the historic Forest of Arden to the northeastern edge of the Cotswolds. As might be expected, this part of Warwickshire is rich in rural delights. Village after village along the Rivers Avon, Arrow or Alne, many relatively untouched since Tudor times, reflect some of the best traditional architecture and scenery to be found in the region. There are also several impressive hilltop views to be had along the way, revealing breathtaking views of the surrounding countryside.

For northeastern Warwickshire, Rugby - home of the famous public school which introduced the game of rugby football to the world - is the largest town, in an area predominated by smaller and very picturesque villages and hamlets.

PLACES OF INTEREST

ARBURY HALL

A visit to **Arbury Hall** fits another piece in the jigsaw of George Eliot's life and times. She was born on the estate, where her father was land agent; in *Mr Gifgil's Love Story* she portrays Arbury as Cheverel Manor, and gives detailed descriptions of many of the rooms in the house,

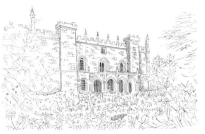

Arbury Hall

including the Saloon and the Dining Room - comparing the latter, unsurprisingly given its grandeur, to a cathedral. The Hall's grounds include a delightful 10 acre garden with a real air of tranquillity.

ARROW

The village of Arrow is interesting to stroll around (despite some development) - as is the pretty stream that divides Arrow and Alcester. Though fruit farming around here is much rarer than it used to be, there are still to be found delicious fresh dessert plums for sale in the late summer and early autumn.

Nearby **Ragley Hall** is a genuine 17th century treasure. The Warwickshire home of the Marquess and Marchioness of Hertford, it is a perfectly symmetrical Palladian house set in 400 acres of parkland and gardens landscaped by Capability Brown. One of England's great

4

Palladian country houses, it was inherited by the eighth Marquess in 1940 when he was only nine. During the Second World War the house was used as a hospital, and thereafter became almost completely derelict. In 1956 the Marquess married, and he and his wife set about making the Hall their home. All the main rooms have been redeco-

Ragley Hall

rated in colours similar to the original ones that would have been used, and the process of restoring and improving continues. Today, with all the interest generated in 17th century style and taste generated by the popularity of the works of Jane Austen as depicted in several television series, a lasting interest and enthusiasm for this 18th century microcosm would seem to be ensured.

This magnificent stately home boasts James Gibb's elegant Baroque plasterwork in the Great Hall, as well as Graham Rust's stunning 20th century mural, 'The Temptation'. A tour takes in Ragley Hall's fabulous collection of treasures from a bygone age, featuring paintings (including some modern art), china, furniture and a goodly assortment of Victorian and Edwardian dolls and toys. The Stables house an impressive carriage collection.

The main formal garden, to the west of the Hall, descends in a series of wide terraces, now entirely occupied by roses. The rest of the garden, covering 24 acres, consists of shrubs and trees interspersed with spacious lawns providing vistas across the 400 acre park. The lake, created in 1625, is now used for fishing, sailing, swimming and water skiing; there is also a lakeside picnic area. The cricket pitch is in regular use. A country trail of about two miles wends its way through the park and the woods, to end at a very popular adventure playground.

The Hall also boasts licensed terrace tea rooms. Special events such as craft fairs, gardeners' weekends, dog trials and outdoor concerts are held throughout the year.

BEDWORTH

This small town was once part of the North Warwickshire coalfield established at the end of the 17th century. Local people were largely responsible for the building of the **Coventry Canal**, running from Coventry to Fradley near Lichfield and completed in 1790, 22 years after work on it began. It was constructed to connect the fast-growing town with the great new trade route, the Grand Trunk - and to provide Coventry with cheap coal from the Bedworth coal field.

French Protestant families fleeing persecution sought refuge here, bringing with them their skill in silk and ribbon weaving. The parish church, completed in 1890, is a good example of Gothic Revival. Its grounds include a scented garden. The open air market and main shopping precinct share the town's central All Saints Square with the splendid Chamberlain almshouses, founded in 1663. Bedworth's award-winning **Miners' Welfare Park** contains some of the finest spring and summer bedding layouts in the region, as well as areas devoted to tennis, bowls, pitch and putt, roller skating and cricket.

CHARLECOTE

The National Trust's **Charlecote Park** is a magnificent stately home occupying extensive grounds overlooking the River Avon. Home of the Lucy family since 1247, the present house was built in the mid-16th century; Thomas Lucy was knighted here by Robert Dudley, Earl of Leicester, deputising for Elizabeth I, who spent two nights here in 1572. The house was comprehensively modernised during the 18th century, but when George Hamilton Lucy inherited it in 1823 he took the decision to 'turn the clock back' and create interiors according to rich Victorian 'Romantic' ideals of the Elizabethan era. The house, apart from the family wing which is still used by descendants of these early Lucys, has not been changed since. The lavish furnishings of the house include important pieces from William Beckford's Fonthill Abbey sale in 1823. A treasure-trove of historic works of sculpture and painting, no visitor can fail to be impressed by the house's sheer magnitude, grace and beauty. The park was landscaped by 'Capability' Brown and reflects his use of natural and man-made features complementing each other. The park supports herds of red and fallow deer (in about 1583 the young William Shakespeare is alleged to have been caught poaching Sir Thomas' deer; years later he is said to have taken his revenge by using Sir Thomas as his inspiration for the fussy Justice Shallow in *The Merry Wives of Windsor*), as well as a flock of Jacobs sheep first introduced here in 1756.

Charlecote Mill is situated on the site of an earlier mill mentioned in the Domesday Book, at which time it was valued at six shillings, eight pence. In 1978 this 18th-century building was restored with the help of volunteers from Birmingham, and the west waterwheel was repaired at the expense of the BBC for their film of George Eliot's novel, *The Mill on the Floss*.

COMPTON VERNEY

Before crossing the Fosse Way, the Roman road that runs from Exeter to Lincoln passes **Compton Verney Manor House**. For many years closed to the public, this magnificent manor has been renovated and is now open to visitors. An exquisite collection of works of art has been assembled, including British portraiture, European Old Masters and modern works, along with a unique collection of British Folk Art. Workshops, evening talks, lectures and special events bring to life the processes and inspiration behind some of these great works. The manor house stands in 40 acres of parkland landscaped by Capability Brown and rich in flora and fauna, with a lake, arbour, stirring stone obelisk, Victorian watercress bed, Cedar of Lebanon, and Adam Bridge. The handsome avenue of Wellingtonias lines what was once the entrance to the estate.

COUGHTON

The parish church of this very pretty village was built by Sir Robert Throckmorton between 1486 and 1518. It has six bells which were restored in 1976 but are still carried in their original wooden frame. Inside there are some interesting oddments: a faceless clock, fish weather vanes and a dole cupboard from which wheaten loaves were distributed to the needy.

The crowning glory of the village is one of the great Tudor houses, **Coughton Court**, home of the Throckmorton family since 1409. The family were very prominent in Tudor times and were instigators of Catholic emancipation, playing a part in the Gunpowder Plot - the wives of some of the Gunpowder Plotters awaited the outcome of the Plot in the imposing central gatehouse. This, and the half-timbered courtyard, are particularly noteworthy, while inside there are important collections of paintings, furniture, porcelain and other family items from Tudor times to the present day. Treasured possessions include the chemise of Mary Queen of Scots and the Throckmorton Coat; the former was worn by Queen Mary at her execution in 1587. The Coat was the subject of a 1,000 guinea wager in 1811. The priest's hole found in the house was constructed by one of the most famous builders of hiding places, Nicholas Owen.

This National Trust property has extensive gardens (a new formal walled garden and bog garden) and grounds, a lake, a riverside walk and two churches to add to the interest. The fountain Pool in the courtyard leads out to formal paths of lime trees. Spring heralds a magnificent display of over 100,000 daffodils and other spring blooms. The grounds also boast a walk planted with willows and native shrubs and trees beside the River Arrow, a new bog garden, a formal orchard and a walled garden project opened in 1996 and maturing into a splendid example of garden 'rooms' set with their own particular plant themes. One herbaceous border is planted with cools blues and yellows, the other with hot reds and orange.

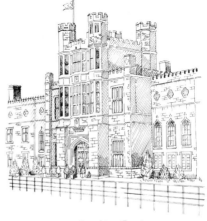

Coughton Court

The Hidden Inns of the Heart of England

6

Also on site there is the Tudor Restaurant serving coffee, lunches and teas, an attractive gift shop and a plant centre. Tel: 01789 400777

A little way east of Coughton, at Kinwarton just south of the B4089, there stands another National Trust property in the shape of **Kinwarton Dovecote**. This circular 14th-century dovecote still houses doves and retains its 'potence', a pivoted ladder by which access is possible to the nesting boxes. Visitors can home in every day from April to October.

DUNCHURCH

'The gunpowder plot village': on November 5th, 1605, the Gunpowder Plot conspirators met at the Red Lion Inn, Dunchurch, to await the news of **Guy Fawkes'** attempt to blow up the English Houses of Parliament. The Red Lion still exists today, as a private residence known as **Guy Fawkes House**. This attractive village with its rows of thatched cottages has a 14th-century church built by the monks of Pipewell Abbey, with one of the oldest parish registers in England.

Such was the considerable trade in looking after travellers who stopped over in Dunchurch during the great coaching days (up to 40 coaches a day stopped here), it is said that every property in the centre of the village was at some time an inn or ale house. For centuries Dunchurch has been a popular stopover point for travellers on the main Holyhead-London road. A coaching stop to take on fresh horses, Dunchurch was also the staging post for pupils, masters, parents and visitors travelling to Rugby School. Many famous and important people have stayed in the village over the centuries, including Princess Victoria, Longfellow, the Duke of Wellington and William Webb Ellis of Rugby Football fame. Today, the village is in a designated conservation area with a lovely village green complete with village stocks and maypole, charming 16th, 17th and 18th century buildings, many of which retain the traditional Warwickshire thatched roofs. In 1996 the village won the prestigious Best Kept Large Village in Warwickshire award.

The Old Smithy which stands on the Rugby Road, is believed to have been the inspiration for Henry Wadsworth Longfellow's poem '*Under the Spreading Chestnut Tree*'.

FARNBOROUGH

The National Trust's **Farnborough Hall** is a lovely honey-coloured stone house built in the mid-18th century and the home of the Holbech family for over 300 years. The interior features some superb plasterwork, and the delightful grounds include a terrace walk, 18th-century temples and an obelisk. Tel: 01295 690002

FENNY COMPTON

This charming village close to **Burton Dassett Hills Country Park** and just half a mile from the **Oxford Canal** provides endless opportunities for scenic walks along the edge of the **Cotswold Scarp**. Burton Dassett Park itself is distinguished by rugged open hilltops topped by a 14th-century beacon with marvellous views in all directions. Henley-in-Arden

Possibly the finest old market town in Warwickshire, its mile-long High Street brimming with examples of almost every kind of English architecture from the 15th century onwards, including many old timber-framed houses built with Arden oak. Little remains today of the Forest of Arden, the setting adopted by William Shakespeare for his *As You Like It*, as its stocks were diminished in the 18th century by the navy's demand for timber, but nothing could diminish the beauty of Henley itself.

The town emerged initially under the protection of Thurston de Montfort, Lord of the

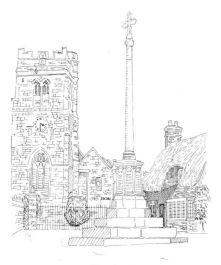

Dunchurch

Manor in 1140. **Beaudesert Castle**, home to the de Montfort family, lies behind the churches of St John and St Nicholas, where remains of the castle mound can still be seen. Famous visitors of the past to this delightful town have included Dr Johnson, his friend James Boswell, and the poet Shenstone.

The 15th-century **Church of St John the Baptist** has a tower which dominates the High Street where it narrows near the ancient Guildhall. The roof of the Guildhall is supported by oak beams which were growing at the time of the Norman invasion, and a wooden candelabra hangs from the ceiling. At one end of the hall is a huge dresser displaying a set of pewter plates dating back to 1677. The charter granted to the town has a royal seal embossed in green wax, kept in its own glass case in the Guildhall.

The town's **Court Leet** still meets yearly with the lord of the manor at its head, as it has for centuries. Members of this distinguished grouping have included the High Bailiff, Low Bailiff, Ale-taster (now there's a job!), Butter-weigher, the Mace bearer, the Town Crier, the Town Constable, the Two Affearers and the Two Brook Lockers. Just outside Henley lies **Beaudesert**, a village even older than its near neighbour Henley, with a good few timber-framed cottages and the beautifully restored Norman church of St Nicholas.

ILMINGTON

Along the northeastern Cotswolds, at the foot of the Wilmington Downs, you'll come to the village of Ilmington. This eye-catching place has several lovely old houses. Its part-Norman church, which features oak furnishings by Robert Thompson of Yorkshire, is approached through a Norman arch. This is truly a hidden place and one of the most picturesque one could hope to find. Lying in the valley between the Campden and Foxcote hills, it is surrounded by green fields and Cotswold countryside. Here there are fine old stone cottages with roses round the doors, and gardens full of colour. The village's name means 'the elm grown hill'. It was made famous on Christmas Day 1934, when the first radio broadcast by George V was introduced by Walton Handy, the village shepherd, and relayed to the world from **Ilmington Manor**, the fine Elizabethan house once owned by the de Montfort family. The remains of a tramway, once the main form of transport to the village, can still be seen.

The nearby **Ilmington Downs** are, at 850 feet, the highest point in the county, commanding fine views of the surrounding country. Across the B4632 you will pass **Meon Hill**, where an Iron Age fort stood dominating the valley.

KENILWORTH

Although the town was here before the Domesday Book was compiled, Kenilworth's name is invariably linked with its castle. Today the remains of this castle stand as England's finest and most extensive castle ruins, dramatically ensconced at the western edge of the town.

Kenilworth Castle's red sandstone towers, keep and wall glow with an impressive richness in the sun, particularly at sunrise and sunset. Here you can learn about the great building's links with Henry V (who retired to Kenilworth after the Battle of Agincourt), King John, Edward II and John of Gaunt. The tales of this great fortress, immortalised (if enhanced) in Sir Walter Scott's novel *Kenilworth* written in 1821, are many and varied. The marvellous Norman keep, the oldest part of the ruins, was built between 1150 and 1175. John of Gaunt's Great Hall once rivalled London's Westminster Hall in palatial grandeur. After Simon de Montfort's death at the Battle of Evesham in

Kenilworth Castle

8

1265, Kenilworth was held by his son. At that time the castle was surrounded by the Kenilworth Great Pool, a lake covering about 120 acres. Henry VIII's army failed in its attempts to storm the castle by using barges to cross the lake. Eventually the castle fell, after six months' siege, when starvation forced de Montfort to surrender.

An audio tour guides you on a revealing journey around the Castle, recounting stories of Kenilworth's turbulent past. There are fine views from the top of Saintlowe Tower, and lovely grounds for exploring and picnicking, as well as beautifully reconstructed Tudor gardens. Special events throughout the year include a festival of Tudor Music, Saxon and Viking exhibitions, medieval pageantry, various re-enactments, plays and operas in the grounds and much more. The remains of **Kenilworth's abbey** can be seen in the churchyard of the Norman parish church of St Nicholas in the High Street. Much of interest was discovered during excavations and there are many relics on display in the church, including a pig made of lead. It is said that this formed part of the roof at the time of the Dissolution, but was then melted down and stamped by the Commissioners of Henry VIII.

KINGSBURY

Kingsbury Water Park boasts over 600 acres of country park, with loads to see and do, including birdwatching, picnic sites, nature trails, fishing and good information centre. There is also a cosy cafe and special unit housing the park's shop and exhibition hall. Also within the park, Broomey Croft Children's Farm makes for an enjoyable and educational day out for all the family, with a wealth of animals housed in renovated early 19th-century farm buildings.

LAPWORTH

Here where the Grand Union and Stratford Canals meet, handsome Lapworth boasts some characterful old buildings. At Chadwick End, a mile west of the A4141, **Baddesley Clinton** is a romantic, medieval moated manor house which has changed little since 1633. Set against the backdrop of the Forest of Arden, this National Trust-owned property has had strong Catholic connections throughout its history. There is a tiny chapel in the house, and secret priests' holes, used to hide holy fathers during

the fiercely anti-Catholic times during the reign of Charles I. The grounds feature a lovely walled garden and herbaceous borders, natural areas and lakeside walks. More modern additions to the site include the second largest ice rink in the country. Lunches and teas are available.

LONG COMPTON

Just a short distance from the Oxfordshire border, this handsome village lies close to the local beauty spot known as **Whichford Wood**. It is a pleasant Cotswold village of thatched stone houses and some antique shops. A mile or so to the south of Long Compton, straddling the Oxfordshire border, are the **Rollright Stones**, made up of the King Stone on one side of the lane, with the other two stone groupings - known as the King's Men and the Whispering Knights - on the other. Legend has it that this well-preserved stone circle is a king and his men, tricked by a sorceress into falling under her spell, and then petrified.

NUNEATON

Originally a Saxon town known at Etone, Nuneaton is mentioned in the Domesday Book of 1086. The 'Nun' was added when a wealthy Benedictine priory was founded here in 1290. The Priory ruins left standing are adjacent to the church of St Nicholas, a Victorian edifice occupying a Norman site which has a beautiful carved ceiling dating back to 1485.

The town has a history as a centre for coal-mining, which began in Nuneaton as early as the 14th century. Other industries for which the town has been famous include brick and tile manufacture and ribbon-making on hand looms. As the textile and hatting industries boomed, the town began to prosper. Today's Nuneaton is a centre of precision engineering, printing, car components and other important trades.

Nuneaton Museum and Art Gallery, located in Riversley Park, features displays of archaeological interest ranging from prehistoric to medieval times, and items from the local earthenware industry. There is also a permanent exhibition of the town's most illustrious daughter, the novelist and thinker George Eliot.

Born to a prosperous land agent at Arbury Hall in 1819, Eliot (whose real name was Mary Ann Evans) was an intellectual giant and free thinker. She left Warwickshire for London in adulthood, and met George Henry Lewes, a writer and actor who was to become her life-long companion. Lewes, married with three children, left his family so that he and Eliot, very bravely for the time, could set up house together. Eliot's novels return again and again to the scenes and social conventions of her youth, and are among the greatest works of English - in particular her masterpiece, *Middlemarch*.

Three miles northwest of Nuneaton, **Hartshill Hayes Country Park** is an ideal place for exploring the developing rural attractions of this part of Warwickshire. Although surrounded by a network of roads, here visitors find only woodland trails and walks, and magnificent views. The park boasts 136 acres of woodland, meadow and open hilltop. Winner of the Forestry Authority's 'Centre of Excellence Award' in 1996, the park boasts three self-guided walks, an informative Visitors' Centre and truly wonderful views. Hartshill itself was the birthplace of the poet Michael Drayton (1563-1631).

Five miles west of Nuneaton, the village of **Ansley** is best known for adjacent **Hoar Park**, which dates back to the 1430s. The existing house and buildings date from 1730, and now form the centrepiece of the 143 acre Park, which contains a handsome **Craft Village**. The Park, as well as being a craft, antique and garden centre, is still a working farm.

ROYAL LEAMINGTON SPA

This attractive town boasts a handsome mixture of smart shops and Regency buildings. The Parade is undoubtedly one of the finest streets in Warwickshire. It starts at the railway bridge, dives between a double row of shops and comes up again at the place marked with a small stone temple announcing 'The Original Spring Recorded by Camden in 1586'. In 1801 very few people knew of the existence of Leamington, but by 1838 all this had changed. By this time the famous waters were cascading expensively over the many 'patients' and the increasingly fashionable spa was given the title 'Royal' by permission of the new Queen, Victoria. **The Pump Rooms** were opened in 1814 by Henry Jephson, a local doctor who was largely responsible for promoting the Spa's medicinal properties. This elegant spa resort was soon popularised by the rich, who came to take the waters in the 18th and 19th centuries. Immediately opposite the Spa itself are **Jephson's Gardens** containing a Corinthian temple which

houses a statue of him. The town's supply of saline waters is inexhaustible, and a wide range of 'cures' is available, under supervision, to this day.

Warwick District Council Art Gallery and Museum in Avenue Road boasts collections of pottery, ceramics and glass, as well as some excellent Flemish, Dutch and British paintings from the 1500s to the present.

RUGBY (DRAYCOTE, BRANDON)

The only town of any great size in northeastern Warwickshire. Rugby's **Market Place** is surrounded by handsome buildings which act as reminders of the town's origins during the reign of Henry III. The Church of St Andrew was built by the Rokeby family after their castle had been destroyed by Henry II. The old tower dates from the 1400s. With its fireplace and 3 foot-thick walls, it looks more like a fortress and was, indeed, a place of refuge.

Rugby is probably most famous for its **School**, founded in 1567. Originally situated near the Clock Tower in the town, it moved to its present site in 1750. Their are many fine buildings, splendid examples of their period, the highlight being the school chapel, designed by William Butterfield. These buildings house treasures such as stained glass believed to be the work of Albrecht Durer, the 15th-century German artist and engraver.

Rugby School

10

There are few places in the world where you can gaze with any certainty over the birthplace of a sport that gives pleasure to millions. The game of Rugby originated here at the school when William Webb Ellis broke the rules during a football match in 1823 by picking up and running with the ball. The **James Gilbert Rugby Museum** is housed in the original building where, since 1842, the Gilberts have been making their world-famous rugby footballs. This Museum is crammed with memorabilia of the game and its development.

James Gilbert Rugby Museum

Rugby Town Trail is a two-hour walk that brings to life the town's history from its Saxon beginnings to the present day. The walk begins and ends at the **Clock Tower** in Market Place. This edifice was intended to commemorate the Golden Jubilee of Queen Victoria in 1887, yet it was not completed until 1889 because over-indulgent citizens had dipped too deep into the Tower funds to feast and drink at the Jubilee. You will see many of the town's main tourist attractions, including the house where Rupert Brooke was born, and his statue in Regent Place. Caldecott Park in the centre of town has beautiful floral displays, trees and a herb garden. Picnicking areas and a play area are two more of the highlights of this lovely park, and there are also facilities for bowls, putting, tennis and boules.

Rugby is bounded by two of the greatest Roman roads, Fosse Way and Watling Street, which meet just northwest of Rugby, at **High Cross**, one of the landmarks of the area.

The town is as far inland as it is possible to get in the British Isles, yet Rugby is an excellent centre for all kinds of water sports and aquatic activities. The **Oxford Canal** winds its way through the borough, and the Rivers Avon, Leam and Swift provide good angling, pleasant walks and places to picnic.

Cock Robin Wood is a nature reserve on Dunchurch Road, near the junction with Ashlawn Road. Here the visitor will find extensive areas of oak, ash, rowan, cherry and field maples, as well as grassy areas and a central pond, a haven for insects, frogs and butterflies.

The **Great Central Walk** is a four-mile ramble through Rugby. Along the way visitors will encounter an abundance of wildlife, plants and shrubs, as well as conservation areas and picnic sites.

Four miles southwest of Rugby, **Draycote Water** is a centre of watersports, fishing, sailing, birdwatching and attractive walks around the reservoir. Fly fishing permits are available from the Fishing Lodge. **Draycote Country Park**, next to Draycote Water, boasts 21 acres for walks, kite flying, picnicking by the lake, and magnificent hilltop views over Draycote Water, one of the largest reservoirs in the region.

Six miles west of Rugby, **Brandon Marsh Nature Centre** is 200 acres of lakes, marshes, woodland and grassland, providing a home and haven for many species of wildlife. There are bird hides, an informative Visitor Centre and a nature trail, as well as guided walks, pond-dipping and changing exhibitions.

RYTON-ON-DUNSMORE

This village is home to the **Henry Doubleday Research Association** at Ryton Gardens. This organic farming and gardening organisation leads the way in research and advances in horticulture. The grounds are landscaped with thousands of plants and trees, all organically grown. Also on site are a herb garden, rose garden, garden for the blind, shrub borders and free-roaming animals. **Ryton Pools Country Park** is a 100-acre country park opened in 1996. The 10-acre Ryton Pool is home to great crested grebes, swans, moorhens and Canada geese. There is also an attractive meadow area for strolling or picnicking, a Visitor Centre, shop and exhibition area. **Pagets Pool** near the northeastern end of the park is one of the most important sites in Warwickshire for dragonflies, with 17 species including the common blue, emperor dragonfly and black-tailed skimmer. Other highlights include guided walks and a model railway run by Coventry Model Engineering Society.

STRATFORD-UPON-AVON

After London, many visitors to England put Stratford-upon-Avon next on their itinerary, and all because of one man. William Shakespeare was born here in 1564, found fame in London and then retired here, dying in 1616. This place where he was born and where he grew up is dominated by the great playwright and poet. Needless to say, the places connected with his life and work have become meccas for anyone interested in the cultural history, not just of these islands, but of the entire world.

Each of the houses associated with the Bard has its own fascinating story to tell, and staff at the houses are happy to guide visitors on a journey encompassing what life might have been in Stratford-upon-Avon during Shakespeare's day.

With the help of a £300,000 grant, the half-timbered house that is **Shakespeare's Birthplace** has been returned to the way it must have looked in his day. Household inventories, books and pictures have been assembled, and a room thought to have been his father John's workshop was been re-created with the help of the Worshipful Company of Glovers.

Shakespeare's Birthplace

Further along, on Chapel Street, stands **Nash's House**. This half-timbered building was inherited by Shakespeare's granddaughter, Elizabeth Hall, from her first husband, Thomas Nash. It now contains an exceptional collection of Elizabethan furniture and tapestries, as well as displays, upstairs, on the history of Stratford. The spectacular Elizabethan-style knot garden is an added attraction. Next door, in New Place, Shakespeare bought a house where he spent his retirement years, from 1611 to 1616. Today all

that can be seen are the gardens and foundations of where the house once stood. An exhibit in Nash's House explains why this, Shakespeare's final home in Stratford, was destroyed in the 18th century. Opposite New Place is the **Guild Chapel**, and beyond this is the Grammar School, where it is believed that Shakespeare was educated.

Hall's Croft in Old Town is one of the best examples of a half-timbered gabled house in Stratford. It was named after Dr John Hall, who married Shakespeare's daughter Susanna in 1607. This impressive house contains outstand-

Hall's Croft

ing 16th and 17th century furniture and paintings. There is also a reconstruction of Dr Hall's 'consulting room', accompanied by an exhibition detailing medicinal practices during Shakespeare's time. Outside, the beautiful walled garden features a large herb bed; visitors can take tea near the 200-year-old mulberry tree or have lunch in the restaurant here.

Hall's Croft is near **Holy Trinity Church**, an inspiration for many poets and artists because of its beautiful setting beside the River Avon. It is here that Shakespeare is buried. Dating partly from the 13th century, it is approached down an attractive avenue of limes. The north door has a sanctuary knocker, used in the past to ensure any fugitive who reached it 37 days' grace. Shakespeare's wife Anne Hathaway and their daughter Susanna and her husband John Hall are also buried here.

Shakespeare is not the only illustrious name to have associations with the town. **Harvard House** in the High Street, dating from 1596, was the childhood home of Katherine Rogers.

12

Her son, John Harvard, went to the American Colonies in the early 1600s and founded the university named after him in 1636. In 1909 Harvard House was restored and presented to Harvard University. It boasts the most ornately carved timbered front-

Harvard House

age in the town. Cared for by the Shakespeare Birthplace Trust, it houses the nationally important Neish Collection of Pewter.

There are many fascinating old buildings in Stratford. The old market site in Rother Street has a history dating from 1196, when a weekly market was granted by King John. In the square is an ornate fountain-cum-clock tower, a gift from GW Childs of Philadelphia in the jubilee year of Queen Victoria. It was unveiled by the actor Sir Henry Irving, who in 1895 became the first Knight of the Stage.

Stratford has become a mecca for theatre-lovers, who flock to enjoy an evening at one of the town's three theatres. The first commemoration of Shakespeare's passing was organised by the actor David Garrick (of Garrick Theatre and the Garrick Club fame), 150 years after the Bard's death. People have been celebrating this illustrious poet and playwright's life and times ever since. The **Royal Shakespeare Company** has an unrivalled reputation both in the UK and worldwide, and wherever the RSC perform,

the audience are certain of witnessing performances of the highest standard. **The Royal Shakespeare Theatre** opened in 1879 with a performance of *Much Ado About Nothing* starring Ellen Terry and Beerbohm Tree. The season was limited to one week as part of a summer festival. It was so successful that, under the direction of FR Benson, it grew to spring and summer seasons, touring the nation in between. In 1925, because of the excellence of the performances and direction, the company was granted a Royal Charter. Sadly, a year later the theatre perished in a fire. At the time, playwright George Bernard Shaw sent a one-word telegram: Congratulations! Apparently the building was a bit of an eyesore, but there are few such buildings in today's Stratford. The company, undeterred, continued by giving performances in cinemas while a worldwide fundraising campaign was launched to build a new theatre, which was opened on 23rd April, 1932, the 368th anniversary of the Bard's birth. A tour of the RSC theatre gives visitors the opportunity to discover what goes on behind the scenes and to see the RSC collection of over 1,000 items.

Quite apart from the industry that has grown around Shakespeare and his life and times, Stratford boasts a number of other world-class attractions. **Stratford's Butterfly Farm** is on Tramway Walk. Here, a specially designed and constructed habitat makes the perfect home for Europe's largest collection of butterflies. This indoor exotic tropical rain forest boasts rare blooms, waterfalls and fish-filled pools, and hundreds of the world's most spectacular and colourful butterflies fly around in perfect freedom. There is also an area devoted to Insect City, where stick insects, beetles, leaf-cutting ants, bees and many more of nature's little miracles can be seen. And for the brave of heart, Arachnoland is home to the deadly and dangerous spiders of the Amazon and elsewhere. Here, the world's largest spider, rain forest scorpion colonies and other 'spinners' can be seen in perfect safety.

The Royal Shakespeare Theatre Summer House on Avonbank Gardens is home to the **Stratford Brass Rubbing Centre**, which contains a large collection of exact replicas of brasses of knights and ladies, scholars, merchants and priests of the past. Admission is free; a small charge is made for the special paper and wax required.

One mile west of Stratford lies Shottery, the birthplace of Anne Hathaway, Shakespeare's wife. Here visitors will find the Elizabethan farmhouse now known as **Anne Hathaway's Cottage**, and can retrace the steps which the courting couple, who married in 1582, might have taken. The epitome of the traditional thatched cottage, this delightful spot has been home to Hathaways since the 15th century, up until some 70 years ago when the Shakespeare Birthplace Trust decided it was time to open up the home to the public. The Hathaway bed, settle and other pieces of furniture owned by the family remain, and there is a traditional English cottage garden and orchard - plants and herbs grown by the Shakespeare Trusts' gardeners can be purchased. Other attractions of this handsome village are the Shakespeare Tree Garden, the tranquil Shottery Brook, and well-laid-out Jubilee Walks.

Three miles northwest of Stratford, in the village of Wilmcote, stands another notable house connected with the poet is that of his mother, situated here in the village of Wilmcote, slightly off the well-beaten tourist track. **Mary Arden's House** is a striking Tudor farmhouse, now home to the Shakespeare Countryside Museum of farming and rural life. Note in particular the bread oven doors, which are made of bog oak, which never burns, and are seen only very rarely now in England. Special events and demonstrations of traditional sheep shearing, weaving and spinning, crook making and other country crafts are held throughout the year, as well as celebrations and entertainments based on accounts from Shakespeare's plays, in particular *A Winter's Tale*. Best of all, however, is the dovecote of the house. Robert Arden, who was lord of the manor, was in this capacity the only villager allowed to have one. It has over 600 pigeon holes and, at nesting time, would house about 3,000 birds.

Wilmcote is also one of the few small villages left which retains its Victorian Gothic railway station.

UPPER TYSOE

From Upper Tysoe there is a lovely walk south over **Windmill Hill** (which actually has a windmill on it), taking you to the church on the edge of **Compton Wynyates Park**, with views of the attractive Tudor manor below - a refreshing bit of brick building in this Cotswold-edge stone country.

UPTON HOUSE

13

Here on the border with Oxfordshire, **Upton House** is a late 17th-century National Trust property built of the mellow local stone. The house was remodelled in 1927-9 for the second Viscount Bearsted to house his growing art collection and also to modernise the premises. The collections in the house are the chief attractions, featuring paintings by English and Continental Old Masters including El Greco, Brueghel, Bosch, Hogarth and Stubbs. Brussels tapestries, Sèvres porcelain, Chelsea figures and 18th-century furnishings are also on display. In the fine gardens, in summer there can be seen the typically English scene of white-clad cricketers; in winter, the Warwickshire Hunt hold their meet.

WARMINGTON

The **National Herb Centre** enjoys a great location on the northern edge of the Cotswolds on the B4100 close to the Warwickshire-Oxfordshire border. A centre for research and development work for the UK herb industry, the site has been developed with an eye towards providing visitors with a fascinating range of activities and sights. The Plant Centre has one of the widest selections of plants, trees and shrubs with herbal uses in the country. The Herb Shop stocks a range of herbs, health foods and gifts, many produced on site.

WARWICK

Over the past ten centuries **Warwick Castle** has witnessed some of the most turbulent times in English history. From the era of William the Conqueror to the grand reign of Queen Victoria, the Castle has left us a fascinating legacy to enjoy today. Dominating the town, it is surely everyone's ideal of a medieval building, one of the country's most splendid castles and certainly one of the most visited. It still serves as a home as well as retaining the greater part of its original masonry. Standing by the River Avon, Warwick is in a good defensive position and became part of Crown lands as recorded in the Domesday Book in 1086. Much of the castle was destroyed during the Barons' revolt in 1264, led by Simon de Montfort, and the majority of the present castle dates from the 14th century. The towers at each end are very impressive - one is known as Caesar's Tower and is shaped rather like a clover leaf.

14

A tour of this palatial mansion takes you from the grim austerity of the original dungeons with their gruesome torture chambers to the gloomy but sumptuous opulence of rooms later adapted for comfortable living. The castle's magnificent State Rooms, once used to entertain the highest members of the nobility, house some superb art treasures including works by Holbein, Rubens and Velasquez. As the castle is owned by Madame Tussaud's, striking waxworks play their part in

Warwick Castle

the displays. In the castle's Ghost Tower, visitors can learn of the dark and sinister secrets surrounding the fatal stabbing of Sir Fulke Greville, said to haunt the premises to this day. In the Great Hall visitors come face to face with Oliver Cromwell's death mask. And the armoury houses one of the best private collections in the country.

The castle exterior is best viewed from **Castle Bridge**, where the 14th-century walls can be seen reflected in the waters of the River Avon. There is a walk along the ramparts, and much to explore within 60 acres of grounds, including a re-created Victorian formal rose garden, the Peacock Gardens and an expanse of open parkland designed by Capability Brown. Events throughout the year include **Medieval Tournaments**, open-air firework concerts and special entertainment days.

A strong link with the castle is found in the **Collegiate Church of St Mary** in Old Square, a splendid medieval church on the town's highest point. Of pre-Conquest origin, the church contains the magnificent fan-vaulted Beauchamp Chapel, built to house the monuments of Richard Beauchamp, Earl of Warwick, and his family. The chapel houses an outstanding collection of Warwickshire tombs, a chapter house and a Norman crypt (complete with

a tumbrel, part of a medieval ducking stool). In summer visitors can ascend the tower to enjoy the excellent views.

The centre of Warwick was rebuilt after a fire in 1694, and though many older buildings survived, the centre is dominated by elegant Queen Anne buildings. A walk around High Street and Northgate Street takes in some of the finest buildings, including **Court House** and **Landor House**. Court House on Jury Street houses the **Warwickshire Yeomanry Museum**, with displays of uniforms, arms, swords, sabres and selected silver, and Warwick Town Museum, which features changing exhibitions.

Some of the town's oldest structures can be found around Mill Street, an attractive place for a stroll, with several antique shops along the way. The **Mill Garden** at the end of Mill Street is home to a delightful series of plantings in a breathtaking setting on the Avon beside the castle. Here visitors will find a herb garden, raised beds, small trees, shrubs and cottage plants including some unusual varieties.

Warwickshire Museum in Market Place occupies a 17th-century market hall housing collections that illustrate the geology, wildlife and history of the county. Notable exhibits include giant fossils, live bees, ancient jewellery and the historic Sheldon Tapestry map of Warwickshire. Changing programmes in the ground floor gal-

The Doll Museum

leries offer exciting exhibitions of acclaimed local and national artists' work.

History of a different kind can be seen at picturesque **Oken's House**, an ancient building once owned by Thomas Oken, a self-made businessman who died childless in 1573 and left his fortune to found almshouses for the poor. Today his home houses The **Doll Museum**, just 100 yards from the castle in Castle Street. This carefully restored Elizabethan house is home to hundreds of dolls, teddies and toys from days gone by. Visitors can have a go at hopscotch or spinning tops, or hunt for Teddy's friends, while video bring the exhibits to life, demonstrating how all the mechanical toys on display work.

One of the most important buildings in Warwick is St John's House, dating from 1666 and considered a very good example of the period. Today the building houses a museum where visitors can find out how people lived in the past. Upstairs is the **Museum of the Royal Warwickshire Regiment**.

Two of Warwick's medieval town gateways survive, complete with chapels. Of these, Westgate Chapel forms part of **Lord Leycester's Hospital**, a spectacularly tottering and beautiful collection of 15th-century half-timbered buildings enclosing a pretty galleried courtyard. Inside, the main interest is provided by the

Lord Leycester's Hospital

Queen's Own Hussars Regimental Museum. This 600-year-old medieval treasure has a unique chantry

15

Chapel, magnificent Great Hall and Guildhall together with other timber-framed buildings, first established by the Earl of Leicester as an old soldiers' home in 1571. The candlelit chapel dates from 1123, and the Regimental Museum of the Queen's Own Hussars is another site of interest in this medieval masterpiece. The historic Master's Garden, featuring a Norman arch and 2,000 year-old vase from the Nile, is a spectacular summer attraction.

In the heart of Warwick, just 400 yards from the castle, the Lord Leycester Hotel occupies Grade II listed buildings steeped in history: in 1694 they halted the Great Fire of Warwick; in the 1700s they housed the Three Tons Inn; and by the 19th century they were elegant townhouses.

Warwick Racecourse in Hampton Street offers flat and National Hunt racing throughout the year. This picturesque racecourse makes a good day out for all the family, with a regular programme of 25 meetings throughout the year. The central grandstand incorporates the first stand built in 1809, among the oldest surviving in the country.

Three miles south of Warwick, set in lovely countryside with views over fields to the River Avon, **Sherbourne Park** is one of the very finest gardens in the county. Highlights of the gardens, which were designed by Lady Smith-Ryland in the 1950s, include a paved terrace covered by clematis, wisteria and a magnolia; an 'orchard' of sorbus trees; a box-edged, rose-filled parterre and the White Garden surrounded by yew hedges. The redbrick house of the Park is early Georgian, and the view is dominated by the parish church, built in 1863 by Sir George Gilbert Scott. Open on certain afternoons and by appointment. Tel: 01926 624255

WELLESBOURNE

Wellesbourne Wartime Museum is located on the site of a wartime airfield. On display are tools, ration books and an exhibit in the style of a contemporary battle operations control room. The **Wellesbourne Watermill** is a genuine brick-built working flour mill dating back to 1834. This restored mill on the River Dene, a tributary of the River Avon, is one of the few in the country which visitors can see working as

16

it did when new. A video presentation prepares visitors for the mill itself, providing an insight into this heritage site. Demonstrations of the art and skill of milling stoneground flour are enacted and explained by the miller, and visitors are encouraged to take part. Apart from the working demonstrations, there are guided walks alongside the river and two ponds, tree trails, and coracle boats along the river. There is also a display of antique farm implements, a craft shop, and a tea room in the wonderful 18th century timber-framed barn where teas and lunches are served.

WOOTTON WAWEN

Handy for walks on nearby **Stratford Canal**, Wotton Wawen also contains some fine timber-framed buildings. Views from the village encompass some outstanding vistas of the surrounding countryside.

The village's name is part Saxon in origin: the suffix 'Wawen' having been added to distinguish the village from other Wottons, and coming from the Saxon thane who held the land prior to the arrival of the Normans.

Situated in a hollow, the village is dominated by its church of St Peter. This impressive structure still has its Saxon tower and stands within a picturesque churchyard which has won the Diocesan 'Best Kept' award several times. The main building is actually three churches in one; there are three completely separate chapels tacked on to each other with a refreshing disregard for architectural design which does not in any way detract from the church's charm. Next to the church stands **Wootton Hall**, dating from 1637. Maria Fitzherbert, wife of George IV, spent her childhood here and is thought now to return in ghostly form as the 'Grey Lady' who has been seen wandering about the Hall.

The Bear 17

Bilton Lane,
Long Lawford,
near Rugby,
Warwickshire
CV23 9DU
Tel: 01788 522297

Directions:

Long Lawford is off
the A428, 2 miles
west of Rugby

The Bear is a modern, smart inn, no more than twelve years old, with a fine reputation in the area. Built of red brick, it combines all that is best in traditional English hospitality with modern decor and up to-the-minute facilities. The inside is carpeted throughout, with gleaming wood furnishings and fixtures, subdued wall lighting, and an atmosphere that speaks of quality, comfort and relaxation. And, without giving anything away, look out for the "Legends Corner"!

The place has been run for over two years now by the partnership of Matt and Vicki Warwick and Ian and Pat Goring. Between them, they've managed to create a delightful inn of great charm - one that won't disappoint the visitor. Head chef Justin Law, does the cooking, and there's an extensive printed menu complemented by a daily specials board. The specialities of the house are the 48 oz steaks and the 30 oz mixed grills, which almost overflow the plates. Not many people finish these, and if they do manage it, a bell is rung, they get their photograph taken, and get a free drink and pudding. Both dishes are cooked to perfection, so maybe ringing that bell isn't so hard to do after all! The inn stocks four real ales - Bombadier, from Charles Wells, Eagle Smooth and two guest ales. You can also buy Fosters, Red Stripe, Carlsberg, Kirin (Japanese, and very strong!), Woodpecker, Strongbow and Guinness.

It's not often you find a modern inn that has bags of character. But The Bear certainly does - one visit will convince you of that.

Opening times: Open all day, six days a week; closed Monday lunchtimes except bank holidays

Food: Served 17.30-21.00 on Monday; 12.00-14.00 and 17.30-21.00 from Tuesday, to Thursday; 12.00-14.30 and 17.30-21.45 on Friday and Saturday; 12.00-21.00 (12.00-16.00 roast dinners only) on Sunday

Credit cards: All major credit cards accepted

Facilities: Car park

Accommodation: None

Entertainment: Quiz night every Sunday at 20.00; Saturday barbecues throughout summer, weather permitting ; pool; darts

Local Places of Interest/Activities: Rugby (historic town) 1 mile; Stanford Hall 7 miles; Coventry (historic city) 19 miles; Draycote Water Country Park (sailing and fishing) 4 miles

18   The Bell Inn

Binton Road,
Welford-on-Avon,
Warwickshire
CU37 8EB
Tel: 01789 750353
Fax: 01789 750893

Directions:

Take the B439 west from Stratford-upon-Avon; after four miles turn left onto a minor road signposted to Welford-on-Avon.

Within a building dating from the 17th century, **The Bell Inn** is at the centre of the picturesque village of Welford-on-Avon, with it's thatched cottages and a delightful lych-gate into the churchyard. Colin and Teresa Ombler have owned the inn for six years, and have succeeded in making a delightful stop for a quiet drink or a meal, (being one of 6 finalists in The Publican Catering Pub of the Year, this year), while exploring Shakespeare Country or the lovely Cotswolds, which are on its doorstep. It has everything a good country pub should have - open log fires which makes the place warm and cozy in winter, low ceilings with exposed beams, flagstone floors and oak furniture. There are always fresh flowers everywhere in summer, and it has a spacious dining area.

So popular is the inn for meals that you are well-advised to book a table in advance. There is a well thought out menu containing everything from sirloin steaks (cooked to your requirements) to delicious salads and sandwiches. On Sunday there is a traditional lunch of roasts and vegetables in season, all prepared on the premises from fresh, local produce when available. The Bell is justly proud of its reasonably-priced wine list, and it has a wide range of ales and ciders to suit all tastes.

The Bell Inn sits at the heart of an area steeped in history, and there are many small, picturesque villages to explore. Within an hour's drive there are towns and cities such as Birmingham, Coventry, Stratford-upon-Avon, Worcester and Evesham. Warwick and Leamington Spa are also close by, and were made famous by the popular TV series "Dangerfield".

Opening Hours: Mon-Thu 11.30-15.00, 18.30-23.00; Fri-Sat 11.30-15.00, 18.00-23.00; Sun 12.00-16.00, 19.00-22.30

Food: Extensive menu with regularly changed specials board. Available daily up to 14.30 lunchtimes (15.00 on Sunday) and 21.30 evenings

Credit Cards: Access; Visa; Master Card; Switch; Solo

Facilities: Large Car Park

Accommodation: None

Local Places of Interest/Activities: Coughton Court (NT), 7 miles; Ragley Hall, 5 miles; Mary Arden's House, 4 miles; Shakespeare's Birthplace, Stratford-upon-Avon, 4 miles; Charlecote Park (NT) 7 miles

Internet/Website:
www.thebellwelford.co.uk
e-mail: info@thebellwelford.co.uk

The Boat Inn | 19

62 Main Street,
Newbold-on-Avon,
Warwickshire
CV21 1HW
Tel: 01788 576995

Directions:

Newbold-on-Avon
is two miles north
of Rugby on the
B4112

This delightful inn is situated only 100 yards from the Oxford Canal, and was formerly the place where the horses which pulled the barges along the canal were stabled. It's a white-washed building dating originally from the 17th century, and has a colourful, welcoming look to it. Inside is equally as delightful, with low ceilings, old panelling, country style furniture and open fires. In fact, just the kind of place to have a meal or a quiet drink. Look out for one area in particular. It has a wonderful and sometimes fanciful collection of memorabilia and objets d'arts around the walls - everything from old bread bins, framed prints, walking sticks, books, jugs and even chamber pots!

The Boat Inn has been under the personal management of Dax and Christine Miller since the beginning of 2001, and it is their first venture in the trade. Dax is an excellent cook, and most of the items on the menu are prepared on the premises by him from good, fresh produce (try his steaks - they are tender and full of flavour). The restaurant area seats 36, and so popular is the place that you need to book if you wish to eat on Saturday or Sunday. You have the choice from two real ales (Marston Pedigree and Boddington), plus Worthington Creamflow, Carling, Stella, Strongbow and Guinness.

This is an excellent, well maintained inn, with comfortable seating and plenty of room in which to relax. But one thing will no doubt worry you about the place. The place is spotlessly clean, so where do they find the time to dust down that amazing collection of memorabilia?

Opening times: Open all day, every day

Food: Served 12.00-14.00 and 18.30-21.30 from Monday to Saturday; 12.00-15.00 on Sunday. No food served on Sunday evening; Mondays and Tuesdays are steak nights

Credit cards: All major credit cards accepted

Facilities: Car park

Accommodation: None

Entertainment: Pub games; occasional entertainment on Sunday evenings; ring for details

Local Places of Interest/Activities: Rugby (historic town) 2 miles; Stanford Hall 6 miles; Coventry (historic city) 10 miles; Draycote Water Country Park (sailing and fishing) 6 miles

20   The Boot Inn

Birmingham Road,
Ansley Village,
near Nuneaton,
Warwickshire
CV10 9PL
Tel: 02476 392349

Directions:

Ansley is on the
B4112, 4 miles west
of Nuneaton

The Boot Inn is an old coaching inn which is steeped in history. It's whitewashed, picturesque front, complete with bow windows, dates from 1688, and its rear, which was once the stable block, dates from the 18th century. It's name was changed to "The Wellington Boot" after the Battle of Waterloo, but this was changed back in the 19th century. The inn is owned and run by Alan and Margaret Fellows, who have retained all the period features while adding modern touches of their own, so that it has become popular with tourists and regulars alike

The interior is equally as appealing and historic. The immense oak beams that give the place its charm are old ship timbers, and during a recent refurbishment, shoes and tools were found in one of the chimney breasts, believed to have belonged to a young sweep who died in the chimney. They were subsequently put on display, and have become a talking point for people visiting for the first time. In addition, the charming lounge was once a bakery, though it is now a comfortable place to relax and enjoy a quiet drink. At least five reals ales are on offer at the bar, including Highgate Mild, Tetley, Bass and two rotating ales. Plus there is Creamflow, Carlsberg, Carlsberg Export, Strongbow and Guinness. The dining area can seat 40 people in comfort, and the food is excellent. You can choose from the menu or the daily specials board, with the inn's fish dishes and home made steak pie being the favourites. On Sunday there's a traditional roast, though booking for this, and for Saturday meals, is recommended. Behind the inn is Oakridge Golf Club, built and co-owned by Alan. It is open to the public.

Opening times: Open lunchtimes and evenings from Monday to Thursday and all day on Friday, Saturday and Sunday in winter; open all day, every day in summer

Food: Served 12.00-14.30 and 17.00-21.30 in winter; served all day in summer; no food is served after 16.30 on Sunday

Credit cards: All major credit cards accepted

Accommodation: 5 rooms (not en suite) available; tariff includes breakfast

Facilities: Car park; golf course; occasional barbecues in summer, beer garden

Local Places of Interest/Activities: Hartshill Hayes Country Park 2 miles; NEC Birmingham 8 miles; Nuneaton (historic town) 4 miles; Coventry (historic city) 8 miles; Arbury Hall (George Eliot associations) 3 miles, Astley Castle 1½ miles, Bosworth Field 5 miles

The Bridge   21

Southam Road,
Napton,
Warwickshire
CV47 8NQ
Tel: 01926 812466

Directions:

Follow the A425 from
Southam towards
Napton for three
miles. The inn is
beside Bridge 111 on
the Oxford Canal.

Canalside inns are one of England's great glories, and **The Bridge** (formerly called the Napton Bridge) is no exception. It sits beside the Oxford Canal, which is a favourite for leisure cruising and waterway holidays. With its rendered brick exterior, the inn is a favourite with locals and holidaymakers alike. The grounds of the inn run down to the busy canal, and there's nothing more relaxing than sitting, drink in hand, watching the canal traffic go slowly past.

The interior is equally as inviting. Mine host Bob Peters has created a comfortable and cozy atmosphere, though all the areas are surprisingly roomy. There's even a separate dining room if you want to try the inn's excellent cuisine. Every year the place is spruced up by giving it a fresh lick of paint, which means that it always looks clean and inviting.

The food is prepared on the premises, and is excellent value, with an extensive and ever-changing menu. But one thing doesn't change, and that's the quality, which is quite superb. But be warned - so popular is the place on a Sunday for the traditional Sunday lunch of roast and vegetables that you are well advised to book in advance!

The village of Napton-on-the-Hill is typically English, with its village green and old church. The "hill" is over 500 feet high, though it looks more because of the surrounding flat countryside. On top is the tower of a derelict mill, which can be seen for miles around.

Opening Hours: 12.00 - 15.00, 18.30- 23.00, Mon-Sat. Sunday 12.00-21.00 in summer and 12.00-16.00 in winter

Food: Extensive menu.

Credit Cards: All major cards

Accommodation: None

Facilities: Canal moorings, play area, large garden, car park

Local Places of Interest/Activities: Rugby 8 miles; Draycote Water 4 miles; Burton Dassett Hills Country Park 6 miles; Heritage Motor Centre at Gaydon 7 miles.

22 The Cock Horse Inn

Old Warwick Road,
Rowington,
Warwickshire
CV35 7AA
Tel: 01926 842183

Directions:

Rowington is on the
B4439, 6 miles
north west of
Warwick

Built of warm red brick, **The Cock Horse Inn** is the epitome of traditional English inns. It dates back to the 18th century, with many interesting features, and up until the 1930s was called simply The Cock. The picturesque outside is echoed in its interior. Low ceilings, an inglenook fireplace and flagstoned floors vie to catch your attention in this charming hostelry. Wendy and David Preston have only been in charge a short while, though Wendy has a wealth of experience in the trade. They want to preserve all that is best about the place - its period fittings, its fine food and its warm welcome - while introducing touches of their own that will enhance its already fine reputation.

There are specials boards and two menus - one for bar lunches, and one for the 28 seat no smoking restaurant, where children are welcome. All feature cooking at its best. The bar lunch menu includes such dishes as steak and ale pie, gammon steak, scampi and chicken chasseur, plus sandwiches, "lite bites" and vegetarian dishes. The restaurant menu offers a fine selection of starters, plus rack of lamb, fillet steak Rossini, fresh fillet of salmon and so much more. So popular is the place that if you want to eat in the restaurant, you are advised to book. There's an extensive wine list, or you can order from a range of four real ales (Flowers, Bass and Ansells and weekly guest ales). The bar also stocks Tetley Smooth, Carlsberg, Stella, Guinness and Dry Blackthorn. This inn is truly a hidden gem. If you decide to visit, you'll be assured of good food, fine drink and a warm welcome from Wendy and David.

Opening times: Open during lunchtimes and in the evening over 7 days, except for summer, when it is open all day on Saturday and Sunday

Food: Bar food is served Monday to Saturday from 12.00-14.00 and 18.00-21.00, and on Sunday from 12.00-16.00 (no food Sunday evenings); the á la carte menu is available in the restaurant Tuesday to Saturday between 18.00-21.00

Credit cards: All major credit cards accepted

Accommodation: None

Facilities: Car park beer garden; children's play area

Entertainment: Live entertainment will be available in the future; ring for details

Local Places of Interest/Activities: Warwick (historic town) 6 miles; Leamington Spa (historic town) 7 miles; Baddesley Clinton (NT) 2 miles; Packwood House (NT) 3 miles

The Fox and Dogs
23

Orton Road,
Warton,
near Tamworth,
Staffordshire
BT79 0HT
Tel: 01827 892448

Directions:

Take the B5000 east from Tamworth, then turn north at Polesworth onto a minor road until you reach Warton, one mile along

The Fox and Dogs is a classic, handsome whitewashed English inn. It's well proportioned front, with two large bay windows, looks out onto the road, and has been welcoming visitors for over 200 years. Before it became a hostelry, it housed a blacksmith's shop, though all evidence of this has long since gone. The inside is a delight. Think olde worlde, and you've got the picture. Stout, gnarled oak beams grace the ceilings, there is a wealth of shining brass and copper (including the table tops), memorabilia crowds every corner, feature walls are bare brick, and an open fire offers a warm welcome in the winter months.

Mine host Sylvia Allbrighton worked in the Fox and Dogs for five years before she and her husband Richard took over not so long ago. Since then they have been working hard on creating a hostelry that is popular with regulars and visitors alike - one that offers a warm welcome, true hospitality and value for money. The food is first class and filling, with the inn specialising in home made dishes such as steak pie (a favourite here!), which are prepared on the premises. You can choose from the menu or a daily specials board, and everything is piping hot, with ample portions. Children are welcome if you're dining, and you can eat throughout the inn, or, in the summer months, in the huge beer garden at the rear. On a Friday, Saturday or Sunday you are well advised to book in advance, as the place is very popular. To accompany your meal, you can choose from a fine selection of wines, or from two real ales (Marston's Pedigree and guest ale). There is also Banks Mild, Banks Smooth, Fosters, Stella, Strongbow and Guinness.

Opening times: All day, every day

Food: Served Tuesday to Saturday (and Mondays in the summer months) 12.00-14.45 and 18.00-20.45; Sunday: 12.00-14.45; no food on Sunday evenings

Credit cards: Cheques and cash only

Accommodation: None

Entertainment: Occasional quizzes; karaoke on the last Friday of the month; live bands out of doors in summer; bonfire on November 5

Facilities: Car park; large beer garden; children's play area

Local Places of Interest/Activities: Twycross Zoo 2 miles; Middleton Hall 6 miles; Ash End House Farm (children's farm) 8 miles

24   The Gaydon Inn

Banbury Road,
Gaydon,
Warwickshire
CV35 0HA
Tel: 01926 640388

Directions:
Gaydon is on the
B4100, 10 miles
north west of
Banbury

The Gaydon Inn is a classic roadside hostelry which is full of history. It was originally a coaching inn, and a favourite meeting place for cut throats and highwaymen. A band of robbers called the Culworth gang were active close to the inn, under the leadership of John Smith, who was subsequently hanged in Northampton. His son, also called John, took up highway robbery as well, and carried out a daring hold-up at the Gaydon Inn. He was hanged at Warwick. And it's thought that another famous Warwickshire highwayman called Tom Hatton frequented the inn as well.

Steve and Lorraine Richens have been in charge since February 2001, and, while retaining all the period features, have brought their own ideas on how to improve the place even further. The food is first class, with ample portions and dishes that are always beautifully cooked. There's a pleasant non smoking dining area that can seat up to 24 people in comfort, though you can eat in the bar area or in the beer garden in summer if you wish. This is a favourite place for dining out, and if you want a meal, you are advised to book for Friday and Saturday evenings and Sunday lunchtime. You can order from a printed menu, or chose from the popular specials board, and children are always welcome. The bar stocks three real ales (Bass, Brew X1 and a rotating guest ale) plus Caffreys, Worthington Creamflow, Tetley Smoothflow, Guinness, Carling, Carlsberg and Stowford Press Cider. You won't find any highwaymen at the Gaydon Inn any more, thank goodness. What you will find is a warm welcome, tradition aplenty, comfortable surroundings, value for money and a wonderful place in which to eat or have a relaxing drink.

Opening times: Open lunchtimes and evenings from Monday to Thursday, and all day on Friday, Saturday and Sunday

Food: Good food is served from 12.00-14.30 and 18.00-21.00 Monday to Saturday ; 12.00-16.00 on Sunday; no food on Sunday evenings

Credit cards: All major credit cards accepted except American Express and Diners

Accommodation: None

Entertainment: Occasional entertainment on Saturdays; ring for details

Facilities: Beer garden; car park

Local Places of Interest/Activities: Heritage Motor Centre in village; Stratford upon Avon 11 miles; Charlecote Park (NT) 7 miles; Burton Dassett Country Park 2 miles

The Great Western 25

Deppers Bridge,
Southam,
Warwickshire
CU47 2ST
Tel: 01926 612355

Directions:

Take the A425 west from just south of Southam; turn left at the roundabout onto the B4451 for Bishop's Itchington; the inn is next to the bridge over the railway, about three miles along the road.

This inn is ideal for people with a love of railways. Not only is it named after a famous old railway company, it sits beside a bridge over the main line from Birmingham and Leamington Spa south to Oxford and London. And to continue the theme, at the foot of the inn garden, there was once a railway station. Outside the inn there is a full-size Hudswell Clarke 0-4-0 DM type D604 diesel shunter of 1936, awaiting restoration. There is even an overhead O gauge model railway on the premises, and suitable Great Western railways prints on the wall.

But even if you're not into railways, The Great Western is still an attractive and popular place for a meal or a quiet drink. The interior decor of green and cream, giving the place a cozy and comfortable atmosphere. It's food is outstanding, and owners Catherine and Laurence Williams have put together an excellent menu from fresh produce, which is sourced locally wherever possible. Dishes include king prawns in filo pastry, steaks, mixed grills, cajun chicken, battered cod and Barnsley chop glazed with a mint and redcurrant jelly. There are also bar meals and snacks, and in the summer months there are cook-your-own barbecue meals in the garden. To accompany your food, there's an excellent selection of wines, beers (including real ale) and spirits.

The Great Western is in an attractive part of Warwickshire, within driving distance of many delightful towns and cities, such as Warwick, Rugby, Leamington Spa, Coventry and Stratford-upon-Avon. The surrounding villages are equally as attractive, many having thatched cottages and medieval churches which are worthy of a visit.

Opening Hours: Mon-Fri 12.00-14.30, 17.30-23.00; Sat 12.00-23.00; Sun 12.00-22.30

Food: Extensive menu

Credit Cards: All major cards

Accommodation: None

Facilities: Climbing equipment for children in the garden

Entertainment: Regular jazz and country music events.

Local Places of Interest/Activities: Burton Dassett Hills Country Park 4 miles; Newbold Cormyn Leisure Centre 6 miles; Leamington Spa Pump Room 7 miles; Heritage Motor Centre at Gaydon 3 miles.

26 | The Queens Head

Main Road,
Newton Regis,
near Tamworth,
Staffordshire
B79 0NF
Tel: 01827 830271
Fax: 01827 830609

Directions:

Take the B5493 south
from Junction 11 on the
M40, and after 3 miles
turn east onto a minor
road for Newton Regis

This substantial inn has been under the personal management of Michael and Debbie Rhodes for the last four years, and during that time they have managed to create a hostelry that combines old world charm with the modern concepts of service and value for money. Parts of the building are over 400 years old, and many period features have been retained. The basic building material is old, red brick, with a whitewashed facade and windows are small paned and picturesque.

Inside **The Queens Head** the theme is continued, with low ceilings, stout oak beams, a wealth of old ornaments, and plates and prints adorning the walls. The furniture is comfortable, with upholstered benches along the walls of the lounge, and the bar is as snug and warm as you would wish. The cuisine is traditional English, with a few foreign influences thrown in. Everything is prepared on the premises from fresh produce, and you can choose from a printed menu or from a daily changing specials board. There is also a vegetarian menu, and children are more than welcome if you're eating. The specialities of the house are its steak and fish dishes, and the regulars will tell you that you can't go wrong if you order one of them! The Sunday roast is also popular. Michael and Debbie don't accept bookings, so turn up early! You can order wine with your meal, or you can choose from four real ales (Bass, Brew X1, Highgate Mild and a rotating guest ale. Other drinks include Worthington Creamflow, Caffreys, Carling, Stella, Guinness, Woodpecker and Strongbow.

Opening times: Open at lunchtimes and evenings over seven days

Food: Good food is served Monday to Saturday between 12.00-14.00 and 18.00-21.30 and on Sunday from 12.00-14.00 and 19.00-21.30; no bookings accepted

Credit cards: Cash and cheque only at present

Accommodation: None

Entertainment: Darts; dominoes; crib; pool table. Quiz night every second Monday at 20.30.

Facilities: Car park; beer garden;

Local Places of Interest/Activities: Tamworth (historic town) 5 miles; Twycross Zoo 4 miles; Battlefield Line (old railway) 6 miles

Internet/website:
e-mail: rhodesqueens@aol.com

The Royal Oak | 27

Whatcote,
nr Shipston-on-Stour,
Warwickshire
CU36 5LF
Tel: 01295 680319

Directions:

Take the A3400
north from
Shipston-on-Stour
for a mile, then
turn right onto the
minor road for
Honington;
Whatcote is about
four miles further
on.

Think of an attractive, village pub, snug in winter and with a welcoming outdoor area for the summer months, and you could be thinking of the **The Royal Oak**. It describes itself as "quite small", but this is surely one of its plus points. It sits at the heart of the small, attractive village of Whatcote, and is built of mellow stone with ivy-clad walls. Inside the country feel is continued with low, beamed ceilings and a roaring fire in the winter months. It is well run and - always a good sign - is popular with the locals. If you visit, you'll be in good company - this is one inn where Oliver Cromwell really did stay in the 17th century!

The Royal Oak's food is delicious and beautifully prepared. It is justly famous for its ribeye steaks, which can be cooked to your requirements. Only the best beef from the Orkney Islands is used. And there's a fine selection of wines, spirits and ales (including real ale) to accompany your meal.

Whatcote is in itself interesting. It's 600-year old church of St Peter must have been the only country church in England to have been destroyed by a German bomb. During the Coventry air raid in 1940, a German plane jettisoned one of its bombs over the village, hitting the church. It has now been carefully rebuilt.

Whatcote is an easy drive from many Midlands towns. Banbury is twenty minutes away, as is Stratford-upon Avon and Leamington Spa. And the small market town of Shipston-on-Stour, four miles to the south, is well worth exploring.

Opening Hours: 12.00 - 15.00 (closed Mon), 17.30 - 23.00; Sun 12.00 - 15.00, 19.00 - 22.30

Food: A limited but well thought out menu.

Credit Cards: All major cards

Accommodation: None

Local Places of Interest/Activities: Edgehill Battlefield 4 miles; Hidcote Manor 5 miles; Rollright Stones 9 miles; Upton House (NT) 4 miles.

28   The Stags Head

Welsh Road,
Offchurch,
nr Leamington Spa,
Warwickshire
CV33 9AQ
Tel: 01926 425801

Directions:

From the centre of Leamongton Spa take the A425 towards Southam. After 2 miles turn left into Offchurch

Traditional English inns don't come any more traditional looking than this. Old white-washed walls, a thatched roof, tall brick chimneys, hanging baskets - **The Stags Head** has got the lot. Not surprisingly, this picture postcard building dates back to the 16th century, with later sympathetic additions, such as a comfortable conservatory. The inside equally as appealing and delightful, with everything spotlessly clean and well maintained, thanks to mine host Mel Best, who has been in charge since May 2000. There are low ceilings, stout oak beams, subdued wall lighting, polished woodwork, open fires, a carpeted lounge that is both comfortable and snug, and a conservatory that has been tastefully furnished and decorated to fit in with the period features. In fact, it's the ideal hostelry in which to have a quiet, relaxing drink or a meal.

The Stags Head has a great reputation in the area for its food, and has a menu and daily specials board that includes many delicious home made dishes, such as salmon fish cakes and juicy steaks. All are beautifully cooked from fresh produce that is sourced locally if possible, and the portions are ample and filling. You can eat throughout the inn, though there is a dedicated dining area and a no smoking conservatory that sits 30 people in comfort. If you're eating, children are welcome. The bar always carries a minimum of three real ales (Bass, Tetley and Flowers I.P.A.) plus John Smith's Smooth, Heineken, Carlsberg, Carling, Guinness and Strongbow. And if you'd like wine with your meal, there's a small but select wine list.

Opening times: Open lunchtimes and evenings from Monday to Thursday, and all day on Friday, Saturday and Sunday

Food: Served is served from 12.00-14.30 and 18.30-12.30 seven days

Credit cards: All major credit cards accepted except American Express

Accommodation: None

Entertainment: Occasional entertainment on Sundays; ring for details

Facilities: Beer garden; car park; conservatory

Local Places of Interest/Activities: Leamington Spa (historic town) 3 miles; Warwick (historic town) 6 miles; Stratford-upon-Avon (historic town) 12 miles; Draycote Water Country Park (sailing and fishing) 7 miles; Newbold Comyn Leisure Centre 2 miles

2 Northamptonshire

PLACES OF INTEREST:

PUBS AND INNS:

The Hidden Inns of the Heart of England

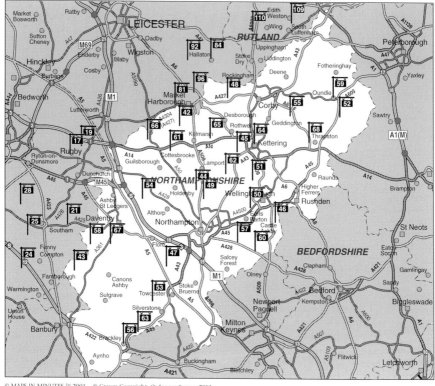

© MAPS IN MINUTES ™ 2001   © Crown Copyright, Ordnance Survey 2001

42	**The Bull's Head**, Clipston		**56**	**The Red Lion**, Brackley
43	**The Carpenters Arms**, Lower Boddington		**57**	**The Red Lion**, Denton
44	**The Coach and Horses**, Brixworth		**58**	**The Red Lion**, Hellidon
45	**The Country House Hotel**, Great Cransley		**59**	**Rose and Crown**, Oundle
46	**The Cuckoo**, Wollaston		**60**	**Rose and Crown**, Yardley Hastings
47	**The Eastcote Arms**, Eastcote		**61**	**The Royal Oak**, Naseby
48	**The Fox Inn**, Wilbarston		**62**	**The Royal Oak**, Walgrave
49	**The Griffin**, Pitsford		**63**	**The Sun Inn**, Whitfield
50	**The Horseshoe Inn**, Wilby		**64**	**Talbot Inn**, Kettering
51	**The Lamb Inn**, Little Harrowden		**65**	**Tollemache Arms**, Harrington
52	**The Montagu Arms**, Barnwell		**66**	**The Wharf**, Welford
53	**The New Inn**, Abthorpe		**67**	**The Windmill**, Badby
54	**The Old Kings Head**, Long Buckley		**68**	**The Woolpack Inn**, Islip
55	**The Old Three Cocks**, Brigstock			

Please note all references refer to page numbers

Northamptonshire

A county whose central location makes it easy to get to, with access from the M1, M6, M40, A1 and A14. Large areas are still mainly rural, with many miles of wide open spaces to explore. Seven long-distance footpaths traverse the county, and there are the same number of well-maintained country parks. Fifteen mapped routes are dedicated to cyclists, so visitors, whether on foot, on a cycle or in a car, will find that planning a tour is an easy task. A full list of the routes is available from Northamptonshire County Council on 01604 237227. The countryside is full of variety, with hills, lakes, rivers, canals and areas of dense woodland that were once royal hunting grounds.

As in most British counties, the village pub is at the centre of local community life, and in the case of Northamptonshire the visitor will sometimes have the opportunity to join in the traditional game of skittles. Country crafts, historic markets and majestic stately homes are other delights to be discovered, as well as some wonderful churches, each with its own character and unique features. The royal heritage is very strong, and the county has two of the three surviving Eleanor Crosses. Monuments at Naseby mark the site of the battle that was a turning point in the Civil War, and in Fotheringhay Castle Mary Queen of Scots was imprisoned and eventually executed. And Althorp, home of the Spencer family and final resting place of Diana, Princess of Wales: always a beautiful family country home and now a place of pilgrimage for thousands of visitors. Sporting enthusiasts will find plenty to interest them, including National Hunt racing at Towcester, football (Northampton Town, Rushden & Diamonds), motor racing at Silverstone, drag racing at Santa Pod ... and the world conker championships at Ashton near Oundle!

Northamptonshire is shaped like a laurel leaf, with the River Nene a distinctive feature. The alluvial soils and gravel terraces of the Nene Valley have been continuously farmed sinc Neolithic times and there are remains of many Anglo-Saxon settlements. Bones of horses, woolly rhinoceroses and mammoths have been unearthed, giving some hint as to the kind of animal life Paleolithic peoples used to contend with. During the Roman occupation, the Nene Valley lay within the most densely populated region of Britain. Today's main centres of population have their own delightful corners, but the county is perhaps even better known for the many picturesque villages that dot the landscape. And whatever one's taste in scenery, there is something for everyone from rolling meadows to spectacular views over seven counties. All this, and much more, awaits the visitor to this delightful and very accessible part of the world.

PLACES OF INTEREST

ALTHORP

The home of the Spencer family since 1508, **Althorp** remains exactly that - a classic family-owned English stately home which the Spencers have stamped with their style ever since John Spencer, a large-scale sheep farmer, acquired the estate. The present house was begun in 1573, and behind the stark tiling of the exterior is a wealth of fine paintings, sculpture, por-

Althorp House

32

celain and furniture. Known widely by connoisseurs for generations, Althorp is now known across the whole world since the tragic death of Diana, Princess of Wales, in 1997. She lies in peace in the beautiful, tranquil setting of the Round Oval, an ornamental lake, surrounded by her family's ancestral heritage. Visits to the house are strictly by advance booking: call 01604 592020.

Canons Ashby House

ASHBY ST LEDGERS

From 1375 to 1605 the manor house at Ashby was the home of the Catesby family, and it was in a room above the gatehouse that Guy Fawkes is said to have met Robert Catesby to hatch the **Gunpowder Plot**. On the 5th of November in 1605 Catesby rode the 80 miles from London in seven hours with the news that the plot had failed. He fled to Holbeach in Staffordshire, where he was shot dead after refusing to surrender. The Church of St Mary & St Leodegarious has much to interest the visitor, including Jacobean box pews, an elaborately carved rood screen, a Norman font, a number of Catesby brasses and, most notably, some medieval wall paintings depicting the Passion of Christ.

AYNHO

A peaceful, picturesque limestone village of leafy lanes and lovely old cottages. The former manor house, **Aynho Park**, is a very grand 17th-century country house in the care of the Country Houses Association. It was originally the property of the Cartwright family, who, it is said, claimed the rents from their tenants in the form of apricots; some apricot trees can still be seen trained into fan shapes and growing on the walls of cottages. The house was burnt down by Royalist troops during the Civil war but was rebuilt by the Cartwrights, who at the same time rebuilt the village church with the proportions as the house, so the church too has the appearance of a country villa. Later changes were made to the house by Archer and Soane. Public rooms and the grounds are open to the public on Wednesday and Thursday afternoons from May to September. **The Wharf** at Aynho on the Oxford Canal has holiday boats for hire and a canalside shop.

CANONS ASHBY

This pretty village contains the Church of St Mary, once part of the Black Canons' Monastery church and much reduced in size at the time of the Dissolution of the Monasteries. **Canons Ashby House**, built from part of the ecclesiastical building after the Dissolution, is one of the finest of Northamptonshire's great houses. Home of the Dryden family since the 1550s and now in the care of the National Trust, it contains some marvellous Elizabethan wall paintings and sumptuous Jacobean plasterwork. The grounds are equally delightful, with yews, cedars and mulberry trees, terraces and parkland. Open afternoons April to October except Thursday and Friday.

CASTLE ASHBY

Two main attractions for the visitor here. **Castle Ashby** is a fine Elizabethan mansion, owned by the Marquess of Northampton, standing in Capability Brown parkland with Victorian gardens and a lake. The building of Castle Ashby was started in 1574 in the area of a 13th century castle that had been previously demolished. The original plan of the building was in the shape of an 'E' in honour of Queen Elizabeth I, and is typical of many Elizabethan houses. About sixty years later the courtyard was enclosed by a screen designed by Inigo Jones. One of the features of Castle Ashby is the lettering around the house and terraces. The inscriptions, which are in Latin, read when translated *"The Lord guard your coming in"* and *"The Lord guard your going out"*. Inside there is some wonderful restoration furniture and paintings of the English and Renaissance schools.

On a much smaller scale the old **Manor House** makes a delightful picture by the church; it has a dungeon and there is a 13th century window with exquisite tracery set in the oldest part of the house near a blocked Norman arch. The poet Cowper loved to wander amongst the trees, some of which are said to have been

Entrance to Castle Ashby

Buchanan family, the hall and gardens are open to visitors on certain days in the summer. Tel: 01604 505808

DAVENTRY

Old and new blend intriguingly in this historic market town, whose streets are shared by dignified Georgian houses and modern shops. A colourful market is held along the High Street every Tuesday and Friday, and in the Market Place stands the Moot Hall, built in 1769 of ironstone. Originally a private house, it became the moot hall, or town hall, in 1806 after the former town hall was demolished. It is now home to the Tourist Information Centre and to Daventry Museum, which illustrates the social history of the town and its environs. It also shows regularly changing arts and crafts exhibitions and contains archaeological finds from **Borough Hill** and some of the equipment used by the BBC when it had a transmitter station on the hill. The oval hill, which rises to 650 feet above sea level, is more than two miles round and covers an area of 150 acres. It was the third largest Iron Age hill fort in Britain and in more recent times was topped by the huge radio masts that transmitted the World Service of the BBC.

Daventry was once an important stop on the coaching routes, and it is said that King Charles II spent several days at the Wheatsheaf Inn before the Battle of Naseby, where he lost the battle and his kingdom. Shakespeare mentions the town in *King Henry IV (Part 1)*, when Falstaff tells Bardolph the tale of a shirt stolen from a 'red-nose innkeeper'. During the coaching era the chief industry of Daventry was whip-making.

Daventry Country Park is a beautiful 133-acre site centred on the old Daventry Reservoir. Coarse fishing, picnic area, adventure playground, nature trails, nature reserve, visitor centre are among the amenities of this great family attraction, which is open daily all year.

DEENE

Surrounded by beautiful gardens and grounds filled with old-fashioned roses and rare trees and shrub stands **Deene Park**. Originally a medieval manor, it was acquired in 1514 by Sir Robert Brudenell and has been occupied by the family ever since; one of the family's most distinguished members was James, 7th Earl of

planted by the Countess Judith herself. The tree that attracts the most visitors is called Cowper's Oak, the branches of which spread twice as far across as the tree is high. There is a tradition that it will never die because Cowper stood beneath it one day during a heavy thunderstorm and was inspired to write his famous hymn: *"God moves in Mysterious Ways"*.

Castle Ashby Craft Centre & Rural Shopping Yard is set in an old farmyard and comprises farm shop and delicatessen, craft shops, pottery, goldsmith's studio, art gallery and tea room.

COTTESBROOKE

In secluded countryside near the site of the Battle of Naseby, **Cottesbrooke Hall** is one of the finest of all the grand houses in the county. The magnificent Queen Anne house, reputedly the model for Jane Austen's *Mansfield Park*, was begun in 1702 and is home to an impressive collection of pictures, porcelain and furniture. The grounds are quite superb, featuring the Statue Walk (statues from the Temple of Ancient Virtue, at Stowe), the Dilemma Garden with old roses and rare trees, the Dutch Garden, the Pine Court and many other charming gardens and courtyards. Owned by the Macdonald-

34 Cadogan, who led the Charge of the Light Brigade at the Battle of Balaclava. Transformed from medieval manor to Tudor and Georgian mansion, Deene Park contains many fine examples of period furniture and some beautiful paintings. The old-

Deene Park

est visible part is an arch of about 1300 in the east of the house; the Great Hall was completed at the end of the 16th century and has a magnificent sweet chestnut hammerbeam roof. Open certain days Easter-August. Tel: 01780 450278/450223

Also near Deene, in the parish of Gretton, is the English Heritage-run **Kirby Hall**, one of the loveliest Elizabethan ruins in England. Now only partly roofed, the hall dates from 1570 and was given by Elizabeth l to her Lord Chancellor and favourite courtier Sir Christopher Hatton. Alterations attributed to Inigo Jones were made in the 17th century. The fine gardens with their peacock population are being restored. A version of Jane Austen's *Mansfield Park* was filmed here in 1998.

EARLS BARTON

A great treasure here is the village **Church of All Saints**, with one of the most impressive Saxon towers in the whole country. It looks today as it did a thousand years ago with its mass of decorations by medieval craftsmen. In 1934 workmen found, embedded in the wall fifty feet from the ground, a horse's tooth. There was a pagan belief that the burial of horses' skulls improved the sound acoustics and that the skulls of forty horses were once laid in rows between the joists with the idea of improving the tone of an organ which stood over them. That wasn't here though - so maybe the tooth was meant to improve the sound a little bit, or more likely a horse belonging to one of the workmen had eaten too many lumps of medi-

Earls Barton Church

eval sugar. Beyond the remarkably well-preserved Norman doorway the most amazing sight is the 15th-century chancel screen, ablaze with hundreds of dazzling butterflies on the wing; next to it is a wonderful, heavily carved Jacobean pulpit in black oak.

FLORE

Called *Flora* in the Domesday Book, the village has a wide green that slopes gently down to the River Nene. **Adams Cottage** was the home of the ancestors of John Adams (1797-1801), President of the United States, whose son was also President. In the 13th-century church are several memorial windows, one of them dedicated to Bruce Capell, an artillery officer who was awarded the Military Cross at the age of 22 for courage and devotion to his wounded men. A simple wooden cross from Flanders hangs on the wall, and his window depicts the farewell between David and Jonathan.

FOTHERINGHAY

The first **Fotheringhay Castle** was built around 1100 by the son-in-law of William the Conqueror; the second in the 14th century by Edmund of Langley, a son of Edward lll. Richard lll was born here; Henry Vlll gave the castle to Catherine of Aragon and it later became the prison and place of execution of Mary, Queen

Church of St Mary and All Saints

of Scots, who was brought here in bands of steel and beheaded in the Banqueting Hall in 1587. Sir Christopher Hatton, a favourite of Elizabeth I whom we have met at Holdenby and Kirkby Hall, was one of the judges who sentenced Mary to death. Following her death, it is said that her jewellery was stolen and hidden in the woodlands around Corby. If so, it lies there still. The castle was pulled down in 1627 and 200 years later a gold ring was found with a lovers' knot entwined around the initials M and D - Mary and Darnley? Perhaps the ring fell from the Queen's finger as she was executed. The evocative site of the castles by the River Nene is rich in atmosphere, and visitors to Fotheringhay should not leave the village without seeing the **Church of St Mary and All Saints**, a 15th-century former collegiate church in a prominent position overlooking the Nene Valley.

Geddington

This attractive village, like many in the county, has known royal visitors: monarchs from the time of William the Conqueror used a summer palace as a base for hunting in the Royal Forest of Rockingham. In the centre of the village is an ornately carved stone cross almost 40 feet high. This is the best preserved of the three surviving **Eleanor Crosses** that marked the funeral procession of Queen Eleanor, who had died at Harby in Nottinghamshire in 1290. Her devoted husband, King Edward I, accompanied the body south to London, and wherever the funeral bier rested, he built a cross. Of all the crosses this, at Geddington, is the most complete. Other crosses were at Lincoln (where the Queen's heart was buried), Grantham, Stamford, Hardingstone in Northampton (this still exists), Stony Stratford, Dunstable, St Albans, Waltham (this still exists), Cheapside and Charing Cross.

Off the A43, on a minor road between Geddington and Grafton Underwood (where there is a monument to the crews of B17 bombers), stands one of the very finest houses in the country. The origins of **Boughton House**, the Northamptonshire home of the Duke of Buccleuch, go back 500 years to a small monastic building; added to down the years, it was transformed into 'a vision of Louis XIV's Versailles'. In addition to the wonderful architecture, Boughton is noted for its French and English furniture, its paintings (El Greco, Murillo, 40 Van Dycks) and its collection of armoury and weaponry. The grounds, which include parkland, lakes, picnic areas and woodland play areas, are open May to September, the house in August only.

Large tracts of the ancient woodland of the region have survived, and in the fields by Boughton House are the remains of more recent planting. The 2nd Duke of Montagu, nicknamed **John the Planter**, had the notion of planting an avenue of trees all the way from the house to his London home. The plan hit immediate trouble when his neighbour, the Duke of Bedford, refused to let the trees cross his estate; instead, the Planter set down many avenues on his own estate, amounting to the 70 miles of the distance to London. Dutch Elm disease destroyed much of his planting, but the old trees are being replaced with limes and beeches.

Guilsborough

A handsome, dignified village where Wordsworth came to stay in the vicarage and, it is said, brought with him the yellow Cumberland poppy that is often seen here. The church has lovely windows by William Morris and Burne-Jones, and Guilsborough Grange has a wildlife park and areas for walking and picnicking. A short distance south of the village, in the tiny community of Coton, **Coton Manor Garden** is a traditional garden originally laid out in 1925 and embracing several delightful smaller gardens. Beyond the garden are a wildflower meadow and a magical five-acre bluebell wood. The nursery propagates over 1,000 varieties of plant, and in the stable yard are a restaurant and tea room. Open Easter-end September.

36

HIGHAM FERRERS

Just off the **Market Place** in this delightful old town, a narrow lane leads to a unique group of ecclesiastical buildings. These include the 13th-cen-

Market Square, Higham Ferrers

tury spired Church of St Mary the Virgin, a chantry and bede house, and a 13th-century market cross. Also here is **Chichele College**, a college for secular canons founded in 1422, named inn honour of a local worthy called Henry Chichele. Born here in 1362, he progressed from baker's boy to Archbishop of Canterbury, a position he filled for 30 years until his death in 1443. His statue looks down from the church tower.

HOLDENBY

The Royal connections go back more than 400 years at **Holdenby Hall**, which was built by Elizabeth I's Lord Chancellor and favourite Sir Christopher Hatton for the purpose of entertaining the Queen. At the time, it was the largest Elizabethan house in England, and, for the diarist John Evelyn, 'one of the most pleasing sights that ever I saw'. It was visited but once by Elizabeth; it later became the palace and eventually the prison of Charles I, who was kept under guard here for five months after his defeat in the Civil War. The house, which appeared as Limmeridge House in the BBC's *The Woman in White*, stands in magnificent grounds which contain a falconry centre, a smaller scale reconstruction of Hatton's original garden, a fully working armoury and a 17th-century farmstead that evokes the sights and smells of life in days gone by. There's a museum, a children's farm and a lakeside train ride, which together with tea in the Victorian Kitchen, make a grand day out for young and old alike, and on Bank Holidays there are always special events and his-

torical enactments. For opening times call 01604 770074.

KELMARSH

Near Junction 2 of the A14, just outside the village of Kelmarsh, **Kelmarsh Hall** is an early 18th-century house designed in Palladian style by an outstanding pupil of Sir Christopher Wren, James Gibbs (who is perhaps best known as the architect of the Church of St Martin in the Fields, London). One of only two surviving houses outside London by Gibbs in this style, it stands in 3,000 acres of farmland, with a lake, beautiful gardens and woodland walks. The Great Hall is the focal point of the house, with many of Gibbs' original features. One of the most attractive rooms is the Chinese Room, where the hand-painted wallpaper, from Kimberley Hall in Norfolk, dates from the 1840s. Open to the public Sunday and Bank Holiday afternoons from Easter Sunday to the end of August. The church opposite the main entrance to the Hall contains fine marble from Rome, some William Morris furnishings and the vaults of the families who have lived at the Hall - the Hanburys, the Naylors and the Lancasters.

KETTERING

An important town standing above the River Ise, Kettering gained fame as a producer of both clothing and shoes. It was in Kettering that the missionary William Carey and the preacher Andrew Fuller founded the Baptist Missionary Society in 1792, giving a new impetus to the cause of foreign missions all over the world. The parish church of St Peter and St Paul, with its elegant crocketed spire, is one of the finest in the country and a landmark for miles around. Much of the old town has been swallowed up in modern development, but there are still a few old houses in the narrow lanes, and the **Heritage Quarter** around the church gives a fascinating, hands-on insight into the town's past.

The **Manor House Museum**, housed in an 18th-century manor house, has impressive collections of social and industrial history, archaeology and geology. Individual items range from a macabre mummified cat to an example of the Robinson car built in Kettering in 1907.

In the adjacent **Alfred East Gallery** a constantly changing programme of exhibitions of paintings, crafts, sculpture, photography and children's work ensures that there will be something new to see on every visit. Among the items on permanent display are works by Alfred East RA and Thomas Cooper Gotch. In between visits to the museum and gallery (both wheelchair-accessible) the Heritage Gardens are a pleasant place for a stroll or a picnic. The Tourist Information Centre is at the same location.

On the A6, on the outskirts of town, **Wicksteed Park** is a 148-acre site of leisure and pleasure, with 40 rides and attractions, including roller coaster, pirate ship, train ride, Mississippi river boat and pitch & putt. There are several catering outlets, shops, a pottery, a photographic studio and two playground areas. Open daily Easter-September, weekends to November.

LAMPORT

Lamport Hall is a fine 16th-century house enlarged in the 17th century by John Webb. Home to the Isham family from 1560 to 1976, it features an outstanding collection of furniture, books, paintings and china. It has gardens and parkland, including the first Alpine garden and

Lamport Hall

the first garden gnomes in England, plus a shop and tea room. It is also the home of the **Hannington Vintage Tractor Club**, which houses a wide variety of vintage tractors and other farm machinery. Open certain days Easter-September. Tel: 01604 686272

NORTHAMPTON

Much of its face is modern, but the capital of the county has a wealth of history for the visitor to discover. At least 6,000 years ago a camp was set up at **Briar Hill**, and more recent traces of early settlements in the area date from between 700BC and 50AD. The Domesday Book of 1086 shows Northampton as a town of 300 houses, comparable in size to Derby or Nottingham. Richard 1 granted the town its first charter in 1189, and by the 13th century it had become a major market town, and its market square, dating from that period, is reputed to be the second largest in the country.

Northampton has for centuries been associated with the shoemaking trade. Tradition has it that in 1213 a pair of boots was made here for King John, and the first large order came in 1642 when 4,000 pairs of shoes and 600 pairs of boots were made for the army. The industry grew rapidly throughout the county and by the end of the 19th century 40% of the population was involved in the shoe trade. People like Philip Manfield and William Barrett were just two of the major players who started their businesses in Northampton and grew them into extensive chains. William Barrett gave his name to the maternity hospital, and Manfield gave his to another of the town's hospitals. St Crispin, the patron saint of shoemakers, is portrayed in several churches, and Northampton Town Football Club are known as the Cobblers. The **Central Museum and Art Gallery** has the world's largest collection of footwear, showing shoe fashions down the centuries and the machines that made the shoes. There is also an outstanding collection of British and Oriental ceramics, leathercraft from around the world and a some fine paintings - Italian 15th-18th century and British. The **Abington Museum**, set in a 15th-century manor house, has a number of interesting exhibits, including a room with 16th-century oak panelling, the county's military history and a 19th-century fashion gallery.

Northampton has two outstanding churches: All Saints, designed by Henry Bell in the Wren style, with ornate plasterwork by Edward Goudge and two organs by JS Walker; and the wonderful Church of the Holy Sepulchre, one of only four remaining round churches in the kingdom. Founded by Simon de Senlis, 1st Earl of Northampton, to commemorate his safe return from the Crusades in 1100, it is often known as the 'soldiers church' and carried battle scars from the Wars of the Roses. It is the oldest standing building in Northampton and is almost identical to the original in Jerusalem.

The most prestigious building in town is certainly the **Guildhall**, a gem of Victorian architecture built in 1864 by Edward Godwin and later extended by Matthew Holding and Arnold Jeffrey. Grand tours of the building take in the old prison cells, the Mayor's parlour, the Great Hall, the Godwin Room and the Council Chamber. The Royal Theatre is another Victorian gem, built in 1884 in opulent Italianate style and home to one of the oldest repertory companies in England. The **Welsh House**, one of the few buildings to survive the disastrous fire of 1675, dates from 1595 and recalls the time when Welsh drovers would bring their cattle to the market.

In 1290 the funeral procession of Queen Eleanor, wife of Edward l, stopped for the night at Delapre Abbey. In the south of town, at **Hardingstone** on the London Road A508, stands one of the three surviving **Eleanor Crosses** of the thirteen originally erected to mark each night of the progress of the mournful cortege to London. See under Geddington for more about the Eleanor Crosses.

Northampton boasts more than 150 parks and open spaces, most notably **Abington Park** with lakes, aviaries and the museum mentioned above; Delapre Park, where the Cluniac Abbey was built in 1145; and **Hunsbury Hill Country Park**, where the Iron Age hill fort can still be seen - this park is also home to the Northamptonshire Ironstone Railway Trust's museum and railway. Sports and leisure facilities are abundant: two of the best are Billing Aquadrome with extensive fishing and moorings and, new in 1999, the **Nene White Water Centre** with facilities for canoeing, rafting, rowing and orienteering.

Four miles north of Northampton, off the A508 just north of the village of Pitsford, **Pitsford Water** is an 800-acre reservoir with trout fishing and boats for hire, sailing, a picnic area, nature reserve and information centre. The reservoir is also accessible from the village of Holcot.

OUNDLE

Best known for its **Public School**, Oundle is a town rich in architectural interest, with many fine buildings of the 17th and 18th centuries. The school was founded by Sir William Laxton in 1556, and an inscription to his memory is written above the 17th-century doorway in Greek, Latin and Hebrew. The medieval church, with its magnificent tower and 200-foot spire, is an impressive sight, and other notable buildings include three sets of almshouses. The museum paints a picture of local life down the years.

Tourists from all over the world visit the historic streets and shops, the school and the tall-spired church of Oundle. The River Nene, the

Memorial Chapel, Oundle School

marina, the theatre, the school, the church and the museum are among the many attractions of this pretty market town.

A mile east of Oundle, a unique attraction at Ashton Mill is the **National Dragonfly Museum**, the only one of its kind in Europe. It highlights the beauty, the wonder and the plight of dragonflies through habitats, exhibitions and videos, and guarantees a visit with a difference that is both fascinating and educational. Open weekends and Bank Holiday Mondays mid-June to end September. Ashton is home

ROCKINGHAM

"450 Years a Royal Castle, 450 years a family home". 900 years of history are contained within the walls of **Rockingham Castle**, built by William the Conqueror on the slopes of Rockingham Hill, overlooking the Welland Valley and the thatched and slate-roofed cottages of the village. The grand rooms are superbly furnished, and the armour in the Tudor Great Hall recalls the Civil War, when the castle was captured by the Roundheads. Owned and lived in since 1530 by the Watson family, the castle was put to atmospheric use by the BBC in the series *By the Sword Divided*, in which it was known as Arnescote Castle. Charles Dickens wrote much of *Bleak House* at Rockingham. For visiting times call 01536 770240.

RUSHTON

One mile west of the village, on an unclassified road, stands **Rushton Triangular Lodge**, described as 'the purest folly in the country'. It was built by Sir Thomas Tresham in 1597 and symbolises the Holy Trinity, with three walls, each with three windows, three gables and three storeys, topped with a three-sided chimney. Thomas Tresham, known as Thomas the Builder, was brought up a Protestant but courageously returned to the Roman Catholic faith of his ancestors. At Rushton Hall, the Tresham family home since the 14th century, he was caught harbouring the renowned Jesuit Edmund Campion and was sentenced to seven years' imprisonment. Responsible for several intriguing buildings, he died soon after proclaiming the first Stuart king and just before his son Francis was arrested as a protagonist in the Gunpowder Plot.

Neighbouring **Rushton Hall**, also dating back 400 years, is described as a 'dazzling example of Tudor and Stuart splendour'. Built by Sir John Tresham, enlarged by Sir Thomas and completed by the Cockayne family, it now houses a Royal Institute for the Blind school, but is open to the public by appointment and for special events. Tel: 01536 710506

SALCEY FOREST

Reached from the A508 at Roade or the B526 between Horton and Stoke Goldington, the 1,250-acre **Salcey Forest** has been owned and managed by the Forestry Commission since the 1920s. Part of the chain of ancient Royal Hunting Forests that stretched from Stamford to Oxford, it produces quality timber while providing a home for a wide variety of animal and plant life, and recreational facilities for the public. There are three circular trails at Salcey, named after the three woodpeckers found there: the Lesser Spotted Trail of a leisurely hour; the Great Spotted Trail of about two miles; and, for the more energetic, the Green Woodpecker Trail of about 2½ hours. The forest is open to visitors all year round.

SILVERSTONE

The home of British motor racing, located off the A43 in the village. The **British Grand Prix** is the highlight of the year, but the circuit hosts a large number of other events, including rounds of the Auto Trader touring car championship and the International Historic Car Festival. Members of the public can test their skills in a single-seater racer, a Lotus Elise, a rally car or a 4x4 off-road vehicle. For details call 01327 850016.

Tucked away on country roads northwest of Silverstone are two of the many interesting churches for which Northamptonshire is famous. **The Church of St Mary at Wappenham** has a sculpture by Giles Gilbert Scott from the renowned family of architects, who had local connections; two fonts; a clock from the 17th century; and brass memorials to the Lovett family. In the neighbouring hamlet of Slapton the church boasts some interesting 14th-century wall paintings; and the village of **Weedon Lois** is the final resting place of Edith Sitwell (1887-1965).

STOKE BRUERNE

A picturesque canalside village at the southern end of the famous Blisworth Tunnel. The canal provides the major attractions, with waterside walks, boat trips to the tunnel and a visit to the fascinating **Canal Museum**. Housed in a converted corn mill, the museum displays 200 years of canal history and life on the narrow boats (many of which are still in use for pleasure trips). The exhibits include working engines, old photographs, waterway wildlife and the tools used by canal workers and boatmen. The museum, which is open throughout the year, has a tea room and a souvenir shop. The canal has a series of locks at this point, and visitors can stop in the car park at the lower lock on the A508 and walk into the village along the towpath, passing seven locks en route. There are shops, pubs and restaurants at this popular place, which is the perfect location for a family day out and an ideal starting point for a canal holiday.

A private drive on the Stoke Bruerne to Shutlanger road leads to **Stoke Park**, a great house standing in a 400-acre estate. Attributed to Inigo Jones, the house was built in Palladian style (the first in this country) around 1630 for Sir Francis Crane, head of the Mortlake Tapestry Works. The main house burnt down in 1886, and only the pavilions and a colonnade remain; but they are an impressive sight and may be viewed externally on afternoons in August or by appointment (Tel: 01604 862172).

SULGRAVE

The best-known attraction here is **Sulgrave Manor**, a Tudor manor house built by the ancestors of George Washington, first President of the United States of America. Lawrence Washington, sometime Mayor of Northampton, bought the manor from Henry VIII in 1539. In 1656, Lawrence Washington's great great grandson Colonel John Washington left England to take up land in Virginia which later became Mount Vernon. This man was the great grandfather of George. The Washington family arms, which are said to have inspired the stars and stripes design of the American flag, are promi-

40

nent above the front door, and the house is a treasure trove of George Washington memorabilia, including documents, a velvet coat and even a lock of his hair. The house is open daily (except Monday) from April to October, and at weekends in March, November and December. A lottery grant has allowed the construction of a series of buildings in the grounds which are part of major educational programmes covering all aspects of Tudor history. The lovely gardens in-

Sulgrave Manor

clude yew hedges, topiary, herbaceous borders and a formal rose garden planted in 1999. There's a gift shop and a buttery serving light refreshments. Other Washington memorials are to be seen in the village church, and nearby are the old village stocks and the remains of a castle mound.

THRAPSTON

The **Medieval Bridge** at Thrapston crosses the **River Nene** on one of its loveliest stretches. The town is surrounded by fine pastureland, created when the flood waters and rich mud subsided after the two Ice Ages. The main attraction in the church is a stone tablet carved with stars and stripes. It is thought by some that this motif was the inspiration for the American flag, being the coat of arms of Sir John Washington, who died in 1624. The church and nearby Montagu House, home of Sir John, are places of pilgrimage for many American tourists.

TOWCESTER

In Roman times the town was called Lactodorum and it stood on the major highway Watling Street (now the A5). The Romans improved the road and built a fort to guard their troop movements. During the Civil War it was the only Royalist stronghold in the area and in the following centuries it was an important stop on the coaching route between London and Holyhead. By the end of the 18th century there were twenty coaching inns in the town, servicing up to forty coaches every day. Charles Dickens stayed at the Saracen's Head, then called the Pomfret Hotel, and immortalised it in The Pickwick Papers. The parish church of St Lawrence, built on the site of a substantial Roman building, is one of the loveliest in the county, with features from several centuries: the crypt, reached by a doorway from the sanctuary, is 13th century, the arcades 13th and 14th. On the arch of the south chapel is a carved jester's head probably from the 14th century, while the massive tower and the font are from the 15th. Close to the church is the **Chantry House**, formerly a school, founded by Archdeacon Sponne in 1447.

Towcester Racecourse is set in the beautiful parkland estate of Easton Neston, the family home of Lord Hesketh. The course, which has its entrance on the A5, came into being in 1876, when the Empress of Austria was staying at Easton Neston and attended an Easter steeplechase held in her honour. The course now stages about 16 National Hunt meetings a year, including a couple in the evening.

WELLINGBOROUGH

This important market and industrial town, known for its iron mills, flour mills and tanneries, sits near the point where the River Ise joins the River Nene. The spire of the medieval All Hallows Church rises among trees in the centre of town, and the other church, whose great tower can be seen on the further bank of the Nene, is the Church of St Mary, built in the first decades of the 20th century. Wellingborough was granted its market charter in 1201 and markets are still held four days a week. In and around the market square are several interesting old buildings, including the gabled **Hind Hotel**. One of its rooms is called the Cromwell Room because it was being constructed while the Battle of Naseby was in progress.

Another fine building is **Croyland Abbey**, now a Heritage Centre with a wealth of local history, and near it is a splendidly restored old tithe barn originally used for storing the manorial tithes. Stone-walled and thatch-roofed, it is 70 feet long and 22 feet wide. It dates from the 15th century and has two great doorways at either side, one of them 13 feet in height. A new attraction in the centre of town is the Millennium Rose Garden at **Swanspool Gardens**. The Embankment at Wellingborough is a great place for a family outing, where a thriving population of swans lives next to the outdoor paddling pool that dates from the 1930s. South of town, **Summer Leys Nature Reserve** is a year-round haven for large numbers of birds. Each May, thousands of people visit the town for the **International Waendel Weekend** of walking, cycling and swimming.

One mile south of Wellingborough, **Great Doddington** faces its neighbour **Wollaston** across the gently flowing Nene, and the proximity of the river led to a local industry making mats from the riverside rushes. Nearby **Beacon Hill** provides really splendid views which, it is said, take in 27 towers and spires on a clear day. Many of the houses here are built of the local brown ironstone.

Another mile southeast, **Irchester** was originally a Roman settlement, a fortified town whose walls were eight feet thick. A Saxon cemetery was also discovered here, and Norman England is represented by the plinths in the church. The six-arched bridge that crosses the River Nene is 14th century and bears the crossed keys of Peterborough Abbey and the wheel of St Catherine. On the B570 is **Irchester Country Park**, 200 acres of woodland walks, wayfaring course, nature trail, picnic meadows and ranger service in a former ironstone quarry.

42

The Bull's Head

Harborough Road,
Clipston,
Leicestershire
LE16 9RT
Tel: 01858 525268
Fax: 01858 525266

Directions:

Take the A508 south from Market Harborough for 3 miles, then turn west onto a minor road; Clipston is 2 miles along this road

The Bull's Head is a real family run inn within the small picturesque village of Clipston. It sits right on the roadside, and with its whitewashed walls, tubs and window boxes brimming over with flowers, quaint sign and small paned windows, it is a real picture post card place. Even the car park at the side is lined with tubs and barrels that burst with colour! The building dates from about 1627, and still retains many original features. The walls are thick, and inside there are old beams, gleaming brass and copper, sturdy country furniture and an overall atmosphere that speaks of history and tradition.

In charge is George and Sue Price, who, along with their daughter and son, have managed to preserve all that is good about the inn while adding refinements of their own.The bar has a fine choice of four cask ales, plus a rotating guest ale, and a range of lagers, stout and cider. They have over 520 different varieties of Whisky and have been named Whisky Pub of the Year 2001. As far as food is concerned, the inn's speciality is chicken and whisky with a Stilton Sauce, though there are many fine main courses on the extensive menu. It's the daughter and son-in-law who do the cooking, and they try to use good, fresh local ingredients wherever possible. In the summer months, you can sit out in the beer garden or patio and watch the world go by as you have a quiet drink. You could also try one of the barbecued dishes that are available then as well!

This is an inn that turns people's heads as they pass. It is everyone's idea of a picture post card traditional village hostelry, and offers a warm and friendly welcome to locals and visitors alike.

Opening hours: Monday: 17.30-23.00; Tuesday to Saturday 11.30-15.00 and 17.30-23.00; Sunday: 12.00-15.00 and 19.00-22.30

Food: Good and filling, with a wide choice, served whenever the pub is open

Credit cards: all cards except American Express and Diners

Accommodation: 3 en suite twin rooms

Entertainment: Occasional theme nights such as murder/mystery and Burns Night

Facilities: Beer garden; patio with occasional barbecues

Local Places of Interest/Activities: Kelmarsh Hall 2 miles; Shire Falconry Centre 7 miles; Lamport Hall 5 miles; Cottesbrooke Hall 5 miles

The Carpenters Arms

43

Hill Road,
Lower Boddington,
Northamptonshire
NN11 6YB
Tel/Fax: 01327 260451

Directions:

Follow the A361 north from Banbury for 5 miles, then turn west onto a minor road signposted for Aston le Walls and Lower Boddington

Set in a picturesque village, **The Carpenters Arms** is a small country inn with an almost classical look dating from the 18th century. Its walls are of mellow, red brick which makes it a very welcoming place indeed. In the summer months hanging baskets and tubs of flowers add colour and character. This is a typical country pub, warm in winter and cool in summer, and is very much a part of the local farming community.

So don't be surprised if you see customers wearing muddy boots and wellies in what is an otherwise spotless inn! This makes for a great atmosphere. The interior is snug and compact, and reflects the fact that the place is family run by husband and wife Mike and Jackie Wakelin. The whole place speaks of efficient, friendly service backed up by that a sense of tradition and continuity.

The food is traditional as well – and it's none the worse for that! Here you can get real pub food at its best, cooked on the premises using fresh produce that is sourced close to hand wherever possible. The portions are generous, sensibly priced, and always tasty and satisfying. The ales are Hook Norton, so you know you're not going to be disappointed, plus there are occasional guest ales if you want to try something different.

In the Carpenters Arms you know that Mike and Jackie are trying just that little bit harder to create a piece of olde England, backed up of course by modern day efficiency and a warm welcome.

Opening hours: 12.00-14.00 and 18.00-23.00 Tuesday to Saturday (open Monday evenings only) and 12.00-14.00 and 18.00-22.30 on Sunday

Food: Competitively priced traditional pub grub, all beautifully cooked, with good portions

Credit cards: Most cards with the exception of American Express and Diners

Accommodation: None

Entertainment: Quiz and theme nights

Facilities: Small beer garden

Local Places of Interest/Activities: Canons Ashby (NT) 5 miles; Banbury (historic market town) 7 miles; Burton Dasset Country Park 5 miles

Internet/Website:
e-mail: thecarps@supanet.com

44 The Coach and Horses

Harborough Road,
Brixworth,
Northamptonshire
NN6 9BX
Tel: 01604 880329

Directions:

Brixworth is just off the A508 at a roundabout, five miles north of Northampton

Set within a small, typically English village that contains one of the finest Saxon churches in the country, **The Coach and Horses** occupies a prime position, and is run by the husband and wife team of Anthea and Les Pike. Though the inn dates from the late 19th century, it has dark stone walls topped off with a picturesque thatched roof that speaks of continuity and tradition.

The interior is equally as attractive, and comprises a bar, lounge and intimate dining area that always seems welcoming. The whole place is spotlessly clean, and attracts a good mix of regulars, from typical country workers to the more professional types who work in nearby Northampton. So there's a good cross section of England here, and an hour spent in the bar can be a rewarding experience as the stories circulate and the laughter starts.

The food varies from Oriental to traditional and local, and the chef, as the regulars will tell you, is someone who likes to experiment, though he invariably gets it just right! The dishes can be washed down with a bottle of wine from the Coach and Horse's small but varied cellar, or by one of the cask conditioned ales from the bar. Plus there's always a guest beer or two on offer.

The surrounding countryside is typically English, with a rich, green landscape of woodland and meadow. And this is a typically English country pub, popular with the locals for a quiet drink, pub lunch or a celebration meal. It's family run, and the pride the family takes in it shows through.

Opening Hours: 11.30-15.00 and 17.30-23.00 all week.

Food: A good menu is available, with everything from Oriental to local. Food is served all day

Credit Cards: Most credit cards with the exception of Diners and American Express.

Accommodation: None

Facilities: Beer garden and patio garden with occasional barbecues

Local Places of Interest/Activities: Althorp Park 5 miles; Brixworth Country Park 1 mile; Cottesbrooke Hall 3 miles; Lamport Hall 2 miles; Coton Manor Garden 5 miles; Holdenby House 4 miles

The Country House Hotel 45

63 Loddington Road,
Great Cransley,
Northamptonshire
NN14 1PY
Tel: 01536 791600
Fax: 01536 791369

Directions:

Great Cransley is half a mile off the A43, 2 miles south of Kettering

On the outskirts of the village of Great Cransley near Kettering you'll find **The Country House Hotel**, a fine, imposing detached villa that has been extended to accommodate a small, upmarket hotel. It is owned and run by Jessica Pohl, who has had many years experience in the hotel and catering trade. She recently returned from Germany to set up an establishment that pays great attention to detail so that guests can experience the best in comfort and service. She has certainly succeeded, and her proud motto is "there are no strangers here, only friends you have not met". The high standards set by the hotel certainly reflect this. It's a welcoming, well appointed place that offers a peaceful retreat or a base from which to explore all that is best about this part of England. It can also host small business conferences of up to ten people, and such things as flip charts, OHP equipment and videos can be provided. Jessica even speaks French, Spanish and German, so overseas visitors - here either for business or pleasure - are especially welcome.

There are 5 en suite bedrooms, each furnished and decorated to an extremely high standard, and each with colour TV, hair driers, trouser press and tea and coffee making facilities. One of them - the master bedroom (which makes an excellent bridal suite) has a small sitting room attached. Jessica can arrange to have flowers, champagne or fresh fruit placed in you room to await your arrival. There's a relaxing lounge bar for residents, and if you book well in advance, she can prepare a set dinner for incoming guests.

The Country House Hotel is beautifully appointed and extremely comfortable. Jessica's attention to detail and wide experience has made this one of the top small hotels in the area. It is situated away from the bustle of the town or city, and yet is handy for all road, rail and air links.

Opening times: All day every day

Food: Food served to residents only; a set dinner can be booked well in advance

Credit cards: Most credit cards accepted

Facilities: Bar area and conservatory; car park; picnic hampers can be arranged; private parties catered for; conference facilities; historic tours of the area can be arranged;

Accommodation: 5 en-suite rooms

Local Places of Interest/Activities: Golf and fishing close by; excellent walking and cycling in the area; Althorp Park 11 miles; Lamport Hall 4 miles; Cottesbrooke Hall 7 miles ; Boughton House 5 miles; Triangular Lodge 4 miles

Internet/website:
www.the-country-house-hotel.co.uk
e-mail:Jessica@thecountryhousehotel.fsnet.co.uk

46 The Cuckoo

120 High Street,
Wollaston,
near Wellingborough,
Northamptonshire
NN29 7RN
Tel: 01933 664351

Directions:

Take the A509 south from Wellingborough for 3 miles. Wollaston is just off the main road, on the left

Wollaston, with its 14th century church with tall spire, nestles in the Northampton countryside just south of the historic town of Wellingborough. **The Cuckoo** sits on an elevated position in the village, and with its three sided front, you can't miss it. It is mostly built of red brick, and sits on a corner, with its sign swinging high over the main road. It's not a particularly old inn, and indeed the building has fulfilled several functions in the past. Nor does look like everyone's idea of a traditional village pub, but husband and wife Graham and Becky Upcraft, who have only been in charge for a few months, have managed to create a homely and welcoming atmosphere which more than compensates. So much so that it's become a firm favourite with the locals, which tells its own story. Inside, there's a lovely lounge, a compact bar and games room where pool is played, and all are comfortable and inviting. This is true English local, unassuming yet special. You can almost feel the welcome as you step over the door.

The food represents great value for money. There's a bar meal menu and an evening one. One of the most popular dishes is good old bangers and mash, and you can't get more traditional than that! The Cuckoo is proud of its cask conditioned ales, and it also features some guest ales if you're looking for a change. It's a great place in which to relax, and there's plenty of room to stretch your legs and pass the time of day with the regulars. You won't be disappointed if you pay it a visit.

Opening hours: 12.00-23.00 Monday to Saturday, and 12.00-22.30 on Sunday

Food: Simple and well cooked on the premises. The prices are very competitive

Credit cards: Cash only at present

Accommodation: None

Entertainment: Quiz nights, charity nights and occasional live music

Facilities: Games area with pool table; families welcome

Local Places of Interest/Activities: Irchester Country Park 3 miles; Santa Pod Raceway (Drag Racing) 3 miles; Higham Ferrers (historic market town with ruins of Chichele College) 5 miles; Sywell Reservoir (fishing) and Country Park 5 miles

The Eastcote Arms

47

6 Gayton Road, Eastcote,
near Towcester,
Northamptonshire
Tel: 01327 830731

Directions:
East of the A5, 3 miles north
of its junction with the A43

Located near the centre of the
small, peaceful village of
Eastcote, **The Eastcote Arms**
is a striking little pub at the
heart of the local community.
It dates from the late 17th century, and is full of character
and history. This is an inn that
was built to last, and it shows! Under the personal supervision of George and Kerrie Scott
and Della and Ted Haskins, it has established a reputation in the area as the inn to visit for
a quiet drink, a bar lunch or an evening meal.

The interior is welcoming and spotlessly clean, and has none of that plastic artificiality
that seems to be creeping up on some of our pubs nowadays. There are two bars and a small
restaurant, and in the winter months an open fire throws a welcoming glow over everything. The owners want to keep it that way – a village pub that has an ambience that is hard
to resist. It serves bar and Sunday lunches, as well as full evening meals, and the menus are
a mixture of traditional fare and the more exotic. The bar lunches, for instance, include
such dishes as Lincolnshire sausage, egg and chips, filled baguettes, soup and jacket potatoes. The evening meals are an experience in themselves. Main courses include deep fried
Camembert, fillet steaks, poached salmon fillet and beef and Guiness served with green
beans and spring onion mashed potato. Sunday lunches include roast beef (of course!) roast
pork and a vegetarian dish of the day.

All of this can be washed down with a selection of award-winning real ales, as the
Eastcote Arms boasts the best beers in the area. There's also a small, intimate wine list for
that special occasion. The owners have some exciting plans for the place, so this is one inn
that should be watched!

Opening hours: Mon-Fri: 12.00-15.00,18.00-
23.00; Sat: 12.00-15.00, 17.00-23.00; Sun:
12.00-16.00, 19.00-22.30

Food: Three superb menus, for bar lunches,
Sunday lunches and evening meals. All the
food is beautifully cooked and presented.
Food is served 12.00-14.00 Tue to Sat, 19.00-
21.30 on Thu, Fri and Sat, and Sun lunches
from 12.00-15.00

Credit cards: All major cards except American Express and Diners

Accommodation: Available towards the end
of 2002

Entertainment: Theme nights and ongoing
activities

Facilities: Award winning garden and beer
garden.

Local Places of Interest/Activities:
Silverstone Motor Racing Circuit 7 miles;
Stoke Park 5 miles; Stowe Gardens (NT) 10
miles; Stoke Bruerne Canal Museum 5 miles;
Canons Ashby (NT) 7 miles

48   The Fox Inn

Church Street,
Wilbarston,
nr Market Harborough,
Leicestershire
LE16 8QG
Tel: 01536 771270
Fax: 01536 518141

Directions:

Wilbarston is just north
of the A427, about four
miles west of Corby

This is a fine looking rural pub, occupying a prime corner site in a village which has earned itself a reputation as being a popular venue for well known musicians to hold rock concerts! It is built of warm, rosy stone, and has a high, steeply pitched roof with two delightful half dormer windows at one end. Thanks to mine hosts Mark Field and Lesley Evans, the place has recently been extensively refurbished and upgraded to a high standard. The building dates from the mid 1700s, and, with its small windows and tall chimneys, has an air of history and tradition about it.

The inside has benefited greatly from the refurbishment, and is cozy and comfortable. The whole place has a homely feel to it, though Mark and Lesley haven't stinted when it comes to efficient, friendly service and all the modern conveniences of a well run establishment. This, coupled with good service and value for money, makes it a popular place for locals and visitors alike to eat and drink. There's a small ornate bar area with copper-topped tables, well-upholstered furniture and soft carpeting on the floor.

Mark is a qualified chef, and is in charge of preparing the inn's excellent food. So popular is it for meals that you are well advised to book beforehand. The menu is well balanced, with both traditional and slightly more exotic dishes on offer, all at unbelievable prices. Try the double loin chop with apple and rosemary stuffing! The bar offers cask ales plus two rotating guest ales, and of course, in a place renowned for its food, there's an excellent wine list

Opening hours: Monday to Friday 12.00-15.00 and 17.00-23.00; Saturday and Sunday: 12.00-23.00

Food: An excellent menu; food is served daily from 12.00-14.00 and 18.30-21.00

Credit cards: all cards except American Express and Diners

Accommodation: 3 double rooms and one family room (sleeping up to 4), all en suite

and all having TV and tea and coffee making facilities

Entertainment: Skittles; darts; occasional quizzes and live music

Facilities: Beer garden

Local Places of Interest/Activities: East Carlton Country Park 1 mile; Shire Falconry Centre 2 miles; Triangular Lodge, Rushton 3 miles; Kelmarsh Hall 7 miles

The Griffin 49

Pitsford,
near Northampton,
Northamptonshire
NN6 9AD
Tel: 01604 880346

Directions:

Pitsford lies just to the east of the A508, about four miles north of Northampton

Situated in the heart of the pretty village of Pitsford, **The Griffin** is under the personal supervision of husband and wife team Paul and Lesley Woolard. It dates from the late 18th century, and its solid stone walls conceal an interior that speaks of the traditions of the English countryside. The bare stone walls are hung with fishing rods, golf clubs and small, old farming implements and prints. The inn, after all, is close to Pitsford reservoir, a favourite haunt of fishermen.

Don't let the idea of bare stone walls put you off. This is a cozy and welcoming inn – warm in winter, when a fire blazes away in the grate, and cool in summer, when the visitor can sit outside in the beer garden and enjoy a cooling pint. The tables are copper topped, and the bar, lounge and dining areas are scrupulously clean.

Lesley does the cooking, while Paul is mine host behind the bar. The food is unpretentious and honest, all with sensible prices. However, the quality (and quantity!) is excellent. This isn't fast food – all boil in a bag and quick frozen – this is simple food that has been thoughtfully prepared and presented. To accompany a bar meal or dinner, there's a selection of six cask ales, plus occasional guest beers. And, of course, if your fancy runs to wine, then there's a wine list that may be small, but is always interesting.

The Griffin is a real village local which is used to welcoming visitors who come for both the fishing and golf. It will give you a warm welcome as well!

Opening Hours: 12.00-15.00 and 17.30-23.00 Monday to Saturday, and 17.30-22.30 on Sunday

Food: A simple menu of good, honest wholesome fayre, served between 12.00-14.00 and 18.00-21.00

Credit Cards: Cash only at present

Accommodation: None

Entertainment: Sunday quiz night

Facilities: Beer garden and golfing society

Local Places of Interest/Activities: Pitsford Reservoir (fishing) and Brixworth Country Park 1 mile; Lamport Hall 4 miles; Northampton and Lamport Railway (privately owned) 1 mile; Holdenby House 4 miles; Althorp 5 miles

50 The Horseshoe Inn

100 Main Road,
Wilby,
near Wellingborough,
Northamptonshire
NN8 2UE
Tel: 01933 272493

Directions:

Take the A509 to the west of Wellingborough, then turn onto the A4500 at a roundabout. Wilby is along this road

You can't miss the village of Wilby. Its church has an octagonal tower crowned by a tall spire. And in the village you'll find **The Horseshoe Inn**, run by husband and wife team of Kathleen and Graham Wright. The inn dates from the late 18th century, and is a four square building on an elevated site. The stonework on the outside has recently been refurbished, which gives it a clean but traditional look.

The interior is spick and span, with a bar, attractive dining area and games room. Kathleen and Graham keep the whole place spotlessly clean, and it's a popular place for the locals to meet and have a drink or a meal. In fact, you would sometimes think it was a community centre rather than a pub, as its list of activities includes such things as jazz every Monday night and quiz nights. Every second Friday there's a special food night, when you can sample such things as Italian food and juicy steak nights (for which you're well advised to book). There seems to be something on every night of the week!

The food can best be described as simple and traditional. Everything is cooked in the inn's own kitchen's by Kathleen, and she takes pride in the fact that she only uses the freshest of ingredients which are sourced locally wherever possible. There's a lively menu, and there's sure to be something on it that will appeal to most tastes. The dishes represent real value for money, and are well presented. On Sundays, a traditional Sunday lunch is served, and it's so popular that you should book beforehand if you wish to come along. The well stocked bar has a fine range of five rotating cask ales, plus the usual lager, Guinness, cider and wine for that special occasion.

Opening hours: Monday to Friday: 11.30-15.30 and 17.00-23.00; Saturday: 11.30-15.30 and 18.00-23.00; Sunday: 11.30-15.30 and 19.00-22.30

Food: Monday-Sunday 12.00-14.30; no evening meals except for 18.00-23.00 on special nights every second Friday

Credit cards: Cash only at present

Accommodation: None

Entertainment: Live music; food nights; quiz nights (phone for full programme)

Local Places of Interest/Activities: Wellingborough (historic town) 1 mile; Santa Pod Raceway (drag racing) 6 miles; Sywell Country Park and Reservoir (fishing) 4 miles; Irchester Country Park and Narrow Gauge Railway Museum 3 miles

The Lamb Inn   51

*Little Harrowden,
near Kettering,
Northamptonshire
NN9 5BH
Tel: 01933 673300
Fax: 01933 403131*

Directions:

Little Harrowden
lies between
Kettering and
Wellingborough,
just west of the
A509

Looking for a typical whitewashed country inn with small-paned windows, a swinging pub sign and a welcoming atmosphere? Welcome to **The Lamb Inn** at Little Harrowden! This is a gem of a place, deep in the heart of the soft, delightful Northamptonshire countryside. Under the personal supervision of mother and daughter team Linda Shadbolt and Melanie Martin, it oozes tradition and history. One look at its recently repainted exterior will tell you that this is an immaculately kept establishment popular with both locals and visitors. It sits close to the heart of the village, and the inside is just as clean and spotless – even the carpets. There is a bar, lounge and 30-seat dining area, and much thought had obviously gone into the planning and furnishing of the whole place. It is cozy and inviting while at the same time giving plenty of space to stretch the legs and relax.

The food is traditional, and always plentiful. Just ask the locals, who invariably do their away from home eating here! Or watch the heaped plates as they're set before the diners. What the visitor gets are family meals prepared by family chefs, and even the most man-sized of appetites is sure to be satisfied. And there's plenty of variety behind the bar – everything from cask conditioned ales and guest beers to wine and spirits.

There's nothing pretentious about the Lamb Inn. What you see is what you get – good, well prepared traditional English food, a wide choice of drinks and a warm welcome in the traditional English manner.

Opening Hours: 12.00-23.00 Monday to Saturday, and 12.00-22.30 on Sunday

Food: Traditional, honest food (and plenty of it), all beautifully prepared and served

Credit Cards: All cards with the exception of American Express and Diners

Accommodation: None

Entertainment: Occasional karaoke and charity nights, and a quiz every other Sunday

Facilities: Beer garden and patio, with occasional barbecues. Children are always welcome.

Local Places of Interest/Activities: Sywell Reservoir (fishing) and Country Park 4 miles; Sywell Aerodrome and Aviation Museum 4 miles; Lamport Hall 7 miles; Boughton House 7 miles

52   The Montagu Arms

Barnwell,
near Oundle,
Northamptonshire
PE8 5PH
Tel: 01832 273726
Fax: 01832 275555

Directions:

Barnwell is three miles south of Oundle, just off the A605

Barnwell is one of the most beautiful villages in Northamptonshire. The cottages are built of old, local stone, and a green-verged stream divides the village in two. Beside one of the picturesque bridges that cross it stands **The Montagu Arms**, built of the same warm stone, and fitting beautifully into the village landscape. Small paned windows, thick walls and tall trees fronting the inn complete what is undoubtedly a picture postcard scene.

The inn dates from the 17th century, when the Montagu family were lords of the manor, and it has an equally appealing interior. Bare stone walls, flagstones on the floor, old beams and a wealth of gleaming wood gives it the unmistakable look of a traditional village inns. But all this doesn't happen by accident. Husband and wife team Ian and Lisa Simmons work hard to keep it this way, and they've created a warm, friendly atmosphere that is apparent as soon as you step over the threshold. Five cask conditioned ales are always available, as well as lager, beer, stout and cider. And, of course, there's a good choice of wines. Justin, Ali and Lisa do the cooking, and use fresh local produce wherever possible. There's sure to be something for everyone in the dishes available. You can have simple bar snacks, or choose from the Á la carte menu. Close to the inn there are four stone built twin chalets, all en suite, and all with TV and coffee and tea making facilities.

The Montagu Arms is justly proud of its warm, cozy atmosphere. Ian and Lisa have got it just right by retaining the olde worlde charm of the inn, while at the same time offering the modern concepts of friendly efficient service and value for money.

Opening hours: Monday to Friday: 12.00-15.00 and 18.00-23.00; Saturday and Sunday: 12.00-23.00

Food: 12.00-14.30 and 19.00-22.00 seven days a week

Credit cards: All credit cards except Diners

Accommodation: 4 en suite chalets next to the inn, with TV and coffee and tea making facilities

Facilities: Beer garden with occasional barbecues in summer

Local Places of Interest/Activities: St Andrew's Church in the village; Brigstock Country Park 5 miles; Lyveden New Bield (NT) 4 miles miles; Elton Hall 5 miles; Deene Park 7 miles; Barnwell Country Park 1½ miles

The New Inn

Silver Street,
Abthorpe,
Towcester,
Northamptonshire
NN12 8QR
Tel: 01327 857306

Directions:

The inn is within Abthorpe, a hamlet on a minor road off the A43, about 3 miles west of Towcester.

Think of the classic English village pub, and you could be thinking of **The New Inn** at Abthorpe, right in the heart of the delicious Northamptonshire countryside. It dates from 1847, and its mellow red brick exterior has hanging baskets, tubs and window boxes everywhere. In the summer the place a riot of colour, and because of this you just can't miss it - nor can you afford to!

The New Inn has recently been taken over by David Hastie and Hazel Ludgate, who are well on the way to creating a pub full of character and charm. The inviting interior is snug and cozy, with a compact lounge/dining area plus bar and taproom. One of the most interesting features is a wall covered in old framed photographs and documents highlighting the history of the area surrounding Abthorpe.

The food is ample and traditional, prepared by Hazel (who's an experienced cook) on the premises from locally sourced ingredients wherever possible Ask one of the locals, and you'll be told that you must try the New Inn's home cooked pies. If, however, you feel adventurous, there's a small but comprehensive menu that offers you something a bit more special. This is a real ale pub (and people come from far and near to sample them) offering Hook Norton beers, plus a small but comprehensive range of wines to accompany your meal.

This is an inn for all seasons - warm and snug in the winter, and cool and welcoming in the summer, when you can sit outside in the beer garden and even, if you're lucky, take part in a barbecue!

Opening Hours: 12.00-14.30 and 18.00-23.00 Monday to Saturday, and 12.00-14.30 and18.00-22.30 on Sunday

Food: Cooked on the premises, and always good. There's a small but comprehensive menu. Try their home made pies and special sausages prepared by local butcher

Credit Cards: Cash only at present

Accommodation: None

Facilities: Beer garden with occasional barbecues

Entertainment: Quiz Night fortnightly on Mondays, and monthly live music on a Saturday evening

Local Places of Interest/Activities: Silverstone Motor Racing Circuit 3 miles; Stowe Gardens (NT) 6 miles; horse racing at Towcester 3 miles; Canons Ashby (NT) 5 miles; Sulgrave Manor 4 miles; Hook Norton Brewery Visitor Centre, Banbury 12 miles; Llama Trekking Centre, Weston 4 miles

54 The Old Kings Head

Harbidges Lane,
Long Buckby,
Northamptonshire
NN6 7QL
Tel: 01327 844195

Directions:

Long Buckby is on the B5385, between the A5 and the A428

Dating from the 17th century, the building that houses **The Old King's Head Inn** was originally a bakery, and you can still see the old oven to this day. For all that, it now manages to look like everyone's picture of a typical village inn – thick, whitewashed walls and attractive small windows, and a thatched roof. It sits about 300 yards from the centre of a large village which once supported a thriving boot and shoe manufacturing industry.

The village is still thriving, and The Old King's Head Inn, thanks to owners John Dunville and Carolyn Marjolin, plays an important part in its life. Every year it hosts Long Buckby's annual pumpkin show, and it has its own football team. The interior of the inn is comfortable and welcoming – a place where visitors can relax and enjoy a quiet drink or a meal. The public bar and the lounge bar are carpeted throughout, and, while looking snug and inviting, still manage to convey a light and airy feeling.

The food is traditional, beautifully cooked and competitively priced. No frills here – just honest, simple fare that will make you smack your lips in anticipation. It's all cooked on the premises by John, using local ingredients wherever possible. Meanwhile, Carolyn is behind the bar serving a wide range of drinks. There are five cask conditioned real ales on offer, ranging from Tetley Cask to Adnam's Broadside, plus occasional guest ales. And, of course, if you're wanting to celebrate, there's a small but select wine list.

Opening hours: 11.00-23.00 from Monday to Saturday and 11.00-22.30 on Sunday

Food: Good, honest tasty meals, served between 12.00-15.00 and 19.00-21.00 Monday to Saturday. Sunday lunches are available between 12.00-15.00, though booking is advisable

Credit cards: Cash only at present

Accommodation: None

Entertainment: Quiz night every Sunday, plus occasional live music. Darts and pool can be played.

Facilities: Beer garden; patio garden; no smoking area

Local Places of Interest/Activities: Althorp Park 3 miles; Holdenby House and Falcon Centre 3 miles; Coton Manor 3 miles; Cottesbrooke Hall 7 miles; Daventry Country Park 4 miles

The Old Three Cocks | 55

High Street,
Brigstock,
near Kettering,
Northamptonshire
Tel: 01536 373736

Directions:

Off the A6116, four miles south east of Corby

Brigstock is an ancient village with an old church and a cross that records the coronation dates of four queens - Elizabeth 1, Anne, Victoria and Elizabeth 11. It also has a delightful inn - **The Old Three Cocks**, which dates from 1881 and is substantial and imposing. The place is popular with both locals and people who travel the A6116, which bypasses the village. Owned by Janet Reader, the inn is well appointed and clean throughout, with a homely feel to it. But it is also bright and airy, with plenty of space to stretch the legs and relax while enjoying a drink or meal. The bar is copper-topped, and positively gleams, as does the woodwork and furniture.

The place is renowned for its three cask ales and guest ales, plus lager, Guinness and cider. There's a restaurant area, and the food is honest and traditional, cooked on the premises and beautifully presented. The kitchen staff pride themselves on the fact that people keep coming back to sample the many dishes that are on offer. The Sunday carvery is extremely popular, and if you want to sample the roasts with all the trimmings, you'd be well advised to book in advance. Janet is the sole proprietor, and takes an active role in every aspect of the inn, including the kitchen. This attention to detail shows throughout the establishment, including five rooms which you can book on a bed and breakfast basis.

As soon as you step inside the Old Three Cocks, you know right away that it is a traditional village local - warm and snug in winter, cool in summer, and with a friendly, open welcome for everyone.

Opening hours: Monday to Friday 11.00-14.30 and 17.00-23.00; Saturday 11.00-23.00; Sunday 12.00-22.30

Food: Monday to Saturday: 12.00-21.00; Sunday: 12.00-14.30 (no evening meals on Sunday)

Credit cards: All credit cards except American Express and Diners

Accommodation: 5 rooms available on B&B basis

Entertainment: Occasional karaoke and theme nights; quiz every second Thursday evening

Facilities: Games room

Local Places of Interest/Activities: Brigstock Country Park 1 mile; Lyveden New Bield (NT) 2 miles; Kirby Hall 5 miles; Boughton House 4 miles; Deene Park 5 miles

56   The Red Lion

11 Market Place,
Brackley,
Northamptonshire
NN13 7AB
Tel: 01280 702228
Fax: 01280 701647

Directions:

From Junction 10 on
the M40, take the
A43 north west for 5
miles, then turn left
into Brackley at the
start of its bypass

Brackley is a small market town with a lot of charm and history. It was founded by a Saxon called Bracca, who made a clearing, or "ley" here, hence the name Brackley. But one thing is for sure - if Bracca were alive today, he would head for the **The Red Lion**! With its unusual frontage in slate and stone, you can't miss this sturdy yet charming inn, the oldest in town. It was certainly in existence, under the ownership of a certain William Cave, in 1772, when the inaugural meeting of a friendly society was held there – and owner Nigel Wiles has the articles and rules book to prove it.

The inn has earned a great reputation as a well-run and friendly inn where you'll always get a warm welcome. The whole place – inside and out – is shortly to be tastefully refurbished, though most of the original features will be retained. There's a public bar, a lounge/ dining area and a function room. The pine tables are very old, and the solid oak floors are original. The inn has a fine selection of real ales, plus guest beers, and a fine wine list. The clientele varies from dark-suited business types to workers in overalls, and they all appreciate the olde worlde atmosphere.

The food is another thing that is appreciated, because it ranges from good old fashioned English cooking to something just a bit more adventurous. Try the home made pies – they are justly famous.

The accommodation is keenly priced, and consists of four individual rooms, which are comfortable and well appointed. It's a great base to explore a town which has history on every street.

Opening hours: 11.00-23.00 from Monday to Saturday and 11.00-22.30 on Sunday

Food: A good and varied selection of meals, from pub lunches to something just that little bit special

Credit cards: to be advised

Accommodation: 4 comfortable rooms

Entertainment: Monthly quiz nights and twice monthly live music

Facilities: Beer garden; no smoking area

Local Places of Interest/Activities: Brackley Town Hall (18th century) within town; Stowe Gardens (NT) 5 miles; Silverstone Motor Racing Circuit 6 miles; Towcester (horse racing) 9 miles; Aynho Park 5 miles

Internet/Website:
e-mail: nigel.redlion@virgin.net

The Red Lion | 57

Main Street,
Denton,
Northamptonshire
NN7 1DQ
Tel/Fax:
  01604 890510

Directions:

Four miles east of
Northampton, off
the A428

This whitewashed inn is set just off the road, within a small village. There's a welcoming porch, above which hangs a lamp, and it seems to give a cheery aspect to the place. The windows are small paned, and altogether the place has a traditional look about it. The building dates originally from the late 18th century, though it was upgraded in the 19th century to how we see it today. The compact interior is best described as a real home from home, with well planned fixtures, dark, country style furniture and comfortable, upholstered benches. The copper and brass sparkle, and the floor is carpeted. Under the management of Jon and Deb Sims, **The Red Lion** has earned a reputation as a great inn to have a relaxing drink, a bar lunch or an evening meal.

Both Jon and Deb enjoy cooking, and this is the place to go if you enjoy well prepared food using really fresh ingredients. Only the finest cuts and freshest fish and chicken find their way into the dishes, which are renowned throughout the area. The portions are generous, and the dishes on the menu represent good, honest value for money. There is also a good selection of drinks at the bar, from cask conditioned bitter to lager, cider and Guinness. There's also a small but select wine list to choose from.

Denton is surrounded by charming Northamptonshire countryside, with leafy lanes, streams and woodland. It deserves to be explored, either on foot or by car, and the Red Lion makes a delightful stopping off place if you decide to do so.

Opening hours: Monday to Friday: 12.00-14.30 and 18.30 to 23.00; Saturday: 12.00-15.00 and 18.30-23.00; Sunday: 12.00-15.00 and 19.00-22.30

Food: Mon-Sun 12.00-14.00 and 18.30-21.00

Credit cards: Cash only at present

Accommodation: None

Facilities: Beer garden with occasional barbecues and front patio

Local Places of Interest/Activities: Northampton (historic town) 4 miles; Santa Pod Raceway (drag racing) 7 miles; Sywell Country Park and Reservoir (fishing) 4 miles; Olney (historic town) 5 miles

58 The Red Lion

Stockwell Lane,
Hellidon, Daventry,
Northamptonshire
NN11 6LG
Tel: 01327 261200
Fax: 01327 264376

Directions:

Take the A425 west
from Daventry for 3
miles. Just beyond the
roundabout at
Staverton turn south
onto a minor road.
Hellidon is 3 miles
along this road.

This is the area to see the soft, rich Northamptonshire countryside at its best. Small fields, woodland, country lanes and streams – it's got the lot. Hellidon itself is a large, handsome conservation village which fits perfectly into the rural scenery, and at its heart is **The Red Lion**. It is a long, two storey pub, and sits complacently on a corner, opposite a patch of green. The walls are of warm locally quarried stone, with lazy, welcoming windows.

The inn is within a sporting area, with golf, tennis and croquet on offer. It's also popular with ramblers, who make good use of the inn. The interior is typically English, with open fires in winter, sporting prints on the bare stone walls and copper topped tables. There's a bar, a lounge bar, function room and dining room, and all are scrupulously clean and comfortable. The Red Lion is one of the few places where you can still play the traditional game of Northamptonshire skittles!

The food is outstanding. Visitors can get everything from a bar meal to a superbly cooked gourmet dinner, and all the food is individually prepared on the premises and beautifully presented. The accommodation too is outstanding. There are eight rooms, and all are en suite, with colour TV and tea and coffee making facilities. The present owners have been running the pub for over fifteen years, and this wealth of experience shows through in everything they do. The Red Lion is a pub to remember!

Opening hours: 12.00-15.00 and 18.00-23.00 Monday to Saturday; 12.00-15.00 and 18.00-22.30 on Sunday

Food: Superb food, a wonderful dinner menu and great value pub lunches

Credit cards: Most cards with the exception of American Express and Diners

Accommodation: 8 en-suite rooms with TV and tea/coffee making facilities

Entertainment: Quiz and occasional live music

Facilities: Beer garden

Local Places of Interest/Activities: Windmill Vineyard on the outskirts of the village; Hellidon Lakes Golf Course 1 mile; Burton Dassett Country park 8 miles; Daventry Country Park 6 miles; Stanford Hall 14 miles

Internet/Website:
e-mail: j.daffurn@aol.com

Rose and Crown

Market Place, Oundle,
Northamptonshire PE8 4BA
Tel: 01832 273284
Fax: 01832 275646

Directions:

Oundle is on the A427, 9 miles
east of Corby; the inn sits in the
centre of the town

Oundle is a town steeped in history, and and
has a famous public school. **The Rose and
Crown** stands right in the heart of the place,
in the old Market Square, and dates from
1724. But the building itself goes right back
to the 15th century, and is a stone built, picturesque, bow windowed structure in keeping with the architecture of a town that has
so much to offer the visitor. It is run by husband and wife team John and Dawn Saunders,
who have tried to keep the inn's unique atmosphere. They play a real" hands on" role,
and this shows in the friendly service and
warm welcome you get as soon as you step
over the door. The inside is beautifully clean,
and in keeping with the ambience of the ex-
terior. Warm log fires in winter spread a cozy glow over over the bar areas, the walls are hung
with old framed hunting scenes, there are ships in a bottle and a charming collection of old
Oundle memorabilia.

The inn has a 50 seat restaurant from which you can get a great view of the parish church's
lofty spire. You can order such dishes as salmon in white wine, chicken breast and Stilton,
and barbecued duck. For a real treat, try the slow baked lamb, which is delicious. There are
also bar lunches and light snacks, which can be washed down with one of the four real ale on
offer, or a bottle of wine from the excellent wine list. The Rose and crown is a traditional
English market town inn that seems to be part of the community. It's popular with both local
people and visitors, and everyone is sure of a warm welcome.

Opening hours: Monday to Wednes-
day:11.00-23.00; Thursday 9.00-23.00; Friday
and Saturday: 11.00-23.00; Sunday: 12.00-
22.30

Food: Monday to Saturday: 11.30-14.30 and
18.30-21.30; Sunday 12.00-16.00

Credit cards: all cards except American
Express and Diners

Accommodation: None

Entertainment: Occasional theme nights

such as murder/mystery and Burns Night

Facilities: Beer garden; patio with occasional
barbecues

Local Places of Interest/Activities: Barnwell
Country Park 1 mile; Elton Hall 4 miles;
Prebendal Manor House (Northamptonshire's
oldest house) 5 miles; Peterborough Cathedral 12 miles; Lyveden New Bield (NT) 4
miles

Internet/Website:
e-mail: roseandcrown@btinternet.com

60 Rose and Crown

4 Northampton Road,
Yardley Hastings,
Northamptonshire
NN7 1EX
Tel: 01604 696276

Directions:

Yardley Hastings is on the A428, seven miles south east of Northampton

Yardley Hastings is one of those idyllic villages that Northamptonshire does so well. It's typically English, with beautiful stone-built cottages, thatched roofs and colourful gardens. The inn itself, which dates from 1748, is totally charming, and built of old, mellow stone that fits perfectly into the serene and beautiful landscape. Inside is equally attractive. Think of a cozy, welcoming English inn, full of history and heritage, and you could be thinking of the **Rose and Crown.** There's a bar, a lounge and a restaurant, all with flagstone floors, oak beams, ornate windows and many original features. No could possibly be disappointed with this inn, as it has a warmth and friendliness visitors rarely forget.

But it takes more than just antiques and old features to turn a pub into a comfortable and relaxing place to have a quiet drink or meal. It has to be worked at, and husband and wife team Tereska and Stephen McAllister have worked hard since they took over in December 2000 to create a place that is a pleasure to visit. The bar is especially attractive, and sells real ales, plus a range of lagers, cider and stout. There's also an excellent wine list, which complements the meals that are available. There's a wide choice of food on the menu, including meat, chicken and fish, and it is all cooked on the premises.

This is a historic inn. In October 1840, John Dunkley, a gamekeeper, was murdered in the vicinity, and an old ballad records the event. The actual planning of the murder took place in the Rose and Crown. No one is suggesting you plan a murder under its roof, but you could do worse than have a drink there when you next plan a visit to the area!

Opening hours: 12.00-14.30 and 18.00-23.00 all week

Food: Lunches: 12.00-14.00; evening meal: 19.00-21.00

Credit cards: All cards except Diners

Accommodation: None

Entertainment: Occasional theme nights, such as blues nights, murder mystery, etc.

Facilities: Beer garden; landscaped garden

Local Places of Interest/Activities: Santa Pod Raceway (drag racing) 6 miles; Castle Ashby (not open to the public) 2 miles; Burton Dassett Country Park 8 miles; Northampton (historic town) 7 miles

The Royal Oak | 61

Church Street,
Naseby,
Northamptonshire
NN6 6DA
Tel: 01604 740164

Directions:

Take the A508 north from Northampton for 9 miles, then, turn left onto the A14. 3 miles along, turn off onto a minor road signposted for Naseby.

Close to Naseby, in 1645, was fought the most important battle in the Civil War. And within the historic village itself you will find **The Royal Oak**, a friendly inn that dates from the 19th century. It is full of charm, with its brightly painted walls and classic roof and windows - a real village local.

Run by the husband and wife team of Debbie and John Stevenson, it offers all the amenities and comfort you would expect from a pub which has a clean, "family" atmosphere. The interior is bright and airy, with a good, well planned floor space, and the seating is comfortable and inviting.

This is an inn that has a reputation for good traditional food. It represents real value for money, and while the dishes could be described as honest and wholesome, they use only the best ingredients, sourced locally if possible. There's also a pensioners' offer of cod, chips and peas for £2.75. There is a good selection of drinks available - everything from a bottle of wine to accompany a meal to cask conditioned ales and occasional guest beers.

The Royal Oak is an inn that is going places. The Stevensons have been in charge for just over a year, and already its reputation is growing. Naseby is close to one of the highest points in Northamptonshire, and when Debbie and John have completed their plans for the inn, it will surely become one of its high points as well!

Opening Hours: 12.00-14.30 and 17.00-23.00 Monday to Saturday, and 12.00-15.00 and 19.00-22.30 on Sunday

Food: A good, simple menu of traditional dishes is available.

Credit Cards: Most credit cards with the exception of Diners and American Express.

Accommodation: None

Facilities: Large beer garden with children's play area. Occasional barbecues

Local Places of Interest/Activities: Site of the battle of Naseby 1 mile; Kelmarsh Hall 3 miles; Stanford Hall 6 miles; Cottesbrooke Hall 6 miles

62 The Royal Oak

Walgrave,
Northamptonshire
NN6 9PN
Tel: 01604 781248
Fax: 01604 780001

Directions:

Walgrave is on a
minor road to the
west of the A43, 7
miles north of
Northampton

This substantial inn stands overlooking the centre of the village, with a car park in front of it. It is built of a light stone, with a well proportioned front and clean, white framed windows. It has been an inn since 1840, though the building itself is much older than that. Walgrave itself is very pretty, and **The Royal Oak** fits perfectly into its charming, olde worlde atmosphere. Inside is open plan, with many period fittings. There are bare stone walls, black beamed ceilings, and in the winter the open fires in the restaurant and bar areas give out a welcoming heat and cozy glow that reflects on the well polished and spotlessly clean furniture.

It is a family run place, and landlord Trevor Jones has tried to create an inn which is popular with both locals and visitors alike. His son Aaron runs the Tollemache Arms in Harrington, so looking after well maintained hostelries seems to run in their blood! Real ales are available at the bar, plus guest ales, and there's a good selection of lager, stout and cider as well. The Royal Oak's food is famous, and Trevor reckons he serves about 600 bar meals a week! The cuisine is traditional British, and the seafood, which is always fresh, is particularly recommended. For bar meals, you can choose from the chalkboard, but if you want something just that little bit special, a gourmet menu is also available. If you want wine to accompany your meal, there's a small but select wine list which will undoubtedly include something that complements your choice of food.

Opening hours: 12.00-15.00 and 18.00-23.00 Monday to Saturday and 12.00-22.30 on Sunday

Food: Served when open

Credit cards: All credit cards except American Express

Accommodation: None

Facilities: Car park; beer garden; function suite; occasional barbecues

Local Places of Interest/Activities: Lamport Hall 3 miles; Pitsford Reservoir (fishing) and Brixworth Country Park 3 miles; Cottesbrooke Hall 5 miles

The Sun Inn 63

Farrer Close,
Whitfield,
Brackley,
Northamptonshire
NN13 5TG
Tel/Fax:
  01280 850232

Directions:

Approx 1½ miles
north of Brackley
off the A43

The attractive village of Whitfield stands on the border between Northamptonshire and Oxfordshire. Within it you'll find **The Sun Inn**, which dates from the 18th century, and is run by the husband and wife team of Janet and Graham Tofte. The old inn is just as attractive as the village, and fits in perfectly with the sturdy stone cottages. This is Olde England at its very best –unhurried, charming and welcoming. The surrounding landscape of fields, woodlands and streams might not be spectacular, but it does impart a sense of peace and continuity.

So too does the pub's interior. Think of a friendly open fire, low beamed ceilings and small copper topped tables, all dimly lit. Think also of a wealth of prints on the walls and quirky objects d'art dotted around, and you'll get an idea of how relaxing it is to have a quiet drink or a meal here. There is a public bar, a lounge, and a 50-place restaurant – all spotlessly clean and comfortable. There is a good selection of cask ales, plus one or two guest ales, and a small selection of choice wines. Janet does the cooking, which is outstanding. The Sun Inn must have the longest menu of any pub in the area, and everything is perfectly prepared and presented. Try the 16 oz. steaks if you need convincing! If it's a simple pub lunch you're after, you can get that as well – and it's just as beautifully cooked.

The inn has ten rooms, four of which are en suite. All have TVs and coffee and tea making facilities.

Opening hours: 11.00-23.00 from Monday to Saturday and 11.00-22.30 on Sunday

Food: A large, comprehensive menu. The food is tasty, and the portions ample

Credit cards: All major cards except American Express and Diners

Accommodation: 10 rooms (4 en-suite) with TV and tea/coffee making facilities

Entertainment: Quiz night every Sunday

Facilities: Beer garden; games room with pool and darts

Local Places of Interest/Activities: Sulgrave 5 miles; Canons Ashby 7 miles; Stowe Gardens (NT) 4 miles; Silverstone Motor Racing Circuit 4 miles

64   Talbot Inn

33 Meadow Road,
Kettering,
Northamptonshire
NN16 8TL
Tel: 01536 514565

Directions:

Kettering is a substantial town about 13 miles north of Northampton. The Talbot Inn is near the centre of the town

Kettering is an industrial town, at one time famous for making shoes and clothing, which still has many quaint, historical corners, especially around the parish

church of St Peter and St Paul. **The Talbot Inn** is on Meadow Road, off the A43 Northampton Road close to the town centre, and has a large frontage in red brick. This is the kind of inn that has a "please step inside" look about it, and if you do, you won't be disappointed. It is well looked after by mine hosts Ann and Kenny Bowen, and enjoys the patronage of local workers, business types and visitors. So there's a good, eclectic mix, which makes for a warm, friendly atmosphere. There's a good sized bar which is cozy and welcoming, a lovely lounge and a restaurant with gleaming cutlery and comfortable seating.

Under the personal supervision of Ann and Kenny, the place has an enviable reputation as a place to relax and have a quiet drink, or to enjoy a bar lunch. The food is good, honest, well cooked and unpretentious, and is all prepared by Ann, using fresh produce wherever possible. The choice ranges from chicken or fish to curries, salads and light snacks, and the prices are reasonable. Sunday lunch is especially popular, and you should book in advance. The Talbot Inn is an award winning real ale pub, with three real ales to choose from plus a good selection of lagers, stout and cider. If you'd like a bottle of wine with your meal, you can choose from a small but varied wine list that's sure to have something that appeals to you. The Talbot Inn is a real English pub, with that traditional feel about it. As soon as you step inside you know that the ales will be refreshing, the food good, and the company friendly and outgoing.

Opening hours: Monday to Saturday:11.00-23.00; Sunday: 12.00-22.30

Food: 12.00-15.00 for seven day (no evening meals)

Credit cards: Cash only at present

Accommodation: None

Entertainment: Quiz nights, Pool, Darts

Facilities: Beer garden; patio

Local Places of Interest/Activities: Manor House Museum within the town; Alfred east Gallery within the town; Wicksteed Park on the edge of the town; Lyveden New Bield (NT) 8 miles; Brigstock Country Park 7 miles; Triangular Lodge, Rushton 3 miles; Boughton House 2 miles

Tollemache Arms | 65

Harrington,
Northamptonshire NN6 9NU
Tel: 01536 710469

Directions:
Harrington lies half a mile north of the
A14, from junction 3

This beautiful country inn dates right back to the time of Henry Vlll, and with its thatched roof and strong walls, it certainly looks quaint and inviting. History has unfolded round it through the years, and indeed its name derives from a well loved vicar of the parish church who retired in the early 1800s. His successor, however, disapproved of strong drink, and bought the inn, installing his coachman as landlord and shutting it on a Sunday.

The welcome at the **Tollemache Arms** is a lot warmer now, thanks to landlord Aaron Jones, a young man with enough drive and experience to turn it into one of the premier inns in the area. The interior reflects the inn's long history, with antiques everywhere, and a cozy yet open and airy atmosphere. The well stocked bar has a wide range of ales and lagers on offer, and there's an excellent wine list. As soon as you enter the inn, you know that food is important here. The tables in the dining room are set with cut glass, linen and shining cutlery. The chef is classically trained, and the à la carte menu caters for the most discerning of palates.

But beware - the restaurant is situated in the area of the inn where our disapproving vicar used to lay out the local dead! There's no evidence that the place is haunted, but if you visit the Tollemache Arms, you're sure to find the fine food and good ale will haunt your memory for some time afterwards!

Opening Hours: 12.00-15.00 and 18.00-23.00 seven days

Food: An excellent menu of distinctive food, including vegetarian, plus bar meals. There are occasional gourmet nights

Credit Cards: Most credit cards with the exception of Diners and American Express

Accommodation: Available shortly, phone for details.

Entertainment: Monthly theme nights

Facilities: Large car park and gardens

Local Places of Interest/Activities:
Harrington Airfield and Museums 1 mile; site of the battle of Naseby 5 miles; Kelmarsh Hall 3 miles; Lamport Hall 4 miles; Rushton Triangular Lodge (English Heritage) 4 miles

66   The Wharf

Welford,
Northamptonshire
NN6 6JQ
Tel: 01858 575075

Directions:

Turn east at Junction 19 of the M1 onto the A14. Five miles on at junction1, turn left onto the A5199. Welford is two miles along the road.

The Wharf stands next to the Welford Bridge, over the River Avon. The Welford arm of the Grand Union Canal stretches to the bottom of the car park. The Building dates from the early 19th century, and over the years has been added to and altered, resulting in an unusual yet delightful building which in some ways resembles a small castle. The Wharf is an attractive example of a typical canalside inn, though it has the added advantage of being located within some delightful countryside. The inside is grand and roomy, with bare brick walls being a particular feature. There's a bar, a comfortable lounge, a restaurant and a piano lounge – all well appointed, and all spotlessly clean and welcoming. You can also sit out in the garden in the summer months, and watch for the canal boats gliding into the marina.

It's no wonder that this is a popular place with the locals. Here they can meet, have a drink and chat, or sit down to a beautifully cooked meal or bar lunch. The menu would please the most fastidious of diners, and all the food is beautifully cooked on the premises from fresh produce. But The Wharf isn't averse to experimenting, and a daily chalk board announces the dishes of the day – all of them tasty, and all well worth sampling. There's also a Sunday carvery. Customers can chose from three different cask ales, and there are regular guest ales as well. Plus there's a small but interesting wine list. The Wharf is run by husband and wife team Trevor and Sue Burberry, who have put a lot of effort into making it what it is today – an inn with character and charm, and one well worth a visit.

Opening Hours: 12.00-23.00 Monday to Saturday, and 12.00-22.30 on Sunday.

Food: An extensive menu, with chalkboards announcing daily specials. Meals are served from 12.00-14.00 and 18.00-21.00 Mon-Sat, and Sunday carvery 12.00-15.00

Credit Cards: All major cards

Accommodation: 2 double rooms en suite; 1 twin en suite, one bunk bed room with separate shower room

Entertainment: Occasional quizzes, theme nights, laser shoots, live music and open air theatre.

Facilities: Beer garden and occasional barbecues

Local Places of Interest/Activities: Welford Marina next to inn; The Soaring Centre (gliding) 1 mile; Naseby battlefield 3 miles; Stanford Hall 3 miles; Northampton and Lamport Railway (privately owned) 6 miles. Foxton Locks 8 miles.

The Windmill 67

Badby,
near Daventry,
Northamptonshire
NN11 3AV
Tel: 01327 702363
Fax: 01327 311521

Directions:

Take the A361 south
out of Daventry for
two miles. Badby
sits just off the
main road, and the
inn is in the heart
of the village

This is a real charmer
of a country inn.
Warm, honey coloured local stone, small-paned windows and a thatched roof. What more
could the discerning customer ask for? Well - quite a lot, actually, and **The Windmill** is sure
to provide it! It was built in 1673 within a pretty village that speaks of history and tradition.
But the inn itself isn't an old fashioned place – it has been tastefully modernised internally by
owners John Freestone and Carol Sutton, and the standard of service and efficiency is first
class. Period features have been retained, and any changes have been sympathetic to the
original ambience and history of the building. When you step through the door of The
Windmill, you know that you're going to be well looked after.

The inn is famous for its food, and there's truly something for everyone – bar lunches
that represent good value for money, and full meals that can be traditional or just that little
bit different, depending on your taste. There's a daily specials board, and the menu features
such dishes as monkfish wrapped in prosciutto ham with a spicy tomato sauce, lambs kid-
neys in wine sauce and pheasant casserole. The bar is well stocked, and cask ales and occasional guest ales are available. There's also a small but enlightened wine cellar for that
special evening meal.

The Windmill has eight rooms, and all have been recently modernised to a high standard.

Opening hours: 11.00-23.00 Monday to
Saturday; 11.00-22.30 on Sunday

Food: Superb food, a wonderful dinner menu
and great value pub lunches, served 12.00-
14.00 and 18.30-21.30

Credit cards: Most cards with the exception
of American Express and Diners

Accommodation: 8 recently modernised
rooms

Entertainment: Quiz and occasional theme
nights

Facilities: Beer garden

Local Places of Interest/Activities:
Silverstone Motor Racing Circuit 12 miles;
Canons Ashby (NT) 5 miles; Sulgrave 8 miles;
Althorp House 7 miles

68 The Woolpack Inn

Kettering Road,
Islip,
Northamptonshire
NN14 3JU
Tel: 01832 732578
Fax: 01832 731843

Directions:

Take the A14 east from Kettering for 6 miles, then turn north onto the A6116. Islip is just off this road, about one mile along

Set in the picturesque and historic village of Islip, whose church has monuments associated with the ancestors of George Washington, you'll find the **Woolpack Inn**. It's a splendid old place, built of mellow local stone, with walls two feet thick in places. It dates from the 16th century, though it has been tastefully added to and altered over the centuries. The outside is particularly pleasing, with hanging baskets and window boxes, leaded bow windows and small dormers dotted along the roof. There's been an inn within its walls since at least 1762, when a John Varley was the registered ale house keeper.

Now run by husband and wife team Sue and Lionel Roberts, the place has managed to retain much of its olde worlde charm, while still offering modern service and real value for money. The interior is spotlessly clean, and the bar is particularly charming and quaint, with much gleaming brass, stone walls, fireplace, and little nooks and crannies just right for a cozy drink and a chat. There are four cask ales on offer, plus lager and cider, and if you want a special meal, the wine list will surely offer something suitable. The dining room seats up to 85 patrons, and the food is a great mixture of traditional and modern, all cooked by Sue on the premises. If it's fast food you're after, forget it. Every dish is individually prepared, and great care is taken to use only the freshest produce. You can eat Thai and Italian dishes here, for instance, and the baked monkfish is a speciality of the house. Adjacent to the inn are ten well appointed chalets, all en suite, with tea and coffee making facilities and TVs. The countryside around Islip is typical of Northampton - green and pleasant, with woodland, streams and winding lanes. The Woolpack Inn is the perfect base from which to explore it.

Opening hours: Monday to Saturday from 12.00-23.00; 12.00-22.30 on Sundays

Food: Monday to Saturday from 12.00-14.30 and 18.00-21.30; lunchtime only on Sunday

Credit cards: All major cards except American Express

Accommodation: 10 en-suite chalets with TV and tea/coffee making facilities

Entertainment: Monthly jazz sessions and a fortnightly quiz

Facilities: Car park; beer garden; function suite being developed

Local Places of Interest/Activities: Lyveden New Bield (NT) 4 miles; Brigstock Country Park 4 miles; Barnwell Country Park 5 miles; Oundle (historic town) 6 miles; Triangular Lodge, Rushton 9 miles; Boughton House 5 miles

3 Leicestershire

PLACES OF INTEREST:

PUBS AND INNS:

The Hidden Inns of the Heart of England

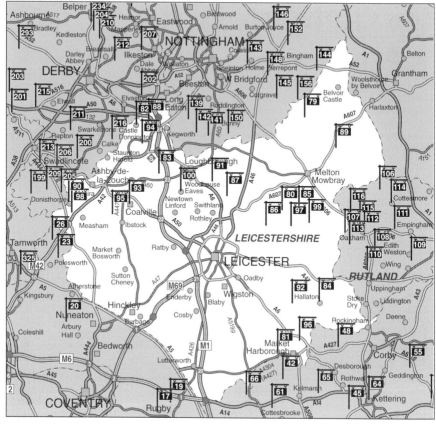

© MAPS IN MINUTES ™ 2001   © Crown Copyright, Ordnance Survey 2001

79	The Black Horse, Hose
80	The Carington Arms, Ashby Folville
81	The Coach and Horses, Lubenham
82	The Cross Keys, Castle Donnington
83	The Delisle Arms, Shepstead
84	The Fox Inn, Hallaton
85	The Fox Inn, Thorpe Satchville
86	The Golden Fleece, South Croxton
87	The Horse & Trumpet, Sileby
88	The Jolly Sailor, Hemington
89	The Marquis of Granby, Waltham-on-the-Wolds

90	The Masons Arms, Donisthorpe
91	The Navigation Inn, Barrow upon Soar
92	The Old Barn Inn, Glooston
93	The Pick and Shovel, Coalville
94	The Plough Inn, Diseworth
95	The Queens Head, Heather
96	The Red Lion, Great Bowden
97	The Saddle, Twyford
98	The Shoulder of Mutton, Oakthorpe
99	The Stag and Hounds, Burrough-on-the-Hill
100	Wheatsheaf Inn, Woodhouse Eaves

Please note all references refer to page numbers

Leicestershire

A pleasant county of fields and woods, ancient earthworks, picturesque villages and some marvellous churches. The towns of Ashby, Coalville, Loughborough, Hinckley, Market Harborough and Melton Mowbray all have great history and character, and the county capital Leicester offers the best of several worlds, with a rich industrial and architectural heritage, a wealth of history, an abundance of open spaces, a firm commitment to environmental issues and an eye to the future with the of a space centre. Loughborough has been famous for making bells for over 100 years, their product pealing from many of England's church towers. At Melton Mowbray, wondrous pies have been made on a commercial scale since 1830. Red Leicester cheese was made in the southern part of the county in the 1700s, but now the only genuine product is made at Melton, which also makes Stilton and, of course, the superlative pies. The most attractive features of this unassuming county are shy and quiet, and have to be sought out, but they amply reward the explorer.

Leicestershire is divided into two almost equal parts by the River Soar, which flows northward into the Trent. It separates the east and west by a broad valley, flowing through historic Leicester in the very heart of the county. Nearly half of the county live in Leicester; the rest are in over 200 villages. All who know Leicestershire know Swithland Wood. The experience of walking through the dense carpet of bluebells inearly summer is without parallel. Charnwood Forest has an area of 60 square miles, but the little mountain region has lost much of its woodland. Even so it remains an area of outstanding natural beauty, rich in flora and fauna of all kinds.

PLACES OF INTEREST

ASHBY-DE-LA-ZOUCH

A historic market town whose name comes from the Saxon Aesc (ash) and Byr (habitation); the ending de la Zouch was added in 1160 when a Norman nobleman Alain de Parrhoet la Zouch became lord of the manor by marriage. in the 15th century Edward IV granted Ashby Manor to his favourite counsellor, Lord Hastings, who converted the manor house into a castle and rebuilt the nearby St Helen's Church. During the Civil War **Ashby Castle** was besieged for over a year by the Parliamentarian Army until the Royalists surrendered in 1646. After the war the castle was partly destroyed to prevent its further use as a centre of resistance and almost wholly forgotten until the publication of Sir Walter Scott's Ivanhoe in 1820. He used the castle as the setting for the archery competition which Robin Hood won by splitting the shaft of his opponent's arrow in the bull's eye. The most striking feature of the imposing ruins is the Hastings Tower of 1464, which visitors can still climb to enjoy the view. The earliest parts predate the conversion and include parts of the hall, buttery and pantry of the 12th-century manor house.

Hard by the castle ruins stands **St Helen's Church**, built by Lord Hastings in the 15th century on the site of an 11th century church. Restored and enlarged in 1880, it contains much of interest, including some exceptionally fine stained glass depicting the life of Christ. There are several monuments to the Hastings family and an unusual relic in the shape of a finger pillory used to punish parishioners misbehaving in church. Ashby de la Zouch Museum contains a permanent display of Ashby history, the highlight being a model of the castle during the Civil War siege.

Ashby was for a while in the 19th century promoted as a spa town; the **Ivanhoe baths** were designed in 1822 by Robert Chaplin in Grecian style and had a 150' colonnaded front with 32 Doric columns. Nearby Georgian terraces, also by Chaplin, stand as testimony to the seriousness of the spa project, but a period of decline set in and the baths closed in the 1880s; they were demolished in 1962. Yet another Chaplin building, the grand railway station, ceased to function as a station when the Leicester-Burton line was axed in the 1960s but was restored in the 1980s for use as offices.

BELVOIR CASTLE

The Leicestershire home of the Duke of Rutland is an imposing home in an equally imposing setting overlooking the lovely Vale of Belvoir. The present **Belvoir Castle** was completed in the early 19th century after previous buildings had been destroyed during the Wars of the Roses, the Civil War and in the major fire of 1816. In the stunning interior are notable collections of furniture and porcelain, silks and tapestries, sculptures and paintings, and also within the castle is the **Queen's Royal Lancers Museum**. The grounds are as splendid as the castle and are used for medieval jousting tournaments on certain days in the summer.

BURBAGE

The village was originally called Burbach, a name that came from the burr thistles that grew in profusion in the fields. The 9th Earl of Kent was an early incumbent, being rector here for 50 years at the Church of St Catherine, whose spire is a landmark for miles around. The River Soar rises in Burbage to begin its winding journey to the Trent. **Burbage Woods** are nationally important because of the spectacular ground flora, and Burbage Common is one the largest areas of natural grassland in the locality. For the visitor there's a network of footpaths, bird observation hide, picnic tables and a visitor centre.

A mile further, and half a mile south of the village of Sharnford, **Fosse Meadows Nature Park** is 140 acres of newly created woodland and flowering hay meadows. A trail points out features of interest.

CASTLE DONINGTON

Originally just Donington - the Castle was added when the Norman castle was built to defend the River Trent crossing. It was demolished by King John to punish the owner for supporting Magna Carta and was rebuilt in 1278.

The **Donington Grand Prix Collection**, in Donington Park, is the world's largest collec-

tion of single-seater racing cars. The five halls contain over 130 exhibits depicting 100 years of motor racing, including several McLarens, Mansell's Williams, BRM, Lotus and Vanwall.

COALVILLE

Originally called Long Lane, the town sprang up on a bleak common when Whitwick Colliery was opened in 1824. The big name in the early days was George Stephenson, who not only established the railway here (in 1832) but also built the churches.

At Ashby Road, Coalville, **Snibston Discovery Park** is built on the 100-acre site of the former Snibston Colliery. Visitors can explore a unique mixture of nature, history, science and technology: topics covered include the industrial heritage of Leicestershire, and former miners conduct a lively surface tour of the colliery. The Science Alive Gallery allows visitors to play with lightning, walk through a tornado or cycle with a skeleton; they can test their strength against a pulley system in the Engineering Gallery and see the clothes of days gone by in the Textile and Fashion Gallery. 'Switch on, Tune in' is an interactive exhibition commemorating 75 years of the BBC.

Three miles south of Coalville, **Sense Valley Forest Park**, at Heather near Ibstock, is a 150-acre site that has been transformed from an opencast mine into a woodland and wildlife haven. The site includes several large lakes and areas of conservation grassland, and the number of species of birds recorded grows each year.

Also a little way south of Coalville is **Donington Le Heath Manor House**, an attractive stone manor that is one of the few of its period (1280) to remain intact. The house has been restored in the style of the Tudor and Stuart periods, and the grounds include period flower and herb gardens. Tea room in the old barn.

Hallaton Village

HALLATON

A picturesque and historic village in the rich grazing lands of the Welland Valley. The village goes a little mad on Easter Monday, when the inhabitants challenge the good folk of neighbouring Medbourne to a bottle-kicking contest. A display of this curious event is on show in the **Hallaton Village Museum**, along with relics from the motte and bailey castle and some unusual agricultural items.

HINCKLEY

Many of the old timbered houses still stand in the town of Hinckley, whose Fair is mentioned in Shakespeare's *Henry IV*. In Lower Bond Street, a row of restored 17th-century thatched cottages is home to **Hinckley & District Museum**, whose displays depict aspects of the history of Hinckley and district; these were framework knitters' cottages, and the hosiery exhibits include a 1740 stocking frame.

It was in Hinckley that Joseph Hansom produced the first hansom cab, which he drove at full gallop along Regent Street to prove that it could not be overturned.

KEGWORTH

A large village with many architectural reminders of its days as a framework-knitting centre. The 14th-century church is really splendid, with fine stained glass and magnificent Royal Arms dated 1684. Topics in the **Kegworth Museum** include the knitting industry, saddlery and air transport and photography.

LEICESTER

Designated Britain's first 'environment city' in recognition of its commitment to green issues and the environment, Leicester has numerous parks and open spaces but also a rich architectural heritage, with no fewer than 350 listed buildings. When the Romans built a town here in the 1st century AD they called it Ratae Corielauvorum, and when they left 300 years later it survived in some form. It was the seat of a Christian bishop in the 7th century, and in the 9th century was conquered and settled by the Vikings along with Lincoln, Nottingham, Derby and Stamford. The city flourished in the Middle Ages when the cloth and wool trades became important, and the coming of the canals and the railways brought further prosper-

ity. The development of road transport changed the face of the city, and modern Leicester is a thriving industrial and commercial city with superb shopping and recreational facilities and a mixture of cultures and communities as rich and diverse as any in the land.

At the heart of Leicester's heritage is **Castle Park**, the old town, an area of gardens, churches, museums and other fine buildings. Here are concentrated many of the city's main visitor attractions. **Castle Gardens**, was an area of marshland by the River Soar until it was drained and opened as gardens to the public in 1926. In the gardens is a statue of Richard III, commemorating his links with the city. Castle Motte is a man-made mound built around 1070 by Leicester's first Norman lord; like the gardens, it is open to the public during daylight hours; interpretation boards explain its history. Adjacent to the gardens are the **Church of St Mary de Castro**, founded in 1107 and still in use. The chancel, stained glass, carvings and tombstones are all well worth taking time to examine. Chaucer was probably married here and Henry VI was knighted in the church in 1426. Next to the church is the Great Hall of Leicester Castle. The Hall was built in the 12th century by Robert le Bossu and used by successive Earls of Leicester as their administrative headquarters; it is open to the public on special event days.

Also in the same space is **Newarke Houses Museum**, a museum of social and domestic history contained in two 16th-century houses. Displays include clocks, toys, furniture, a 1940s village grocers shop and a reconstructed Victorian street scene. Leicester's diverse cultural heritage is represented by the **Jain Centre**, the only one of its kind in the Western world, housed in a converted 19th-century Congregational chapel; and the **Guru Nanak Gurdwara**, a Sikh temple and museum.

Across the road from the Jain Centre is the **Jewry Wall and Museum**; the Wall is the oldest Roman Civil building in Britain and was part of the public baths, whose foundations are still visible. The museum chronicles the history and archaeology of the city and the county from Roman times to 1485. The adjacent St Nicholas Church dates back to Anglo-Saxon times, and despite later alterations Saxon work and re-used Roman bricks can be seen in the walls and tower.

74

The Church of St Martin, which was in existence before 1086, was extended in the 14th and 15th centuries, restored in the 19th century and hallowed as the Cathedral of Leicester in 1927. Stained glass and carvings are impressive, and the memorial to Richard III is a highlight.

One of the very finest buildings in Leicester is the **Guildhall**, built around 1390 for the Guild of Corpus Christi and used as the Town Hall from the late 15th century to 1876. Concerts and theatrical performances are held regularly in the Great Hall. Across the road from the Cathedral is **Wygston's House**, a part-timber-framed building, one of the oldest in the city, which now houses displays of fashion, textiles and crafts from around the world, along with a reconstruction of a 1920s drapers shop. This museum section also has an activity area where children are encouraged to dress up in replica historical costumes. Leicester City Museums also include The **New Walk Museum and Art Gallery**, with displays covering natural history, geology, ancient Egypt and a fine German Expressionist collection; Belgrave Hall and Gardens, a Queen Anne house whose rooms reflect Edwardian elegance and Victorian cosiness; and the Abbey Pumping Station, an 1891 station with massive beam engines and several exhibitions. In Western Park, **Ecohouse** is an environment-friendly show home featuring energy efficiency, sustainable living and an organic garden. The **National Space Science Centre**, a multi-million pound landmark project supported by the Millennium Commission, opens to visitors in spring 2001. the centre will house a planetarium, a research centre, artefacts from space and the only Challenger Learning Centre outside the United States.

The newly opened **Charnwood Museum** displays the natural and local history of Charnwood, the district around Loughborough that includes the majestic Charnwood Forest. In Queen's Park stands the imposing **Carillon and War Memorial**. The carillon tower, the first to be built in Britain, was built in memory of the men of Loughborough who gave their lives in World War I and contains a unique carillon of 47 bells, covering four chromatic octaves, under the care of the borough carilloner. Carillon recitals are given in the summer months. Visitors who climb the 138 steps to the viewing gallery are rewarded with magnificent views of the Charnwood scenery. The **Museum of Armed Forces** in the park has displays relating to the Great War and is open seven days a week. Loughborough's Church of All Saints is a large and beautiful medieval building in the heart of the ancient town centre. Exceptional features include the 15th-century roof and clerestory and the grand Somerset Tower.

For many visitors to Loughborough, the most irresistible attraction is the **Great Central Railway**, Britain's only main line steam railway. Its headquarters are at Loughborough Central Station, where there is a museum, a working signal box and a collection of historic steam locomotives. The station, with its ornate canopy over the island platform, is worth a visit in its own right, and is in regular demand from film companies - it was used a few years ago for the filming of *Shadowlands*. The line runs ten miles to Quorn and Birstall, crossing the Swithland Reservoir viaduct, and the service operates every weekend and Bank Holiday throughout the year and weekdays from June to September. A meal on the move makes the trip even more memorable: traditional lunch on the Silver Jubilee

---

LOUGHBOROUGH

Bells have long been an important part of life in Loughborough, whose bells have pealed round the world since 1858, when the bell foundry of John Taylor moved from Oxford. The **John Taylor Bell Foundry Museum**, part of the world's largest working bell foundry, covers all aspects of bellfounding from early times and show the craft techniques of moulding, casting, tuning and fitting up of bells. The museum is open all year, including some weekends, and tours of the foundry itself can be arranged with notice. Tel: 01509 233414

Steam on the Great Central Railway

every Saturday and Sunday; dinner on the Charnwood Forester and Master Cutler Saturday and Sunday evenings. Tel: 01509 230726

Opposite the Central station is the town's original station, where Thomas Cook's famous excursion of 1841 arrived.

In the **Phantom & Firkin**, Loughborough's only brew pub, visitors can see how traditional cask ales are made. Call 01509 262051 for details of free brewery tours.

Loughborough market is one of the finest street markets in the country; full of tradition and atmosphere, it is held in the market place and adjacent streets every Thursday and Saturday. Two days in November see the annual Loughborough Fair, with stalls, shows, rides and other attractions.

LUTTERWORTH

John Wycliffe was rector here under the tutelage of John of Gaunt. His instigation of an English translation of the Bible into English caused huge dissent. He died in 1384 and was buried in the church here, but when he was excommunicated in 1428 his body was exhumed and burned and his ashes scattered in the River Swift. Close to the church, **Lutterworth Museum and Historical Society** contains a wealth of local history from Roman times to World War ll. Outside the village is **Stanford Hall**, home of the Cave family since 1430. The present hall was built by Smiths of Warwick in the 1690s and contains fine pictures, antique furniture and family costumes. The grounds include a wallled rose garden, nature trail, souvenir shop and craft centre. A major, if less expected attraction, is the motorcycle museum.

MARKET BOSWORTH

Market Bosworth has been a Britain in Bloom winner for the years 1995-1998. This market town is of course most famous as the battle site for the turning point in the Wars of the Roses - Richard III (Duke of York, the 'White Rose' county) was routed here by 'Red Rose' forces (Henry Bolingbroke, later Henry IV, of Lancaster) and killed in 1485. This was the battle immortalised in Shakespeare's play Richard III, where the king is heard to cry 'My kingdom for a horse.' Richard's defeat led to the reign of the Tudor dynasty, Shakespeare's patrons and perhaps, therefore, the impetus behind his less-than-complimentary portrayal of Richard, which is disputed by historians to this day. Today's Market Bosworth occupies a delightful rural setting, offering many opportunities for good walks and gentle recreation.

Market Bosworth Country Park is one of many beautiful open spaces in the area. Another is **Bosworth Water Trust's Leisure and Water Park** on the B585 west of town. This is a 50-acre leisure park with 20 acres of lakes for dinghy sailing, boardsailing and fishing. At nearby Cadeby is the unusual combination that is the **Cadeby Light Railway & Brass Rubbing Centre**, comprising a narrow-gauge steam railway, model and miniature railways, a steam road engine and a brass rubbing centre in the church. More railway nostalgia awaits at Shackerstone, 3 miles northwest of Market Bosworth, where the **Battlefield Railway** offers a steam-hauled nine-mile round trip from Shackerstone to Shenton through the delightful scenery of southwest Leicestershire. At Shackerstone is an impressive museum of railway memorabilia, locomotives and rolling stock. Service summer weekends, sometimes diesel railcar.

Five miles northwest of Market Bosworth, on the A444 Burton-Nuneaton road, **Twycross Zoo** is an ideal family attraction, home to a wide variety of animals including gorillas, chimps, orang-utans, gibbons, elephants, lions and giraffes. Pets corner, adventure playground, penguin pool, and in summer donkey rides and train rides. Open daily throughout the year.

On a side road parallel to the A444 three miles north of Market Bosworth a village with the wonderful name of **Barton-in-the-Beans**. The county was apparently once known as 'bean-belly' Leicestershire, on account of the large reliance on the bean crops that formed part of the staple diet in needy times. The beans were said to have been sweeter and tenderer than anywhere else and consequently they were considered for human and not just animal consumption.

MARKET HARBOROUGH

Halfway between Leicester and Northampton at a crossing point of the River Welland, Market Harborough was created as a planned market town in the mid-12th century. The booths that filled its market place were gradually replaced by permanent buildings, and many of these, along with the courts that led off the High Street, still stand. In 1645 Charles l made Market Harborough his headquarters and held a council of war before the Battle of Naseby. The development of turnpike roads - the motorways of their day - led to prosperity and the establishment of coaching inns in the town, many of them still in business. The canals and the railways trans-

Old Grammar School, Market Harborough

formed communications and manufacturing industry became established, the most notable company being RW & H Symington, creators of the Liberty Bodice. The town trail takes in the major buildings, including the 14th-century parish **Church of St Dionysius** with its superb limestone broach (the church has no graveyard as it was until the early 20th century a daughter church of St Mary in Arden with the status of a chapel). The **Old Grammar School** is a timber-framed building with an open ground floor; built in 1614 to serve the weekly butter market and 'to keepe the market people drye in time of fowle weather', it later became a school, a role which it kept until 1892. The factory of the Symington Company, which grew from a cottage industry of staymakers to a considerable economic force in the town, now houses the Council offices, the library, the information centre and the **Harborough Museum**, which incorporates the Symington Collection of Corsetry. Among the town's distinguished past residents are William Bragg, whose nephew and son shared the Nobel Prize for Physics in 1915; Jack Gardner, who was British Empire and European Heavyweight boxing champion between 1950 and 1952; and Thomas Cook, who spent ten years of his life here

and was married in the town. While travelling one day by road to Leicester he conceived the idea of an outing using the then newly opened railway. He organised the excursion from Leicester to Loughborough on July 7 1841; the fare of a shilling (5p) included afternoon tea. Cook later moved to Leicester, where he is buried at Welford Road cemetery.

One mile north of Harborough, in the village of Foxton, the most famous site on the county's canals is the **Flight of ten locks** on the Grand Union Canal. In the **Canal Museum**, the remains of a steam-powered boat lift of 1900 have been restored, and there are several other buildings and bridges of interest (including a swingbridge) in this pretty village.

Melton Mowbray

The very name of this bustling market town makes the mouth water, being home to the pork pie, one of the most traditional of English delicacies. The Melton hunt Cake is another local speciality, and Stilton, 'king of English cheeses', is also made here. The cheese has the longest history, dating back possibly as far as the 14th century. In the 1740s Frances Pawlett from Sproxton came to an arrangement with the landlord of The Bell Inn at Stilton to market the cheese she had helped to develop. Melton Mowbray became the market centre for Stilton and from 1883 to 1914 three specialist fairs were held each year - 12,672 cheeses were sold at the first! A 16lb Stilton takes 17 gallons of milk to produce and a minimum of two months to mature. Hand-raised pork pies have been made here since 1831 and since 1851 in the oldest surviving bakery, **Ye Olde Pork Pie Shoppe**, where visitors can watch the traditional handraising techniques and taste the pies and the Hunt cake. Markets have long been a feature of life in Melton Mowbray, and the Domesday

Nottingham Street, Melton Mowbray

Book of 1086 records the town's market as the only one in Leicestershire. Large street markets are held on Tuesdays and Saturdays in the Market Place, and impressive butter and corn crosses still stand at two of the town's former market points. The **Carnegie Museum** tells the story of Melton through the ages, including 'Painting the Town Red', an occasion in 1837 when the Marquis of Waterford and his pals decided to decorated the town with red paint after a night's drinking. Chief victims were Swan Porch (an inn on the market place) and the keeper of the tollgate. St Mary's Church, considered the largest and stateliest parish church in the whole county, dates from 1170. It has a particularly imposing tower and impressive stained glass windows. Malcolm Sargent, later Sir Malcolm, began his distinguished career here as organist and choirmaster.

MOIRA

Contrasting attractions here. The **National Forest** is a truly accessible, multipurpose forest for the nation that is transforming 200 square miles in the Heart of England. Spanning parts of Derbyshire and Staffordshire as well as Leicestershire, the forest is providing a full range of environmental, recreational and social benefits for current and future generations. The Heart of the National Forest Visitor Centre, located off the B5003 Ashby-Overseal road, is the hub of the whole forest, featuring interactive displays, themed trails, demonstrations, a lakeside restaurant, shop, garden and plants centre, amphitheatre and a number of craft workshops. The site adjoins **Sarah's Wood**, a 25-acre farmland site transformed into a woodland and wildlife haven, with trails and paths suitable for wheelchairs and a children's play area. Near Donisthope, 2 miles south of Ashby, **Willesley Wood** was one of the first National Forest planting sites and is now an attractive 100-acre area of mature woodland, a lake and meadows. One of the walks leads to Saltersford Valley, which features woodland sculptures, a lake and a picnic area.

The industrial heritage of the region is remembered in the **Moira Furnace**, an impressive, perfectly preserved blast furnace built in 1804 by the Earl of Moira. The site includes lime kilns, a casting shed and engine house, and a range of craft workshops, woodland walks, nature and industrial trails, country park and children's playground.

NEWTOWN LINFORD

Bradgate Country Park is the largest and most popular in the county, welcoming well over a million visitors every year. The 850 acres of the park were created from Charnwood Forest 700 years ago as a hunting and deer park, and the scene is probably little changed since, a mixture of heath, bracken, grassy slopes, rocky outcrops and woodland - and the deer are still there. Man-made features of the park include a well-known folly called **Old John Tower**. Built around 1784 by the 5th Earl of Stamford, it stands nearly 700 feet above sea level and affords fine views.

Also here are the ruins of **Bradgate House**, built of brick at the beginning of the 16th century. This was the home of the Grey family and it was here that Lady Jane Grey was born in 1537. In 1553 she married Lord Dudley, son of the Duke of Northumberland, and on the death of her cousin Edward VI she was proclaimed Queen of England in the same year. Nine days later she lost her crown to Mary Tudor, eldest daughter of Henry VIII, and in the following year she was executed for treason. The story is that the foresters at Bradgate cut off the heads of the oaks in the park as a mark of respect; pollarded oaks can still be seen here. Just north of the park is Swithland Wood.

ROTHLEY

This commuter village on the eastern edge of Charnwood Forest has two greens, one fringed with some lovely rural cottages. In Rothley Park, **Rothley Temple** was built by the Knights Templar in the 13th century and its chapel is considered to be among the finest of all their surviving works. The temple was eventually incorporated into Rothley Court, seat of the Babington family; the most famous member of the family, Thomas Babington Macaulay, was born here in 1800. William Wilberforce, a family friend, worked on his Bill for the abolition of slavery while staying here. In 1960 the Court became a hotel. Gaslit **Rothley station** on the Great Central has a splendidly restored parcels office and a signal box that was brought from Wembley to replace the original. The line passes Rothley Brook, which was a canal in Roman times, on its way to the southern terminus just beyond Birstall. There are ambitious plans here, including the construction of a station mod-

78 elled on Marylebone, the erstwhile London terminus of the line.

STAUNTON HAROLD

There's a fine crafts centre here, with 16 craft workshops within a magnificent Georgian courtyard. Crafts at **The Ferrers Centre** include contemporary furniture, ceramics, coppersmithing and forge, picture framing and sign studio, designer clothing and textiles, automata, stained glass, china restoration, stone carving and silver jewellery. Gift shop, gallery and tea room on site. Staunton Harold Hall and Holy Trinity Church are surrounded by the beautiful parkland and lakes of the Staunton Estate. The Palladian-style hall is not open to the public, but the church is open for afternoon visits April to September daily except Thursday and Friday. In the care of the National Trust, the church is one of the few to have been built during the Commonwealth period in 1653 and retains the original pews, cushions and hangings, together with fine panelling and a painted ceiling.

Staunton Harold Reservoir, covering over 200 acres, has two nature reserves, fishing, sailing and a visitor centre with exhibitions and 3-D models. Footpaths and nature walks provide a link with the nearby 750-acre Calke Abbey park at Ticknall, near Melbourne. The National Trust's **Calke Abbey** is a baroque mansion built in 1701-3 which has remained virtually unchanged since the death of the last baronet, Sir Vauncey Harpur-Crewe, in 1924. Interior highlights include an 18th-century state bed, while in the pleasant grounds are walled gardens, an 18th-century stable block and a Gothic-style church.

SUTTON CHENEY

Bosworth Battlefield is the historic site of the Battle of Bosworth in 1485, where King Richard III was defeated by the future King Henry VII. The Visitor Centre gives a detailed insight into medieval times with the aid of models, replicas and a film theatre, and also on site are a picnic area, a country park and a battle trail, a self-guided trail of 1¾ miles which takes the visitor round the field of battle, passing the command posts of Richard and Henry. Huge flags are frequently flown from these sites, adding colour and poignancy to the scene. Visitors can see the well where Richard drank during the battle, and pause at the memorial stone on the spot where Richard died. A fascinating addition to the site is a display of weapons from the Tudor period, found on t e *Mary Rose*, one of Henry VIII's warships, which sank in Portsmouth Harbour in 1545.

SWITHLAND

Swithland quarries produced roofing material from Roman times until about 1887, and other uses of the dark blue slate included the making of fireplaces and gravestones. Cheaper Welsh slate, easily brought in by rail, put paid to these quarries and the pits in Swithland Wood are now filled with water. **Swithland Wood**, which is part of Bradgate Country Park (qv) is a remnant of the original Charnwood Forest and has Ancient Woodland status. **Swithland Reservoir**, opened by Leicester Corporation in 1894, is very grand, with lots of ornamentation on the valve tower, pump house and entrance lodge, and a Greek temple topping the treated water tank! A viaduct carries the Great Central Railway over the reservoir, which had to be drained for its construction. Swithland's 13th-century Church of St Leonard has a brass memorial to a certain Agnes Scott, who lived in the 15th century as a hermit in Charnwood Forest.

WOODHOUSE EAVES

The village takes its name from the edges, or eaves, of Charnwood Forest. The views are superb, especially from the summit of **Beacon Hill Country Park**, one of the highest points in Leicestershire. The park comprises 180 acres of woodland and bracken, and near the top are the remains of a Bronze Age settlement.

The Black Horse

Bolton Lane,
Hose,
near Melton Mowbray,
Leicestershire
LE14 4JE
Tel: 01949 860336

Directions:

Take the A606 north west from Melton Mowbray for 6 miles, then turn east onto a minor road, passing through Long Clawson; Hose is 2 miles further on

Hose is a small village in the beautiful Vale of Belvoir with a 13th century church. It was a large settlement at one time, and extensive earthworks to the north indicate just how large it was. Now it has shrunk to no more than 150 houses. But it does have one of the best inns in the area – **The Black Horse**, a red brick building that dates from the 19th century. It's an attractive building which is full of character, and has been added to over the years.

The inside is a gem, and spotlessly clean. It has recently been tastefully refurbished, and is compact and cozy, with a wealth of gleaming brass and copper. Two open log fires that keep the place snug and inviting on a cold winter's day. The 30 seat restaurant is panelled in oak, and its menu offers a wide range of wonderfully cooked dishes. The cuisine is traditional, with one or two hints of the East that make the dining there an interesting experience. The place is run by husband and wife team Mick and Gail Aram, with Gail doing the cooking. She likes to use good, local produce (even the herbs she uses are from the inn's own gardens!) and the portions are good and filling. She cooks game in season, and sources her fish from Grimsby, which means that it is always fresh. The locals love her range of sauces and fruit-based side dishes. If you would like a treat, order her rack of lamb in a claret sauce - absolutely delicious!

Six real ales are on offer at the bar (three resident, three guest), as well as a range of beers, stouts, lager and cider. There is also a good selection of wines which would complement any meal.

This is an inn that is sure to please the most discerning customer. Warm and snug in winter, cool and welcoming in summer, and with an ambience that is second to none.

Opening hours: Monday to Saturday: 12.00-14.30 and 19.00-23.00; Sunday 12.00-16.00 and 19.00-22.30

Food: Served when open, except on Monday, Tuesday and Sunday evening

Credit cards: Most cards accepted

Accommodation: None

Entertainment: Quiz nights on a regular basis; skittle alley; darts

Facilities: Car park, large enclosed beer garden and patio

Local Places of Interest/Activities: Belvoir Castle: 6 miles; Melton Mowbray (historic town) 6 miles; Woolsthrope Manor (birthplace of Sir Isaac Newton) 12 miles

80 The Carington Arms

Ashby Folville,
near Melton
Mowbray,
Leicestershire
LE14 2TE
Tel/Fax:
  01664 840228

Directions:

Take the B6047
south from Melton
Mowbray for 5
miles, then turn
west onto a minor

Ashby Folville is a charming and picturesque village typical of this part of Leicestershire, at one time famous for its trees, and now visited for the magnificent parish church of St Mary, with its Maud Bassett tomb. Within the village you'll find the equally charming **Carington Arms**, situated on a corner site. It is long and low, and dates from the early 19th century, though it looks older. With whitewashed walls, a mock Tudor gable, and neat, well proportioned windows. It has all the appearance of a typical village local, and indeed that's exactly what it is. It's a favourite haunt of visitors and regulars alike, who appreciate it's unhurried atmosphere coupled with efficient, friendly service. Step over the threshold of the inn and you leave the hustle and bustle of modern life behind you.

In charge is husband and wife team William and Joan Wakeford, who have worked hard to make the Carington Arms what it is today. The interior is smart and well maintained, with square, solid pine tables in the dining area, which seats 20, and comfortable furnishings. On offer at the bar are four real ales, three resident and a rotating guest. Plus, of course, there's a fine range of beers, lager, stout and cider. Joan does the cooking, and the menu could best be described as "English traditional". She takes a pride in using only the freshest produce, with most of it locally sourced if possible. Regulars will tell you to try her delicious steak and ale pie or venison in red wine. If you want to eat on Friday, Saturday or Sunday you should book in advance to avoid disappointment.

Opening hours: Monday to Friday: 12.00-14.30 (closed Wednesday lunchtime) and 19.00-23.00; Saturday: 12.00-15.00 and 19.00-23.00; Sunday: 12.00-15.00 and 19.00-22.30

Food: Served every lunchtime between 12.00-14.30 (except Wednesday); served in the evenings between 19.00-21.00 (except Sunday). Monday evenings-summer only

Credit cards: All major cards except American Express and Diners

Accommodation: None

Entertainment: Quiz night every Tuesday; occasional theme nights

Facilities: Car park; beer garden; occasional barbecues in summer

Local Places of Interest/Activities: Melton Mowbray (Historic town) 5 miles; Burrough Hill Country Park 4 miles; Leicester (historic city) 9 miles

Internet/website:
e-mail: joanWakeford@aol.com

The Coach and Horses | 81

54 Main Street, Lubenham,
Leicestershire LE16 9TF
Tel: 01858 463183

Directions:

3 miles west of Market
Harborough on the A4304
road to Lutterworth

The Coach and Horses is a
truly handsome inn on the village's main street. It was built
in about 1670, and has a handsome, gabled frontage in
warm, golden stone which has
recently been cleaned, and
half dormer windows which
add a touch of tradition to the
place. The windows are small
paned and picturesque, and
the whole place speaks of past times when coaches, pulled by a team of straining horses,
plied the roads of Britain. It is run by husband and wife team Geoff and Liz Sykes, and they
have created an inn that is full of atmosphere and history. The interior is especially charming. There's a cozy, welcoming bar with a roaring fire, a neat lounge and a separate restaurant that is open and airy. The floors are reclaimed timber, and the tables in the bar are of
wood and iron. There are even fine leather couches where you can lie back and stretch your
legs!

Geoff is the chef, and he has put together an excellent and inventive menu which
features a combination of traditional English and new world cooking There's also a specials
board, and the signature dish is bangers and mash made from sausages from the local butcher
(who boasts 100 different flavours) acompanyed by cheesy leek mash with rich onion gravy.
Geoff also has occasional fresh fish nights, where only the finest and freshest seafood is
used. One of the features of the inn is a special deal on food for OAPs. On offer at the bar are
two cask conditioned ales plus a guest ale, and the usual lager, stout and cider. If you require
a bottle of wine, there's a small but comprehensive wine list. The Coach and Horses offers
good old fashioned British hospitality, great food at reasonable prices, and a choice of drinks
that will surely satisfy the most demanding of tastes.

Opening hours: Monday to Saturday: 11.30-
15.00 and 17.00-23.00; Sunday: 17.00-22.30

Food: Excellent, well prepared food is served
Monday to Saturday: 12.00-14.00 and 18.00-
21.30; Sunday 12.00-14.30

Credit cards: all main cards except American
Express and Diners

Accommodation: None

Entertainment: Occasional theme nights,
and the inn is always looking for new ideas!

Live music; quiz on Tuesday evening

Facilities: Beer garden; family garden with
summer barbecue

Local Places of Interest/Activities: Foxton
Locks 1½ miles, Kelmarsh Hall 5 miles;
Market Harborough (historic town) 3 miles;
Lutterworth (historic town) 10 miles; East
Carlton Country Park 8 miles;

Internet/Website:
thecoachandhorses@lubenham.fsbusiness.com

82

The Cross Keys

90 Bondgate,
Castle Donington,
Leicestershire
DE74 2NR
Tel: 01332 812214

Directions:

Leave the M1 at
Junction 24 and
take the A50 west
for two miles; take
the unmarked road
south signposted
Castle Donington

The Cross Keys is housed in a building which is over 300 years old, right in the heart of this large village. It's a substantial, whitewashed inn with well proportioned windows, tall chimneys, hanging baskets and a car park to the side. Irene and James Glenister became mine hosts in 2000, after having looked after a students' union bar in Derby. Their aim to preserve the best period features of this old, traditional hostelry, while offering friendly service and a warm welcome to locals and visitors alike.

The interior is exactly how an old inn's interior should be - cozy and inviting, with dark, low beams, subdued lighting, and polished, comfortable furniture. There's carpeting on the lounge floor and old tiles in the bar, making for that olde worlde, traditional look. There's a selection of real ales behind the bar - Marston's Pedigree, Bass, Theakston's Best, and up to three rotating guest ales. You can also choose from Theakston's Mild, Carling, Stella, Fosters, Becks, John Smiths Extra Smooth, Guinness and Strongbow.

Irene does the cooking, and everything is freshly prepared on the premises using the best of ingredients. Meals are only available at lunchtimes through the week, and you can choose from a menu that features traditional pub food that can satisfy the heartiest of appetites. Irene's watchword is good, old fashioned value for money, and no one could be disappointed with the quality or ample portions.

The Cross keys is a sporty pub, and sponsors the local rugby A and B teams, plus the cricket team. It's the ideal place to stop off for that quiet drink or bar lunch. Irene and James are sure to give you warm welcome!

Opening times: Open lunchtimes and evenings from Monday to Friday; open all day Saturday and Sunday

Food: Good, traditional food is served from 12.00-14.00 Monday to Friday; no food at the weekend

Credit cards: Cash and cheques only at present

Accommodation: None

Facilities: Fruit machine; quiz machine; pub games

Local Places of Interest/Activities: Donington Park (motor racing) 1 mile; American Adventure (theme park) 10 miles; Shipley Country Park 10 miles; Elvaston Castle Country Park 4 miles; Calke Abbey (NT) 5 miles; East Midlands Airport 1 mile

The Delisle Arms　　83

Ashby Road,
Shepshed,
near Loughborough
Leicestershire
LE12 9BS
Tel: 01509 650170

Directions:

Leave the M1 at
Junction 23 and
travel west for 1 mile
along the A512;
Shepshed is to the
north of this road, 1
mile along.

Shepshed sits to the west of Loughborough, close to the M1. At one time it was called "the largest village in England", but it now has town status. Its parish church, St Botolph's, is an ancient building dating originally from the 13th century, and around the ancient market place there are still some thatched houses. **The Delisle Arms** sits just off the M1, on the A512, on the edge of the town, making it an ideal stopping off point for people travelling along the motorway. The building dates from the late 19th century, and is a handsome, stone pub with ornate windows.

Inside, it is spacious and airy, while still having the intimate feel that gives a hostelry its character and atmosphere. There are oak beams, fine carpets and comfortable, upholstered furniture. Excellent use is made of the space, and under the tenancy of Tracie Dyche, it is a favourite place for the locals to have a quiet, relaxing drink or a meal. The food is excellent, with a menu that owes more to restaurant fare than pub fare, while still maintaining pub prices. Choose from a specials board that changes daily, and watch out for monthly specials. Tracie is in charge of the cooking, and a great job she makes of it! Everything is piping hot and well presented, with portions that represent good value for money. At the bar, you can order real ale, or choose from a range of draught beers, lager, cider and stout. And, of course, if you want wine with a meal, you can buy it by the bottle or by the glass.

Opening hours: Monday to Saturday:11.30-23.00; Sunday: 12.00-22.30

Food: Served 12.00-14.30 every day

Credit cards: Switch, Visa and Mastercard

Accommodation: None

Entertainment: Tuesday: quiz night; Thursday: disco night; Friday: karaoke night

Facilities: Beer garden; children's play area; games room

Local Places of Interest/Activities: Mount St Bernard Abbey 3 miles; Loughborough (historic town) 4 miles; East Midlands Airport 5 miles; Bradgate Country Park 6 miles

84 The Fox Inn

North End,
Hallaton,
Leicestershire
LE16 8UJ
Tel: 01858 555278

Directions:

Follow the B664 north east from its junction with the A427 east of Market Harborough for 4 miles. Turn west onto an unmarked road at Medbourne, and Hallaton is 2 miles along it

Leicestershire has some beautiful, verdant countryside - all quiet lanes, quaint cottages and picturesque villages. And they don't come any more picturesque than Hallaton. There's a village green, an old butter cross and thatched houses. Plus, every Easter Monday there's the annual "Bottle Kicking", or "Hare Pie Scramble", when opposing teams from Hallaton and nearby Medbourne try to kick a wooden bottle towards the parish boundaries.

There's also a fine hostelry – **The Fox Inn**, run by husband and wife team Enrique and Jennifer Varela. It's an imposing inn, with parts dating back to the 17th century., though it has been added to over the years. And though the place has recently been refurbished, the interior is equally as imposing. There are terracotta tiles on the floor, gleaming brass, old wood and a general feeling of coziness, history and continuity. There's a well appointed bar, a comfortable lounge, and a restaurant. Jennifer does the cooking, and takes pride in the fact that her food is renowned throughout the area, especially her juicy fillet, sirloin and T-bone steaks. She sources her meat locally, and insists that all her ingredients are as fresh as possible. You can order bar food, or from the full á la carte menu. Behind the bar you'll find two real ales, plus a rotating guest ale, and a choice of draught beers, lager, cider and stout. And in a place where food is important, there's an excellent wine list.

Hallaton is a historic place, and, with its 13th century church, is well worth a visit. If you go there, be sure to pay a visit to the Fox Inn as well!

Opening times: Monday to Saturday: 11.00-15.00 and 18.00-23.00; Sunday: 11.00-15.00 and 18.00-22.30

Food: Superb food is served at lunchtime and in the evenings

Credit cards: Most credit cards accepted except American Express and Diners

Accommodation: None

Facilities: Beer garden; large car park; children's play area; duck pond and lawns

Local Places of Interest/Activities: East Carlton Country Park 5 miles; Eyebrook Reservoir (trout fishery) 4 miles; Market Harborough (historic town) 7 miles

The Fox Inn · 85

Thorpe Satchville,
near Melton Mowbray,
Leicestershire
LE14 2DQ
Tel/Fax:

01664 840257

Directions:

Thorpe Satchville is on
the B6047, 6 miles
south of Melton
Mowbray

Thorpe Satchville is set amid typically rolling English countryside, with woodland, winding country lanes and picturesque thatched cottages. **The Fox Inn** may not be thatched, but it is a charming inn, located in the heart of the village, and a focus for local life. It was built in the the early 1900s of mellow, red brick, with whitewashed walls at the front and large, airy windows. Overall, it is a stylish inn, typical of its period and with a quaintness and warmth that belies its age. In charge is Celia Frew, who has brought a wealth of experience to running what is a cozy and popular village local.

Three real ales are on offer at the bar, including an absolutely stunning one called Robin a Tiptoe, which is only sold in this pub and nowhere else. Why? Because Mrs Frew brews it herself in a nearby micro brewery. You can also, of course, pick from a good range of beers, cider, stout and lager.

The inside is stylish and airy, with good use made of the available space. A bar divides the lounge from the public area, and the whole place is clean and well maintained. The food is simple and always cooked to perfection. You can have a choice of light lunches, though the locals will no doubt advise you to go for the inn's famous mixed grill. And if you want to work off the extra pounds you put on, you could always have a game of skittles in the hostelry's own skittles alley.

There are no frills about the Fox Inn. What you see is what you get - a good, honest selection of drinks (not forgetting John o' Gaunt!), and sensibly priced, delicious meals that will satisfy the heartiest of appetites.

Opening hours: Open seven days 12.00-15.00 and 18.30-23.00 (except Monday lunchtime)

Food: Served when open, except Mondays

Credit cards: Cash and cheques only at present

Accommodation: None

Entertainment: Games room, skittle alley; pool, petanque

Facilities: Car park

Local Places of Interest/Activities: Burrough Hill Country Park 2 miles; Melton Mowbray (historic town) 6 miles; Leicester (historic city) 12 miles Rutland Water 10 miles

86 The Golden Fleece

Main Street,
South Croxton,
Leicestershire
LE7 3RL
Tel: 01664 840275
Fax: 01664 840548
Directions:
South Croxton is
on a minor road off
the B6047, 7 miles
north east of
Leicester city centre

South Croxton is a small, mainly farming, community in the rich farmlands of Leicestershire. It has a medieval church made of local ironstone, plus the delightful **Golden Fleece**, an inn of real charm. It sits right on the village street, and is a long building with hanging baskets and window boxes that add colour to the scene in the summer months. Parts of the building date from the late 18th century, though the facade dates from 1837.

You know that this is a hostelry of real quality and character by just looking at it. When you cross the threshold, this opinion is confirmed. The furnishings and fittings are more hotel-like that pub-like. There's plush and luxurious seating, carpets which combine with the many period features that have been retained, and an atmosphere that speaks of quiet comfort and friendliness. In charge is the husband and wife team of James and Rita Osborne, who with Samantha and Kay, bring to the inn many years experience in the trade.

Three real ales are on offer at the bar - two resident and a guest ale. There's also a range of draught beers, cider, stout and lager. If you wish to eat, you can also order wine by the glass or bottle.

The light and airy dining area seats 40 in comfort, and the resident chef has created a menu that combines the best of British and Continental cuisine. He enjoys a challenge, and is always expanding the menu so that the choice of dishes on offer will have something to please everyone. Everything he uses is fresh, and bought locally if possible, so you know you are getting the best. The Golden Fleece offers English hospitality at its best. If you visit, you'll be sure of a warm welcome from James, Rita, Samantha and Kay.

Opening hours: Monday: 19.00-23.00; Tuesday to Sunday: 12.00-15.00 and 18.00-23.00;

Food: Served Tuesday to Thursday from 18.30-21.00; Friday and Saturday: 18.30-22.00; Sunday: lunchtimes only

Credit cards: All major cards accepted except Diners

Accommodation: None

Facilities: Beer garden with occasional barbecues

Entertainment: Monthly live music

Local Places of Interest/Activities: Melton Mowbray (historic town) 7 miles; Leicester (historic city) 7 miles; Burrough Hill Country Park 5 miles

Internet/website:
www.golden.fleece@barbox.net

The Horse & Trumpet

87

*Barrow Road,
Sileby,
Leicestershire
LE17 7LP
Tel & Fax:
01509 812549*

Directions:

Sileby lies on a
minor road
between the A6
and A46, 6 miles
north of Leicester
city centre

Within the large village of Sileby, with its fine church of St Mary, is **The Horse & Trumpet**, under the personal management of Peter and Anna Higgins. It stands in a row of buildings that is known to be the oldest in Sileby. Though parts have been rebuilt over the years, the inn still retains many period features, both inside and out. The walls are of old, mellow stone, and the inside is comfortable furnished and well maintained, with gleaming woodwork, brass and copper that sparkles and walls that are of bare stone. It's an inn that caters for all tastes, with a large, welcoming public bar, neat, well appointed lounge and a dining area that is spotlessly clean.

The food is cooked by Anna, and represents astonishing value for money. It is traditional English cuisine, with simple dishes that are full of flavour. The portions are ample and hearty, and the service in the dining area is efficient without being hurried. Everything is prepared on the premises from fresh ingredients, and Anna likes to use products that are sourced locally wherever possible. She'll even cook to your preferred taste. In the summer months, you can order from the occasional barbecues that are held on the inn's patio. This, for obvious reasons, is where local people eat and drink, which is a recommendation in itself. Nobody is going to rush you here!

The inn runs occasional special food and theme nights, which are always popular. You can have a choice of four real ales - one a rotating guest - plus there's a fine selection of draught beers, lager, stout and cider. If you like, you can order wine with your meal, either by the glass or bottle. Peter and Anna have worked hard to make the Horse & Trumpet one of the most popular and lively inns in the area. They'd like to welcome you to the Horse and Trumpet so that you can judge for yourself.

Opening hours: 11.00-23.30 Monday to Saturday; 11.00-22.30 on Sunday

Food: Served when inn is open, apart from Sunday, when food is served at lunchtime only

Credit cards: Cash only at present

Accommodation: None

Entertainment: Quiz night every Monday; karaoke and live music twice a month

Facilities: Patio with occasional barbecues in summer

Local Places of Interest/Activities: Melton Mowbray (Historic town) 10 miles; Bradgate Country Park 5 miles; Leicester (historic city) 6 miles; Great Central Railway (Loughborough) 5 miles

88 The Jolly Sailor

Main Street,
Hemington,
Derbyshire
DE74 2RB
Tel: 01332 810448

Directions:

Off the A50,
between Castle
Donnington and
Kegworth

Peter and Margaret have been in the licensed trade for over 20 years, and have owned **The Jolly Sailor** for the last eleven. Hemington is a true hidden village, tucked away in the countryside close to the Nottinghamshire border, but it is well worth seeking out to sample the delights of this lovely inn. Though it looks comparatively new, Peter has looked into the history of the place, and discovered that the building actually dates back to at least the 17th century, though the inn is first mentioned in 1873. Parts of it may have been old cottages lived in by basket weavers.

Children are welcome in this very smart hostelry, which is very clean and presentable indeed. The interior is in keeping with its early origins, and has old beams hung with pint pots and an open fire in the comfortable and well appointed lounge. The restaurant, which is non smoking, is light and airy, with salmon pink walls and carpeted floors that will enhance any dining experience.

There are separate bar and restaurant menus, and a wide choice of home made dishes are available, including fish, meat and poultry. The restaurant seats 22 in comfort, though if you want to eat there, you should book to avoid disappointment. However, no food is served on Sundays or Mondays, except at bank holidays. If it's a drink you want, then the bar has no less than seven real ales on offer, including Bass, Marston's Pedigree, Abbot, Mansfield, M&B Mild and two guest ales. Also available is Tetley's Smooth, Carling, Harp and Stella lagers, Blackthorn cider and Guinness. And. of course, there's a range of wines and spirits. The Jolly Sailor is a first class establishment that is spotlessly clean, and offers good value for money in comfortable surroundings. You're sure of a warm welcome from Peter and Margaret if you pay them a visit.

Opening times: Open lunchtimes and evenings from Monday to Friday and all day on Saturday and Sunday

Food: Lunches are served 12.00-14.00 from Tuesday to Saturday; evening meals are served 18.00-22.30 Friday and Saturday

Credit cards: Most credit cards accepted

Accommodation: None

Facilities: Car park

Local Places of Interest/Activities:
Donington Park (motor racing) 3 miles; Calke Abbey (NT) 7 miles; East Midlands Airport 1 mile; Staunton Harold Church (NT) 8 miles

The Marquis of Granby 89

*Waltham-on
-the-Wolds,
nr Melton Mowbray,
Leicestershire
LE14 4AH
Tel: 01664 464212*

Directions:

Take the A607 north east from Melton Mowbray; Waltham on the Wolds is just off this road 5 miles along

Waltham-on-the-Wolds is a charming village of old stone cottages, some of which are thatched. It was an important place at one time, as it used to have a weekly market and annual horse and cattle fairs. It is home to **The Marquis of Granby**, a charming yet substantial corner site inn that dates from the 17th century. Over the years, it has been tastefully modernised, and now offers first class service and hospitality to regulars and visitors alike. It has recently been refurbished throughout, and is a wonderful mixture of period detail and modern facilities. It has a huge floor space, with a carpeted restaurant, a delightful flagstoned lounge and bar, and a games room.

In charge is Melanie Dawson, who had a wealth of experience in the trade before taking over at the beginning of 2001. She is committed to good old fashioned friendly service, a warm, welcoming atmosphere and genuine value for money. The restaurant seats 60 people in comfort, and has a varied menu which includes full business lunches, bar snacks and evening meals, all of which can be cooked to your individual taste. If you'd like a glass or bottle of wine with your meal, Melanie will be glad to oblige, as the wine list is comprehensive and popular.

At the bar, you can order from a wide range of drinks, including three cask ales and a rotating guest ale, beers, stout, lager and cider. These can be consumed in the bar or lounge, where the seating is comfortable and the ambience relaxing. Melanie knows what a customer expects from an inn, and is determined to provide it. She has great plans for the place, and her next project is to provide good accommodation so that visitors can stay the night on a B&B basis or use the inn as a base for exploring the surrounding area.

Opening hours: Monday to Friday: 11.00-14.30 and 17.30-23.00; Saturday and Sunday: 12.00-23.00

Food: Simple, beautifully cooked food is served from Monday to Saturday between 12.00-14.00 and 18.00-21.00, and on Sunday between 12.00-2.00

Credit cards: Cash only at present

Accommodation: Available shortly -phone for details

Entertainment: Quiz night on Wednesday; theme nights on demand (phone for details)

Facilities: Beer garden; skittle alley; occasional barbecues

Local Places of Interest/Activities: Belvoir Castle 6 miles; Melton Mowbray (historic town) 5 miles; Grantham (historic town) 9 miles; Woolsthrope Manor (birthplace of Sir Isaac Newton) 8 miles

90 The Masons Arms

1 Church Street,
Donisthorpe,
Leicestershire
DE12 7PX
Tel: 01530 270378

Directions:

Leave the M42 at Junction 11 and travel north west for a mile and a half on the A444. Donisthorpe is on a minor road to the east of the A444.

Donisthorpe is an old mining village right on the Leicestershire-Derbyshire border. The mines have long gone, but the place is rightly proud of its traditions and industrial heritage. At the heart of the village you'll find the picturesque **Mason Arms**, an inn that has the look and feel of bygone days, even though it only dates from 1934. It was built on the site of an earlier inn, and is an attractive place, with walls of mellow red brick and a half timbered gable. The roof is steeply pitched, and the overall effect is of a typical English inn - warm and welcoming to both locals and visitors alike.

Sharon Moorecroft has only recently taken over as mine host, though she brings a wealth of experience to the job, having been in the trade for over ten years. The interior has an ambience and atmosphere that continues the traditional look of the exterior. It is spotlessly clean, with polished woodwork, gleaming brass and comfortable seating. Just the kind of place where you can enjoy a relaxing drink or a meal! There is a good range of quality ales, such as Marston's Pedigree (which is a real ale), Worthington Creamflow, Bass Mild, Guinness plus lager and cider. Plus, of course, there is a wide range of spirits and wines. The food is good and filing, with generous portions. You can chose from the menu or from the specials board, and there's a popular Sunday lunch, for which you are advised to book in advance. Sharon herself does the cooking, and she uses fresh ingredients wherever possible.

The Masons Arms is a distinctive, quaint pub which belies its modern origins. Sharon has great plans for it, and already she has put some of them into action, making it a great place to stop if you're touring the area.

Opening hours: Monday to Saturday: 12.00-23.00; Sunday: 12.00-22.30

Food: 12.00-15.00 and 19.00-23.00 every day; Sunday lunches served 12.00-15.00

Credit cards: Cash and cheques only at present

Accommodation: Small campsite for campers and tourers behind the inn

Entertainment: Live bands or karaoke on Saturdays from 21.00; quiz from 21.00 on

Sunday evenings; free pool and juke box on Tuesdays from 19.00; music sessions on every second Wednesday evening - bring your own instrument

Facilities: Car parking; secluded beer garden

Local Places of Interest/Activities: Calke Abbey (NT) 6 miles; Ashby de la Zouch (historic town) 3 miles; Twycross Zoo 4 miles; Donnington Park (motor racing) 10 miles

The Navigation Inn 91

Mill Lane,
Barrow upon Soar,
nr Loughborough,
Leicestershire
LE12 8LQ
Tel: 01509 412842

Directions:

Barrow upon Soar
sits to the east of
the A6, 3 miles
south of the centre
of Loughborough

The Navigation Inn, as its name implies, sits on the banks of a canal - in this case the Grand Union Canal. It is an attractive, red brick building, whitewashed at the front with a well proportioned facade facing the road. It boasts hanging baskets and window boxes full of flowers in the summer months, and beside it is a small, picturesque hump-backed bridge over the canal, again made of old red brick, giving the whole scene a picturesque feel to it. The inn dates from the early 19th century, and in charge is Chris Lee, who has had many year's experience in the trade. He has created a relaxed and charming place to enjoy a drink or a meal, either within the inn, or on the patio on the banks of the canal. The interior is well maintained and spotless, with gleaming brass and copper, open fires, and snug looking tables and chairs. Both the business community and the locals appreciate the ambience of the place,

The Navigation Inn serves pub food at its best. All the produce used is sourced locally wherever possible, and all the dishes are beautifully cooked and presented. The main courses include jumbo battered cod, giant Yorkshire pudding, ham and eggs, steak and kidney pie, lasagna and chicken curry. Or you can go for the speciality of the house - the chicken combo, with an 8oz chicken breast and six pieces of wholetail scampi. There's also a good selection of filled baguettes, baked potatoes and rolls. If you have children with you, then a children's menu is available, as are vegetarian dishes such as vegetarian wedges and vegetable burgers. On a Sunday there is a Sunday roast with all the trimmings available every lunchtime Four real ales and a rotating guest ale are on offer at the bar, plus draught beers, lager, stout and cider. And, of course, there's wine if you wish it to accompany your meal. The inn was mentioned in the CAMRA Good Beer Guide 2000. All in all, this is a lovely hostelry that will always give you a warm, friendly welcome.

Opening hours: Monday to Saturday:12.00-23.00; Sunday: 12.00-22.30

Food: Served lunchtimes only from 12.00-14.30

Credit cards: All major cards accepted except American Express and Diners

Accommodation: None

Facilities: Waterside patio; function room

Local Places of Interest/Activities: Mount St Bernard Abbey 7 miles; Loughborough (historic town) 3 miles; East Midlands Airport 9 miles; Bradgate Country Park 4 miles; Leicester (historic city) 8 miles

92 The Old Barn Inn

Andrew Lane,
Glooston,
Nr Market
Harborough,
Leicestershire
LE16 7SO
Tel: 01858 545215

Directions:

Follow the B6047 north from Market Harborough. Two miles beyond its junction with the A6 (a roundabout), turn east onto an unmarked road; Glooston is 2 miles along this road

Glooston is a small, picturesque village sitting in some lovely countryside, and at its heart is **The Old Barn Inn**. Though it looks more recent, it is in fact a former coaching inn which dates back to the 16th century. A closer inspection of the building will easily reveal this, and so will the interior. It has many period features, which all contribute to an inn that speaks of a history of hospitality that goes back at least 500 years. There are quaint, low beams, thick walls that keep the place warm in winter and cool in summer, and old pine tables. There are some modern features as well, but husband and wife team Philip and Clare Buswell have managed to blend everything in to create a cozy and welcoming atmosphere.

Though off the beaten track, and a true "hidden inn", it is popular with both locals and tourists, who come to sample the fine ales and food. In fact, its food is outstanding. The restaurant is a no smoking area, and is spotlessly clean, with linen tablecloths, gleaming cutlery and cut glass on every table. It has a full á la carte menu, and Philip, who does the cooking, insists that every ingredient he uses is as fresh as possible. The speciality of the house is seafood, and the quality of the dishes on offer would would not be out of place in a smart London restaurant! And, of course, if you want a bottle of something special to go with your meal, there's a good choice of fine wines. Behind the bar you'll find four real ales on offer, two of which are guest ales which vary weekly. Plus there is draught beer, lager, stout and cider.

The Old Barn Inn exudes quality. It continues the good old traditions of fine food, good drink and a warm welcome to everyone.

Opening times: 12.00-14.30 and 18.30-23.00 Monday to Saturday; 12.00-14.30 and 19.00-22.30 on Sunday

Food: Lunches served 12.00-14.30 (not Mondays except Bank Holidays)

Credit cards: Most credit cards accepted except American Express and Diners

Accommodation: 2 en suite, double rooms

Entertainment: Occasional themed seafood nights

Facilities: Beer garden

Local Places of Interest/Activities: East Carlton Country Park 7 miles; Eyebrook Reservoir (trout fishery) 7 miles; Market Harborough (historic town) 5 miles

The Pick and Shovel

2 High Street,
Coalville,
Leicestershire
LE67 3ED
Tel/Fax:
01530 835551
Directions:

The inn is in the centre of Coalville, which is 11 miles west of Leicester city centre on the A511

Coalville, as its name implies, is a former mining town in the Leicestershire coalfield. Originally called Long Lane, it was founded in the 1830s to house the miners from the nearby Whitwick Colliery. Thanks to the hard work of husband and wife team Tracey and Allan Hood, **The Pick and Shovel** is one of Coalville's most popular and friendly hostelries. It is a substantial corner building dating from around 1837, so must be one of the town's original buildings. Its well proportioned front and handsome windows hide an interior that echoes those earlier times, as many period features have been retained. The original oak and stone flooring is still there for instance, and the low, beamed ceilings of the bar and lounge have subdued lighting, which adds to the feeling of age and tradition. The furniture is handsome and sturdy, with thick oak tables and and leather benches. In the winter months, open fires give off a warming, cheery glow. This is the kind of place where you'd want to linger over a quiet drink or meal!

The food can best be described as simple, honest pub fayre, always beautifully cooked and presented using local produce where available. The portions are hearty, and everything on the menu represents astonishing value for money. To accompany a meal, you can choose from two real ales (Banks and Marstons Pedigree), or from a selection of draught beers, cider, lager and stout. Wine is also available by the bottle or glass. The inn is famous in the area for its live entertainment, and many well known bands have performed here in the past, playing music that will appeal to all age groups.

Opening hours: Monday to Saturday: 11.00-23.00; Sunday: lunchtime and evening

Food: Served on Monday from 12.00-16-00; Tuesday to Thursday from 12.0-14.30 and 16.30-19.00; no food served on Sundays

Credit cards: cash only at present

Accommodation: None

Entertainment: Wednesday: karaoke night; Thursday: disco night; Friday and Saturday: live bands

Local Places of Interest/Activities: Snibston Discovery Park (industrial heritage museum) within town; Mount St Bernard Abbey 2 miles; Donnington le Heath (manor house) 1 mile; East Midlands Airport 8 miles

94   The Plough Inn

33 Hallgate,
Diseworth,
Derbyshire
DE74 2QJ
Tel: 01332 810333
Fax: 01332 811915

Directions:

Take the A453 north from Junction 23A for 1 mile, then turn west onto the A453; after a mile, turn south onto the unmarked road for Diseworth

Diseworth is only a mile from the hustle and hurry of the M1, yet is a peaceful, picturesque village that speaks of tradition and history. And yet it has one, thoroughly modern, claim to fame - it was the first English village to have its own website, away back in 1995.

The Plough Inn is one of two inns in the village. The building as you see it today has undergone many changes and additions, though parts of it go back as far as the 13th century, according to experts from Nottingham University who surveyed it in 1988. A "modernisation" in the 1970s covered up a lot of period features, such as old beams, herringbone pattern brickwork, even old rooms, and it wasn't until a complete restoration in 1997 that they were revealed again. The lounge is aptly called the "Duck Lounge", and if you enter it, don't forget to duck as you do so!

The place is now run by Lynne and Peter Hammond, who are determined to maintain the inn's unique atmosphere and sense of history. In the winter, you can relax in front of a roaring open fire, and in the summer you can take your drink out into the beer garden and watch the world go by, or sit in the conservatory. The bar has a fine selection of ales and beers, including four real ales - Bass, Marston's Pedigree and two rotating ales. Also available are Worthington Creamflow, Carling, Stella, Guinness and Strongbow.

You can eat throughout the inn, though there is a cozy, 20-seater restaurant called, appropriately enough, The Snug Restaurant, which is non-smoking. If you're eating, children are welcome. There's an across the board menu, with good honest dishes featuring. Try the home made pies - they're delicious!

Opening times: Lunchtimes and evenings

Food: Monday to Saturday 12.00-14.00 and 18.00-21.00; Sunday: 12.00-14.00 (no food served on a Sunday evening)

Credit cards: Most credit cards accepted except American Express

Accommodation: None

Facilities: Car park; beer garden

Local Places of Interest/Activities: Donington Park (motor racing) 3 miles; Calke Abbey (NT) 5 miles; East Midlands Airport 2 miles; Staunton Harold Church (NT) 5 miles

The Queens Head | 95

5 Main Street,
Heather,
near Coalville,
Leicestershire
LE67 2QP
Tel: 01530 260544

Directions:

Take the A447 south from the west roundabout on the Coalville bypass; after 3 miles turn west onto a minor road and head for Heather, 1 mile along it

The Queens Head is a substantial, picturesque inn made of red brick, with half timbering above and a steep pitched slate roof. It is a substantial, gabled building with many delightful features, such as an arched doorway, a sturdy chimney and small paned windows on the first floor, that adds a sense of tradition and history to the streetscape. Under the management of husband and wife team Di and Pete Deacon, it has gained and maintained an enviable reputation, and is popular with both visitors to the village and with regulars.

It dates from the 18th century, when times were more expansive, and there wasn't the hustle and bustle of today's stressful living. For that reason, it is the perfect place for a quiet, relaxing drink or a leisurely meal. In fact, it has a definite 50s feel to it, which, though it might not be intentional, still adds to the ambience of the place. The furnishings are simple and comfortable, and Di and Pete make sure that everywhere is spotlessly clean and polished.

The Queens Head boasts two real ales in winter and three in summer, plus a fine range of draught beers, stouts, cider and lager. And. of course, wine is always available by the glass or bottle. Di does the cooking, and a grand job she make of it! This is value for money, traditional cuisine, with hearty portions and a good choice of dishes. The locals will tell you to try one of the range of home made pies, and you might be well advised to listen to them! If you want to eat on a Sunday evening, you must book in advance. This is a snug hostelry that continues the great tradition of hospitality that is found everywhere in England. Di and Pete work hard to make sure that a visit to their inn is an enjoyable experience. Try it - you won't be disappointed.

Opening hours: Monday to Friday: 12.00-14.30 and 18.00-23.00; Saturday: 12.00-14.30 and 18.30-23.00; Sunday 12.00-14.30 and 19.00-22.30

Food: Served seven days 12.00-14.00 and 18.30-21.00; must book on Sunday evenings

Credit cards: all major credit cards

Accommodation: None

Entertainment: 3-day village music festival last week in July

Facilities: Beer garden; games room

Local Places of Interest/Activities: Snibston Discovery Park (industrial heritage museum within Coalville) 3 miles; Donnington le Heath (manor house) 1 mile; Market Bosworth Country Park 6 miles

Internet/website:
e-mail: qheadh@aol.com
website: www.queensheadheather.co.uk

96   The Red Lion

Main Street,
Great Bowden,
nr Market Harborough
Leicestershire
LL16 7HB
Tel: 01858 463858

Directions

Great Bowden is 1 mile
north east of Market
Harborough, on a
minor road off the A6

The Red Lion has earned a great reputation as an inn which appreciates real ale. No less than six are on offer at any one time in the trim bar - four resident brews and 2 guest brews. The building is on a prime site in the village, with a long frontage that is both picturesque and welcoming. Richard and Amanda Kitson have only been in charge for a short while, and they have great plans for the place. Already they have refurbished the interior, preserving the best of the period features and adding touches of their own that make this a comfortable pub in which to have a drink or meal. There's an excellent bar and lounge area, with old oak beams, soft carpeting and intimate, subdued lighting. The bar itself is huge, and it positively bristles with draught dispensers and taps.

The menu is, at the moment, limited, but this is sure to change. Everything on it is home cooked by Amanda. The dishes are a fine blend of English traditional cuisine with the best of Continental, using fresh, local products wherever possible. Locals will no doubt tell you that you should try Amanda's beef stew with dumplings, which is delicious! You can eat in the 30 seat restaurant area, in the 30 seat lounge, or, in the summer months, in the rear yard.

Apart from the real ales, there's a great selection of draught bitters, stout, lager and cider, and, of course, wine is always available with your meal if you wish. The wine list is small but comprehensive, and you're sure to find something to your taste.

This is an inn that is going places. Richard and Amanda's next big task is to completely refurbish the inn's frontage, which, when completed, will be magnificent. It will the warm welcome and friendly service that awaits you as you step over the threshold.

Opening hours: Monday to Thursday: 12.00-15.00 and 18.00-23.00; Friday and Saturday: 12.00-23.30; Sunday: 12.00-22.30

Food: Served during opening hours

Credit cards: All major cards except American Express and Diners

Accommodation: None

Facilities: Massive car park; beer garden; rear yard with al fresco dining

Local Places of Interest/Activities: Market Harborough (historic town) 1 mile; East Carlton Country Park 5 miles; Rockingham Motor Speedway 8 miles; Rockingham Castle 8 miles; Kelmarsh Hall 6 miles

The Saddle

Main Street,
Twyford,
nr Melton Mowbray,
Leicestershire
LE14 2HU
Tel: 01664 840237

Directions:

On the B6407, 6 miles south of Melton Mowbray

The Saddle is a delightful roadside inn sitting alongside the B6407. It is renowned in the area for its ales, its good food and its friendliness. It dates from the 17th century, and it retains many period features that make it a pleasure to visit for a drink or a meal. The inside is quaint and appealing, with a marvellous copper topped bar, comfortable seating and an ambience that speaks of a bygone, gentler age. It is thoughtfully decorated throughout, and is spacious enough to let you stretch out and relax with a drink before you on the table.

The place is looked after by husband and wife team Peter and Rosemary Featherstone, who have managed to create a place of great character, history and charm - one that is appreciated by locals and visitors alike. The bar offers a fine range of drinks, including three real ales, draught beers, cider, stout and lager, as well as spirits, wine by the glass or bottle and a selection of soft drinks and mixers. In fact, there's something for everyone.

Both Peter and Rosemary do the cooking, and the food is simple, hearty, sensibly priced and always immaculately cooked on the premises. Don't expect fast food here! Expect instead high quality and an eye for detail. The comfortable, airy restaurant is spotless, and can seat up to 40 people. The portions are large, and if you visit, try their fish, which is as fresh as it can be, or their juicy steaks, which fill the plate and will satisfy the largest of appetites.

Peter and Rosemary have a hands on approach to running The Saddle. They want to make your visit as friendly and welcoming as possible, and they'll go out of their way to do so!

Opening hours: Monday to Friday: 12.00-14.30 and 17.00-23.00; Saturday: 12.00-15.00 and 18.00-23.00; Sunday: open all day from 12.30-22.30

Food: Simple, beautifully cooked and served all week between 12.00-14.30 and 18.00-21.00

Credit cards: All major cards except Diners

Accommodation: None

Entertainment: Occasional discos and karaoke nights

Facilities: Beer garden; petanque court

Local Places of Interest/Activities: Burrough Hill Iron Age Fort: 3 miles; Burrough Hill Country Park: 3 miles; Oakham (historic town) 8 miles; Rutland Water 10 miles; Melton Mowbray (historic town) 6 miles; Leicester (historic city) 10 miles

98 The Shoulder of Mutton

*6 Chapel Street,
Oakthorpe,
Swadlincote,
Derbyshire
DE12 7QT
Tel: 01530 270436*

Directions:

Oakthorpe sits west of the A42, two miles north of Junction 11, where it merges with the M42

Seen on a summer's day, when its hanging baskets and tubs froth with colour, and its white, half timbered walls reflect the sunlight, you would surely agree that **The Shoulder of Mutton** is one of the most beautiful and picturesque pubs in Derbyshire. It's a real local - popular with the people of the village and with visitors who turn off the A42 to sample its delights. It is owned and run by Julie Mole, who, in a real career move eight years ago, gave up long distance lorry driving to become mine host. It is something she has never regretted, and neither have her customers! The pub dates from the late 18th century, and has all the hallmarks of a bygone, more leisurely time. Here you can stretch your legs and enjoy a drink, or have an quiet evening meal.

This isn't to say that the inn isn't efficiently run. It is - and Julie makes sure that the modern concepts of good service, efficiency and value for money are to the fore. Children are welcome, and she makes sure that her customers are well looked after, and already a new dining area is being built, as well toilet facilities.

Keenly priced bar lunches and evening meals are available, and all are freshly prepared on the premises from local, seasonal produce wherever possible. There's a well stocked bar serving real ale, Marston's Pedigree, Caffrey's, and so on, plus cider, lager, spirits and wines.

The Shoulder of Mutton is the hub of village life. You'll find that a warm welcome awaits you in its cozy interior, which has country-style furniture and comfortably upholstered wall benches.

Opening hours: Open all day

Food: Served all day; bar lunches and evening meals available

Credit cards: Cash and cheques only at present

Accommodation: None

Facilities: Car parking; disabled facilities

Entertainment: Live entertainment on Saturday evenings; phone for details

Local Places of Interest/Activities: Calke Abbey (NT) 7 miles; Staunton Harold Church (NT) 7 miles; Burton upon Trent (historic town) 4 miles; Twycross Zoo 7 miles

The Stag and Hounds | 99

4 Main Street,
Burrough-on-the-Hill,
Leicestershire
LE14 2JQ
Tel: 01664 454181

Directions:

Take the B6047 south from Melton Mowbray for 6 miles, then turn east onto a minor road at Twyford. The village is 2 miles along this road

Burrough-on-the-Hill is famous for the Iron Age fort that tops a nearby hill. But it was nearly a village without a pub until husband and wife Alan and Audrey Noble took over the 18th century **Stag and Hounds** some time ago. Now this picturesque inn, with its well proportioned front and leaded windows, is a favourite with locals and tourists alike, who come to sample its warm welcome and its good food and drink.

The interior could best be described as a real home from home. It is cozy and clean, with bags of atmosphere. There's an intimate little bar, a no smoking restaurant, and a comfortable lounge within which you can relax, stretch you legs and forget the strains of modern living. The bar carries a fine stock of draught beers, lagers, stout and cider, plus three real ales, so there's sure to be something you'll appreciate.

The inn's food is simple, flawless, and very reasonably priced considering the quality. It's all cooked by Audrey, who always insists on the freshest produce and ingredients available The bar menu caters for light meals and snacks, while the restaurant menu and blackboard specials carry more substantial dishes, such as duck in sherry sauce, steak and Stilton pie, pork in cider, turkey supreme with parsley dumplings and various juicy steaks. If you're stuck for choice, try the red snapper in an orange and chive sauce if it's available! There's also a good range vegetarian dishes, and the starters include prawn cocktail, soup, brie wedges with a salad garnish and garlic mushrooms. So popular is the food here that you're advised to book in plenty of time for the weekends.

Thanks to Alan and Audrey's hard work, the Stag and Hounds is a lovely inn, with a welcoming atmosphere, a great range of drinks and some of the best food in the area.

Opening hours: 12.00-14.30 and 18.00-23.00 seven days

Food: Served during opening hours Tuesday to Sunday; no food served on a Monday

Credit cards: All major cards except American Express and Diners

Accommodation: Will advise on local B&Bs; please ring for details

Entertainment: Quiz night every Tuesday; occasional karaoke nights; crib, dominoes and darts

Facilities: Beer garden

Local Places of Interest/Activities: Burrough Hill Iron Age Fort: 1 mile; Burrough Hill Country Park: 1 mile; Oakham (historic town) 6 miles; Rutland Water 8 miles

100   Wheatsheaf Inn

Brand Hill,
Woodhouse Eaves,
near Loughborough,
Leicestershire
LE12 8SS
Tel:01509 890320
Fax: 01509 890891

Directions:

The village of
Woodhouse Eaves sits
on a minor road 3
miles south of
Loughborough and 3
miles east of the B591

The charming village of Woodhouse Eaves lies within an area known as Charnwood Forest. Behind it, Beacon Hill rises up to over 800 feet. It was here that one of the beacon fires was lit during the time of Elizabeth 1 to warn of the approach of the Spanish Armada. The **Wheatsheaf Inn** sits at the heart of this picturesque and historical village, and is built of the local golden Charnwood stone. It dates from the 18th century, and is a former coaching inn. It fits in perfectly with its surroundings, and has thick walls, small windows and an overall feeling of quaintness.

The interior is a labyrinth of interconnecting rooms and passages. There are open fires, country style furniture and all the atmosphere of a true country pub - one that offers you a warm welcome as well as good food, good drink and good cheer. There are four real ales on offer at the bar, plus draught bitter, mild, stout, lager and cider. You can even ask for the inn's own label wines, which are a good red and white.

The inn is a family run concern, with Richard and Bridget Dimblebee in charge, so the food is all prepared on the premises to your own taste. No boil-in-the-bag or frozen ingredients here! Just honest, fresh produce that is sourced locally wherever possible, and an eating experience that will long be remembered. The cuisine can best be described as the best of English with French and Italian influences, with the fish dishes being especially good. You can eat in the pub itself, or in a bistro upstairs, which is smart and comfortable, with an ambience that adds to the eating experience.

Opening times: Monday: Monday to Friday: 12.00-14.30 and 18.00-23.00; Saturday: 12.00-15.00 and 18.00-23.00; Sunday: 12.00-15.00 and 19.00-22.30

Food: Monday to Friday: 12.00-14.30 and 19.00-21.30; Saturday: 12.00-14.l30 and 19.00-22.00; Sunday (lunches only): 12.00-14.30

Credit cards: All credit cards except American Express

Accommodation: None

Entertainment: Monthly classical evening and barbecues on Monday evenings in the summer months

Facilities: Car park; courtyard; large lawns; beer garden

Local Places of Interest/Activities: Beacon Hill Country Park 1 mile; Leicester (historical city) 7 miles; Loughborough (historical town) 3 miles; Great Central Railway 2 miles; Bradgate Country Park 3 miles

4 Rutland

PLACES OF INTEREST:

PUBS AND INNS:

The Hidden Inns of the Heart of England

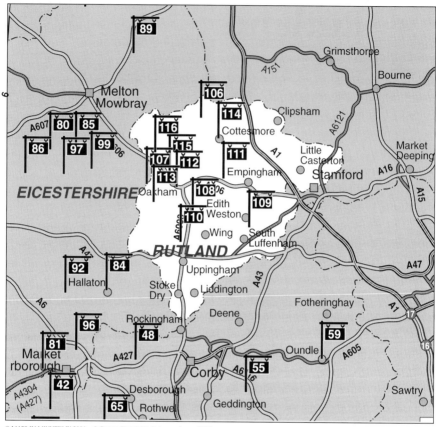

© MAPS IN MINUTES ™ 2001   © Crown Copyright, Ordnance Survey 2001

106 The Black Bull, Market Overton	**112** The Odd House, Oakham
107 The Fox and Hounds, Kossington	**113** The Old Plough Inn, Braunston-in-Rutland
108 The Horse and Jockey, Manton	
109 The Horse and Panniers, North Luffenham	**114** The Sun Inn, Cottesmore
110 The Kingfisher, Preston	**115** The Wheatsheaf, Oakham
111 The Noel Arms, Whitwell	**116** The Wheatsheaf Inn, Longham

Please note all references refer to page numbers

Rutland

For many years Rutland battled with great vigour to retain its independent status as the smallest county in England, but in 1974 it was amalgamated with its big neighbour Leicestershire. A campaign that started locally and was soon carried on nationwide reversed this decision, and Rutland is on its own again. Rutland, like the counties that surround it, has villages of thatch and ironstone clustered round their churches. Its central feature is Rutland Water, which extends over 3,300 acres and is the largest man-made reservoir in Europe. Started in 1971 to supply water to East Midlands towns, it was created by damming the valley near Empingham.

The result is an attractive five-mile stretch of water with many recreational facilities, picnic sites and nature reserves. The motto of the county is, appropriately, 'multum in parvo' ('much in little'), and indeed in Rutland the visitor can enjoy the bustle of the market towns, the quaint villages, and the varied delights of Rutland Water and the countryside; the visit can be quiet and restful, or as energetic as you like, with a day on the water, one of the best cycling days out in Britain (on traffic-free waterside tracks) or a hike along one of the long-distance paths that run across the county. The Viking Way, the Hereward Way and the Macmillan Way all converge on Oakham, the capital town.

PLACES OF INTEREST

CLIPSHAM

The chief treasure of this little hamlet is the heraldic glass in the north chapel. It was shattered during the Wars of the Roses at nearby Pickworth and was brought here. Half a mile east of the village (follow the Brown tourist signs) is Yew Tree Avenue, a half-mile avenue of 150-year-old yew trees clipped into various designs.

COTTESMORE

The Rutland Railway Museum is the big attraction here. The working steam/diesel museum is based on local quarry and industrial railways. Call 01572 813203 for details of steam days and gala days. A little further along the B668 is the village of Greetham on the Viking Way, one of the three long-distance walks that converge on Oakham.

EDITH WESTON

This village takes its name from Edith, wife and then widow of Edward the Confessor, who gave her this part of the county as a gift. A peaceful spot in the heart of really lovely countryside on the south shore of Rutland Water.

Near the village, off the A606 and A6121, stands Rutland's best-known landmark. Normanton Church, on the very edge of Rutland Water, was formerly part of the Normanton Estate and now houses a display dedicated to the construction of the reservoir by Anglian Water and a history of the area. Open April to September. The estate was the property of the big local landowner Sir Gilbert Heathcote, sometime Lord Mayor of London, who pulled down the village of Normanton to enlarge his park and moved the villagers to nearby Empingham.

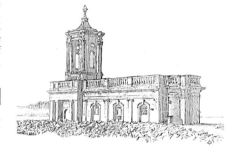

Normanton Tower, Rutland Water

104

EMPINGHAM

This pleasant little town is dominated by the tower and spire of St Peter's Church, whose interior features include fragments of ancient glass. At Sykes Lane, North Shore, just west of Empingham, is the Rutland Water Butterfly Farm & Aquatic Centre. A great place to spend a few hours, with 5,000 square feet of walk-through jungle that is home to free-flying butterflies and tropical birds. Other creatures at the centre include koi carp, terrapins, iguanas, tarantulas, tropical creepy-crawlies and monitor lizards. Open daily April to October.

LIDDINGTON

A quiet village where English Heritage oversees the Bede House. This house of prayer was once part of a retreat for the Bishops of Lincoln, and was later converted to almshouses. The fine 16th-century rooms can be visited daily from April to October. The small gardens contain a notable herb garden with over 60 herbs, both culinary and medicinal.

LITTLE CASTERTON

At Tolethorpe Hall, just off the A1 and close to the Lincolnshire border, the Stamford Shakespeare Company performs on an open-air stage in an idyllic woodland setting facing a 600-seat covered auditorium. Performances take place in June, July and August at what must be one of the finest open-air theatres in Europe.

OAKHAM

Lying in the Vale of Catmose, Oakham is Rutland's county town, where the visitor can learn something of the county's past and appreciate the very agreeable nature of its present.

Just off the Market Place is Rutland Castle, a romantic, evocative fortified manor house built between 1180 and 1190, with the earliest surviving example of an aisled stone hall in the country. A unique feature is a collection of over 200 horseshoes hanging all around the walls of the hall. The custom, dating back to the 12th century, demanded that any royalty or peer of the realm visiting the castle should present a horseshoe as a forfeit to the Lord of the Manor, and there they hang, all shapes and sizes, including examples presented by Queen Elizabeth

l and Queen Elizabeth ll. The oldest on display was given by Edward IV.

All Saints Church is the spiritual centre of town, a fine parish church with a 14th-century tower. On the capitals in the nave are striking carvings of traditional subjects, including dragons, the Green Man, Adam and Eve, and Reynard the Fox.

Rutland County Museum, in a splendid 18th-century riding school in Catmose Street, has displays of farm equipment, machinery and wagons, domestic collections and local archaeology. The riding school belonged to the Rutland Fencibles, a volunteer cavalry regiment raised in 1794 and now remembered in a gallery in the museum. The Tourist Information Centre is in Flore's House, one of the oldest buildings in Oakham. It dates from the late 14th century and was built by William Flore and his son Roger, who was a wealthy merchant and four times Speaker of the House of Commons. Notable natives of Oakham include the infamous conspirator Titus Oates, born here in 1649. He had the major hand in inventing the 'Popish Plot' of 1678, in which he claimed to have uncovered a secret Jesuit plot to assassinate Charles ll and return the Catholic church to power. Many innocent Catholics were killed as a result of this alarm, but Oates, when the truth was discovered, did not escape lightly. He was sentenced to yearly whippings and was not freed until 1688; he died in obscurity in 1705. A more recent and altogether more likeable Titus Oates was the crack northern steeplechaser of that name who won many big races in the care of Gordon W Richards at Penrith.

Oakham was also home to the famed midget Jeffrey Hudson, 'the smallest man from the smallest county in England', who worked for the Duke and Duchess of Buckingham at nearby Burley, a couple of miles north-east of Oakham. Once when Charles l and his Queen Henrietta Maria were guests at Burley a huge cold pie was placed on the table before them and when the pie was cut open out popped Jeffrey Hudson. The Queen was so delighted with the midget, who grew to 39 inches at his tallest, that she took him back to the royal court, where he became a popular figure and was knighted. But he was also a very vain person who made many enemies, killing one of them in a duel. He was twice captured by pirates and sold as a slave. His first master, the Duke of Buckingham, paid a ransom for his freedom, but Jeffrey soon left for London, where he was accused of complicity in Titus Oates' Popish Plot and imprisoned.

The Market Place is still very much at the heart of life in Oakham, and the twice-weekly market (Wednesday and Saturday) attracts visitors from the whole of Rutland and beyond. Oakham School was founded in 1584 by Archdeacon Robert Johnson, who also founded Uppingham School. Many of the original buildings survive, and one of the more recent is the school chapel, built in 1924 as a World War I memorial.

On the outskirts of town, the road to Uppingham crosses Swooning Bridge, where condemned felons going on their last journey from the town gaol first saw, on top of a small rise called Mount Pleasant, the gallows from which they were about to hang.

One mile east of Oakham, the village of Egleton is home of Anglian Water's Birdwatching Centre, located on two storeys on the west shore. It has an osprey platform with CCTV.

Four miles further east, Exton is a charming village in one of the largest ironstone extraction areas in the country. **Barnsdale Gardens**, in The Avenue, offers unusual garden plants and also has a coffee shop. It was designed and owned by Geoff Hamilton.

SOUTH LUFFENHAM

A village on the River Chater, whose church has a 14th-century tower with a crocketed spire. One of its bells is dated 1563 and is probably the oldest in the county. The most famous rector of the church was Robert Scott, who was the incumbent for four years before becoming Master of Balliol College, Oxford. It was at Balliol that he produced, with Henry George Liddell, the impressive and weighty Greek Lexicon that is essential to any classical studies. At nearby North Luffenham, Robert Johnson, who founded the schools at Oakham and Uppingham, is buried in the churchyard. A short drive south along the A6121 is the village of Morcott, where the well-preserved windmill is a fine sight. A Norman church is at the heart of this pleasant village of charming old houses.

STOKE DRY

There are monuments in the church at Stoke Dry to the Digby family, one of whose number, Sir Everard Digby, was born in the village in 1578 and executed for his part in the Gunpowder Plot. The village overlooks Eyebrook Reservoir, a 300-acre trout fishery in an idyllic location in the Welland Valley, by the border with Leicestershire and Northamptonshire. Good bank and boat fishing from April to October.

UPPINGHAM

This picturesque stone-built town is the major community in the south part of the county. It has a long, handsome high street and a fine market place (Friday is market day). The town is known for its bookshops and art galleries, and most of all for its school. Uppingham School was founded here in 1584 by Archdeacon Robert Johnson (who also founded Oakham School) and became one of the leading public schools when the renowned Dr Edward Thring was headmaster during the 19th century. When he arrived it was a very small concern with just two masters and 30 boys. He extended enormously the size and the scope of the school, introducing new subjects like modern languages and encouraging the study of art and music.

It was the good Dr Thring who in 1876 moved all the boys (by now some 300) to a temporary home by Cardigan Bay in Wales when Uppingham was struck by a rampant fever. He wrote extensively on educational matters, championed education for girls and founded the Headmasters Conference. The oldest rooms, the 18th-century studies, the Victorian chapel and schoolrooms and the 20th-century great hall, all Grade l or Grade ll listed, can be visited on a guided tour on Saturday afternoons in summer.

WING

The little village of Wing is best known for its medieval Turf Maze, made of foot-high turf banks and measuring 40 feet across. Once a fairly common sight, these mazes were a popular way of recreating the mazes of the ancients and also served as a not-too-serious penance for minor wrongdoings.

106   The Black Bull

Market Overton,
Rutland
LE15 7PN
Tel: 01572 767677
Fax: 01572 767291

Directions:

Take the B668 north east from Oakham for 4 miles; turn north onto an unmarked road just before Cottesmore; Market Deeping is 2 miles along this road

Market Overton is a delightful village deep in the heart of the soft, verdant Rutland countryside. Sir Isaac Newton's mother was born here, and it is believed that a sundial in the church was presented by Sir Isaac himself. **The Black Bull** adds to the picturesqueness of the place, as it is a part thatched building dating mainly from the 16th century. In fact, this is everything a village inn should be - colourful in summer when the flowers at the front of the inn are in bloom, and warm and cozy in the long winter months.

John and Val Owen have been running the place for the last 15 years. In that time, they have conserved all that is good and traditional about the inn, while adding a few modern touches, such as efficient service and superb food. The inside has thick red carpeting, low oak beams and subdued lighting, and there are one or two surprises, such as the tromp l'oeil owls and cats on the doors - the work of a local Rutland artist.

A blackboard tempts the palate with a range of superb dishes, using only the finest produce - fresh fish from Grimsby and meats from local butchers. And there's a range of seasonal game pies which have such Walt Disney names as Bambi, Donald and Thumper, with the main ingredient in each being self evident! But it's fish that predominates, and all the dishes are beautifully prepared by the two professional chefs. The home made puddings are excellent, and are brought to the table for you to choose. There's also a popular Sunday roast, with a choice of meats - so popular in fact, that you're advise to book beforehand. The inn boasts six cask ales plus a guest ale, and there's an excellent wine list. plus, of course, you can order beer, lager, stout or cider.

They say that the Black Bull was built to accommodate the workmen who built Market Overton church. If this is true, and the inn was as good then as it is now, they must have had a wonderful time!

Opening hours: Monday to Saturday: 12.00-15.00 and 17.30 to 23.00; Sunday: 12.00-15.00 and 17.30-22.30

Food: Lunches are served between 12.00-14.30; dinners are served 18.00-21.00

Credit cards: Most credit cards accepted except American Express and Diners

Accommodation: 3 en suite rooms with colour TV and tea and coffee making facilities

Local Places of Interest/Activities: Oakham (historic town) 2 miles; Rutland Water 4 miles; Stamford (historic town) 11 miles; Burrough Hill Country Park 8 miles; RAF Cottesmore (yearly tattoo) 2 miles

Internet/website:
email: jowenbull@aol.com

The Fox and Hounds

Knossington,
near Oakham,
Rutland
LE15 8LY
Tel: 01664 454676

Directions:

Follow an un-
marked road west
from the A606 in
Oakham for just
over 3 miles until
you arrive at
Knossington

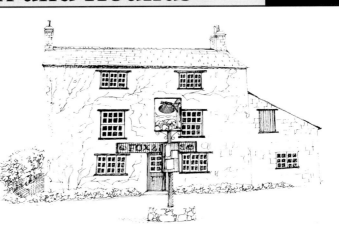

The rolling uplands west of Oakham are noted for their lovely villages. One of the best is Knossington, with its picturesque parish church of St Peter, which dates from the 12th century. It's now a conservation village which is steeped in history, having been within the estates of Owston Abbey before passing at the Dissolution of the Monasteries to Lord Gregory Cromwell, son of Thomas Cromwell, Earl of Essex. The almshouses - founded in 1711 and rebuilt in 1821 - are very picturesque and well worth seeing.

At the heart of the village is **The Fox and Hounds**, run by Rob Bishop and Terri Martin. It is a neat, well maintained building that fits perfectly into its tranquil surroundings, and dates originally from the 18th century. Inside Rob and Terri have tried to preserve the period fittings, while at the same time adding modern touches of their own that enhances the inn's reputation for good food, drink and hospitality. The interior is compact and immaculately clean, and has a cozy. comfortable public bar, adjoining lounge and well appointed restaurant. The food is excellent, and cooked on the premises by Terri. She is particular about the produce she uses, and everything must be fresh and wholesome. It is also beautifully presented, and would appeal to the educated palate. Having said that, try their special fish and chips - you'll not have tasted anything like it before! It's the way this traditional dish should be cooked. If it's a drink you're after, there are three real ales to choose from - one resident and two guest. Plus there's a fine range of beers, lagers, cider and stout.

In the winter months, you can heat yourself at a roaring open fire, while in summer you could sample food from the occasional barbecues that are organised in the beer garden. It's a true village local, though popular with people from further afield who have visited and invariably come back for more.

Opening hours: Monday to Friday: 12.00-15.00 and 18.00-23.00; Saturday: all day; Sunday: 12.00-22.30

Food: Served when open

Credit cards: Most credit cards accepted except American Express and Diners

Accommodation: None

Entertainment: Quiz night every Thursday;

monthly live music

Facilities: Beer garden; occasional barbecues; petanque

Local Places of Interest/Activities: Oakham (historic town) 3 miles; Rutland Water 5 miles; Burrough Hill Country Park 3 miles; RAF Cottesmore (yearly tattoo) 7 miles

108 The Horse and Jockey

St Mary's Road,
Manton,
Rutland
LE15 8SU
Tel: 01572 737335

Directions:

Two miles south of
Oakham, just off
the A6003

Standing on a busy crossroads site, **The Horse and Jockey** is a lovely country inn and roadhouse dating from 1802 with later additions. It is stone built and substantial, with small paned windows and a well proportioned front - just the sort of place that offers a warm welcome to everyone. It is owned and managed by Keith Stanley, who takes a keen interest in all aspects of the place, and who knows every one of his regulars by their first names.

The interior has a look of tradition and coziness about it, and is spotlessly clean. There's a small lounge with a neat public bar, a comfortable dining area and a games area. All are maintained to a high standard, and all are popular with the locals and the passing trade alike. In addition, there are four rooms to let on a B&B basis - two en suite (a double bedroom and a family bedroom) and two twins which share a WC and bathroom.

Two cask ales are available from the bar - Banks Bitter and Marston's Pedigree, plus a selection of draught beers, lagers, stout and cider. The inn serves genuine English cuisine, with everything fresh. There are two menus - a Monday to Saturday one, and a Sunday one. Through the week, you can have such dishes as lasagna verde, breaded scampi, toasted sandwiches, vegetarian dishes, ploughman's lunches or filled rolls; on Sunday you can also have a Sunday roast, with all the trimmings, though you're advised to book for this.

The Horse and Jockey is the ideal base from which to explore this part of England. It's close to the olde worlde market towns of Oakham, Uppingham and Stamford, and Peterborough, with its magnificent cathedral, is only half an hour away.

Opening hours: Open 7 days 11.30-14.30 and 19.00-23.00 (seasonal)

Food: Served during opening hours, apart from Sunday evening

Credit cards: Cash only at present

Accommodation: 4 rooms (2 en-suite); 1 double, 1 family, 2 twin

Entertainment: Pub games such as darts and dominoes

Facilities: Beer garden

Local Places of Interest/Activities: Oakham (historic town) 3 miles; Uppingham (historic town) 3 miles; Rutland Water 1 mile; Wing Turf Maze 1 mile; Peterborough (historic city) 20 miles

Internet/website:
website: www.horseandjockey.net
e-mail: info@horseandjockey.net

The Horse and Panniers | 109

Church Street,
North Luffenham,
Rutland
LE15 8JN
Tel: 01780 722124
and 722125

Directions:

North Luffenham is
south of Rutland
Water, just north of
the A6121

The Horse and Panniers is an unusual but strikingly beautiful little inn, built round three sides of a small courtyard within the lovely village of North Luffenham. With its thick walls of warm, local stone, dormer windows and almost crooked roof with high chimneys, it is everybody's idea of a traditional English village inn - full of character and history, and a focal point of local life. It was built in 1643, and every stone seems to breath tradition and hospitality.

Every effort has been made by mine host Chris Milburn to preserve all that is good about the place. The floor is of small, neat segmented slabs, and there are low beams, a huge open fire, and copper and brass that positively gleams. The place is spotless, and so cozy and welcoming that you'll have a difficult job tearing yourself away after a visit! The bar has no less that five real ales on tap, so you'll be spoiled for choice when you come to order a drink. And, of course, there is a great range of spirits and wine, plus beers, lager, stout and cider on draught.

The menu is a combination of traditional English dishes and meals with a mediterranean and international flavour. All the food is freshly prepared daily on the premises.   If you want a special treat, try the Horse and Pannier's seafood dishes - the place is renowned for them. You can eat indoors, or, in the summer months, you can dine al fresco in the 40 seater courtyard, which sprouts a fine display of colourful umbrellas when the sun is shining! There's also the occasional barbecue, where good, hearty food is cooked and served. All in all, the inn exudes tradition, good service, a warm welcome and value for money meals.

Opening hours: 12.00-15.00 from Monday to Friday (closed Tuesday afternoon) and 12.00-23.00 on Saturdays and Sundays

Food: Served 12.00-1500 and 18.30-21.30

Credit cards: Most credit cards accepted except Diners

Accommodation: None

Entertainment: Occasional jazz nights and theme nights

Facilities: Beer garden; occasional barbecues; patio

Local Places of Interest/Activities: Stamford (historic town) 6 miles; Rutland Water 2 miles; Kirby Hall 7 miles; Deene Park 7 miles; Wing Turf Maze 3 miles

Internet/Website:
www.thehorseandpanniers.co.uk

110 The Kingfisher

9 Uppingham Road,
Preston,
Rutland
LE15 9NW
Tel: 01572 737256
Fax: 01572 737866

Directions:

Preston is on the
A6003, 4 miles
south of Oakham

The look of this inn belies its age. The building dates from around 1893, though it looks older, and it fits in perfectly with the rest of the picturesque village of Preston. In charge are mother and son team Sue and Luke Healey, and they have created a wonderful inn ("The Kingfisher") and an equally wonderful restaurant ("Nines") that is a hub of village life. The bar/lounge has a welcoming and open ambience, something that didn't happen by accident. Sue and Luke have worked hard to get the atmosphere of the place just right! It is comfortable and relaxing, with an open fire to cheer you up on the coldest of days. The intimate restaurant is spotless - the ideal place to have a bar lunch or evening meal.

The bar offers three real ales, two resident and one guest, plus a range of draught beers, lagers, stout and cider. The food is always freshly cooked, using produce that is always carefully sourced to make sure it is the best available, and the inn takes great pride in its presentation. One dish in particular - Rutland bangers and mash - is a firm favourite with locals and visitors alike, who seem always to return to **The Kingfisher and Nines Restaurant**. It even offers a unique "fax-u-back" service for discerning diners. You fax the inn about its daily specials, and it will fax you back telling you what's on the specials board for that day!

Next to the inn are three studio apartments which are let on a self catering basis, making this place an ideal base to explore an area of England that is steeped in history. It's a family run establishment which is friendly and inviting, and which welcomes children. There's even a "secret garden" which they can explore. If you visit, Sue and Luke will go out of their way to make you welcome.

Opening hours: Monday to Saturday:12.00-15.00 and 19.00-23.00; Open all day Sunday

Food: Served during opening hours

Credit cards: All major cards except American Express and Diners

Accommodation: 3 studio apartments, 2 sleeping four people, and 1 sleeping 6

Entertainment: Occasional race nights for charity

Facilities: Beer garden; children's play area; secret garden

Local Places of Interest/Activities: Oakham (historic town) 4 miles; Wing Turf Maze 1 mile; East Carlton Country Park 5 miles; Rockingham Motor Speedway 8 miles; Rockingham Castle 8 miles; Kelmarsh Hall 6 miles

Internet/website:
e-mail: sue.thekingfisher9s@tinyworld.co.uk

The Noel Arms

Whitwell,
Rutland
LE15 8BW
Tel: 01780 460334
Fax 01780 460531

Directions:

Whitwell is 4 miles
east of Oakham, on
the A606

Within Rutland, England's smallest county, you'll find Whitwell, Rutland's smallest village! It sits almost on the shores of Rutland Water, which is Europe's largest man made lake. And to make the place even more special, it is twinned with one of Europe's largest cities - Paris! It's a charming village, built mostly of warm, local stone. And at the heart of the village life you'll find **The Noel Arms**, a large hostelry of great character and charm, with a partly thatched roof and thick walls. It dates mainly from 1876, though parts may be a lot older than this.

Mark and Jo Bailey are in charge, and have put together an interior which is a soothing blend of old and new. The floors, for instance, are part carpeted, while the rest is in old, stone slabs. This is a spacious inn which makes excellent use of its size. There are two large lounges plus two restaurants, all having well spaced tables and chairs so that you can make yourself comfortable while relaxing over a meal or drink. Open fires burn in the wintertime, throwing a cozy glow over everything, while in the summer months you can eat from occasional barbecues that are held on the terrace.

The food is excellent. You can have a bar snack, or sit in one of the restaurants and have a full dinner. The menus are changed seasonally, and you can chose from a wide range of dishes which are beautifully cooked from fresh, local produce wherever possible. Try the smoked mackerel in a dill and tarragon dressing with mixed leaves - delicious! There's an excellent wine list to accompany the meals, and the bar carries four real ales plus a guest ale. And, of course, you can have draught lager, stout of cider if you require it. There are also eight rooms en suite rooms with TV and tea and coffee making facilities that can be booked on a B& B basis.

Opening hours: Open between 8.00-11.00 seven days

Food: Served all day

Credit cards: Most credit cards accepted except American Express and Diners

Accommodation: 8 en suite rooms with colour TV and tea and coffee making facilities

Entertainment: Occasional jazz and blues nights

Facilities: Large car park; beer garden; occasional barbecues; children's play area

Local Places of Interest/Activities: Oakham (historic town) 4 miles; Rutland Water on the doorstep; Stamford (historic town) 6 miles; Burrough Hill Country Park 10 miles; RAF Cottesmore (yearly tattoo) 3 miles

112   The Odd House

1 Station Road,
Oakham,
Rutland
LE15 6QT
Tel: 01572 7222225
Fax: 01572 722187

Directions:

Oakham is Rutland's county town, and is 10 miles west of Stamford, on the A606

Oakham is the quintessential English market town - compact, full of lovely old buildings, and with a long, lively history that goes right back into the mists of time. The name has nothing to do with the oak tree; it derives from the town's founder, one Occa, a Saxon lord who may have had a manor here. It's in Oakham, on a corner site, that you'll find **The Odd House**, a substantial stone inn that remains almost unchanged from when it was built many years ago. Richard and Catherine Burley have been in charge for over 2 years, and during that time the hostelry has gained a fine reputation for its food, drink and hospitality. Richard and Catherine have kept it well maintained over the years, and it has retained a lot of period features. The glow from open log fires highlight the comfortable, polished furniture and lend an air of tradition to the place. There are low beamed ceilings, a cozy bar, a comfortable lounge seating 50 in total, all spotlessly clean and welcoming. There's also an adjacent barn which is a wonderful venue for darts and pool.

The bar stocks two real ales plus a range of beers, stout, lager and cider. If you want wine to accompany a meal, there's an excellent and comprehensive wine list. The Odd House has a wide range of excellent value meals on its menu. The emphasis is on fresh, simple dishes that are superbly cooked using fresh produce. If you want a treat, try the mixed grill of steak, kidney, sausage, gammon and lamb and pork chops, and all the trimming you could wish for. It's a hearty plateful, and it tastes out of this world!

The Odd House is a popular place with the people of Oakham If it had been around at the time of Occa, there's no doubt that he, too, would have found his way there to experience the warm welcome and the good food and drink!

Opening hours: Monday to Saturday: 11.00-23.00; Sunday: 11.00-22.30

Food: Served from 12.0-22.00 Monday to Saturday and 12.00-20.00 on Sunday

Credit cards: Most credit cards accepted except American Express and Diners

Accommodation: None

Entertainment: Quiz night every other Sunday

Facilities: Large car park; beer garden; petanque

Local Places of Interest/Activities: Rutland Castle (great banqueting hall) in the town; Rutland Water 2 miles; Stamford (historic town) 10 miles; Burrough Hill Country Park 7 miles; RAF Cottesmore (yearly tattoo) 4 miles

The Old Plough Inn | 113

Church Street,
Braunston-in-
*   Rutland,*
Rutland
LE15 8QY
Tel: 01572 722114
Fax: 01572 770382

Directions:

Braunston is 3 miles
west of Oakham, on
a minor road

Braunston is a real slice of olde England, being one of Rutland's most picturesque and charming villages. **The Old Plough Inn** occupies a prime corner site in the village, and is a handsome, red brick building which dates from the 18th century with later additions. Hanging baskets and window boxes are alive with colour during the surer months, creating a picture postcard scene. The interior is equally as attractive, with large public and lounge bars that combine warmth and coziness with plenty of space. It is immaculately clean and well maintained, with plenty of old brass, memorabilia, dark woodwork and oak trimmings. This is the kind of pub where you want to sit down, stretch out and let the cares of the outside world drift away.

A recently built conservatory/restaurant overlooks the garden and patio to the rear, where excellent food is served. There's a great selection of quick snacks, or you can choose from the full menu. There are also speciality food nights throughout the year featuring such things as "Sizzler Nights", "Fish Specialties" and "Salad Nights". Many tasty, beautifully cooked items are on offer, and the chef's reputation has undoubtedly been enhanced by the fish and steak dishes. For this reason, booking is advisable. To accompany a meal there's a fine selection of wines, or you can choose from one of the five cask ales at the bar - one of them a rotating guest ale, or from the range of beers, lagers, stout and cider. Husband and wife team Dave and Claire Cox have been in charge for only a short time, though they both have extensive experience in the trade. They have great plans for the place, and offer a warm and friendly welcome to anyone wishing to visit.

Opening hours: Monday to Friday 12.00-15.00 and 18.00-23.00; Saturday and Sunday: 12.00-23.00

Food: Served Monday to Saturday 12.00-15.00 and 18.00-21.00; Sunday lunch from 12.00-15.00; special food nights (ring for details)

Credit cards: All major cards except American Express and Diners

Accommodation: None

Entertainment: Quiz club every Monday evening; ongoing theme and speciality nights

Facilities: Beer garden; patio and garden; occasional barbecues

Local Places of Interest/Activities: Oakham (historic town) 2 miles; Rutland Railway Museum, Cottesmore 6 miles; Uppingham (historic town) 5 miles; Rutland Water 2 miles; Wing Turf Maze 4 miles

114 The Sun Inn

Cottesmore,
Rutland
LE15 7DH
Tel: 01572 812321

Directions:
Cottesmore is 4 miles east of Oakham, on the B668

This picturesque little inn sits in the typically English village of Cottesmore, home to an RAF base and a fascinating railway museum. It has all the attributes of a cozy and welcoming hostelry - thatched roof, thick, whitewashed walls and small, ornate windows.

The building dates back to at least 1643, so it has had a long tradition of offering all that is best in English hospitality. It is owned and run by David Johnson, an experienced chef, and he has tried to preserve the period features that make **The Sun Inn** so special. The interior reflects the inn's old worlde charm, with stone flagged floors, solid pine furniture and beamed ceilings. There's a large rear function area, and a flagged courtyard which add to the amenity of the place.

The food, of course, is outstanding, and is a combination of traditional English cuisine with Mediterranean influences. You can chose from a bar snack menu or a full á la carte menu which contains such dishes as gravadlax with lemon, roast vegetable lasagna salad, ribeye steak in a barbecue sauce, seared salmon fillet baked with citrus oil and sirloin grilled with Rutland cheddar and Worcestershire sauce. The speciality dish is traditional Yorkshire fish & chips deep fried in beef dripping. The sweets are equally as tempting - apple crumble, sticky toffee pudding, chocolate parfait or caramelised lemon tart, all served with double cream or ice cream.

You can order wine from a comprehensive wine list that complements the dishes on the menus, and the bar carries a wide range of beers and spirits. Three cask ales are on offer, one of them a rotating guest ale, plus the usual draught beers, lager, stout and cider.

This is an inn that is perfect for a quiet drink, a bar snack or a full meal. It takes its food seriously, and if you wish an evening meal, you'd be well advised to book in advance.

Opening hours: Open 7 days 11.30-14.30 and 19.00-23.00 (seasonal)

Food: Served during opening hours, apart from Sunday evening and Mondays

Credit cards: All major cards

Accommodation: None

Facilities: Beer garden, petanque courts

Local Places of Interest/Activities: Rutland Railway Museum in the village; Cottesmore RAF base (yearly tattoo) 1 mile; Oakham (historic town) 4 miles; Rutland Water 3 miles; Stamford (historic town) 8 miles

The Wheatsheaf 115

*2/4 Northgate,
Oakham,
Rutland
LE15 6QS
Tel/Fax:
   01572 756797*

Directions:

Oakham is
Rutland's county
town, and is 10
miles west of
Stamford, on the
A606

Even though it appears to be a well kept secret, **The Wheatsheaf** is one of Oakham's finest assets. It's a whitewashed, handsome building that sits close to the old church, in a market town that is everyone's idea of olde Englande - fine architecture, history aplenty and a sense of tradition that goes right back to when it was founded by one Occa, a Saxon lord. The inn dates from the 18th century, with some additions, and reflects the elegance and charm of the period, while making use of the best of modern features. The interior has retained many of its splendid original features, such as the original oak floorboards, while other areas have thick flagstones and carpeted floors.

The bar is snug and cozy, while the no smoking lounge has large, comfortable leather couches and potted plants to add that homely touch. Paul and Leslie Bassett are the husband and wife team in charge, and they make doubly sure that the high standards they have introduced in decor, food and drink are rigidly adhered to. The eating area, which is also non smoking, seats 48 in comfort, and the food can best be described as restaurant food at pub prices. Food is only served at lunchtime, but you can order a snack or a full meal, and all are cooked to perfection and great value for money. There's a small, hidden patio and garden area to the rear, and you can take your meal out here if you wish. Five real ales are available at the bar, four regulars and a guest, plus lagers, draught beer, stout and cider. Plus of course, you can order a bottle of wine with your meal.

Opening hours: Open seven days from 11.30-14.30 and 18.00-23.00

Food: Served at lunchtime only

Credit cards: Cash only at present

Accommodation: None

Entertainment: Occasional quizzes and theme nights; ring for details

Facilities: Patio; garden area

Local Places of Interest/Activities: Rutland Castle (great banqueting hall) in the town; Rutland water 2 miles; Stamford (historic town) 10 miles; Burrough Hill Country Park 7 miles; RAF Cottesmore (yearly tattoo) 4 miles

Internet/Website:
e-mail: wheatsheaf.oakham@amserve.net

116   The Wheatsheaf Inn

2 Burley Road,
Langham,
Oakham,
Rutland
LE15 7HY
Tel: 01572 723394

Directions:

Take the A606 north from Oakham for 2 miles; Langham is just off the main road, to the east

Nestling at the edge of the village of Langham, **The Wheatsheaf Inn** is a traditional, stone built and whitewashed inn set some way off the main road, fronted by an extensive car park and a small beer garden. The main building dates mainly from the 18th century, though there have been additions over the years.

This is a real village local, with a welcoming bar, a lounge and a well appointed restaurant that seats 24 in comfort. There are open fires, polished brass, and many period features that make it a comfortable and welcoming place - one where you can relax away from the bustle of everyday life. Chris Samuel and Caroline Norris are mine hosts, and they've tried to preserve all that is traditional about the place, while at the same time offering good service and value for money. Look out for the unusual bar top - it's been cut from a single long length of carved and curved oak.

Two cask ales are on offer behind the bar, plus a range of draught beers, stout, lager and cider. And, of course, an extensive range of spirits and wines is available as well. Caroline that does the cooking, and a grand job she makes of it! The fare is traditional and hearty, and cooked using good, fresh produce wherever possible. The portions are generous, and all the dishes are sensibly priced. In the summer months, there are occasional barbecues in the beer garden.

This is an inn that is popular with locals and visitors alike. It has that homely, traditional feel to it that all village inns should have. As soon as you step inside, you know that Chris and Caroline will make you welcome.

Opening hours: Monday to Saturday: 12.00-15.00 and 17.30 to 23.00; Sunday: 12.00-22.30

Food: Good, hearty fare served at lunchtimes and in the evenings

Credit cards: Most credit cards accepted except American Express and Diners

Accommodation: None

Entertainment: Live music every month; occasional theme nights

Facilities: Car park; beer garden; occasional barbecues

Local Places of Interest/Activities: Oakham (historic town) 2 miles; Rutland Water 3 miles; Stamford (historic town) 11 miles; Burrough Hill Country Park 5 miles

5 Nottinghamshire

PLACES OF INTEREST:

PUBS AND INNS:

The Hidden Inns of the Heart of England

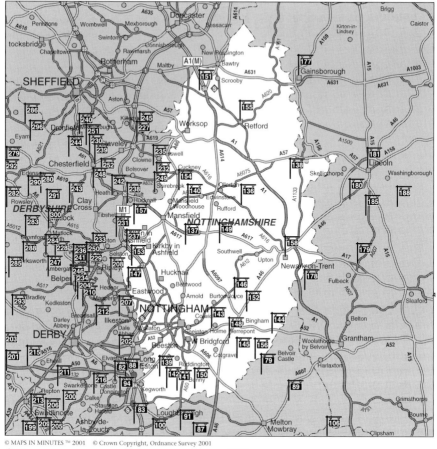

© MAPS IN MINUTES ™ 2001   © Crown Copyright, Ordnance Survey 2001

136	Angel Inn, Kneesall	**148**	Plough Inn, Cropwell Butler
137	Black Bull Inn, Blidworth	**149**	The Plough Inn, Farnsfield
138	Brownlow Arms, High Marnham	**150**	The Plough Inn, Wysall
139	The Cuckoo Bush, Gotham	**151**	The Red Hart Hotel, Blyth
140	The Dog and Duck, Old Clipstone	**152**	The Royal Oak, Car Colston
141	The Generous Briton, Costock	**153**	The Shepherds Rest, Lower Bagthorpe
142	Three Horseshoes, East Leake	**154**	The Swallos , Warsop
143	The Manvers Arms, Radcliff-on-Trent	**155**	The Turks Head, Retford
144	The Manor Arms, Elton	**156**	The Unicorns Head, Langar
145	Martins Arms Inn, Colston Basset	**157**	The White Lion, Huthwaite
146	The Old Volunteer, Caythorpe	**158**	The White Swan, Newark-on-Trent
147	The Old Wine Vaults, Eastwood		

Please note all references refer to page numbers

Nottinghamshire

The county of Nottinghamshire lies mainly on the low ground basin of the River Trent between the peaks of Derbyshire and South Yorkshire and the lowlands of Lincolnshire. It is a county of contrasts, with a good deal of industry but also a strong rural heritage as well as the remains of the famous Forest of Sherwood. It is also the home of the legendary Robin Hood, whose influence can be seen throughout the county; the visitors (and they come from all over the world) can capture the atmosphere of far-off times with a walk in Sherwood Forest, or a trip to Nottingham Castle to see The Tales of Robin Hood; they can try their hand at archery or witness the jousting and merriment at the Robin Hood Festivals in Sherwood Forest Country Park.

The Industrial Revolution saw the mechanisation of the lace and hosiery industries of which Nottingham was a centre and on which many of the surrounding towns and villages were dependent. Mills sprang up in the towns, taking the industry out of the home and causing many families to migrate from their villages to find work in the mills. Coal, which played such an important role in this mechanisation programme, had been mined for many years to the west of Nottingham but, after the mid-19th century, the scale of the mining operations expanded dramatically. Thus the nature of the area changed: the towns grew, with quickly built rows of terraced housing for the new factory and mill workers, and the rural villages lost many of their inhabitants. Today, however, something of a reversal is taking place with many people, working in the city, moving out into the villages to the south of Nottingham to find a quieter home life.

The southeastern area of the county, south of the great Roman road, Fosse Way (now known as the A46), is a mass of small rural villages and hamlets. In the south, bordering the county of Leicestershire, these ancient settlements overlook the Vale of Belvoir and it was here that Thomas Cranmer, in the village of Aslockton, spent his early years. Further north, on the banks of the River Trent and also near the county border with Lincolnshire, lies the historic town of Newark-on-Trent. With Newark a Royalist stronghold and the local gentry on the side of Cromwell, there were many local skirmishes and here, as elsewhere, country houses and other buildings were destroyed by both sides.

Industrial Nottinghamshire is an area, once part of the great Forest of Sherwood, which for centuries played a key part of the coal mining industry, though that industry has all but disappeared today. As Nottingham and the surrounding towns and villages grew as centres of the textile industry, so the need for reliable energy sources grew. Rural market towns expanded into industrial towns and their whole character changed as quick and cheap terraced housing was built for the influx of workers coming to jobs in the mills and the mines. The landscape also changed, with forests being cleared to make way for buildings and mines. Transportation was also important and the Erewash Canal was started in 1777 to take coal from the fields to the River Trent. Once a hive of activity, the canal fell into disrepair in the 1920s but it is now, once again, bustling, though this time with pleasure craft. Into this harsh life DH Lawrence was born in 1885; his father was a miner at the Brinsley pit and the family lived in a terraced house in Eastwood. Drawing on his childhood experiences, Lawrence's novels give a true insight into the lives of those living in a colliery town at the beginning of the 20th century. By contrast, the landowners made their fortunes and there are several fine houses in the area, including Newstead Abbey, the home of the poet Lord Byron.

The northern area of the county is centred around the old market towns of Mansfield, Worksop and Retford, and the famous - and infamous - Sherwood Forest. It is from this quiet and, basically, rural area that the origins of the United States of America can be traced. During the late 16th century, in the villages of north Nottinghamshire, those opposed to Elizabeth I's policy of Church government began to form themselves into the Pilgrim movement, held together in their firm belief in the freedom from State control of religious matters. The members of the Separatists group increased and they held their meetings in secret to escape persecution. By 1608, their persecution by James I became so great that the Pilgrim Fathers, as they were later to be called, fled to Holland. Some years later, in 1620, they sailed from Plymouth to America on board the *Mayflower*, landing at Cape Cod. From there they sent out an expedition to find a suitable settlement and, at a place now known as Forefathers Rock, in Plymouth, the New World was established.

PLACES OF INTEREST

ARNOLD

On the outskirts of Nottingham, and almost part of it, Arnold was very much part of the local lace and hosiery industry and, in 1860, the firm I and R Morley built their factory here. Still standing today, though the company ceased operation in 1963, **Morley's Hosiery Factory** is a fine example of mid-Victorian industrial architecture. It stands two storeys high, with eight bays and a large central clock, and an elaborate extension of three storeys was added in 1885.

Bestwood Country Park, which has been described as 'Nottinghamshire's best-kept secret', comprises 650 acres of land that covers everything from heath to water meadow and is home to a wide variety of wildlife. Miles of woodland trails make it a great place for walkers, and it is also a popular spot with birdwatchers. Open throughout the year. Greenwood Bonsai Studio, by the A614 on the outskirts of Arnold, is one of the largest established bonsai centres in the world. Famous sons of Arnold include the artist Richard Bonington (1802-1828) and the civil engineer Thomas Hawksley (1807-1893).

BESTWOOD

It was while staying at **Bestwood Lodge** that Richard III heard of Henry Tudor's invasion of Wales in 1485. The king left his lodge and was killed defending his crown at the Battle of Bosworth Field. The village's royal connections did not, however, die with King Richard. Bestwood was also a favourite hunting ground of Charles II and he enjoyed staying here with Nell Gwynne. The present Bestwood Lodge was built on a low hill by the 10th Duke of St Albans. Begun in 1862, the lodge is a grand house with flying buttresses, gables, and chimneys, and its best feature is undoubtedly the loft entrance tower with its high pyramidal roof. Also at Bestwood can be found the **Model Aviation Centre**, a museum which specialises in accurate models of aircraft of up to half the scale of the original machine. As well as seeing the finished models, visitors can watch them fly and also see models in various stages of construction.

BUNNY

This pretty village has a wealth of lovely architecture and owes much of its charm to the eccentricities of its former 18th-century squire, Sir Thomas Parkyns. A man obsessed with the sport of wrestling, he employed two full time professionals to spar with him at **Bunny Hall**. He also organised an annual tournament in the village to promote local wrestling talent and this event continued nearly 70 years after its originator's death. In St Mary's Church, which was designed by Sir Thomas, his memorial graphically illustrates his commitment to the sport. It depicts the squire standing victorious over his defeated opponent on a wrestling mat, while Old Father Time stands by, perhaps as referee. The village has some ancient woodland, **Bunny Wood**, which was mentioned in the Domesday Book. Consisting mainly of elm, oak, and ash, the woodland is also home to over 30 species of birds and it is managed by the Nottinghamshire Wildlife Trust.

COLWICK

A large area, some 250 acres, around old gravel workings has been converted into **Colwick Country Park**, where, as well as expanses of water offering facilities for sailing, rowing, and fishing, there is also a nature reserve. This country park was once part of the estate surrounding Colwick Hall, which is now a hotel. Originally the home of the Byron family, the ornate country house came into the hands of the Muster family in the 17th century. Colwick Park is the setting of Nottingham racecourse, which stages some 20 meetings each year (now flat racing only).

COTGRAVE

The discovery of an Anglo-Saxon burial ground on **Mill Hill**, Cotgrave's highest point, confirms that there has been a settlement here for many centuries. The excavation team uncovered the skeletons of nearly 100 people, including several children, and the remains have been dated to around the mid to late 6th century. Cotgrave is probably best known as the home of **Cotgrave Colliery**, which opened in 1963 and was a showplace mine for a number of years.

CUCKNEY

An estate village to the country seat of the Dukes of Portland, Welbeck Abbey, Cuckney is made up of farm workers cottages. Along with Clumber House, Thoresby Hall, and Rufford Abbey, Welbeck Abbey makes up the four large estates in this area of Nottinghamshire which has become known as **The Dukeries**. It was the 5th duke who began, in 1854, an extensive building programme that turned Welbeck into what is seen today. The most impressive of his additions was the riding school, the second largest in the world, complete with a peat floor and gas jet lighting. The building is now in the hands of the Ministry of Defence and it is used as an Army training college, though the abbey and the grounds have been maintained in perfect condition. The Dukeries Adventure Park and Picnic Area, on the Welbeck estate, provides all manner of supervised outdoor activities including rock climbing.

A keen racing man, the 6th Duke bred racehorses at his own stud in the nearby estate village of **Holbeck**. The winner of many big races, including the three colts' Classics, the Duke's famous St Simon is still remembered in the rac-

ing world today. As well as holding great house parties, the Duke built, in 1915, a beautiful new church in the village. **St Winifred's Church** is named after his wife.

St Winifred's Church, Holbeck

Back in Cuckney itself, there is a large mound in the churchyard which represents the site where, in the mid-12th century, Thomas de Cuckney built a castle. Excavations on the site in the 1950s found the remains of hundreds of skeletons, thought to be from the 7th century and the Battle of Heathfield between Edwin of Northumbria and Penda of Mercia.

EASTWOOD

Very much an industrial town, dominated by the coal mining industry, Eastwood is best known as the birthplace, in 1885, of David Herbert Lawrence. The Lawrence family home, a two up, two down, terrace house in Victoria Street is now the **DH Lawrence Birthplace Museum**, furnished in a late 19th-century style with which the Lawrence family would have been familiar. There are also some household items on display which belonged to the family and anyone visiting the museum will see that the house's front window is larger than others in the same street. This is where Mrs Lawrence displayed the children's clothes and other linen

122

items which she made and sold to supplement the fluctuating wages brought home by her miner husband. **Durban House**, built in 1876 as the offices of a coal company, has been restored to the 'handsome brick building almost like a mansion' that Law-

DH Lawrence Birthplace Museum

rence wrote about in *Sons and Lovers*. It is now a heritage centre with a focus on Lawrence's connections with Nottinghamshire. Lawrence died at Vence, in the south of France, in 1930.

The **Erewash Canal**, completed in 1779, runs close to Eastwood and it provided an efficient form of transport for the coal away from the numerous pits in this area. At **Shipley Lock**, in the town, an aqueduct carries the canal over the River Erewash and it was constructed by first building the aqueduct and then diverting the river to run underneath. In the 1980s, following years of neglect, the canal was cleared and made suitable for use by pleasure craft whilst the towpath was resurfaced and it is now a pleasant and interesting walk.

Just east of the town lies the village of **Greasley**, where traces of a fortified manor house built in the 14th century by Nicholas de Cantelupe can still be seen. It was the same Cantelupe who, in 1345, founded Greasley Priory for the Carthusian order. The house fell into disrepair after the Dissolution and many of the village buildings have some of the prio-

ry's stone in their construction. Each year, in May, a procession of local clergymen, followed by their congregation, walk from the local Roman Catholic church to the priory ruins to hold a service.

EDWINSTONE

Lying at the heart of Sherwood Forest, the life of the village is still dominated by the forest, as it has been since the 7th century. Edwin, King of Northumbria, who gave the village its name, died in the Battle of Hatfield in 632 and the village is said to have grown up around the church which was built on the spot where he was slain. In 1912, a cross was erected to mark his grave by the Duke of Portland. From then on until the time of the Domesday Survey, Edwinstowe remained small. Following the Norman Conquest, the village found itself within the boundaries of the Royal Hunting Forest of Sherwood and it became subject to the laws of the forest. Dating from the 12th century, the Church of St Mary was the first stone building in Edwinstowe and legend has it that it was here that the marriage took place between Robin Hood and Maid Marian. A stone in the churchyard marks the grave of Dr Cobham Brewer, author of the renowned *Dictionary of Phrase and Fable*.

A little way up the road leading northwards out of Edwinstowe is the **Sherwood Forest Country Park & Visitor Centre**. The legendary home of Robin Hood is Sherwood Forest, and visitors still flock to see the great hollow tree which the outlaws purportedly used as a meeting place and as a cache for their supplies. The

The Major Oak, Sherwood Forest

Major Oak, which is located about 10 minutes walk along the main track in the heart of the forest, is supported by massive wooden crutches and iron corsets, so it presents a rather forlorn sight. There is no denying that it is at least 500 years old, and some sources would claim it to be more than double that figure. The Visitor Centre houses two exhibitions, Robin Hood's Sherwood Forest and Forests of the World, and the park has a year-round programme of events, including the renowned festival in August. Not far from Edwinstowe, off the A6075, is the Sherwood Forest Farm Park, a naturalist and animal lover's delight. Enjoying a peaceful setting in a secluded valley on the edge of Sherwood Forest, the Farm Park boasts no fewer than 30 rare and threatened species of farm animal and is beautifully laid out, with ornamental ponds and three wildfowl lakes. Residents include rare breed animals, wallabies, fallow deer, water buffalo and Kune pigs, and there is also a tearoom, gift shop and picnic area. Among many other attractions in the forest are the **Fun Park**, just minutes from the Visitor Centre, and the **Sherwood Pines Forest Park**, with waymarked trails and a range of cycle routes (cycles can be hired). **Sherwood Forest Art and Craft Centre** is located in the former coach house and stables of Edwinstowe Hall.

Pronounced Renoth locally, this former mining village of Rainworth, six miles east of Edwinstone, offers two very different places of interest. **Rainworth Water**, a series of lakes and streams, which attracts walkers, naturalists, and fishermen, is also the site of a bird sanctuary founded by the naturalist Joseph Whitaker. Rainworth's other claim to fame is its fish and chip shop, which found itself on the front pages of the national newspapers in the early 1980s as the place where the notorious murderer the Black Panther was caught.

Blidworth is a small forest village, seven miles south of Edwinstone, and closely associated with the legend of Robin Hood. Maid Marian is thought to have lived here before her marriage to the outlaw; at **Fountaindale** are the remains of **Friar Tuck's Well** and, nearby, the site of his home where his fight with Robin is said to have taken place; and, finally, Will Scarlett is reputedly buried in St Mary's churchyard. Near the village there are two Forestry Commission areas of woodland which both offer the opportunity for walks and picnics: **Blidworth Bottoms** and **Haywood Oaks**, where some of the largest oak trees in Sherwood can be found.

HOLME PIERREPONT

Holme Pierrepont Hall is an early Tudor manor house with some rooms restored and furnished in the style of the early 17th century; the ceiling of one of the first-floor bedrooms has been removed to reveal the impressive roof construction. Also worthy of a visit is St Edmond's Church, situated adjacent to the hall. The home of several interesting Pierrepont family monuments, including a 14th-century brass to an unknown lady, the church retains some features of the original 13th-century building behind its 19th-century exterior.

Holme Pierrepont is today more widely known as the home of the **National Watersports Centre**. Built to Olympic standards, it has a 2,000-metre rowing course and a wild water slalom course, all man-made from the carefully landscaped pasture and quarries which once dominated the area.

MANSFIELD

Lying close to Robin Hood country and near Lord Byron's splendid ancestral home, this old market town has plenty to offer the visitor. In the heart of the town, a plaque and new tree mark the historic centre of Sherwood Forest and the famous place where Robin Hood first encountered Friar Tuck lies just outside the town at Rainworth Water. The old market place, which still holds markets on Mondays, Thursdays, Fridays, and Saturdays, is the centre of Mansfield and around the square can be seen some of the town's more interesting buildings. Pride of place goes to the impressive Gothic **Bentinck Monument** erected in 1848 in memory of Lord George Bentinck. The younger son of the

Bentinck Monument, Mansfield

124

Duke of Portland, Bentinck was a long serving Member of Parliament and a great friend of Disraeli. Funds for the memorial were raised by public subscription but they unfortunately ran out before the finishing touch, a statue of Bentinck himself, could be placed in the central space. The original market cross, dating from the 16th or 17th century, stands in Westgate. The Moot Hall, built in 1752 by Lady Oxford, and Waverley House, which lies close by and dates from the same period, are an interesting mixture of architectural styles.

During the 17th century, Mansfield was noted for its nonconformist leanings and in Stockwell Gate is the **Old Meeting House** and parsonage, which date from the early 18th century. Much altered over the years and with some splendid William Morris stained glass added, this is one of the oldest chapels still in use in the county. There has been a place of worship on the site of the present parish Church of St Peter and St Paul since the time of the Domesday Book. The church standing today was built over many years and some of its stones are thought to have come from a Saxon building.

Just to the northwest of the market place, **Mansfield Museum & Art Gallery** concentrates its collections largely on local interest, including a model of a Roman villa that once stood at nearby Mansfield Woodhouse. The collection spans the centuries from that early occupation right up to more recent times, with pictures and artefacts relating to the industry of the town and surrounding villages. The adjoining art gallery also carries a local theme and features works by artists of the area including the watercolourist AS Buxton, who is well known for his works of Mansfield.

Further west, on the outskirts of the town centre, lies the **Metal Box Factory**, which grew out of a mustard business that was established in the 1830s by David Cooper Barringer. In order to keep the mustard dry, the company began to store the powder in metal boxes and not the traditional wooden crates and, by the late 19th century, the market for decorated metal box packaging had grown so great that the company decided to concentrate on the production of the boxes rather than the milling of mustard.One feature though, which anyone approaching Mansfield cannot fail to miss, is the enormous railway viaduct which dominates the skyline. Built in 1875, the 15 immense stone arches cut through the heart of the town and it is one of the largest viaducts in any English town.

Three miles west of Mansfield lies the village of Teversal, the fictional home of Lady Chatterley and the nearby woodlands of the Hardwick Estate (the Hall lies in Derbyshire) were the meeting place for her and the gamekeeper. The Carnarvon family pew in the ancient church has some particularly beautiful carvings which give it an appearance of a four-poster bed. **Teversal Trails** is a beautiful network of walks with a sculpture trail and a visitor centre with refreshments and exhibitions.

MANSFIELD WOODHOUSE

Before the opening of Sherwood Colliery in 1903, Mansfield Woodhouse was a small and quiet rural village of farms and labourers' cottages. However, the village also had a remarkable number of large, grand houses as the area was considered to be a fashionable place to live.

Opposite The Cross, in the heart of Mansfield Woodhouse, stands one of these fine houses, the **Georgian Burnaby House**. Still retaining many of its original, elegant features, the house was obviously built for a prosperous family and, during the mid-19th century, it was occupied by the Duke of Portland's land agent. On the other side of the road stands a stump which is all that remains of the Market Cross which was erected here after a great fire in 1304. At the bottom of the street lies the oldest building in Mansfield Woodhouse, **St Edmund's Church**. Most of the original church was lost, along with the parish records, when fire swept through the village in the early 14th century. The present church was built on the same site though it underwent some severe restoration in the 19th century. Lying not far from the church is a manor house known as Woodhouse Castle because of the battlements which were added to the building in the early 1800s. Dating from the 17th century, this was the house of the Digby family and, in particular, General Sir John Digby, Sheriff of Nottingham.

Another building of note is the essentially 18th-century **Wolfhunt House**, just off the High Street. The unusual name is derived from a local legend which suggests that the land on which the house is built once belonged to a man who was employed to frighten away the wolves in Sherwood Forest by blowing a hunting horn.Newstead

The grand mansion, **Newstead Abbey**, which lies just to the east of the village, was the home of the poet Lord Byron and his ancestors for many years. Originally, Newstead was a true place of worship when, in the late 12th century an Augustinian priory was founded here by Henry II in atonement for his part in the death of Thomas à Becket. However, most of the medieval remains that can still be seen date from building work which was carried out some 100 years after the abbey's foundation. The abbey was bought in 1539 by Sir John Byron, who converted the monastic buildings for his own private use. Much of the original building was destroyed, but a statue of Christ still stands above the main entrance hall and there is a statue of the Virgin and Child in the gable. One of the more colourful characters within the family, the 5th Lord Byron, known as Devil Byron, not only enjoyed playing with a warship on the lake but was involved in the killing of one of his neighbours during a drunken brawl in a London tavern: though his lordship was acquitted of murder. By the time the 5th Lord Byron died the scullery was the only room in this huge mansion that did not have a leaking roof, and this was were his body was found. The poet Lord Byron, the 5th lord's great nephew, then succeeded to the title and began, with some success, to make some of the rooms habitable but he too ran out of money and was forced, in 1817, to sell the house. The abbey welcomes many visitors throughout the year and the grounds contain a wealth of hidden places. There is a secret garden, a beautifully carved fountain decorated with fantastic animals, the elaborate memorial to Byron's dog Boatswain, and the large lake where the 5th lord re-enacted naval battles. The house, home to the Byron Museum, is well worth a visit and a tour around the many rooms reveals a whole host of splendid treasures.

NEWARK-ON-TRENT

Historically, Newark-on-Trent has always been a strategic point: it lies close to the Roman road, Fosse Way, and also guards the first upstream crossing of the River Trent. Though there is no evidence of a Roman settlement here, the remains of pottery and coins found in the vicinity of the castle suggest that there was possibly a fort here at one time. The Saxons certainly settled here and part of their defences for the town have been excavated. It was, however, the Danes who began the formation of Newark-on-Trent as it is known today.

By the time of the Domesday Survey, the name Newark, a corruption of New Work, was being used. This name was either used to refer to the rebuilding of the town following the Danish invasion or it could have been a reference to the new town defences that were constructed around that time. Occupying a strong defensive position beside the River Trent, **Newark Castle** was founded in the 12th century by Alexander, Bishop of Lincoln. Over the next 300 years, the castle saw extensive improvements made to its original construction and, in 1483, it was taken from the bishops of

Newark Castle

Lincoln by Henry VII, who leased it to a succession of noblemen until the time of the Civil War. The Castle was largely destroyed by the Parliamentarians after the Civil War; the remains include one of the finest Norman gatehouses in the country. In the adjacent Gilstrap Centre, the story of the Castle is told in a fascinating exhibition. **The Governor's House** is the place where the governors of Newark lived during the Civil War and also the place where Charles I quarrelled with Prince Rupert after the prince had lost Bristol to Parliament. This wonderful timber framed building was restored in the late 19th century and during the work a medieval wall and some beam paintings were revealed along with some graffiti dating from 1757.

Also in the heart of Newark is Nottinghamshire's finest parish church, the huge Church of St Mary Magdalene, its spire dominating the town and acting as a local landmark. Notable features in the church, which evolved over 300 years from the 12th century, include the Treasury, the chantry chapel, the restored font and the Dance of Death painting. **Newark Museum**, housed in a former school which dates back to 1529, has exhibitions of prehistoric artefacts and Roman finds, coin hoards and Civil War siege plans, along with local crafts from fishing reels to corsets. A large Anglo-Saxon cemetery, discovered in Millgate, is also on display. Newark's position on the River Trent played an important part in its development during the Industrial Revolution, when goods were transported along the River Trent from Nottingham to the North Sea and a wealth of warehouses grew up along the riverbank. Commercial water traffic declined to almost nothing in the second half of the 20th century but one of the old warehouses is now the home of the **Millgate Folk Museum**. Three floors in a Victorian building show the agricultural, industrial and social life of Newark, with streets, shops and rooms faithfully recreated. The Mezzanine Gallery at the museum displays the work of local artists, designers, photographers and craftspeople.

A planned circular walk, starting at the **Gilstrap Centre**, takes in many of the town's Victorian buildings, including the Italianate Corn Exchange, the Castle Brewery, the Queen Anne-style London Road Hospital and the Ossington Coffee Palace.

A major attraction on the northeast side of town, with easy access from the A1, A46, A17, A1133 and the new by-pass, is the **Newark Air Museum**, which has 45 aircraft on display, the majority under cover in the Display Hall. Opened in the 1960s, the museum also has a great deal of aviation memorabilia, relics, and uniforms on display. One of the largest privately managed collections in the country, the museum spans the history of aviation.

NOTTINGHAM

The county town, Nottingham, in the southwestern corner of the county, is by far its largest town, and is generally regarded as the capital of the East Midlands, often called the Queen of the Midlands. A lively mix of the old and new, Nottingham has a colourful history which span-s the ages - from Anglo-Saxon times to the industrial expansion of the 19th century. Today, this blend of ancient and modern makes Nottingham a place worthy of lengthy exploration. The settlement of Nottingham was founded by a 6th-century Anglo-Saxon chief

with the unfortunate name of Snot. He and his people carved out dwellings in the soft local sandstone and the settlement thrived to become Snottingham, which later changed into its currently more acceptable form.

A natural place for a tour to start is the **Castle**, but the castle standing today is not the one which played such a part in the many films dedicated to the legend of Robin Hood; that was already in a state of disrepair by the time of the Civil War and was destroyed soon afterwards. However, the legendary tales of the outlaw hero and his merry band of followers is still very much alive in the city and throughout the county. Commanding an imposing position, high above the city centre and situated on a rocky outcrop, the original castle was built after the Battle of Hastings by William the Conqueror and William Peveril, with additions in the following centuries. Its elevated position, overlooking the city and the River Trent, made it one of the foremost castles in Norman England and it played host to many important visitors. Edward IV proclaimed himself king from here and, later, his brother Richard III built new state apartments and lived at the castle for most of his reign. Thereafter, though, the castle gradually fell into disrepair until Charles I came to Nottingham in 1642 and raised his standard at the castle at the start of the Civil War. Unfortunately, the king found little support for his cause in the city and he moved on to Shrewsbury, leaving the castle in the hands of the Parliamentarians. Over the course of the war, the Royalists made several attempts to recapture the castle but Cromwell's supporters held out. After the fighting was over the castle building was rendered uninhabitable and it was finally demolished in 1674 by the Duke of Newcastle who went on to build his palace on the site. Some of the remains of the early castle are still visible,

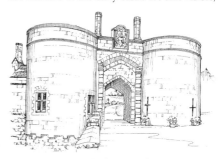

Nottingham Castle

including the 13th-century gatehouse and parts of the moat and outer bailey.

The Duke's palace, rebuilt after it was ransacked by supporters of the Reform Bill in 1831, is home to the **Castle Museum**, opened by the Prince of Wales in 1878, which was also the first municipal art gallery in the country outside London; the collection today is particularly noted for its fine selection of Victorian paintings. The museum has a fine collection of silverware and ceramics and the Story of Nottingham, a mix of displays and audio visual presentations, is well worth a visit.

At the base of Castle Rock, set back into the sandstone, lies the famous **Trip to Jerusalem Inn**, where the crusaders are said to have stopped for a pint to fortify themselves before their long journey to the Holy Land. Dating back to around 1189, it is said to be the oldest pub in England; it was once the brewhouse for the castle and from here travellers to the Holy Land bought their ale. In the pub's cellars, but with its entrance further along the road in

Trip to Jerusalem Inn

Peveril Drive, is Mortimer's Hole, a cave hewn out of the sandstone rock which leads to the castle. It is through this passageway that Edward III crept to capture Roger Mortimer. Later sentenced to death, Mortimer's ghost is said to haunt the cave.

Also at the base of Castle Rock is the **Brewhouse Yard Museum - The Museum of Nottingham Life**, set in a group of 18th-century cottages; it presents a realistic look at life in Nottingham over the past 200 years, with displays that include a Victorian kitchen and a number of shops.

Also in the vicinity is a charming medieval building that is home to the **Lace Centre**, which holds lace-making demonstrations and

offers a vast selection of high quality lace for sale. A little way across the city, in High Pavement, is the newly opened **Museum of Nottingham Lace**, which tells the story of lace from its early days as a cottage craft, through the time of the Industrial Revolution to the high-tech industry of today. There are live demonstrations of working lace machines and displays of hand lace, along with video displays and audio guides. The

Nottingham Lace Market

Lace Shop is stocked with attractive things to buy, and the Visitor Centre is a good place to start a tour of Nottingham's historic **Lace Market** district. Back near the Castle, the **Costume and Textile Museum** features costume displays from 1790 to the mid-20th century, all beautifully presented in period rooms. There are also many other exhibits on show, including tapestries; knitted, woven, and printed textiles; and fashion accessories through the ages. The museum is housed in a terrace of brick houses that was constructed, in 1788, by Cornelius Launder, a former High Sheriff.

The present redbrick building of St Nicholas' Church replaces the medieval church which stood here until 1643 and the days of the Civil War. It was from this church's tower that Royalists fired upon the castle in an attempt to regain control and, after the attack, the Parliamentarian governor of the castle ordered the church's destruction so no further attacks could take place. Rebuilding of the church was completed in 1682 and, inside, at the east end of the south aisle, there is a tombstone to Lawrence Collin, the master gunner of the Castle during the Civil War.

North of the Castle, at a roundabout on Maid Marian Way, The **Tales of Robin Hood** offers a chance to travel back in time to experience the sights, sounds and smells of medieval England in cable cars. Visitors can try their hand at archery and see whether they can become an honorary outlaw. In the Central Library Building, **Angel Row Gallery** is the region's leading contemporary art and craft gallery, with new works by local, national and international artists.

Beneath Broad Marsh Centre, one of the city's major shopping precincts, lie the **Caves of Nottingham**, a popular attraction which opened in 1994. The city is built on sandstone and throughout Nottingham's history the rock has been tunnelled to provide first shelter and then hiding places. Now, thanks to local voluntary groups, these man-made caves have been saved for future generations. The most spectacular cave in the system, the Pillar Cave, dates back to 1250 and contains the remains of the country's only underground tannery. During the Middle Ages, the city was an important leather

Caves of Nottingham

producer but the caves were also commonly used as pub cellars: the constant temperature being ideal for the storage of beer and wine. They have even been used as dwellings, and served as air raid shelters during the blitz of World War II: one of the caves has been left as a reminder of the wartime days.

Nearby, the **Galleries of Justice** tell the story of justice in England down the centuries. The setting is an original courthouse and county jail, and the experience is made all the more vivid by hands-on exhibits.

Located near the bottom of the same road (High Pavement) is Nottingham's largest parish church, St Mary's. It was probably founded in Saxon times, but the current building dates from the 15th century, with 19th- and early 20th-century additions which include windows by a series of renowned stained glass makers. Also inside is a Bishop's Throne carved in 1890, when it was thought that the church would become the cathedral for the diocese of Southwell.

Nottingham is particularly famous for its **Goose Fair**, which gained its name from the large flocks of geese that were sold here around Michaelmas. Mentioned in a charter dated 1284, the Goose Fair is still held today on the first Thursday in October. On the edge of The Park, an old royal hunting ground that was developed for housing in 1827, stands the Roman Catholic cathedral of St Barnabas. Built in 1841 by Pugin, the exterior is rather severe although the spire is very fanciful. Inside, much of Pugin's original decoration has been replaced though his stained glass windows remain in the aisle.

As in many other industrial towns, the late 18th century saw the building of canals to serve the expanding populations and aid the transportation of goods. Nottingham was no exception and, in 1796, the Nottingham Canal was completed, thus linking the town with many of the country's more well-known waterways. Almost 15 miles in length and rising, by a series of 20 locks, some 130 feet, the canal ran from the River Trent, through the centre of Nottingham, to the Cromford Canal at Langley Mill, in neighbouring Derbyshire. Today only some seven miles and three locks are left, including a substantial stretch through the city. A walk along the banks of the canal gives an insight into the life of Nottingham in the last century and there is also much of interest to those who revel in industrial archaeology.

Along the Nottingham Canal, and still with its own basin found under an arch for easy loading and unloading, is the **Canal Museum**. Dating from the mid-19th century, this four storey building was the warehouse for one of the largest firms of canal carriers, Fellows, Morton, and Clayton. The firm went into liquidation in 1948 and this magnificent building has been restored and refurbished to house many displays and

Nottingham Canal Museum

models which illustrate the history of the Trent Valley. The story, from rise to decline, of the country's network of canals and navigable waterways is also told and includes a reconstruction of an area of the warehouse as it would have appeared in its heyday.

JM Barrie, the author of *Peter Pan*, lived in Nottingham and it is said that an urchin he met while walking in Clifton Grove was the inspiration for his leading character.

RETFORD

The town has grown in importance over the centuries, from the granting of its market charter by Henry III in 1246, to the prosperity bought to it by the railway and canal links. The town is made up of East Retford and West Retford, lying on opposite banks of the River Idle. Of the two, West Retford is the older and it is presumably this parish which received a mention in the Domesday Book as Redforde. East Retford was established in 1105 on the other side of the river as a place where tolls could be collected from people make the river crossing. An attempt was made, in the 18th century, to make the river navigable from Retford to Bawtry but this was unsuccessful though the diversion of the Great North Road through the town, in 1766, did bring more prosperity to Retford.

The **Market Square** was laid out in the late 18th century after the rerouting of the Great North Road through the town. Still at the heart of the life of Retford today, with a bustling market every Thursday and Saturday, the square is surrounded by many of the town's most noteworthy buildings, including some fine Georgian houses. The grand and rather chateau-like Town Hall was built in 1868 to replace the Georgian hall which stood on the northeast side of square. Outside the Town Hall can be found the **Broad Stone**, which is probably the base of an old parish boundary cross. Tradition has it that during the times of the plague in Retford, in the mid-16th and mid-17th centuries, coins were placed in a pool of vinegar in the hollow in the top of the stone to prevent the disease from spreading whilst trading was taking place at the market.

Cannon Square now occupies the site of East Retford's ancient market place and it is also home to one of Retford's more unusual attractions: a Russian cannon. Dating from 1855 and weighing over 2 tons, the cannon was captured by British soldiers at Sebastopol and was brought to Retford at the end of the Crimean War. The townsfolk paid for its transportation and, in 1859, after arguments raged about its siting, it was placed in the square and named the Earl of Aberdeen after the incumbent Prime Minister. During World War II the cannon was threatened with being melted down to help the war effort and it was only saved after a Retford gentleman bought it and hid it until the war was over.

Not far from Cannon Square is, reputedly, the oldest chemist's shop in the country still on its original site. Opened in 1779, **Norths Chemists** first belonged to a local vet, Francis Clater, whose books on animal medicine and treatment were bestsellers for over 100 years.

One of the town's most infamous visitors was the highwayman Dick Turpin and several historic inns still stand as a reminder to the great days of the stage coach. Another man who stood and delivered here, though in a more respectable fashion, was John Wesley, who conducted many of his open air meetings in East Retford.

When in Retford, it is well worth visiting the **Bassetlaw Museum & Percy Laws Memorial Gallery** in Amcott House, Grove Street. This

130

imposing late 18th-century town house is noted for its finely executed internal plasterwork and elegant wrought iron staircase, which the restoration has returned to their full Georgian splendour. The museum has a distinct local emphasis, with displays of local archaeology, civic, social and industrial history, and fine and applied art.

Two miles south of Retford, the small hamlet of Eaton was once part of the estate of the Dukes of Newcastle, which incorporated several other nearby villages. The land known as Eaton Wood, now managed by the Nottinghamshire Wildlife Trust, was mentioned in the Domesday Book as an area of pasture woodland and some of the ancient ridges and furrows can still be seen. A wood of mainly ash, elm, and hazel with some oak, **Eaton Wood** is more important for the plant life it sustains such as moschatel, yellow archangel, and several orchids.

Five miles east of Retford stands a village whose correct name is North Leverton with Habblesthorpe which has been described in the Guinness Book of Records as the longest multiple place name in England. The two villages were united in 1884. The 12th-century village Church of St Martin is reached via a bridge over a stream whilst the Wesleyan Sunday school, near the crossroads, was built in 1838.

However, by far the most outstanding feature in the village is the **Windmill**, built in 1813 when it was known as the Subscription Mill. Despite rebuilding work over the years, it remains an attractive sight and it is also the only working windmill in the county. The windmill is open to visitors and freshly ground flour can be bought.

RUDDINGTON

This historic village was once the home of many hosiery workers and several of their cottages still remain here. An old factory and some cottages now house the **Framework Knitters' Museum**, showing the life and work of a Victorian knitting community. Of the 25 hand frames seen here today, most are fully operational and there is an opportunity to buy samples made at the museum. A major attraction in Rushcliffe Country Park is the **Nottingham Transport Heritage Centre**, with a steam railway, a miniature railway and classic bus rides. There's also a souvenir shop and cafeteria.

RUFFORD

Rufford Country Park is an area of woodland and parkland around the remains of a 12th-century **Cistercian Abbey** founded by Gilbert de Gant as a daughter house to the Cistercian Rievaulx Abbey. By the middle of the 14th century the abbey was already in decline, and when Henry VIII started to dissolve the monasteries

Rufford Abbey

in 1536, it was one of the first to go. The Crown granted the abbey to the powerful Talbot family, and George Talbot, 6th Earl of Shrewsbury, transformed it into a country house. The remaining ruins of the abbey are said to be haunted by the ghost of a giant monk with a skull-like face: there is written evidence in the parish register for Edwinstowe that a man died of fright after catching sight of this unholy visitor!

In 1626, the house was bought by the Savile family, who lived here until the 1930s, and it was they who carried out many of the improvements. In the stone undercroft is an exhibition focusing on the lives of the monks, while the stable block houses an impressive craft centre. There is also an important ceramics centre, a craft centre and a craft shop, and every year the Craft potters Association holds its '**Earth and Fire**' summer fair in the abbey grounds. The grounds themselves are well worth a visit, with formal gardens, an arboretum, woodlands with avenues and pathways, a lake with varied bird life, the remains of two ice houses and the graves of some of the Savile family's animals (notably that of the 1872 Derby winner, Cremorne). There's a choice of eating places, the Savile Restaurant and the less formal Coach House, and two shops.

Seven miles southeast of Rufford, the large, 17th-century rectory in the village of Cromwell is now home to the **Vina Cooke Museum of Dolls & Bygone Childhood.** Appealing to adults and children alike, there are all manner of children's toys on display but, perhaps the most fascinating are the handmade dolls which depict celebrities and famous historical characters. Handmade dolls and other crafts for sale.

SCROOBY

Scroppenthor existed here before 958, the year that King Edgar granted the land rights to Oscytel, the Archbishop of York. But Scrooby's greatest claim to fame is through William Brewster, who was a founder member of the Pilgrim Fathers.

It was at Cambridge that Brewster's radical ideas on religion were formed and his spell in the Netherlands, with its toleration of religious views, gave him a new perspective. He returned to England, settling in Scrooby, and, in 1598, he was summoned before the ecclesiastical court for poor attendance at St Wilfrid's Church, which was to lead him on the path to Separatism and the freedom of religion from control by the State. His outspoken views eventually forced him to resign his post and he became outlawed for his ideas. Imprisoned for a short time in Boston, Lincolnshire, Brewster made his way back to Amsterdam. After some years he returned, again, to England and, in 1620, he left again on board the *Mayflower* with a group of like-minded people. He was by now an elder of the Separatist Church and the group later became known as the Pilgrim Fathers. Brewster and his colleagues founded a colony in Plymouth, New England and he died in America, in 1644, at about the age of 77. Bassetlaw District Council have devised **The Mayflower Trail**, which takes in **Babworth**, where **All Saints' Church** contains many interesting items recalling the Pilgrim Fathers; Scrooby; **Austerfield**, birthplace of William Bradford, one of the leading Fathers; and Gainsborough, where the Hickman family of Gainsborough

Old Hall were sympathetic to the Separatist Movement.

For such a small village, Scrooby has a wealth of other interesting features. There is a stone walled pinfold near the churchyard where stray-

All Saints' Church, Babworth

ing cattle or sheep were rounded up and released on payment of a fine. The Pilgrim Fathers Inn dates back to 1771, although it was originally called The Saracen's Head. The Monks Mill, which stands on the old course of the River Ryton, is now a private dwelling and despite the name it has never had any close associations with a monastery.

SHERWOOD FOREST

Sherwood Forest is known to old and young alike, all over the world, thanks to the tales of **Robin Hood** and the various stories, films, and, television series based on this legendary hero of the people. Sherwood, the shire wood of Nottinghamshire, was once part of a great mass of forest land which covered much of central England, stretching from Nottingham in the south to Worksop in the north and from the Peak District to the Trent Valley in the east.

It was likely that William the Conqueror, during his reign, designated Sherwood a **royal forest.** The Norman kings were passionate about their hunting and, to guard their royal forests, there were a set of rigidly upheld laws, to conserve the game (known as the venison) and vegetation (known as the vert). No one, even those

132

with a private estate within the royal forest, was allowed to kill or hunt protected animals, graze domestic animals in the forest, fell trees, or make clearings within the boundaries without the express permission of the king or one of his chief foresters. It is little wonder then, that with such strict rules imposed upon them, that the people turned to the likes of Robin Hood and others who defied the laws and lived off the king's deer. Though villagers were severely punished for breaking the forest law, the Norman kings were well known for frequently offering exemptions from the rule to favoured noblemen as well as local monastic houses.

It was not until the Tudor and Stuart monarchs came to the throne in the 16th century that things began to change and the laws relaxed. Less obsessed with hunting than their predecessors, the kings granted permission for the felling of trees and the clearing of land for agricultural purposes and so the landscape of the forest began to change. Eventually, the royal forest was broken up and the land given to various aristocratic families in the area. The great oaks of the forest were felled in their thousands for shipbuilding and also to fuel the iron industry. Later, in the 19th century, the decline of the forest areas increased with the sinking of mines in the forest. Starting on the southern and western fringes of Sherwood Forest the collieries gradually moved inwards turning once small rural communities into mining villages. The peak of destruction of the wooded areas was reached during World War I. Where once the forest covered a large part of the county, only a few pockets of wood and heathland remained, chiefly the area around Edwinstowe.

Following World War I, the Forestry Commission was set up to replenish the depleted stocks of wood and a programme of planting began. Since World War II, when the forest areas were used again, there has been a great change in the fortunes of Sherwood.

SNEINTON

This suburb of Nottingham is, perhaps, best remembered as the birthplace, in 1829, of William Booth, the founder of the Salvation Army. The small terraced house, where he and his family lived until 1831, is still standing in Notintone Place and, in front of the building, is a statue of the great man. it is now home to the **William Booth Birthplace Museum**, which is part of the William Booth Memorial Complex and is open by appointment only (Tel: 0115 950 3927).

At the age of 16, William Booth gave his first sermon in a house in Kid Street and it was just a year later that he became a Methodist preacher. In 1849, he left Nottingham for London and became a Methodist minister but, finding the church structures too constraining, he started, in 1865, the Christian Missions which, in 1878, became the Salvation Army. In Windmill Lane stands the **Green's Mill & Science Centre**, a fully operational 19th-century windmill that was once owned by the mathematician and physicist George Green. Visitors can see grain being ground and also test their skills in the adjacent science centre, which stages hands-on experiments with light, magnetism and electricity.

SOUTHWELL

An elegant market town, Southwell also boasts a fine **Cathedral**, which may sound implausible to the uninitiated, but the lovely 12th-century Minster was elevated to the status of cathedral in 1884, when the new Diocese of Southwell was created. This has given rise to the building often being referred to as the village cathedral. The two west towers, with their pyramidal roofs, make a striking landmark as they stand proud, dominating the cathedral green. Inside, the choir screen is quite stunning, bearing no less than 200 human carvings, and the eagle lectern, which stands in the choir, was salvaged from the lake at Newstead Abbey in 1750. It had been thrown there by the monks to protect it from the looting that occurred during the Dissolution and was presented to the

Southwell Minster

minster in 1805. In the Chapter House are some beautiful carvings, some of which date from the 13th century. The 'Leaves of Southwell' is a magical work with carvings of dogs, rabbit and pigs hidden in the foliage. The Angel Window is a much more recent feature. To the south of the minster can be found the ruins of the palace of the archbishops of York which dated from the 14th and 15th centuries. Parts of the old palace, closest to the minster's south doorway, have been incorporated into the present **Bishop's Palace**.

Southwell itself has many fine buildings and a wealth of fascinating places to discover. Among these are the Prebendal houses where the secular canons resided, sequestered alleyways, and charming coaching inns like the Saracen's Head where Charles I spent his last hours of freedom before his final surrender. At the time of the king's final visit the inn was called the King's Head but the name of this wonderful 16th-century inn was changed after Charles's execution.

Southwell has claims to be the birthplace of the **Bramley apple**. The story goes that in the early 19th century, two ladies planted some apple pips in their cottage garden in the nearby village of Easthorpe. Nature took its course and one of the seedlings grew into a tree. By this time, Matthew Bramley owned the cottage and the quality of the tree's fruit began to excite public interest. Mr Henry Merryweather, a local nurseryman, persuaded Bramley to let him take a cutting, which he consequently propagated with enormous success. Permission had been granted on the condition that the apples took Mr Bramley's name and not the two ladies'! The garden centre and tea room of H Merryweather Sons incorporates the **Bramley Apple Exhibition**, and visitors should not leave town without sampling a Southwell Galette, a scrumptious pastry confection of hazelnuts, sultanas, and, of course, Bramley apples.

The now disused railway line from Southwell to Mansfield, which was first opened to trains in 1871, is now an attractive and comfortable footpath known as the **Farnsfield to Southwell Trail**. As well as the varied plant and wildlife that can be found along the 4½ mile walk, there is also plenty of industrial archaeological interest including the Farnsfield Waterworks of 1910, a late 18th-century cotton mill, and Greet Lily Mill, a corn mill on the banks of the River Greet.

Norwood Park is the only one of the four original parks around Southwell which remains today. The property of the Archbishops of York, the park remained in the possession of the Church until 1778 and, though a house was built here in Cromwell's day, the present building dates from 1763. Open to visitors during the summer months, the house has a very lived in feel and, as well as many 17th- and 18th-century family portraits, there is also a fine collection of china. The surrounding parkland was laid out in the 18th century at the same time as the ice house and temple were built and the lime avenue planted.

The charming cottages in the industrial village of **Calverton**, six miles southwest of Southwell, date back to the early 19th century and they were the homes of framework knitters. Carefully restored by the Nottinghamshire Building Preservation Trust, the cottages originally formed three sides of a rectangle, though one side is now missing. Unusually, the large windows which provided the light for the knitters are found on the ground floor where, elsewhere, they are usually on an upper storey. Framework knitting was the main industry of the village, and of many others, at that time. The stocking knitting frame was invented in nearby Woodborough by William Lee in 1589. The **Calverton Folk Museum** is a four-roomed stocking-knitter's cottage with displays of the hosiery industry and Victorian clothing and furniture.

Also at Calverton is **Painters' Paradise**, a series of gardens that have been designed with the artist in mind. Covering some 38 acres, the gardens, which have elements based on Monet's garden at Giverny, include woodlands, meadows, butterfly gardens, and a special disabled garden with raised flower beds. Old farming implements are used as props and there are several gazebos so that people can paint in comfort.

UPTON

A famous son of the village was James Tenant, the man who cut the world renowned Koh-I-Noor diamond. The most impressive building here is Upton Hall, a stylish Grecian villa with a central dome and elegant colonnade, built in the early 19th century. The Hall has, since mov-

134

ing from Clerkenwell, London, in 1972, been the headquarters of the **British Horological Institute**, where visitors can see a fascinating display of clocks, watches, and other horological pieces in the Watch & Clock Museum. Exhibits include the first successful electric clock, the watch worn by Captain Scott on his Antarctic expedition, the first self-winding wristwatch and the original 'six-pip' generator. Open from 1.30 to 5 precisely on weekdays, plus Sunday in summer. Each year the Hall holds the National Exhibition of Time.

WOLLATON

Built in the 1580 by Robert Smythson, **Wollaton Hall** was the home of the Willoughby family. Francis Willoughby, head of the family at that time, had made his money from local coal mines and he wanted to construct a grand and lavish house. The cost of the scheme and the failure of other business interests nearly bankrupted the family, but luckily the extravagant front facade of classical columns, busts of philosophers and mythological characters, and flamboyant gables remain. The hall now houses many items of interest though only three rooms have been restored to their former grandeur: the great hall, the entrance hall, and a beautiful salon. The building is also home to a Natural History Museum which is based on the collection of a Willoughby who was a noted naturalist of the mid-17th century. The hall's outbuildings have been transformed into the Nottingham Industrial Museum and the city's major industries are all represented. There are bicycles, from boneshakers and penny-farthings through to Raleigh and Humber models, and the progression to the motorcycle is given space in the form of the Brough machines of the 1920s and 1930s. It was whilst riding a Brough motorcycle that TE Lawrence had his fatal crash in

1935. Textiles, and particularly stocking frames and knitting machines, can be found here as can machinery from the pharmaceutical industry. Finally, the local coal mines are also represented and there is a particularly fine example of a horse winding gin from 1844 on display in the courtyard.

Several prize fighters are natives of Nottinghamshire and Wollaton was the home of John Shaw. Contesting only two prize fights, John was probably the least known and he died, in 1815, of wounds he sustained whilst fighting with the Lifeguards at the Battle of Waterloo.

WORKSOP

The outskirts are dominated by modern housing, but there are some fine Georgian buildings to be found in Bridge Street. One of the real attractions of Worksop is the **Priory Gatehouse**, which is best approached from Potter Street, where the full glory of the 14th-century building can be seen. Its great niches house large and beautifully carved statues and the immense entrance is rather reminiscent of a cave opening. Originally the portal to a large Augustinian monastery, the gatehouse together with the Church of St Mary and St Cuthbert is all that remains. There is also a wayside shrine, which makes it a unique ecclesiastical attraction. Today, the upper floor of the gatehouse houses an art gallery and exhibitions are put on here regularly.

Mr Straw's House is a National Trust property with a unique appeal. The semi-detached turn-of-the-century house and a million pounds were left to the Trust by William Straw in his will and the Trust was surprised to find that it had acquired a time-warp. Inside, everything had been preserved from 1932, when William Straw senior, a grocer and seed merchant in Worksop, died. Seven years later his wife died and the two sons, William Jr and Walter, lived a bachelor existence at the house. Walter, who took on the family business, died in 1976 and his brother, after a spell teaching at the City of London College, eventually returned to look after the house; he died in 1990. In all those years, little had changed: their parents' bedroom was closed up and everything left as it was; a 1932 calendar still hung on the wall; their father's hats were still perched in the hall; and his pipes and tobacco pouch were ready by the fireside. Now the Trust have a unique record of social history of those times with a display of

Wollaton Hall

items that reflects life as it was in the 1930s and the earlier decades of this century.

One remnant of the northern part of Sherwood Forest lies near the town. **Hannah Park Wood**, which covers some 14 acres, is mainly made up of oak and beech but there is also a small section of yew trees.

Worksop Museum, situated in Memorial Avenue, is housed in a large purpose-built gallery within the library and museum provided by the Carnegie United Kingdom Trust which was opened in 1938. Within the museum are small exhibitions relating to the history of Worksop and the neighbouring area of The Dukeries, together with a larger display on the Pilgrim Fathers, whose roots lay in north Nottinghamshire. Presiding over the Pilgrim Fathers Exhibition is a life-size model of Pilgrim Elder, William Brewster, one of the leaders of the movement.

The 3,800 acres of The National Trust's **Clumber Park** provide a great variety of activities to keep visitors happy throughout the year, whether it's walking, cycling, orienteering, birdwatching, or shopping for plants and gifts. Part of Nottinghamshire's Dukeries, Clumber was formerly home to the Dukes of Newcastle. The house was demolished in 1938, but many fascinating features of the estate remain, including a Gothic Revival chapel, a classical bridge and a walled kitchen garden which contains the longest glasshouses in National Trust ownership, with vines, figs and a garden museum. The park, which also has a large caravan and camping site, lies 4½ miles south-east of Worksop, a mile from the A1.

Creswell Crags Visitor Centre, four miles southwest of Worksop, is the start point of fascinating tours of the largest of the caves that lie in a narrow limestone gorge. Archaeologists have found flint tools and animal bones dating from the last Ice Age, and in the Visitor Centre are exhibitions and displays of life more than 10,000 years ago. Open daily February to October, Sundays only November to January.

136

Angel Inn

Main Street,
Kneesall,
near Ollerton,
Nottinghamshire
NG22 0AD
Tel: 01623 861078

Directions:

Kneesall is on the
A616, 4 miles south
east of Ollerton

Neat whitewashed
walls at ground floor
level, old red brick
on the first floor - that's **The Angel Inn** at Kneesall. It dates from the 18th century, and is a very picturesque hostelry indeed. It has changed little over the years, and with its well proportioned front and large bay windows, it makes a delightful picture. To the rear is a large, well kept lawn with a play area for children.

This is a great place to have a quiet drink or a meal. Under the personal supervision of Paul and Rachael Clarke, it has earned an enviable reputation in the area for its food, its drink and its warm welcome. The interior is spacious and well laid out, and everything is spotlessly clean and well maintained. The tables are of pine, and they contrast beautifully with the thick red carpeting on the floors. There's a comfortable lounge, a cozy tap room and a restaurant, with seating for over 100 people. Rachael is in charge of the cooking, and the food, naturally enough, is superb, representing great value for money. The inn is famous in the area for its steaks, with over ten different kinds to choose from. Try the juicy 20 oz T bone steaks with all the trimmings - they're absolutely delicious! There are other dishes on offer, of course, and all are cooked to perfection using only the finest produce. You can choose from the printed menu of from the daily specials board. There's always something that is sure to please. Wine is available by the glass or bottle, or you can choose from three real ales at the bar, plus draught bitter, mild, stout, lager and cider.

Opening times: Monday to Saturday: 11.30-15.00 and 18.00-23.00; Sunday:11.30-15.00 and 18.00-22.30

Food: Served 12.00-14.00 and 18.00-22.00 seven days

Credit cards: All credit cards except American Express and Diners

Accommodation: None

Facilities: Car park; beer garden; rear lawn with play area

Local Places of Interest/Activities: Newark-on-Trent (historic town) 9 miles; Southwell (historic city with cathedral) 6 miles; Rufford Country Park (abbey ruins) 4 miles; White Post Modern Farm Centre (children's farm) 6 miles

Black Bull Inn

Blidworth,
Nottinghamshire
NG21 OKH
Tel: 01623 792291
Fax: 01623 793622

Directions:

Follow the A617 east
from Mansfield for 4
miles, then turn
south onto the
B6020; Blidworth is
2 miles along this
road

Within the heart of Sherwood Forest you'll find the large village of Blidworth. It was near here at Blidworth Bottoms, legend tells us, that Maid Marion first met Robin Hood. Certainly, the village is mentioned in the Domesday Book, complied in the l lth century, where it is called Blidworth.

And within the village today you'll find the **Black Bull Inn**, which dates, according to a stone over its side entrance, from 1877. It's a charming building in mock Tudor, with a well proportioned front that sits right on the street. Husband and wife team Mark and Sharon Henry have been in charge for only a short while, and already they have great plans for it. Quite simply, they want to make it the best pub in the area - one that is a favourite with locals and visitors alike - and they are well on the way to achieving this. The interior is charming, with a cozy tap room, a comfortable lounge and a dining area that is both comfortable and spacious.

The focal is "traditional English", with many favourites on the menu. Everything is cooked by Sharon on the premises using the best ingredients available, and already her Sunday lunches have a fine reputation in the village. At the bar, you can choose from three real ales - two resident and a guest, and you can also choose from draught mild, bitter, lager, stout and cider.

This is a pub that is going places. Mark and Sharon will give you a warm welcome should you choose to visit!

Opening times: Monday to Saturday: 11.00-15.00 and 17.00-23.00; Sunday: 12.00-1500

Food: Served 11.00-14.30 and 17.00-19.30 Monday to Saturday; Sunday: lunches only

Credit cards: Cash only at present

Accommodation: None

Entertainment: Traditional music session every Wednesday night; monthly live music (phone for details)

Facilities: Skittle alley; beer garden; barbecues in summer

Local Places of Interest/Activities:

Mansfield (historic town) 5 miles; Papplewick Pumping Station 3 miles; Southwell (cathedral city) 7 miles; Newstead Abbey 3 miles; White Post Modern Farm centre 3 miles

138 Brownlow Arms

**High Marnham,
Nottinghamshire
NG23 6SG
Tel: 01636 822505**

Directions:

The village of High
Marnham is on a
minor road between
the A1 and the
A1133, 10 miles
west of Lincoln city
centre

The Brownlow Arms is a picturesque pub built from warm red brick, close to the banks of
the River Trent. The original building is Grade 11 listed, and dates from the 17th century.
However, in 1993, it was badly damaged by fire, though a careful and tasteful restoration
has brought it back to life again as a delightful place to have a drink or meal. To the front is
a smart patio, which is a popular spot in the summer months, as there is a lawn which
slopes down to the banks of the River Trent.

The inside is equally as picturesque as the outside, and mine hosts John and Eunice
Fletcher want to keep it that way. There's a cozy bar, a comfortable lounge and a lovely little
restaurant area, all having wood and stone floors. The walls are covered in mementos and
prints of the local area, and the shelves are full of gleaming brass and copper ornaments,
which all add to the ambience of the place. Two cask ales on offer at the bar, as well as two
guest ales. You can also choose from a selection of draught bitters, mild, lagers, stout and
cider.

The food is cooked on the premises from good fresh produce. There's a menu plus a
specials board, and the chef goes to great lengths to change the specials daily, offering new
dishes that are sure to please. The speciality of the house is a 16 oz steak, cooked to your
requirements, with all the trimmings.

Opening times: Monday to Saturday: 12.00-
1500 and 18.00-23.00; Sunday: 12.00-1500
and 18.00-22.30

Food: Served 12.00-14.30 and 18.00-21.00
seven days

Credit cards: All credit cards except American
Express

Accommodation: None

Entertainment: Live music in the summer
months

Facilities: Car park; camping on the front
lawn

Local Places of Interest/Activities: Lincoln
(historic city) 10 miles; Sundown
Adventureland (children's theme park) 5
miles; Newark-on-Trent (historic town)10
miles

The Cuckoo Bush

Leake Road,
Gotham,
Nottinghamshire
NG11 0JL
Tel: 0115 983 0306

Directions:

Gotham is on a
minor road to the
east of the A453, 7
miles south of
Nottingham city
centre

Gotham (pronounced "Goat-ham") is a famous village. It was here that the villagers feigned madness in the 12th century to get out of paying taxes to King John, and the story of planting bushes round a tree to prevent a cuckoo from flying off, or trying to take the reflection of the moon out of a pond, have become famous.

Not quite as famous, but still well known in the surrounding area, is **The Cuckoo Bush**, a lovely, brick built inn in the village whose name celebrates one of the escapades. Anne and John Lowe have been the leaseholders for the last seven years, and it is thanks to their management that the inn has developed an enviable reputation for its hospitality, its good food and drink and its value for money.

The interior is stunning. There are low ceilings with dark beams, comfortable furniture, subdued lighting, and a wealth of framed prints, plates, horse brasses, clocks and memorabilia everywhere. The floors are carpeted, there are open fires, and all in all, it is everybody's idea of a cozy village pub.

You can order food from a menu or a chalk board which displays the day's specials. Anne is in charge of the kitchen, and the cuisine can best be described as traditional English. The Sunday roasts are justly famous, and you'd be advised to book if you require Sunday lunch. At the bar, you can order from a drinks list that includes two real ales (Bass and Marston Pedigree) plus Worthington Creamflow, Caffreys, Stones, M&B Mild, Carling, Stella, Guinness and Scrumpy Jack.

This is the kind of inn where you would be advised to take your time over a quiet drink or a delicious meal. No one feigns madness in Gotham any more – they all have the good sense to realise that they have a fine hostelry in their midst!

Opening times: Open lunchtimes and evenings from Monday to Friday, and all day at weekends

Food: Served every lunchtime from 12.00-14.00 and on Thursday and Friday evenings from 17.30-20.00

Credit cards: Cash and cheque only at present

Accommodation: None

Entertainment: Occasional music and quizzes (ring for details)

Facilities: Car park; beer garden; patio

Local Places of Interest/Activities: Nottingham (historic city) 7 miles; Loughborough (historic town) 7 miles; Whatton House 6 miles

140 | The Dog And Duck

Main Road,
Old Clipstone,
Nottinghamshire
NG21 9BT
Tel: 01623 822138

Directions:

Old Clipstone is on the B6030, 5 miles east of Mansfield town centre

Old Clipstone sits in the heart of what was Sherwood Forest. King John was fond of hunting in this part of Nottinghamshire in the 12th and 13th centuries, and some scant ruins are often pointed out as "King John's Palace", where he stayed. Today the village is a peaceful and unhurried place, with a popular inn called The Dog and Duck. It's a delightful, white-washed building dating from the early 19th century, and is the ideal place to have a drink or a meal.

Under the careful guidance of Joe and Tracy Poskitt, who took over in 1999, it has established itself as one of the best hostelries in the area. Ramblers, hikers and cyclists (the National Cycle Route passes the pub) have already discovered this, and make full use of its excellent facilities. There are no smoking areas, and its beamed ceilings and country style furnishings make it a warm and comfortable place, one with lots of atmosphere and character. It has four real ales on offer – Old Speckled hen, Directors, Marston Pedigree and a rotating guest ale, plus it served John Smith Smooth, Home Mild and Bitter, Fosters, McEwans, Guinness, Woodpecker and Strongbow.

The home cooked food is excellent. The inn's speciality is steak and chips, with, as Tracy and Joe are quick to point out, real chips and not the frozen variety! You can also order Cajun and Mexican dishes. There's a printed menu and a daily specials board, plus separate menus for senior citizens and children. And if you have any special dietary requirements, the inn will try to accommodate you if you give them plenty of notice.

Tracy and Joe have great plans for The Dog and Duck, and already they have refurbished the place to a very high standard. The watchwords here are value for money, and if you visit, you won't be disappointed.

Opening times: Monday to Thursday: open lunchtimes and evenings; Friday to Sunday: open all day

Food: Monday to Saturday: 12.00-14.30 and 18.00-21.00; Sunday lunches: 12.00-15.00

Credit cards: All major cards accepted

Accommodation: There are limited facilities for caravans and camping

Entertainment: Quiz night every Monday at 21.30; sports quiz every Wednesday at 21.30; live entertainment on Saturday or Sunday;

occasional "physic suppers and show" (ring for details)

Facilities: Car park; children's play area; indoor play area

Local Places of Interest/Activities: Mansfield (historic town) 5 miles; Sherwood Forest Country Park and Visitor Centre 2 miles; Rufford Country Park and Abbey 3 miles; Newstead Abbey 8 miles

The Generous Briton | 141

Main Street,
Costock,
near Loughborough,
Nottinghamshire
LE12 6XD
Tel: 01509 852347

Directions:
Costock is off the A60,
4 miles north of
Loughborough

Within the village of Costock, with its lovely little couch of St Giles, you will find the wonderfully name **The Generous Briton**. It is housed in a handsome, well proportioned three-storeyed building of warm old brick which dates from about 1732. The windows are small paned with white wood surrounds, and the whole place speaks of a long tradition of offering hospitality and a warm welcome.

Neil Rogers and Patricia Slaney are mine hosts, and they have created an inn that reflects everything that is good about English hospitality. The interior is warm and welcoming, with solid wood floorboards, terracotta tiles, original oak beams and open fires which cheer in the winter. The bar is well stocked with a wide range of drinks, with three real ales on offer, one of them being the ever popular Mansfield Cask. Plus there is draught beer, a choice of lagers, Guinness and cider. This is the place to go if you want a quiet. relaxing drink after a hectic day!

It's also the place to go if you want good honest food. The cuisine is hearty and traditional, representing the best in English cooking. There's an extensive menu of mouth watering dishes, plus a specials board that changes daily. If you don't fancy a meal, you can order from a range of snacks instead. Patricia prepares all the food, and is proud of the fact that she buys her meat from the local butcher, where she knows she is getting quality. All the other ingredients are fresh as well, including the fish which goes into her excellent and tasty seafood dishes. You know you're getting the very best of food, at the keenest prices, when you visit The Generous Briton!

Opening hours: Monday to Saturday: 11.00-14.30 and 17.30-23.00; Sunday: 12.00-22.30

Food: Served daily (except Sunday) between 12.00-2.00 and 18.00-20.30; food only served at lunchtime on Sunday

Credit cards: Cash only at present

Accommodation: None

Entertainment: Occasional theme nights; phone for details

Facilities: Beer garden

Local Places of Interest/Activities: Nottingham (historic city) 9 miles; Loughborough (historic town) 5 miles; Great Central Railway (Loughborough) 5 miles; East Midlands Airport 7 miles

142   Three Horseshoes

Brookside,
East Leake,
near Nottingham,
Nottinghamshire
LE12 6PB
Tel: 01509 856321
Fax: 01509 853321

Directions:

Follow the A60 south from Nottingham city centre for 8 miles then turn west onto a minor road at Costock. East Leake is 1 mile along this road

The village of East Leake, and its near neighbour West Leake, get their names from the Anglo Saxon word for a water meadow - "leche". They both sit on the banks of the Soar, with East Leake having a particularly fine church which was restored in the 19th century, and within which you will find an eight foot "vamp horn", which led the bass singing during church services.

Also in the village is the red brick **Three Horseshoes**. The previous inn, which dated from Victorian times, was lost in a fire, and the present building replaced it in the early 60s. Under the management of Alan and Joanne Tynan, it continues the fine tradition of good drink, good food and hospitality offered by its predecessor. The interior is large and roomy, with plenty of space to stretch your legs and enjoy a quiet drink. There are carpets on the floor, and a dining area that can seat 50 in complete comfort. The Three Horseshoes serves good, honest English cuisine which represents great value for money, as the portions are hearty - just the thing if you're hungry! There's a printed menu and a specials board containing a range of dishes to suit all tastes. Everything is home cooked, to your own particular taste if required, and the in prides itself on the freshness and quality of the produce that goes into every dish.

The bar has a range of three real ales - one resident and two rotating guests - as well as draught bitter, mild, stout, lager and cider. Plus. of course, you can order wine by the glass or bottle. So there's sure to be something to please everyone.

Opening times: Monday to Friday: 12.00-14.30 and 17.00-23.00; Saturday: 12.00-23.00; Sunday: 12.00-22.30

Food: Served Monday to Saturday 12.00-14.30 and 17.00-20.30; Sunday: 12.00-15.00

Credit cards: All major credit cards except American Express and Diners

Accommodation: None

Entertainment: Quiz night every Wednesday; Saturday evenings: live artists (phone for details)

Facilities: Front beer garden; car park; games room

Local Places of Interest/Activities: Nottingham (historic city) 9 miles; Loughborough (historic town) 5 miles; Donnington Park (motor racing) 8 miles; East Midlands Airport 6 miles

The Manvers Arms | 143

Main Road,
Radcliffe-on-Trent,
Nottinghamshire
NG12 2AA
Tel: 01159 332404

Directions:

Take the A52 east from Nottingham city centre for 6 miles and you will arrive at Radcliffe-on-Trent

Radcliffe-on-Trent sits on a steep cliff above the River Trent, hence its name, and you can get some wonderful views across open countryside. Within the village, and across from the church, you'll find a lovely inn called **The Manvers Arms**, named after Earl Manvers, a former lord of the manor. It was formerly called The White Horse, and dates mainly from the 17th century. Unfortunately, part of it was burnt down in the early 1800s and rebuilt. But this doesn't detract from its overall attractive appearance – an attractiveness that is continued in the inn's cozy and welcoming interior. Everything is spotlessly clean, with open fires that throw a cozy glow over everything in the winter months, carpeted floors and comfortable furniture.

You can eat anywhere in the pub, and the food is always piping hot, well presented and delicious. You can order from a daily specials board or from the printed menu, and the cuisine is traditional English, with a range of dishes that is sure to please everyone. There's a roast at Sunday lunchtime which is very popular, though you don't have to book. Wine is available by the glass or bottle, and two real ales (Marston Pedigree and a rotating guest ale) can be bought at the bar. Also available is John Smith Smooth, Theakston's Best and mild, Websters, Kronenbourg, Fosters, Carlsberg, Guinness and Strongbow.

The watchwords at The Manvers Arms are value for money. Samantha and Richard Patterson have been the tenants since the year 2000, and through their hard efforts and attention to detail, they have created a wonderfully successful hostelry that is popular with both visitors and locals alike.

Opening times: Open all day, every day

Food: Served Monday to Saturday from 12.00-20.00, and on Sunday from 12.00-17.00; no food on Sunday evening

Credit cards: Most credit cards accepted

Accommodation: None

Entertainment: Quiz night every Sunday and Wednesday evening; live entertainment or karaoke every Saturday evening; occasional entertainment on weekday evenings (ring for details)

Facilities: Car park; beer garden with children's "mini Manvers" (pop, crisps, etc); summer barbecues

Local Places of Interest/Activities: Nottingham (historic city) 5 miles; Grantham (historic town) 17 miles; Southwell (cathedral city) 12 miles

144 The Manor Arms

Main Road,
Elton,
Nottinghamshire
NG13 9LB
Tel: 01949 850272
Mobile:
07885 941777

THE MANOR ARMS

Directions:

The inn sits right on the A52 at Elton, 13 miles east of Nottingham city centre

Situated by the side of the A52, **The Manor Arms** dates from the late 1800s, and was once a coaching inn called the Norton Arms. It's a handsome building in old, mellow, red brick, with sleepy shutters on the upper windows and tubs of flowers at the entrance. Mine hosts are Paul and Nadine Hornigold, who have created a wonderful stopping off point for food or a quiet drink. Many famous people, including Tom O'Connor, Richard Todd and Michael Whittaker have done just that at some time or other!

The interior is snug and inviting, with plush seating and rich mahogany panelling in the bar which once graced a luxury liner. The 24-seat restaurant at the rear is finished in dark oak, and is welcoming and airy. The place is famous for its food, with Paul being in charge of the kitchen. He tries to combine the best of English cuisine with plenty of Mediterranean and Eastern influences. You can order a full three course lunch, a simple snack or even just a bowl of chips. Paul has connections with Grimsby, so the fish dishes are prepared using only the freshest of produce. For this reason, Tuesday night is always fish and chips night! Or, if you want something just that bit special, try the lemon sole stuffed with crabmeat, or the fillet of salmon with a lobster sauce. But if you prefer meat, you can also order such dishes as juicy fillet steaks or chicken tikka masala.

The pub serves Mansfield beers, and there are always two real ales on offer, plus bitter, mild, lager, stout and cider. In 1993 the inn won the "Host of the Year" award from Mansfield Breweries, and since then both Paul and Nadine have been offering a warm welcome to everyone who steps over the threshold.

Opening times: Monday: 18.00-23.00; Tuesday to Sunday: 11.30-15.00 and 18.00-23.00

Food: Served 12.00-14.15 and 18.00-21.00 (no food served on Monday evening)

Credit cards: All major cards accepted except Diners

Accommodation: None

Entertainment: Sunday night quiz

Facilities: Beer garden; patio

Local Places of Interest/Activities: Nottingham (historic city) 13 miles; Grantham (historic town) 9 miles; Belvoir Castle 6 miles

Martins Arms Inn | 145

Colston Bassett,
Nottinghamshire
NG12 3FD
Tel: 01949 81361
Fax: 01949 81039

Directions:
Colston Bassett is
on a minor road, 9
miles south east of
Nottingham, and 3
miles east of the
A46

Colston Bassett is Nottinghamshire's best known village, and sits on the edge of that beautiful area known as the Vale of Belvoir. At the heart of this mainly estate owned conservation village, is the **Martins Arms Inn**, a hostelry that matches it for fame, charm and picturesqueness. It is a listed building, and has featured on TV many times. It has also won many awards, including Les Routiers Inn of the Year in 2000. Though the building dates from the early 18th century and is grade 11 listed, it didn't become an inn until the early 19th century, and was named after the then owner of the estate, Henry Martin.

Lynne Stafford Bryan and Jack Inguanta have owned it since 1990, and preserved all its fine period features and atmosphere. There's a cozy bar, a lounge and a dining room that seats 30 in comfort. You can eat anywhere in the inn, even in the one acre garden in the summer months, but if you wish to eat in the beautiful dining room you're advised to book at least two weeks in advance, so popular is it. Jack is an executive chef, and is in charge of a kitchen that is famous in the area. He has put together an outstanding menu that will appeal to everyone, and represents amazing value for money. There is a great wine list, and the bar offers no less than seven real ales (Timothy Taylor Landlord, Black Sheep, Bass, Green King IPA, Marston Pedigree and two rotating guest ales) plus Black Dog Mild, Stella, Carling, Murphys, Worthington Creamflow and Strongbow cider.

Having a meal or a drink at the Martins Arms Inn is an experience not to be missed, and something to brag about later on! And while you're there, why not pop into Lynne's antique shop next to the pub? It's open daily between 11.am-19.30, and you're sure to pick up an old print, an ornament or a piece of silver that will adorn your home

Opening times: Open 12.00-15.00 and 18.00-23.00 Monday to Saturday; 12.00-15.00 and 19.00-22.30 on a Sunday;

Food: Served 12.00-14.00 and 18.00-22.00 Monday to Saturday, and 12.00-14.00 on Sunday

Credit cards: Most credit cards accepted except American Express and Diners

Accommodation: None

Facilities: Car park; large one acre garden

Local Places of Interest/Activities: Nottingham (historic city) 9 miles; Grantham (historic town)13 miles; Belvoir Castle 8 miles; National Watersports Centre, Holme Pierrepont 7 miles

146   The Old Volunteer

*Caythorpe,
near Lowdham,
Nottinghamshire
NG14 7EB
Tel: 01159 663205*

Directions:

8 miles north east of
Nottingham city
centre, on a minor
road off the
junction of the
A612 and the A6097

Caythorpe sits close to the River Trent, and is a pleasant country village surrounded by some charming rural scenery of fields, country lanes and woodland. Within the village you'll find a lovely inn – the **Old Volunteer**, run by Jo and Jay. At one time this fine building, which dates from the late 1800s, was a gentleman's residence, and its well proportioned front still has echoes of earlier times, when life was lived at a gentler pace. The inside is neat, tidy and spotlessly clean, with comfortable furnishings, two open fires, well polished wood and a warm, welcoming atmosphere. It's the kind of rural inn that England does so well – a place where office manager, plumber, doctor and farm worker can come together over a quiet drink and solve the problems of the world!

Though there's no set menu, and food isn't normally served, Jo and Jay will cater for parties of golfers, cricketers and other sportsmen and women who visit, and their food is excellent, with good, hearty platefuls which are always cooked to perfection and delicious. They also keep an excellent cellar, and offer three real ales at the bar – two resident and one guest. There's also a fine selection of draught lager, stout, bitter, mild and cider. And, of course, if you're behind the wheel, you can choose from a wide range of soft and low alcohol drinks.

The Old Volunteer is an inn that is sure to please. The locals are friendly, and Jo and Jay will go out of their way to offer you a welcome that is second to none.

Opening times: Monday to Thursday: 16.30-23.00; Friday to Sunday: 12.00-23.00

Food: Only served to parties on special occasions

Credit cards: Cash and cheques only at present

Accommodation: None

Facilities: Car park; beer garden with occasional barbecues in summer

Local Places of Interest/Activities: Nottingham (historic city) 8 miles; Southwell (historic city with cathedral) 5 miles; Newark-on-Trent (historic town) 9 miles

Internet/website:
e-mail: johnstaddon@btconnect.com

The Old Wine Vaults | 147

Church Street,
Eastwood,
Nottinghamshire
NG16 3BP
Tel/Fax: 01773 715856

Directions:

Eastwood is 8 miles west
of Nottingham city
centre, off the A610

Eastwood is famous as the birthplace, in September 1885, of DH Lawrence. He was born in a small red brick house in Victoria Street which is now a museum and heritage centre dedicated to his memory. And close by, near the church, you'll find the delightful **Old Wine Vaults**, an inn that was certainly here at the time, as it is the oldest in the town, dating from 1771. It has been added to and extended over the years, but still retains an "olde worlde" feeling, with many wonderful period features, such as the original oak flooring, still intact. The bar is snug and warm, with subdued lighting, while the lounge and adjoining dining area are inviting and spacious. The furniture is dark and comfortable, with well spaced tables and chairs that give you plenty of room to relax.

Mine hosts are Andy Dale and Clive Bennett, who are new to the trade but are determined to turn the Old Wine Vaults into a lively and friendly pub that caters for all tastes. It is renowned for the quality of the two cask ales on offer at the bar, as well as the draught bitter, mild, stout, lager and cider. And, of course, there is a wide range of soft drinks if you're driving.

The food is "family friendly" in content, with the menu containing a great range of popular dishes that are sure to appeal, all cooked to perfection, all beautifully presented and representing good value for money. Try the inn's steak and real ale pies - they're famous in the area. You won't be disappointed!

Opening times: Monday to Saturday: 10.30-23.00; Sunday: 12.00-22.30

Food: Available when open

Credit cards: Cash only at present

Accommodation: None

Entertainment: Live music on Saturday evening; Karaoke on Wednesday and Sunday evening; Soul and Motown music on Thursday

Facilities: Car park; beer garden; large children's play area; rear garden

Local Places of Interest/Activities: D.H. Lawrence Heritage Centre close by: Nottingham (historic city) 8 miles; American Adventure Park 3 miles; Ilkeston (historic town) 3 miles evening

Internet/Website:
e-mail: oldwinevaults@ntl.world.com

148 Plough Inn

Main Street, Cropwell Butler,
near Nottingham,
Nottinghamshire NG12 3AB
Tel: 01159 333124

Directions:
Off the A46, 7 miles east of Nottingham city centre

Just off the heavy traffic of the A46, you'll find the quiet, picturesque village of Cropwell Butler. It is an ancient village, and was formerly called Crophill Botiller, named after an early land owning family called Botiller, who came from Lancashire. Within the village is the **Plough Inn**, which dates from about 1800, and is built of warm, local stone. It has always been a hostelry, and is now a popular place with the locals of the village and beyond. Alyson and Mick Draper have been tenants since 1999, and they're helped by their daughter Michelle. The interior is spotlessly clean, with a cozy bar, a comfortable lounge and a dining area that can seat 50 in absolute comfort. Some areas are non smoking, and there is disabled access and disabled toilets.

The food is traditional English, and the inn has a printed menu and a daily specials board. The dishes are all beautifully cooked and represent wonderful value for money. The inn prides itself in using only the freshest ingredients, so you know you'll be getting a meal that is both tasty and filling. There's also a Sunday carvery, although you would be advised to book to avoid disappointment. Of course, you'll be wanting to have a drink with your meal, and the bar offers three real ales (Tetley, Directors and Speckled Hen) plus John Smith Smooth, Ansell Mild, Guinness, Carlsberg, Kronenbourg and Strongbow. Wine is also available, both by the bottle and glass.

This is a delightful, old world inn, full of character and charm. Alyson and Mick have worked hard to make it warm and welcoming, and if you pay it a visit, you're sure to agree.

Opening times: Mon-Tue 18.30-23.00; Wed-Fri 12.00-14.30, 18.30-23.00; Sat 12.00-15.00, 18.00-23.00; Sun 12.00-16.00, 20.00-22.30;

Food: Served Wednesday to Saturday from 12.00-14.00; à la carte from 18.30-21.30; Sunday carvery is open 12.30-14.30

Credit cards: Most cards accepted except American Express

Accommadtion: None

Entertainment: Quiz every Monday evening at 21.00; gourmet evenings every 4 to 6 weeks (booking required); ring for details

Facilities: Car park; beer garden; bus parties catered for by arrangement

Local Places of Interest/Activities: Nottingham (historic city) 7 miles; Belvoir Castle 9 miles; National Watersports Centre, Holme Pierrepont 5 miles

The Plough Inn   149

Farnsfield,
near Southwell,
Nottinghamshire
NG22 8EA
Tel: 01623 882265
Fax: 01623 882265

Directions:

Farnsfield is on a
minor road off the
A614, east of
Southwell

If you find yourself close to the splendid little city of Southwell, with its medieval cathedral, why not pay a visit to Farnsfield, two miles east of the place? It's an attractive village, and at its heart is **The Plough Inn**. This substantial hostelry, with its well proportioned front, whitewashed walls and hanging baskets, is the classic village pub, and is housed in a building which is well over 250 years old.

Under the personal management of husband and wife team June and Bob Reeves, it still offers the best in hospitality. The interior is everything a village local should be, with low ceilings, the original stout beams, carpeted floors and a mass of brightly polished brass and copper adorning the walls and shelves. The whole place imparts a feeling of coziness, while still having plenty of space in which to stretch your legs and relax. At the bar, you can order from a good range of ales and beers, including three cask ales and the usual draught bitter, mild, stout, lager and cider. Plus, of course, wine by the glass or bottle.

The food represents astonishing value for money. Everything is guaranteed to be cooked on the premises from produce which is locally sourced if possible. There are very few frozen foodstuffs here - just the freshest ingredients money can buy. So don't expect fast food. Your meal will be cooked especially for you, in the way you like it. June is in charge of the kitchen, and takes a pride in all the dishes she prepares, especially her home made pies, which include beef and bacon, corned beef and potato and steak and kidney. Ask the regulars - they'll vouch for the fact that they're tasty and beautifully cooked.

Opening times: 11.00-15.00 and 17.30-23.30 Monday to Friday, and all day Saturday and Sunday

Food: Served between 12.00-14.00 and 17.30-19.30; lunches only are served on Sunday

Credit cards: Cash only at present

Accommodation: None

Entertainment: Quiz every Monday evening

Facilities: Car park; barbecue in summer; children's play area

Local Places of Interest/Activities: Southwell (cathedral city) 2 miles; Southwell Racecourse (horse racing) 3 miles; Newark-on-Trent (historic town) 8 miles; White Post Modern Farm Centre (children's farm) 2 miles

150   The Plough Inn

Main Street,
Wysall,
Nottinghamshire
NG12 5QQ
Tel: 01509 880339

Directions:

Wysall is 6 miles
north east of
Loughborough, on
a minor road two
miles east of the
A60

Within the picturesque village of Wysall you'll find one of those inns that seem to epitomise the English village pub. It's **The Plough**, and it's a real gem. It sits above the village street, and is a whitewashed building with small paned windows, tubs of flowers in the summer months, and a look that speaks of warm hospitality and friendliness.

It has been owned since 1999 by Pearl and Michael Edge, and they are determined to preserve all that is good about it. The bars are cozy, with exposed beams, comfortable furniture and open fires that in the winter months throw a warm glow over everything. And in the summer months you can sit out in its south facing patio and enjoy a quiet drink or a pub lunch.

There's a fine range of drinks available at the bar, from real ales to soft drinks if you're driving. In fact, no less than five real ales are on offer – Bass, Timothy Taylor Landlord, London Pride, Old Speckled Hen and Green IPA. There's also Worthington Creamflow, Caffreys, Stella, Carling, Strongbow and Guinness. In fact, there's something to suit everyone.

The Plough also offers delicious pub lunches with platefuls that are sure to satisfy the heartiest of appetites. There's a printed menu and a special board, and both contain a wonderful selection of dishes that represent great value for money. There's everything from a juicy steak with all the trimmings to a sandwich or filled roll. Children are welcome, and there's no booking needed.

This is a pub which is worthwhile seeking out. It's a great favourite with the locals, and if you pay a visit, it's sure to become one of your favourites as well!

Opening times: Open all day, every day

Food: Served 12.00-14.30; no evening meals

Credit cards: Please advise

Accommodation: None

Entertainment: Quiz every Tuesday evening at 20.30

Facilities: Car park; large patio to the front

Local Places of Interest/Activities: Nottingham (historic city) 8 miles; Loughborough (historic town) 7 miles; National Watersports Centre, Holme Pierrepont 7 miles

The Red Hart Hotel
151

Bawtry Road,
Blyth,
Nottinghamshire
S81 8HG
Tel: 01909 591221

Directions:

Blyth is close to
Junction 34 of the
A1(M), where it
merges with the A1,
5 miles north west of
Worksop

The Red Hart Hotel is one of those inns that just asks to be visited! Situated within the village of Blyth, which was on the A1 before it was bypassed, it is a former coaching inn that dates back to the 18th century at least. It is a handsome building of red brick, with two delightful bay windows that add an old world charm to it. Alicia and Aziz Koluman, the licensees, have plenty of experience in the trade, both here and in Turkey, and have been in charge since April 2001.

This is the place to visit if you want outstanding food at surprisingly realistic prices. Thanks to Aziz's undoubted talents in the kitchen, the place has a great reputation for its cuisine, which is a mixture of English and Continental. Within the 25-seat Graceland restaurant you can order from a wonderful menu that includes fillet steak with cream sauce and tarragon, prawn risotto, tuna steak with a Mediterranean dressing, sea bass served with garlic potatoes, tomato, fried mushrooms, seasonal garnish and lemon sauce, rack of lamb, and a host of other cordon bleu dishes that are all cooked to perfection. Aziz prides himself in using only the finest and freshest of ingredients in season, and the presentation, as you would expect, is immaculate. There is also a small menu covering restaurant and bar starters, and a great selection of sweets. So popular is the Red Hart Hotel that you have to book in advance for the no smoking restaurant.

Wine is available, or you can order from a range of three real ales at the bar (Marston Pedigree, Stones and a rotating guest ale), plus Stella and Carling lager, Scrumpy Jack cider, Guinness and Caffreys.

Opening times: Open all day, every day

Food: Breakfasts served from 9.00; lunches served from 11.00-closing time; restaurant opens each evening at 19.00, with à la carte menu

Credit cards: All major credit cards accepted

Accommodation: 4 rooms upstairs (soon to be all en suite)

Entertainment: Quiz every Wednesday evening; monthly live entertainment and themed food evenings (ring for details)

Facilities: Good off-road parking; function room with separate bar

Local Places of Interest/Activities: Roche Abbey (ruins) 5 miles; Worksop (historic town) 5 miles; Bawtry (historic canal port) 4 miles; Clumber Park (NT) 8 miles

152 The Royal Oak

The Green,
Car Colston,
near Bingham,
Nottinghamshire
NG13 8JE
Tel: 01949 20247

Directions:

Car Colston is 1 mile west of the A46, 3 miles north of its junction with the A52

Car Colston, with its red brick cottages and old church, is undoubtedly one of the prettiest villages in Nottinghamshire. It sits in the Vale of Belvoir, a truly beautiful part of England noted for its woodland, its lush fields and its delightful country lanes. At the heart of the village is the **Royal Oak**, and inn that is as sturdy and traditional looking as its name suggests. It has a well proportioned frontage that overlooks the local village green cricket pitch, so a quiet drink here could mean a ringside view! Robin and Shirley are in charge, and they have created an interior that is cozy and welcoming, with oak tables and chairs, handsome windows and prints adorning the walls. The floor is carpeted, and the whole place is immaculately clean. It's the ideal spot for a meal or a relaxing drink.

The bar stocks two real ales plus bitter, mild, lager, stout and cider. And if you fancy a meal, you can order wine by the glass or bottle. The dining area is comfortable and spacious, and seats 30. Shirley is the cook, and the food can best be described as traditional English. She cooks everything in the inn's own kitchen from ingredients that are as fresh as possible. The portions are ample, and everything tastes absolutely delicious. Close to Car Colston is the village of Colston Bassett, the home of Stilton cheese, so it seems appropriate that one of the most popular dishes on the menu at the Royal Oak is its Stilton paté. Or you could try its steak and mushroom pie - a firm favourite with the locals!

If you visit the Royal Oak you'll be sure of a warm welcome from Robert and Shirley. Why not pop in and see for yourself?

Opening times: Tuesday to Friday: 11.30-15.00 and Monday to Friday18.00-23.00; Saturday: 11.30-16.00 and 17.30-23.00; open all day on Sunday in the summer

Food: Served during opening hours (no food served on Monday or Sunday evening)

Credit cards: Cash and cheques only at present

Accommodation: Caravan and camp site

Entertainment: Skittle alley; cricket during summer months (front lawn is the cricket pitch)

Facilities: Car park; beer garden; barbecue in summer

Local Places of Interest/Activities: Nottingham (historic city) 9 miles; Belvoir Castle 9 miles; Grantham (historic town) 13 miles

The Shepherds Rest | 153

Lower Bagthorpe,
Nottinghamshire
NG16 5HF
Tel: 01773 810506

Directions:

Leave the M1 at
Junction 27 and
follow the A608 west
for one mile. Turn
north onto the B600
then west into
Lower Bagthorpe

Within the conservation village of Lower Bagthorpe you'll find a lovely pub called the **Shepherds Rest**. It's a Grade 2 listed building, and is a former coaching inn that dates from the 18th century. The building has been added to over the years, of course, but it still retains an air of quiet charm and dignity that harks back to less hectic times. And as you would expect from a place that has a long tradition of hospitality, the service is superb and the welcome is warm. The cozy bar and comfortable lounge have slate floors and old, upright beams, while the 20 seat restaurant is comfortable and quaint, with enough space to make a meal really enjoyable.

In charge are Carol and Ivan Bell. Ivan, by his own admission, is a bit of a wine buff, and has a fine range of famous labels and vintages. So the inn is very "wine focused". If you're eating, there will always be something that will complement your meal! Plus, of course, the bar carries a range of three cask ales, and the usual bitter, mild, stout, cider and lager.

The chef at the Shepherds Rest is highly qualified, and offers an á la carte menu with dishes on it that cost no more than a good pub lunch! Try the fish or steak - they're renowned in the area. All the produce used is fresh and sourced locally if possible, and the presentation is wonderful.

This is a truly hidden inn, and one that deserves to be visited. It's only a short drive from the motorway, but any detour will be richly rewarded!

Opening times: Open 7 days between 12.00-23.00

Food: Served 12.00-14.00 and 19.00-21.00 7 days; food served lunchtime only on Sunday

Credit cards: All major cards accepted except Diners

Accommodation: None

Entertainment: Occasional wine tasting

nights and themed cooking nights (phone for details)

Facilities: Car park; beer garden; children's play area

Local Places of Interest/Activities: Newstead Abbey 5 miles; Mansfield (historic town) 8 miles; Nottingham (historic city) 11 miles; DH Lawrence Museum (Eastwood) 3 miles

154

The Swallows

Cottage Lane,
Warsop,
Nottinghamshire
NG20 0HC
Tel: 01623 842258

Directions:

Warsop is 4 miles
north of Mansfield
town centre, on
the A60

The Swallows is a pub that dates from the 1950s, and has been in the same family for many years. The eldest daughter, Deborah Todd, now runs it, and she keeps it spotlessly clean and tidy. It sits in a quiet semi-residential area, about three quarters of a mile from the centre of the small town of Warsop, and is a neat, red brick building with, for all its age, an attractive and charming air about it. Surrounding it is a large car park. The inside is modern and welcoming, and Deborah has made sure that it is well maintained, with an atmosphere that positively welcomes visitors. The Red Lounge is especially charming, with, as you might expect, red seating, red curtains, red carpets, red stools and so on.

Lunches are available on request, and are excellent value for money. Here you'll get the best in "pub grub", with platefuls that will satisfy the heartiest of appetites. Many popular dishes are available, as well as snacks, and all the ingredients used are as fresh as possible. It's all cooked on the premises, and if you order a meal here, you know you won't be disappointed. Sunday lunches, with a set menu of two courses, are popular with the locals, which is always a good sign. The bar carries a wide range of draught beers, including real ale, bitter, mild, stout, lager and cider. If you're driving, you can also order from a great selection of soft drinks and alcohol free lager.

So if you're anywhere near Warsop, pop into The Swallows for a quiet drink or a lunch. Deborah and her friendly staff are always ready to offer you a warm welcome.

Opening times: Monday to Friday: 12.00-13.30 and 19.00-23.00; Saturday and Sunday: 12.00-15.00 and 19.00-23.00

Food: Lunches served between 12.00-14.00

Credit cards: Cash only at present

Accommodation: None

Facilities: Car park; beer garden with children's play area

Local Places of Interest/Activities: Mansfield (historic town) 4 miles; Sherwood forest Country Park 3 miles; Hardwick Hall (NT) 7 miles; Rufford Country Park and Abbey Ruins 5 miles

The Turks Head   155

Grove Street,
Retford,
Nottinghamshire
DN22 6LA
Tel: 01777 702742

Directions:

Retford is on the
A638, 7 miles east of
Worksop; the inn is
situated 2 minutes
walk from the
centre of the town

The Turks Head Inn is a handsome hostelry close to the centre of Retford. With its ground floor built of warm local stone, its half timbered upper floor, its red pantiled roof and its archway at the side, it presents an altogether delightful picture of what a traditional coaching inn must have looked like all those years ago. Mike and Denise Norris have recently taken charge of the inn, though they have over 20 years experience in the licensing trade, and they have created a place that is full of old world charm and atmosphere.

The interior is cozy and warm, and makes the ideal ambience for a drink or a tasty lunch. The walls are panelled, there are roaring fires in the winter, and the floors are richly carpeted. At the bar you can order from a range of three real ales (Tetley and two rotating guest ales) plus you can have Theakstons, Guinness, Stella, Fosters, Carling and Strongbow on draught. Both Mike and Denise cook, and their dishes represent the best in traditional English fare, though Mike's lasagna, which he admits is Italian, is famous throughout the area! You can choose from a printed menu, and all the dishes are prepared on the premises using fresh produce which is sourced locally if possible.

The inn has five rooms to let, including two large family rooms, which are all upstairs, and the price of letting includes a hearty breakfast. If you want to spoil yourself, The Turk's Head is the place for you. You'll get a warm welcome from Mike and Denise!

Opening times: Lunchtimes and evenings, seven days

Food: Served 12.00-14.30; no evening meals

Credit cards: Cash and cheques only at present

Accommodation: 5 rooms, including two large family rooms

Facilities: Car park

Local Places of Interest/Activities:
Gainsborough (historic town) 9 miles; Sundown Adventureland (children's theme park) 6 miles; Sherwood Forest Country Park and Visitor Centre 9 miles; Rufford Country Park and Abbey 11 miles

Internet/website:
e-mail: mike.norris@tinyonline.co.uk

156 The Unicorns Head

Main Street,
Langar,
Nottinghamshire
NG13 9HE
Tel: 01949 860460

Directions:

Take the A52 east from Nottingham and turn south onto a minor road after Elton; follow the signs for Langar

On the edge of that beautiful part of England called the Vale of Belvoir you'll find the quiet village of Langar. And situated in the heart of the village is **The Unicorns Head**, one of the most picturesque inns in Nottinghamshire. It is a Grade 2 listed building, and you can tell just by looking at it that history and tradition abound here. It dates from the 17th century, and is a former coaching inn which has retained much of the character and atmosphere of former times, when life was more leisurely and lived at a slower pace.

Many period features are to be found inside, and all have been lovingly preserved by Mick and Joy Mathews and their daughter Claire and son-in-law David. There are low ceilings, oak beams, cream walls, exposed brick, and nooks and crannies galore that are just right for relaxing and enjoying a quiet drink. The "village bar" is cozy and warm, the lounge is comfortably furnished and the restaurant is an absolute delight.

David is in charge of the kitchen, and he produces dishes that can best be described as "English traditional" with one or two that hint of the Mediterranean or the East. You can choose from lamb's liver with bacon, Dublin Bay mussels, Parma ham encased in tortellini pasta with cracked black pepper, tagliatelle pasta carbonara and chicken satay, and so on. Everything is cooked to order using the freshest of ingredients, so this isn't the place for fast food! To accompany your meal, you can choose from a comprehensive wine list, or you can order from the bar. On offer are four cask ales, plus John Smith bitter, Becks, Miller Draught and Kronenbourg.

Along the road from The Unicorns Head is Langar Airfield, home to the British Parachute School. So why don't you take a leaf out if its book, and "drop in" at The Unicorns Head for a drink or a meal?

Opening times: Monday to Friday: 11.00-15.00 and 18.00-23.00; Saturday: 11.00-23.00; Sunday: 12.00-22.30

Food: Monday to Thursday 12.00-14.00 and 18.00-21.00; Friday: 12.00-14.00 and 18.00-22.00; Saturday: 12.00-22.00; Sunday 12.00-21.00

Credit cards: All major cards accepted except American Express and Diners

Accommodation: None

Entertainment: Quiz night every Thursday

Facilities: Car park; beer garden; childrens play area

Local Places of Interest/Activities: Nottingham (historic city) 13 miles; Grantham (historic town) 11 miles; Belvoir Castle 6 miles; British Parachute School (Langar Airfield) 1 mile

Internet//Website:
e-mail: email@unicornshead.co.uk website: www.unicornshead.co.uk

The White Lion
157

Main Street,
Huthwaite,
Nottinghamshire
NG17 2RH
Tel: 01623 441599

Directions:

Huthwaite is on the
western outskirts of
Sutton in Ashfield,
which is 3 miles
from Mansfield
town centre

Close to Junction 28 on the M1 is the village of Huthwaite, on the outskirts of the small town of Sutton in Ashfield. It's a pleasant place and sits almost on the Nottinghamshire and Derbyshire border. It's here that you'll find the **White Lion**, a large, well proportioned inn built of stone that is well worth a visit. It's a family run pub, with Angela Flude and her two daughters and son in charge, that has that traditional look that speaks of friendly service and value for money. It was built in 1887, and the interior is everything a pub should be. There are oak beams, masses of floor space (with plenty of carpeting!), upholstered seating, and masses of highly polished brass and copper everywhere.

The inn has a lovely little restaurant which can seat up to 30 in comfort, and the food is simple, tasty' traditional and always home cooked. You can order a full meal or just a bar snack. The freshness of the ingredients that go into the wonderful selection of dishes is always guaranteed, and the helpings are ample, making this a real value for money hostelry! At the bar there's a wide selection of drinks available, from real ale to draught bitter, mild, stout, cider and lager, plus of course, a selection of soft drinks if you're driving.

This is the ideal place to stop for a delicious lunch or evening meal, or even just to stretch your legs, relax and have a quiet drink with friends.

Opening times: Monday to Friday: 12.00-14.30 and 17.00-23.00; Saturday 12.00-23.00; Sunday 12.00-22.30

Food: Monday to Friday: served between 12.00-14.30 and 17.00-20.30; Saturday: food all day; Sunday: 12.00-16.00

Credit cards: All major cards accepted except American Express and Diners

Accommodation: None

Entertainment: Tuesday and Sunday evenings: bingo; golf society; skittle alley

Facilities: Car park; beer garden with occasional barbecues; children's play area

Local Places of Interest/Activities:
Mansfield (historic town) 4 miles; Hardwick Hall (NT) 3 miles; Stainsby Mill (NT) 4 miles; Newstead Abbey 6 miles

158 The White Swan

50 Northgate,
Newark-on-Trent,
Nottinghamshire
NG24 1HF
Tel: 01636 704700

Directions:

The inn sits near the heart of Newark-on-Trent , a large town 15 miles south west of Lincoln

The White Swan has all the appeal and charm of a period inn, and sits on a prestigious corner site near the centre of the town of Newark-on-Trent. It dates from the 18th century, and has a wealth of half timbering which gives it a picturesque and charming aspect. Even its chimneys have a half timbered look about them to blend in with the walls! This is a typical English town pub - warm and welcoming in winter and cool in summer, with a dimly lit interior that suggests all that is best in English hospitality. The ceilings are low and dark-beamed, the lounge is large and airy, and the taproom is cozy and comfortable - a wonderful place to have a drink and a chat with the locals!

Under the personal supervision of Andrea Eyre, it has an enviable reputation in the town as a place to eat and drink. Andrea's husband, Robert, is in charge of the cooking, and offers a range of dishes that are simple, beautifully cooked, honest and great value for money. Try one of the home made pies, or choose from the range of desserts - you won't regret it! This is pub food at its very best, with hearty platefuls that will satisfy anyone. Only the freshest ingredients are used, and everything is bought locally if possible.

At the bar you'll find three cask ales and a rotating guest ale, all brewed in the traditional way, and all wonderfully kept by Andrea. You can also choose from a range of draught bitters, mild, cider, stout and lagers, and, of course, if you'd like wine with your meal, you can buy it by the bottle or glass.

Opening times: Monday to Saturday: 12.00-15,00 and 19.00-23.00; Sunday: 12.00-1500 and 20.00-22.30

Food: Monday to Thursday: 12.00-14.00; Friday and Saturday: 12.00-14.00 and 19.00-21.00

Credit cards: Cash only at present

Accommodation: None

Entertainment: Quiz night every Sunday; outdoor skittle alley

Facilities: Beer garden; car park; barbecues in summer months; children's play area

Local Places of Interest/Activities: Southwell (historic city with cathedral) 7 miles; Lincoln (historic city with cathedral) 15 miles; Vina Cooke Museum of Dolls and Bygone Childhood (Cromwell) 5 miles

Internet/Website:
e-mail: andieyre@aol.co.uk

6 Lincolnshire

PLACES OF INTEREST:

PUBS AND INNS:

The Hidden Inns of the Heart of England

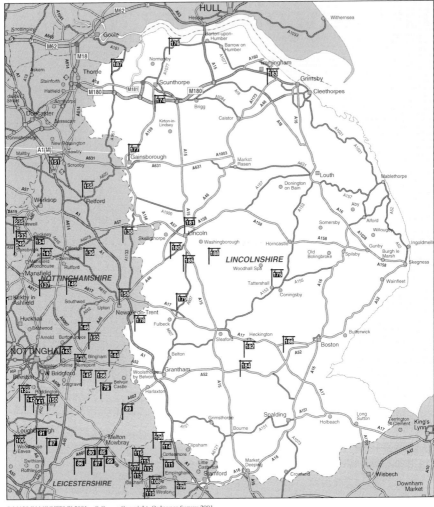

© MAPS IN MINUTES ™ 2001   © Crown Copyright, Ordnance Survey 2001

174 The Bird In The Barley, Messingham	**182** The Nags Head, Helpringham
175 The Black Horse, Tattershall	**183** The Old Farmhouse Hotel, Stallingborough
176 Butchers Arms, Winterton	
177 The Elm Cottage, Gainsborough	**184** Plough Inn, Horbling
178 The Five Bells, Claypole	**185** Thorold Arms, Harmston
179 The George Hotel, Leadenham	**186** Wheatsheaf Hotel, Swineshead
180 The Lincoln Green, North Hykeham	**187** White Hart Hotel, Crowle
181 Monks Abbey Hotel, Lincoln	**188** White Horse Inn, Metheringham

Please note all references refer to page numbers

Lincolnshire

South Lincolnshire offers a variety of places and sights that no traveller or tourist should miss. Stamford, on the western edge of the county, is one of the most attractive towns in the whole country - the most attractive, according to John Betjeman. Moving eastwards into the Fens, the reclaimed land has a rich agricultural yield, with potatoes and sugar beet among the most prolific crops, and Spalding is the centre of the world-renowned Lincolnshire flower industry. Towards the Wash, the rich silt farmland and the salt marshes have become the natural habitat for thousands of wildfowl and wading birds - and those who watch them!

Grantham is the most important town in southwest Lincolnshire, with a population of around 30,000 and a pedigree in the field of engineering. Cross the River Witham out of the town and the attractions of a bustling town are replaced by the appeal of country walks, country mansions and stone villages. A popular local recipe (or rather several recipes) is for Grantham gingerbread, which is traditionally baked in walnut-size balls.

Southeast Lincolnshire takes in historic Boston through Poacher Country and across to the seaside, and the three well known holiday resorts of Skegness, Ingoldmells and Chapel St Leonards. This part of the county is particularly rich in folklore, and with its long coastal boundary smuggling took place on a regular basis in the 17th and 18th centuries, often for consignments of 'hollands', or gin. A stay in this region can be as peaceful or as boisterous as you like, quiet walks in the countryside or letting your hair down at the seaside. Further up the eastern coast the visitor will find more seaside magic at the resorts of Mablethorpe, Trusthorpe and Sutton-on-Sea. Inland, the Domesday Book town of Louth and Alford beckon with their mixture of history and modern amenities, and throughout the area there's every incentive to take the air, with great walking in a variety of landscapes: the Wolds include some of the most beautiful yet undiscovered countryside in England.

The majestic county capital dominates west Lincolnshire, offering almost endless opportunities for exploring the layers of history that have contributed to its unique appeal. But this area, called North Kesteven, also beckons with wide open spaces, show gardens and gentle strolls along the river banks. The RAF connection is particularly strong, and motorists can explore this heritage by taking the Airfield Trail that takes in the bases - some still operational - at such places as Bracebridge Heath, Waddington, Coleby Grange, Digby, Cranwell, Wellingore and Swinderby.

As for north Lincolnshire, delights include a wide variety of thing to see and do as one moves from holiday resorts to the majestic scenery along the Humber Estuary, the modern wonder of the Humber Bridge and, in the west, the Isle of Axholme, which really was an inland island before the 17th century Dutch draining schemes.

PLACES OF INTEREST

ABY

Claythorpe Watermill & Wildfowl Gardens are a major draw for visitors of all ages. Features of this lovely riverside setting include enchanted woods, hundreds of birds and animals, a tea room and a gift shop. Open daily March to October. The mill itself, long since drawing its pension, was built in 1721. At nearby **Swaby** are a long barrow and a nature reserve in Swaby Valley that is designated a Site of Special Scientific Interest.

162

ALFORD

Often described as Lincolnshire's Craft Centre, Alford is a flourishing market town with a real sense of history. **Alford Manor House**, with brick gabling and thatched roof, is a folk museum where visitors are invited to step back into the past and take a look at local life through shops, a veterinary surgery, a Victorian schoolroom and a History Room with a collection of Roman finds and displays from the salt works that once flourished in this part of the world. An even more tangible link with the past is provided by **Alford Tower Mill** on the Mablethorpe side of town, built by local millwright Sam Oxley in 1837. Standing a majestic six floors high, it has five sails and four sets of grinding stones. It retired in 1955, but after loving restoration is now back in operation. Tel: 01507 462136.

The Church of St Wilfrid dates from the 14th century and was extensively restored and enlarged by Sir Giles Gilbert Scott in 1869. Tuesday is market day in Alford, with the craft market on Fridays in summer, and every August a festival attracts a growing variety of arts and crafts on display, joined nowadays by dancers, singers, poets and actors. The Alford town crier scatters his decibels every Tuesday in summer.

BARROW-ON-HUMBER

The birthplace of John Harrison, who in 1735 won a huge prize for inventing a ship's chronometer that would pinpoint the ship's longitude. The story of Harrison's achievement is told in the recent bestseller *Longitude*. Harrison is buried in Hampstead, but Barrow's Church of the Holy Trinity has a portrait of the inventor, and a sundial made by his brother James stands in the churchyard. A picnic site by the A1077 on the way to Barton provides a great view of Humber shipping, the bridge and the outline of Hull across the estuary.

A minor road leading from Barrow to East Halton brings the motorist to **Thornton Abbey**, whose isolated railway station suggests that it was once a popular spot for day trippers. The Abbey is a ruined Augustinian priory founded in 1139. A superb brick gatehouse, built some 200 years later, is the highlight of the massive remains.

BARTON-UPON-HUMBER

Barton was the point from which most boats made the crossing to Hull, and by the 11th century it was the most important port in North Lincolnshire. Continued prosperity is evident in the number of grand Georgian and Victorian buildings, and today it has never thrived more, standing as it does at the southern end of the impressive **Humber Bridge**. This is Europe's longest single-span suspension bridge and was opened by the Queen in 1981. There are viewing areas at both ends of the bridge, which has a pedestrian walkway.

Around the Bridge are important nature reserves. **Barton Clay Pits** cover a five-mile area along the river bank and offer a haven for wildlife and recreation for sporty humans. **Far Ings**, with hides and waymarked trails, is home to more than 230 species of wild flowers, 50 nesting bird species and hundreds of different sorts of moths. Back in town, **Baysgarth House Museum** is an 18th century mansion with a collection of 18th and 19th century English and Oriental pottery a section on country crafts and an industrial museum in the stable block. The surrounding park has a picnic area, play area and various recreational facilities. Barton has two distinguished churches, St Peter's with its remarkable Saxon tower and baptistry, and St Mary's with superb nave arches and elaborate west door. Chad Varah, founder of the Samaritans, was born in Barton, and Sir Isaac Pitman of shorthand fame taught here and married a local girl.

The A1017 running west of Barton meets the B1204 at South Ferriby, and the route down towards the M180 passes through the village of **Horkstow**. Two miles west of the road stands another suspension, on a more modest scale than the Humber Bridge, of course, but also remarkable in its way. It was designed and built by Sir John Rennie in 1844 to cross the River Ancholme to the brick kilns. It is certainly one of the world's oldest suspension bridges. Carrying on towards Brigg, at the junction of the B1204 and B1206, is the village of **Elsham** and real delight in the shape of **Elsham Hall Country and Wildlife Park**. This family-run enterprise in the grounds of an 18th mansion includes a small zoo, children's farm, garden centre, craft centre, café and theatre.

BELTON

Honey-coloured Ancaster stone was used in the building of **Belton House**, home of the Brownlows for many generations before being acquired by the National Trust in 1983. The house dates mainly from the end of the 17th century, and its rooms (15 are open to view on certain days in the summer) are filled with treasures and fine art. The grounds are a great attraction in their own right, and many hours can be spent in the pleasant grounds, Dutch and Italian gardens, orangery and deer park.

The adjacent Church of St Peter and St Paul contains many Brownlow family monuments, and Canova's statue of Religion.

BOSTON

An important port on the River Witham, from Roman times a major centre of import and export. Trade reached its height in the Middle Ages, when the port was second only to London in paying tax dues. Boston's most famous landmark is St Botolph's Church, whose tower, popularly known as **Boston Stump**, rises to 272 feet.

St Botolph's is the largest parish church in England, begun in 1309 and built mainly in the Decorated style of architecture. Light, airy and spacious, the church is full of eccentric carvings in wood and stone, and above the south door the library, founded in 1635, has a superb collection of medieval manuscripts. On the church green is a statue of Herbert Ingram (1811-1860), an MP for Boston and the founder of the *Illustrated London News*. The **Guildhall Museum** in South Street is a handsome brick building of the 15th century which served as the Town Hall for 300 years.

The most important event in Boston's history took place in 1607, when a group of Puritans, trying to escape to religious freedom in the Netherlands, were betrayed by the captain of their ship and arrested. They later reached the Netherlands, where they stayed for 12 years before sailing to America as the Pilgrim Fathers. The cells where the ringleaders were held are the most popular attraction at the museum, which also has numerous exhibits ranging from archaeological finds to a portrait of the botanist Sir Joseph Banks, who sailed with Captain Cook and who introduced sheep into Australia. Other significant Boston buildings include the 13th century Blackfriars, originally the refectory of a Dominican friary and now an arts centre; Fydell House, a handsome 18th century house which now contains an adult education centre; and the restored **Maud Foster Windmill**, the tallest working windmill in the UK, which mills daily when the wind blows. Boston is at its bustling busiest on Wednesdays and Saturdays, when the centre is taken over by colourful street markets.

BOURNE

An abbey was founded here in the 12th century, and the Abbey Church of St Peter and St Paul is one of the very few connected with the Arrovasian sub-division of the Augustinian order. Behind the church is a working mill that is the **Bourne Heritage Centre**. Hereward the Wake possibly started life in Bourne, but William Cecil (later Lord Burghley) certainly did, and so did Raymond Mays, who was responsible for the pre-war ERA racing cars and the post-war BRMs. Red Hall, a sturdy Elizabethan mansion in red brick, spent some of its more recent life as part of Bourne's railway station (the line closed in the 1960s) and is now a community centre. A mile west of town on the A151 stands **Bourne Wood**, 400 acres of long-established woodland with an abundant and varied plant and animal life. Once part of the great forest of Brunswald, it's a great place for walking or cycling, and has some interesting modern sculpture in wood and stone. The waters around Bourne and the Deepings are credited with curative properties, and the Blind Well, on the edge of the wood, is said to be efficacious in dealing with eye complaints.

BURGH-LE-MARSH

Set on a small hill above what used to be marshland, Burgh is a delightful spot within very easy reach of the resorts and the Wolds. **Dobson's Mill**, with the unusual arrangement of five left-handed sails, was built in 1813 and worked until 1964. A year later the County Council bought it and have ensured that it is well looked after. The Church of St Peter and St Paul is notable for its colourful clock face with the inscription 'Watch and Pray for Ye Know not When the Time is', a fine peal of eight bells and an impressive wooden eagle lectern carved by local barber and antiquarian Jabez Good.

164

BUTTERWICK

Butterwick is bypassed, so this marshland village is a haven of peace. The Church of St Andrew is an old brick and stone building that was extensively restored in 1800.

A walk in this remote, uncluttered area takes in White Loaf Hall, where the first white loaf baked in England was apparently made. Freiston Shore was intended to be a holiday resort, and once supported two hotels and a racecourse. But never quite made it, and the arrival of the railway at Skegness ensured that it never would. South of here, at the end of Hobdole Drain, is Boston Haven, the Pilgrim Fathers memorial and picnic area.

CLEETHORPES

South of Grimsby and almost merged with it, Cleethorpes developed from a little village into a holiday resort when the railway line was built in the 1860s. Like so many Victorian resorts, it had a pier (and still has). The pier was opened on August Bank Holiday Monday 1873, when nearly 3,000 people paid the then princely sum of sixpence (2½p) for admission. The toll was reduced the next day to a much more reasonable penny (½p), and it is recorded that in the first five weeks 37,000 people visited. The pier, like many others, was breached during the Second World War as a defence measure to discourage enemy landings, and it was never restored to its full length. On the seafront near the pier stands **Ross Castle**, a folly put up in 1885 that marks the original height of the clay cliffs. Among the attractions for visitors to Cleethorpes are **Pleasure Island**, **Jungle World**, an indoor tropical garden; the **Humber Estuary Discovery Centre**; and the **Cleethorpes Coast Light Railway**, a narrow-gauge steam railway that runs along the front from Easter to September.

CONINGSBY

The centre of this charming village, which started life as a Danish settlement, is dominated by the church tower of St Michael, notable for its enormous single-handed clock; at over 16' in diameter, this 17th century clock has claims to be the largest working example of its kind. RAF Coningsby is home to the **Battle of Britain Memorial Flight**, formed in 1957 to com-

memorate the service's major battle honour. Spitfires, Hurricanes and a Lancaster are on show at the centre.

CROWLAND

The Abbey attracts visitors from all over the world, but it's also worth pausing awhile at the medieval **Trinity Bridge**. It dates from the 14th century and owes its unique triangular shape to the fact that it once stood over the confluence of two rivers. An unidentified stone figure, once in the Abbey, guards one end of the bridge.

1999 saw the 1300th anniversary of the arrival of St Guthlac at Crowland in an area that was then entirely marsh and wetland. The small church and hermitage established there was later to become **Croyland Abbey**, one of the nation's most important Benedictine monasteries. The present Church of St Bartholomew, though still impressive, is a small part of the great buildings that once occupied the site. Nothing but some oak foundations remain of the first abbey, which was destroyed by Danish invaders. The monastery was rebuilt in Saxon style in about 950, when the community began to live according to the Rule of St Benedict.

Crowland Abbey Rectory

The second abbey was completely destroyed by fire in 1091 and some 70 years later the third abbey was built in the Norman style. Parts of this abbey can still be seen, notably the dogtooth west arch of the central tower, the west front of the south aisle and the font built into the south pier of the tower's east arch. Fire again caused massive damage in 1143 and the restoration work undertaken by successive abbots was in part undone during the Dissolution of the Monasteries. A visit to the church today is a fascinating experience and among the many interesting features are the Norman font, the fine roof vaulting, the 15th-century statues on the west front and the superb bells (Croyland had the first tuned peal in England).

THE DEEPINGS

Market Deeping and **Deeping St James**, once important stops on the London-Lincoln coaching route, stand almost as one on the River Welland at the southern end of the county. The parish church at Deeping St James is impressive in its proportions, a legacy of Benedictine wealth, and features a hude, a small shelter, rather like a sentry box, which would keep the vicar dry at the graveside. The oddest building is the Cross, the original market cross, which was converted to a lock-up for village drunks in 1809; three stone seats with chains can be seen through bars in the door. A point of interest in nearby Deeping Gate is a fine old bridge (dating from 1651) that crosses the Welland. Market Deeping's church is dedicated to St Guthlac of nearby Crowland, while at **West Deeping** the major buildings are the 13th-century church and a Grade II Listed moated manor house that once was owned by Henry VII's mother. North of the village, across the A16, lie **Tallington Lakes**, a 200-acre site of water-filled pits where the action includes fishing, sailing and windsurfing.

DONINGTON-ON-BAIN

Country roads lead westward into wonderful walking country at Donington-on-Bain, a peaceful Wolds village on the Viking Way. This welltrodden route, which was established in 1976 by Lincolnshire County Council, runs 140 miles from the Humber Bridge to Oakham and is waymarked by Viking helmet symbols. While in Donington, have a look at the grand old water mill and the 13th century church. There is a story that old ladies used to throw hassocks at

the bride as she walked up the aisle, but that custom was ended in 1780 by the rector when he was hit by a misdirected hassock!

FULBECK

Fulbeck Hall, home of the Fane family since the 17th century, is filled with the family's collection of art and treasures, and an Arnhem exhibition commemorating the time when the Hall was commandeered for the planning of the Arnhem offensive. The Hall is set in 11 acres of formal Edwardian gardens.

GAINSBOROUGH

Britain's most inland port, visited more than once by the Danes, who took advantage of its position on the Trent. The most important building is the **Gainsborough Old Hall**, part 15th century, with extensions at the end of the 16th. The hall is linked with the Pilgrim Fathers, who met here secretly on occasions, and with John Wesley. Perfectly preserved, it has the original kitchen and a superb Great Hall. All Saints Church is of considerable interest, being the only Georgian town church (except for the earlier spire) in Lincolnshire. In Beaumont Street stands Marshall's Britannia Works, a proud reminder of Gainsborough's once thriving engineering industry.

GRANTHAM

This ancient market town was a Saxon Settlement in the 6th century, and when the Domesday Book was compiled it was recorded as a Royal Manor. It remained a royal possession until1696. When the River Trent was bridged at Newark the main road came through Grantham and greatly increased its importance; the coming of the railways accelerated its growth. The crowning glory of the town is undoubtedly **St Wulfram's Church**, originally built in the 8th century and dedicated to a 7th century missionary. The spire was the first of the great spires to be built, when put up between 1280 and 1300. At 282', it is the sixth highest in the country. Among many treasures is a rare 16th century chained library of 150 volumes.

Grantham House, at Castlegate, is a National Trust property dating from the 14th century and standing in pleasant grounds sloping down to the River Witham - a country house in a town. Call 01909 486411 for details of visiting times. **Grantham Museum** provides a fascinating, in-depth look at local history - social, agricultural, industrial - and has special sections devoted to Sir Isaac Newton, born locally and educated at the town's King's School, and Margaret Thatcher, the town's most famous (or infamous, depending on your political persuasion) daughter. When elevated to the peerage she took the title Baroness Thatcher of Kesteven - the area in which Grantham is located. She still retains close links with the town and declared: "From this town I learned so much and am proud to be one of its citizens". The Guildhall Arts Centre is a grand Victorian building that once included prison cells, which are now used as the box office of the centre. Another Grantham landmark is the Conduit, built by the Corporation in 1597 as the receiving point for the fresh water supply that flowed from springs near Barrowby.

GRIMSBY

The fisherman Grim, well known in medieval sagas, heads the field of possible founders of Grimsby, which from humble origins developed into the world's largest and busiest fishing port. The coming of the railways allowed the rapid transportation of fresh fish to all parts of the kingdom, and new fishing and commercial docks were built. The heyday has now passed, and some of the fish docks are finding a new purpose as a marina for leisure yachts.

The story of the boom days is told in vivid detail in the **National Fishing Heritage Centre** in Alexandra Dock, where visitors can get a dramatically real feel of a fisherman's life on the high seas with the aid of exhibits, tableaux and the Ross Tiger, a classic fishing trawler from the 1950s. The Time Trap, housed in prison cells in the Town Hall, recreates the seamier side of life on dry land, and has proved a very popular annexe to the Heritage Centre. As we went to press, it was not known whether the Time Trap would continue.

Many of the older buildings in Grimsby have had to make way for modern development (some of it very imaginative and exciting), but the Town Hall, built in 1863, still stands to give a civic dignity to its surroundings. The most prominent building is the 300-foot Dock Tower, built in Italianate style. It stored water (33,000

gallons) to operate the hydraulic system that worked the lock gates. Another imposing edifice from earlier days is Victoria Mills by Corporation Bridge, a large Flemish-style flour mill that was converted into flats a few years ago. Away from the centre, by the banks of the River Freshney, is Freshney Park Way, 300 acres of open space that attracts walkers, cyclists, anglers and birdwatchers.

Why do Grimsby Town Football Club play all their games away? Because the Mariners' ground is actually in Cleethorpes!

GRIMSTHORPE

The castle, which stands on the A151 between Bourne and Colsterworth, is the ancestral home of the Willoughby family. Parts of the 13th century castle were incorporated into the main 16th century buildings, including King John's Tower. Vanbrugh twice remodelled the north front and also designed the impressive 33-metre hall. The grounds, which were landscaped by the ubiquitous Capability Brown, include a 40-acre lake, Tudor gardens and a deer park. The state rooms and chapel house are open to the public at certain times.

GUNBY

Gunby Hall (National Trust) is a square-set three-storey building made of local red brick, built in 1700 in the style of Wren. It was long associated with the Massingberd family, whose portraits, including several by Reynolds, are on display along with some very fine English furniture. The walled garden is particularly charming, and beyond it the Church of St Peter (not NT) contains some life-size brasses of early Massingberds.

HARLAXTON

Harlaxton Manor, approached by a handsome drive off the A607, is a superb combination of Elizabethan, Jacobean and Baroque styles, and its gardens were designed as a walk round Europe, with French-style terraces, an Italian colonnade and a Dutch-style ornamental canal. The views across the Vale of Belvoir are spectacular

HECKINGTON

There's plenty of variety and interest here, in particular the tall Church of St Andrew, the Victorian almshouses and the magnificent eight-sailed windmill by the railway station. When built in 1830 its sails numbered a modest five, but the eight sails were taken from a nearby mill and installed after storms damaged the mill in 1890. This lovely piece of industrial archaeology rises to five floors and can be visited at weekends and certain other times. A few steps away, the Pearoom is a contemporary craft centre housed in a barn-like brick building.

HORNCASTLE

The town was called *Banovallum* in Roman times, and parts of the Roman wall still survive, with one part incorporated into the library on Wharf Road. Today's buildings date mainly from the 18th and 19th centuries, and the Kings Head is one of the few remaining mud and stud constructions in the town. A famous Horncastle resident was William Marwood, cobbler and public executioner. Among his customers (not for shoes) were the Phoenix Park murderers, whom he went to Dublin to send out of this world. His little cobbler's shop is in Church Lane near the Church of St Mary. The Horse Fair may no longer exist, but each June the Horncastle Town and Country Fayre is a popular event, and the town is noted for its many antique shops. A drive thorough the Wolds around Horncastle takes in small, picturesque villages such as Fulletby, Oxcombe, Salmonby and Tetford. There are some really lovely views, as some of the hills, notably Nab Hill and Tetford Hill, rise well above 400 feet.

IMMINGHAM

A small village that grew and grew with the creation of docks in the early years of this century. The heart of the original village is St Andrew's Church, dating from Norman times. The Docks were opened by King George V in 1912 and rapidly grew in importance, especially when the Great Central Railway switched its passenger liner service from Grimsby. The Docks expanded yet further when the Humber was dredged in the late 1960s to accommodate the new generation of giant tankers. Immingham Museum traces the links between the Docks and the railways. In 1607 a group of Puritans set sail from Immingham to the Netherlands, and a memorial to this occasion - the **Pilgrim Father Monument** - stands on a granite plinth hewn from Plymouth Rock. It stood originally at the point of embarkation, but is now located near the church.

LINCOLN

167

Lincoln is one of England's most beautiful and treasured cities, with 2,000 years of history to be discovered and enjoyed. The Roman walled city has left traces behind at Newport Arch and along Bailgate, where cobblestones in the paving show where the columns of the forum once stood. No 29 Bailgate, a private residence, boasts four giant pillars as well as a section of road believed to have been built by the Romans when they arrived in about 42BC. These ruins were discovered during the Victorian era, along with a Roman urn and other artefacts. The long-time owners had a family tradition of allowing visitors to see the pillars, but the property has recently changed hands - let's hope the new owners keep up the tradition.

The **Cathedral** and the **Castle** date from the Norman invasion, and there are some fine Norman buildings on a lesser scale in Steep Hill and the Strait. **Jews House**, which dates from about 1170, is thought to be the oldest domestic building in England to survive intact. Its neighbour is Jews Court, both reminders of the time when there was a thriving Jewish community in Lincoln. Medieval splendour lives on in the black and white half-timbered houses on High Bridge, and in the old city Gateways, while the residences in the Cathedral Close and Castle Square are models of Georgian elegance.

The **Lincoln Heritage Trail** takes in Lincoln's 'Magnificent Seven' tourist attractions. **Lincoln**

Jews House

168

Cathedral, started in 1072, dates mainly from the 12th and 13th centuries. One of the largest cathedrals in the country, and in a suitably dramatic setting, it is dedicated to the Blessed Virgin Mary. Among its many superb features are the magnificent open nave, stained-glass windows incorporating the 14th century Bishop's Eye and Dean's Eye, and the glorious Angel Choir, whose carvings include the Lincoln Imp, the unofficial symbol of the city. **Lincoln Castle** dates from the same period as the Cathedral, and visitors can climb to the ramparts, which include Observatory Tower, to enjoy fine views of the city. Interesting features abound, notably the keep, known as Lucy Tower, Cobb Hall, where the public gallows were located, and the Victorian prison whose chapel has separate pews like upright coffins. The building also houses an original version of Magna Carta. **The Lawn**, originally built in 1820 as a lunatic asylum, and standing in the heart of the main tourist area, is an elegant porticoed building whose attractions include an archaeology centre, tropical conservatory (the old swimming pool) and aviation museum. It is set in eight acres of beautiful grounds and gardens.

Lincolnshire's largest social history museum is the **Museum of Lincolnshire Life**, which occupies an extensive barracks built for the Royal North Lincoln Militia in 1857. It is now a Listed building and houses a fascinating series of displays depicting the many aspects of Lincolnshire life. The Domestic Gallery turns the clock back to the beginning of the century, showing what life was like in a middle-class home; settings include a nursery, bedroom, kitchen, parlour and wash house. The Transport Gallery shows the skills of the wheelwright and coachbuilder in such items as a carrier's cart and a horse-drawn charabier (hearse). It also contains a fully restored 1925 Bullnose Morris and a Lincoln Elk motorcycle. In the Agricultural and Industrial Gallery notable exhibits

include a First World War tank built by William Foster of Lincoln; a 20-ton steam ploughing engine; a steam traction engine and a number of tractors. Commercial Row features a builder's yard, a printing press, a village post office and several shops.

The **Usher Gallery**, built in 1927 with funds bequeathed by a Lincoln jeweller, James Ward Usher. It is a major centre for the arts, with collections of porcelain, glass, clocks and coins. It also houses an important collection of works by Peter de Wint and works by Turner, Lowry, Piper, Sickert and Ruskin Spear.

The imposing ruins of the **Bishops Old Palace**, in the shadow of the Cathedral, show the sumptuous lifestyle of the wealthy bishops through splendid apartments, banqueting halls and offices.

Ellis Mill is the last survivor of a line of windmills that once ran along the Lincoln Edge, a limestone ridge stretching some 70 miles from Winteringham by the Humber to Stamford on the county's southern border. This tower mill dates back to 1798 and is in full working order.

The **Toy Museum** on Westgate is a sheer delight with its fascinating collection of old toys, crazy mirrors and slot machines, and the Road Transport Museum (see under North Hykeham) has a fine collection of vintage cars, lorries and buses. Many parts of Lincoln involve steep hills, so visitors should not try to rush around the sights too quickly. Almost every building has something to offer in terms of historical interest, and tired pedestrians can always consider the option of guided tours by open-top bus, or a trip along the river.

Lincoln stages several major annual events, including a flower festival in the Cathedral, the Lincolnshire Show at the Showground just north of the city, and the Jolly Water Carnival on Brayford Pool in the centre of the city. Raising money for charity is the purpose behind this aquatic event, which includes rowing and sailing races and a procession through the streets.

Four miles west of the city on the B1190 stands **Doddington Hall**, a very grand Elizabethan mansion completed in 1600 by the architect Robert Smythson, and standing now exactly as then, with wonderful formal gardens, a gatehouse and a family church. The interior contains a fascinating collection of pictures, textiles, porcelain and furniture that reflect four centuries of unbroken family occupation.

Museum of Lincolnshire Life

LONG SUTTON

A sizeable town surrounded by lots of little Suttons. One of the best reasons for a visit, and a great place for a family day out, is the **Butterfly and Falconry Park**. Besides hundreds of butterflies in tropical houses and daily displays of falconry, the park has an animal centre, honey farm, ant room, insectarium and reptile land. A mini-assault course challenges the kiddies, and there's picnic area and a tea room.

St Mary's Church is unusual in having a lead spire, whose height (over 160') made it a useful landmark for sailors.

The area leading to the Wash is a favourite place with walkers and naturalists, especially bird-watchers. One of the most popular routes is the **Peter Scott Walk** (Sir Peter lived in one of the two lighthouses on the River Nene near Sutton Bridge. **King John's Lost Jewels Trail** covers 23 miles of quiet country roads and is suitable for motorists and cyclists. It starts at Long Sutton market place and passes Sutton Bridge, where the king is said to have lost his jewels in the marsh in 1216.

LOUTH

Set on the Greenwich Meridian on the eastern edge of the Wolds in an Area of Outstanding Beauty, Louth is an historic market town where an 8th century abbot went on to become Archbishop of Canterbury. The remains of a 12th century Cistercian Abbey can be found on private land east of the town. Notable existing buildings include the museum on Broadbank (look for the amazing carpets that were shown at the 1867 Paris Exhibition) and the ancient grammar school, but the whole town is filled with attractive buildings, many of them tucked away down narrow streets. A plaque in Westgate Place marks the house where Tennyson lodged with his grandmother while attending the school. The vast Church of St James has the tallest spire of any parish church (nearly 300 feet). A cattle market is held in Louth on Fridays, and a general market on Wednesdays, Fridays and Saturdays.

MABLETHORPE

The northernmost and 'senior' of the three holiday resorts that almost form a chain along the fragile coast, which has frequently been threatened by the waves, and whose outline has changed visibly down the years. Long popular with day trippers and holidaymakers, it offers all that could be asked of a traditional seaside town, and a little more. Tennyson stayed regularly at Marine Villa, which is now called Tennyson's Cottage. One of the most popular attractions is the **Animal Gardens Nature Centre & Seal Trust** at North End. This complex houses creatures of all kinds, with special wild cat and barn owl features, and includes a seal and seabird hospital, lynx caves and a nature centre with many fascinating displays. Open every day from Easter to October.

MARKET RASEN

The little River Rase gives its name to this market town at the western edge of the Wolds. Growing in importance down the years, it prospered even further when the railway line was built. It was certainly a far cry from being 'the sleepiest town in England', as Charles Dickens once declared. Much of the central part is a conservation area, and the best known buildings are De Aston School, St Thomas's Church with a 15th century ironstone tower, and the impressive Centenary Wesleyan church. Market Rasen racecourse, 75 years old, will stage 19 meetings (all jumping) in 1999, including Ladies' Night evening meeting on Saturday July 31st.

NORMANBY

Normanby Hall and Country Park. The Hall was built in 1825 for the Sheffield family and extended in 1906. The interior is decorated in Regency style, and displays include eight rooms that reflect the changes made down the years. There are also two costume galleries. The Park has plenty to see and enjoy, including a deer park, duck ponds, an ice house in the middle of the miniature railway circuit, a Victorian laundry and a walled garden. The **Farming Museum** majors on rural life in the age of the heavy horse, and among the displays are traditional agricultural equipment and transport, and country crafts.

OLD BOLINGBROKE

Old Bolingbroke is the site of **Bolingbroke Castle**, whose impressive remains are still being restored. Originally built in the reign of William I, it later became the property of John of Gaunt, and his son Henry, later Henry IV, was born in the castle. Besieged by Parliamentary forces in 1643, it fell into disuse soon after.

SCUNTHORPE

Scunthorpe changed from a rural farming community to a centre of the steel industry after 1860, when large deposits of ironstone were found beneath the five villages that made up the parish: Appleby, Ashby, Brumby, Crosby and Frodingham. An ironmonger's cottage is incorporated into **North Lincolnshire Museum & Art Gallery**, next to Frodingham church. Displays of geology, archaeology and social history. The main grand house in these parts is Brumby Hall, built in the 17th and 18th centuries.

SKEGNESS

Skegness has been popular with generation after generation as a holiday resort catering for all ages. A port in Tudor times, it was planned as a resort by the Earl of Scarborough, and the arrival of the railway in 1873 really put it on the map, making it accessible for thousands. The pier (now sadly truncated) and St Matthew's Church were built for holidaymakers, and in 1936 Billy Butlin opened his first holiday camp. The town's mascot is the Jolly Fisherman, and the story behind him is an interesting one. In 1908 the Great Northern Railway bought an oil painting of the fisherman for £12. After adding the famous slogan 'Skegness is so Bracing', they used the painting as a poster to advertise trips from King's Cross to Skegness (fare 3/- or 15p). 90 years later the same Jolly Fisherman is still busy promoting Skegness as a holiday resort. There are two statues of him in town, one at the railway station, the other in Compass Gardens.

Besides the obvious attractions of the beach and all the traditional seaside entertainment, Skegness has some places of special interest, including **Church Farm Museum**, a former farmhouse that is home to a collection of old farm implements and machinery, re-created village workshops, a paddock of Lincoln Longwool sheep and a fine example of a Lincolnshire 'mud and stud' thatched cottage. **Natureland Seal Sanctuary** on North Parade provides interest and fun for all the family with its seals and baby seal rescue centre, aquarium, tropical house, pets corner and Floral Palace, a large greenhouse teeming with plant, insect and bird life. Serious birdwatchers should head

south along the coast to **Gibraltar Point National Nature Reserve**, a field station among the salt marshes and dunes with hides, waymarked routes and guided tours.

North of Skegness lie the smaller resorts of **Chapel St Leonards** and Ingoldmells. Just beyond the latter is **Hardy's Animal Farm**, a working farm with an adventure playground.

SLEAFORD

A market town of some 10,000 souls, some of whom have the pleasure of worshipping in the fine old parish church of St Denys, with its beautiful traceried windows. Nothing but a single piece of stone remains of the castle that dominated the town many centuries ago. On the southern edge of town stand the Maltings, an industrial complex built at the turn of the century. Cogglesford Watermill is an 18th century construction restored to working order and housing an exhibition about its past.

A few miles east of Sleaford, at **North Rauceby** on the A17, stands **Cranwell Aviation Heritage Centre**, which tells the story of the nearby RAF College and of the numerous RAF bases in the region.

SOMERSBY

Tennyson's birthplace, and the village and surrounding area are full of associations with the poet. The church contains several memorials to Tennyson, whose father is buried in the churchyard. In the tiny neighbouring village of **Bag Enderby** John Wesley is said to have preached under the tree on the village green; the hollow trunk still stands.

Other places to visit near Spilsby include the **Fenside Goat Centre**, a working dairy goat farm at **Toynton All Saints** (1 mile south off the A16), and the **Northcote Heavy Horse Centre** at Great Steeping, 3 miles east of town on the B1195. Here visitors spend happy hours meeting the horses and enjoying wagon rides, longer country rides and various demonstrations.

SPALDING

A peaceful market town that is the centre of Lincolnshire's flower growing industry. the annual **Tulip Parade** in early May is a great event in the town's life, attracting many thousands of visitors and culminating in a colourful procession of floats. These floats stay on display for a time at **Springfield Gardens** (World of

Flowers), where 30 landscaped acres include marvellous show gardens, a carp lake and a sub-tropical palm house.

The town is an interesting place to stroll around, with Georgian terraces lining the River Welland and many other buildings showing strong Dutch influence. Before the days of mass car-owning, the popularity of the Tulip Parade used to bring in most of its visitors by train, and the sidings north of the station were regularly filled with excursion trains. As a result, Spalding boasts one of the longest iron footbridges in Lincolnshire. Two, actually, because another equally impressive construction stands south of the station, spanning the main line and a now defunct branch line.

The present parish church of **St Mary and St Nicholas** was built by the Benedictine Priory which existed in Spalding from 1051 to its dissolution. In the early 16th century it is reported that elaborate plays were performed in the Sheep Market to raise funds for the Church repairs. In 1674 the St Thomas Chapel became home to the Grammar School. It has been altered and added to over the years and was extensively restored in 1865-7. recent additions include modern stained glass windows and decorations on the Chancel ceiling.

At **Pinchbeck**, a couple of miles north of Spalding, the **Spalding Bulb Museum** depicts the growth of the bulb-growing industry down the years with the aid of tableaux and artefacts, as well as audio-visual and seasonal working demonstrations. Open from April to October. Off West Marsh Road, the **Pinchbeck Engine** is a restored beam engine that was built in 1833 for fen-draining purposes and worked until 1952, draining anything up to 3.5 million tons of water in a year. In 1988 the Drainage Board and South Holland Council took the decision to restore this superb piece of machinery and it now operates regularly, the centrepiece of a land drainage museum that is open daily from April to October. Another massive draining machine is on display at Pode Hole pumping station. A different diversion at Pinchbeck is Spalding Tropical Forest, open throughout the year.

The grandest building in the Spalding area is **Ayscoughfee Hall**, at Churchgate on the Peterborough road, a well-preserved medieval mansion standing in attractive gardens by the river. It houses the Museum of South Holland, whose galleries span Spalding history, drainage and land reclamation, agriculture and horticulture.

A permanent display records the life story of Captain Matthew Flinders RN, who was born in nearby Donington in 1774 and who explored and charted much of the Australian coastline. The Hall, which has been altered many times since its origins in the 15th century, also contains a

Ayscoughfee Hall

collection of stuffed birds belonging to the Spalding Gentlemen's Society. In the garden stands a lonely war memorial at the end of an ornamental lake.

A great find 5 miles east of Spalding, in Whaplode St Catherine, is the **Museum of Entertainment**, a fascinating collection of mechanical musical instruments, and gramophone and phonograph records. One of the stars of the show is a theatre organ from the Gaumont, Coventry.

SPILSBY

A pleasant little market town with a population of about 2,000, set near the southern edge of the Wolds. Market day is Monday, and there's an annual May Day carnival with dancing round the May Pole in the market square. The Church of St James has many interesting features, including tombs and memorials of the Willoughby family and a monument to Spilsby's most famous son, the navigator and explorer Captain Sir John Franklin, who lost his life in charge of an expedition that discovered the North West Passage. A handsome bronze of the great man stands in the square. The stately pillared Court House and prison is now a theatre.

STAMFORD

Proclaimed as 'the finest stone town in Eng-

171

land', Stamford was declared the country's first Conservation Area in 1967. Its origins are probably in the Saxon period, though one of the numerous local legends tells of a settlement and seat of learning founded in the 8th century BC by the Trojan king of Britain, King Bladud. It is the handsome Georgian architecture that gives today's town its wonderful character, in private houses and in majestic public buildings such as the Town Hall, the Assembly Rooms, the theatre and the renowned George Hotel, whose gallows sign spans the main street. The churches, diminished in number down the centuries, are all worth visiting, particularly St Mary's, with a spectacular spire and some marvellous stained glass; St Martin's, built in 1430 in late Perpendicular style; and St George's, long associated with the Order of the Garter - one of its windows is decorated with the order's mottoes and garters. 13th century All Saints Church, notable for its multiple arched wall arcading and semi-detached tower and spire, was extensively rebuilt in the 15th century by John and William Browne, prosperous wool merchants who are commemorated in the church by life-size brasses. Its most distinguished vicar was the archaeologist and antiquarian William Stukeley. St Leonard's Priory, founded by the Benedictine order in the 11th century, is a fine example of Norman architecture, with an ornate west front and north-side arcade.

Famous people connected with Stamford include Sir Malcolm Sargent, who is buried in the town's cemetery. The cross on his grave is inscribed with the Promenader's prayer. Daniel Lambert, the celebrated giant, was in Stamford on many occasions, often staying at the George, and when he died in 1809 at the Waggon and Horses Inn he tipped the scales at almost 59 stones. One of the many stories associated with him is that he would challenge people to race along a course which he would choose. He then set off along the George's corridors, filling them wall to wall and preventing the challenger from passing! He is buried in a detached part of St Martin's churchyard; his grave is an oft-visited Stamford landmark, and one of the most popular exhibits in **Stamford Museum** is a life-size model of him, in one of his own suits, alongside a besuited model of General Tom Thumb. The museum sets out the history and archaeology of Stamford, and includes an industrial sec-

tion featuring agricultural implements and machines, and the short-lived locally produced Pick motor car. Glazed Stamford ware was highly regarded in the Middle Ages, and a collection forms part of the medieval display. It was manufactured in the town from about 850 to the 13th century, while for a short period in the Victorian era terracotta ware was produced; this, too, is on display. A rather more specialised museum is the **Stamford Steam Brewery Museum** displaying original 19th century brewery equipment.

St Martin's Church contains the tomb of William Cecil, the first Lord Burghley, who commissioned **Burghley House**, which stands on the B1443 a mile south-east of Stamford. This sumptuous Elizabethan pile, with 18 state rooms, houses some outstanding 17th century Italian paintings, superb tapestries and a major collection of Oriental porcelain. The extensive park that surrounds the house was designed by Capability Brown and is the setting for the annual Burghley Horse Trials.

TATTERSHALL

Separated from Coningsby by Butts Bridge, Tattershall is known all over the world for the proud keep of **Tattershall Castle**, built in brick in the 1440s on the orders of the Lord Chancellor, Ralph Cromwell, on the site of an existing castle. The keep has four floors, each with a great chamber and smaller rooms opening into the corner turrets. The building was rescued from near ruin by Lord Curzon, who bequeathed it to the National Trust on his death in 1925. Call 01526 342543 for opening times of the castle and its gatehouse, which houses a museum and a shop. In the shadow of the castle is **Tattershall Country Park**, set in 365 acres of woods, parks and lakes and offering all sorts of sporting facilities.

Also at the top of any visitor's list is the magnificent collegiate Church of Holy Trinity, commissioned by Ralph Cromwell in 1440 and completed 40 years later. It is built of Ancaster stone and features some notable brasses and a floor stove dedicated to Tom Thumb, whose house is in the market square. Just off the square are the remains of the college building.

Other major points of interest in the area are **Dogdyke Steam Pumping Station** at Bridge Farm, Tattershall Bridge, the last working steam drainage engine in the Fens; and another pumping station, combined with the **Tales of the River Bank** visitor centre, at Timberland, reached along the River Witham at Tattershall Bridge. All you need to know about the Fens is explained here.

WAINFLEET

Formerly a thriving port, Wainfleet now finds itself several miles from the sea. Narrow roads lead off the market place with its medieval stone cross, making it a good place to explore on foot. It's best known as the home of the family-run Bateman's Brewery, but the most interesting building is Magdalen College School, built in dark red brick in 1484 for William of Wayneflete, Bishop of Winchester and Lord Chancellor to Henry VI. This worthy first founded Magdalen College Oxford and later established the college school in the town of his birth. It continued as the college school until 1933 and now houses the public library and a small museum.

WILLOUGHBY

Travelling from Skegness along the A158 (passing Gunby Hall - see previous chapter) and B1196, the motorist will soon come across Willoughby, best known as the birthplace of Captain John Smith. A farmer's son, he was born in the village in 1580 and educated in Louth. He left England as a young man and, after a spell as a mercenary in Europe, set sail with others for Chesapeake Bay in 1607. His adventures as a slave at the hands of the Red Indians, his rescue by Pocohontas and his return with her to England are universally known in words and songs, and Willoughby retains strong memories in the church, where a memorial window was a gift from America, and in the Willoughby Arms, where a plaque and accounts of his adventures may be seen. At neighbouring **Mawthorpe** there is a nature reserve and a privately run museum dealing with aspects of rural life and featuring a collection of tractors and farm equipment. The old railway line to the coast, long since devoid of track, is now a thriving wildlife area. Great walking country.

WOODHALL SPA

Woodhall became a spa town by accident when a shaft sunk in search of coal found not coal but mineral-rich water. In 1838 a pump room and baths were built, to be joined later by hy-

dro hotels. The arrival of the railway accelerated its popularity, but down the years the spa fell into disuse and the associated buildings collapsed. One interesting survivor of the good old days is the kinema in the Woods, originally a tennis pavilion. The **Cottage Museum** on Iddsleigh Road, also the Tourist Information Centre, tells the story of the establishment of the town as a spa resort. Woodhall Spa had close connections with 617 Squadron, the Dambusters, in the Second World War, and the Petwood Hotel was used as the officers' mess. Memorabilia of those days are displayed in the hotel's Squadron Bar. The **Dambusters Memorial** in Royal Square is in the form of a model of a breached dam.

There are several sites of interest outside the town. To the north stand the ruins of a hunting lodge called the **Tower on the Moor**, associated with Tattershall Castle. Standing all alone on Thimbleby Moor in the hamlet of Reeds Beck, is a 36' high memorial to the Duke of Wellington, erected in 1844 and topped by a bust of the Iron Duke. The column is at the site of Waterloo Woods, where an oak forest was planted just after the Battle.

At **Kirkstead**, off the B1191, stands a towering piece of brickwork, the only visible remains of a 12th century Cistercian Abbey. Close by is the fine 13th century Church of St Leonard. **Near Bardney**, a few miles north on the B1190, are found the ruins of Tupholme Abbey, whose refectory stands between two farmhouses.

WOOLSTHORPE-BY-BELVOIR

Woolsthorpe's Church of St James is made of ironstone and is well worth a visit. The place that really must be seen, though, is **Belvoir Castle**, seat of the Dukes of Rutland since the time of Henry VIII, and the fourth castle to occupy the site since Roman times; it was completed early in the 19th century. The Grand Hall and state rooms are magnificent, and they house a treasure trove of furniture, porcelain, silks, tapestries, sculptures and paintings by such artists as Gainsborough, Reynolds, Poussin and Holbein. The Castle also houses the Museum of the Queen's Royal Lancers. The grounds, which provide wonderful views of the Vale of Belvoir, are a marvellous setting for special events, among which the medieval jousting tournaments are always popular.

174 The Bird In The Barley

*Northfield Road,
Messingham,
near Scunthorpe,
Lincolnshire
DN17 3SQ
Tel: 01724 62994
or 01724 764744*

Directions:

Messingham is 3
miles south of
Scunthorpe town
centre on the A159

In the quiet village of Messingham, three miles south of Scunthorpe, but a thousand miles away form the hustle and bustle of the town, you'll find **The Bird In The Barley**, a quaintly named inn with a great reputation. It is comparatively modern, having been in existence for only fifteen years. Before that the building was two houses and a garage!

But it continues the great tradition of English hospitality, and under the management of Chris and Debbie Cass, it has become one of the most popular inns in the area - a great place for a quiet drink or a meal. The inside must be seen to be believed. No echoes of a garage here. Instead you would imagine you had stepped into a centuries old pub, with low beamed ceilings, walls of bare brick, open fireplaces, country style furniture and soft wall lighting that gives the whole place a rich, welcoming look.

In charge of the kitchen is the resident chef Gail. You can eat throughout the pub, which has seating for 60 in absolute comfort. But so popular is the place that you're well advised to book in advance at all times. The cuisine is traditional English, with one or two foreign influences. You can order from the printed menu or a specials board, and if you want to treat yourself, try the speciality of the house - its great steak pie!

To accompany your meal you can have wine by the bottle or glass, or you can order from a fine selection of ales at the bar. Marston Pedigree is its resident real ale, plus there is a rotating guest ales as well, or you can choose from two keg bitters, Stella, Fosters, Woodpecker or Scrumpy Jack.

Opening times: Open lunchtimes and evenings form Monday to Saturday, and all day Sunday

Food: Served Monday to Saturday from 12.00-14.00 and 18.00-21.00; Sunday from 12.00-21.00

Credit cards: All major cards accepted except American Express

Accommodation: None

Entertainment: Occasional - ring for details

Facilities: Car park (coaches welcome); 2 beer gardens

Local Places of Interest/Activities: Scunthorpe 3 miles; Epworth (birthplace of John Wesley) 7 miles; Normanby Hall 7 miles; Gainsborough (historic town) 10 miles

The Black Horse | 175

17 High Street,
Tattershall,
Lincolnshire
LN4 4LE
Tel: 01526 342113

Directions:
Situated on the main road in Tattershall, which is on the A153 1 mile west of Coningsby

Thanks to mine hosts Diane Whitfield and Martin Warley, **The Black Horse** in Tattershall is a great place to have a quiet drink or a meal. They have been in charge since 1999, and have created an inn that is both comfortable and inviting - one that is appreciated both by locals and visitors alike. The building is solid, with a well proportioned, whitewashed front. It dates from the late 18th century, and was a former coaching inn with stables at the rear.

The interior has a great atmosphere, and Diane and Martin have made sure that it is always cozy and welcoming. The place is spotlessly clean and well maintained, with country style furniture and an array of memorabilia that adds that special touch. The Black Horse's food is tasty, beautifully cooked, and always good value for money. You can choose from the printed menu or from the specials board, which changes daily. Diane sees to this side of things, and her juicy steaks are especially popular. She takes great care when choosing the produce and ingredients that go into the dishes on offer, and they are as fresh as possible. On a Sunday, roasts are available with all the trimmings, and if you're eating, children are more than welcome. But you can also order snacks such as sandwiches and baked potatoes if you don't feel up to the hearty portions she serves. And to accompany your meal you can have wine, or choose from the beers and ales available at the bar. There's Speckled Hen, which is a real ale, as well as John Smiths Smooth, Fosters, McEwans, Miller, Woodpecker and Guinness.

Opening times: Open all day, every day

Food: Served 12.00-14.30 and 19.00-23.30

Credit cards: Cash and cheque only at present

Accommodation: None

Entertainment: Live entertainment most Saturday evenings - ring for details; indoor pub games

Facilities: Car park

Local Places of Interest/Activities:
Tattershall Castle (NT) close to village; Lincoln (historic cathedral city); Battle of Britain Memorial Flight close to village; Lincolnshire Aviation Heritage Centre 8 miles

176   Butchers Arms

High Street,
Winterton,
Lincolnshire
DN55 9PU
Tel: 01724 732269

Directions:

Winterton is 6
miles north of
Scunthorpe town
centre, just west of
the A1077 on the
B1027

Winterton is in North Lincolnshire, and visited nowadays chiefly for its fine church, which has a part Saxon tower. But also in this small quiet town is **The Butchers Arms**, an inn which is well worth a visit if you require a quiet drink or a meal. It sits in the High Street, and is a handsome, whitewashed building with good proportions and a welcoming feel to it. It was a former coaching inn, and is believed to be well over 350 years old.

Nowadays, under the management of husband and wife team John and Carol Hewitt, it still offers all that is best in traditional English hospitality. In fact, its motto is"good food, good beer and good cheer". The interior is warm and friendly, with oak beams, comfortable seating, bare walls, open fires and a wealth of memorabilia on the walls and on shelves. Children are welcome in the dining area, which seats 34,. It is especially attractive, with red upholstery on the seating and thick carpeting on the floor. You can order from a bar food menu, which contains such dishes as beef in Guinness pie, chicken cordon bleu, sirloin steak and seafood platter, or from a restaurant menu, which offers a range of steaks, chicken in red wine sauce, salmon and so on. And there's also a specials board which changes daily. Every Sunday the inn serves four different roasts., and choice of vegetarian dishes is also available. As everything is cooked to order, don't expect fast food in the Butchers Arms!

You can order wine by the glass or bottle, and at the bar there's a good range of drinks available. The two real ales on offer are Ruddles County, John Smith Cask and a rotating guest ale. Other draught drinks include John Smith Smooth, Chestnut Mild, Stella, Carling, Fosters, Woodpecker, Scrumpy Jack and Guinness.

Opening times: Open every lunchtime and evening

Food: Served 12.00-14.00 and 18.30-21.30 seven days; booking is advisable on Friday, Saturday and Sunday

Credit cards: Cash and cheques only at present

Accommodation: None

Entertainment: Quiz every Thursday evening at 20.45; karaoke every other Wednesday evening at 20.30; free pool on Monday nights

Facilities: Large car park, safe childrens play area

Local Places of Interest/Activities: Scunthorpe 6 miles; Normanby Hall 3 miles; Humber Bridge 7 miles; Julians Bower, Alkborough (turf maze) 4 miles

The Elm Cottage 177

138 Church Street,
Gainsborough,
Lincolnshire
DN21 2JU
Tel: 01427 615474

Directions:

The town of
Gainsborough is on
the A159, 13 miles
south of
Scunthorpe

Legend says that King Alfred, before he ascended the throne, visited Gainsborough in the 9th century to marry Elswitha, daughter of a local chief. If he had visited today, he would almost certainly have paid a visit to **The Elm Cottage**, an inn that evokes a gentler age, when things moved at a more leisurely pace. Its age has never been ascertained, though it is known that at one time it was thatched. The interior is lovely, and can rightly claim to be "olde worlde". Otto Krakow has been mine host for only a short time, though he has had several years experience in the licensing trade. He's determined to preserve the inn's unique period features and atmosphere. Here, people can meet, chat, have a drink and eat a meal while the frenetic pace of modern life passes them by.

There's an across the board menu, with many old favourites on it. The cuisine is traditional and English, and all the better for it! All the dishes are prepared on the premises, using only local produce at its freshest where possible. One of the most popular nights to eat is on a Friday, which is, as the locals will tell you, "steak night", when big juicy steaks with all the trimmings are on offer. The portions are generous, and everything is always beautifully cooked and presented. The dining area is no smoking, and children are welcome.

If you want wine with your meal, you can order by the glass or bottle, and, of course, there's a fine selection of beers and ales at the bar. You can have John Smith Cask, Worthington, Tetley, Stones Creamflow, Bass Mild, Guinness, Stella, Carling and Woodpecker Cider.

Opening times: Open all day, every day

Food: Served between 11.45-15.00 every day, and between 17.00-19.00 on Tuesday and Friday

Credit cards: Cash only at present

Accommodation: None

Entertainment: Quiz every fourth Tuesday evening; occasional entertainment on Friday

and Saturday evenings; ring for details

Facilities: Car park

Local Places of Interest/Activities: Gainsborough Old Hall within town; Dambusters Heritage Centre within town; Epworth (birthplace of John and Charles Wesley) 9 miles; Sundown Adventureland (children's theme park) 7 miles

178 | The Five Bells

Main Street,
Claypole,
near Newark-on-Trent,
Nottinghamshire
NG23 5BJ
Tel: 01636 626561

Directions:

Claypole is 5 miles south of Newark-on-Trent, on a minor road off the A1

The former coaching inn of **The Five Bells** takes its name from a feature of old parish church that stands in the village. The inn was taken over in 1999 by Martin and Kay Finney, who have over 15 years of experience in the licensing trade, and they're making a great job of running what is a picturesque and welcoming hostelry. It is built of mellow red brick, with small paned windows that add a dash of history and tradition to the place, and dates from the early 1800s.

The former stables have been converted into three rooms – one family room and two twin rooms, all en suite, and all with TV and tea and coffee making facilities. This makes the inn an ideal base to explore the surrounding area. The interior is everything a country pub should be - warm, cozy and welcoming, with a comfortable lounge done out in plush red where you can relax and let the cares of the world go by, and a spotless restaurant area. Kay does the cooking, and the inn is famous for its good food. You can order full meals and snacks, including filled baguettes, omelettes, pasta with wild mushrooms, chicken tikka, and beef and ale pie. If you want a real treat, try Kay's char grilled Lincolnshire steaks.

Drinks include three cask ales - one of them a rotating guest ale - and Martin tries to make sure that most of them are local brews. He reckons that the inn served at least 100 different cask ales in a year! Other draught beers are also available, of course, as well as lager, stout and cider. And if you wish to have wine with your meal, there's a small but comprehensive selection available.

Opening times: Monday: 17.30-23.00 (closed Monday lunchtime); Tuesday to Friday: 11.00-15.00 and 17.30-23.00; Saturday and Sunday: open all day

Food: Lunchtimes -Mon-Sat 12.00-14.00; Sun 12.00-17.00; evenings 18.00- 21.00 (except Tuesday and Sunday)

Credit cards: All credit cards except American Express and Diners

Accommodation: 2 family twin rooms and one family room, all en suite and with TV and tea and coffee making facilities

Entertainment: Quiz night every Wednesday

Facilities: Car park; beer garden; children's play area; pool table, dart board

Local Places of Interest/Activities: Newark-on-Trent (historic town) 5 miles; Southwell (historic city with cathedral) 9 miles; Vina Cooke Museum of Dolls and Bygone Childhood (Cromwell) 8 miles

Internet/Website:
e-mail: kaymey@fivebells.fsnet.co.uk

The George Hotel 179

Leadenham,
Lincolnshire
LN5 0PN
Tel: 01400 272251
Fax 01400 272091

Directions:

The hotel is in the
centre of Leadenham,
which is on the A607,
12 miles south of
Lincoln city centre

The George Hotel is a handsome building in three storeys built of warm, golden stone. It was probably names after King George 111, so dates from the late 18th or early 19th century. It was a coaching inn, and still has all the looks and feel of a time when people lived at a more leisurely pace. It has entertained many famous people in its time, including Douglas Bader, Captain R. Hinchliffe and Lawrence of Arabia, who wrote part of the "Seven Pillars of Wisdom" in what is now the restaurant. Mike and Karen Willgoose have owned the place for over 30 years, and during that time have created what must be one of the best inns around.

The interior is crammed with old world charm, and the Tudor Restaurant especially - with its linen and its sparkling glasses and cutlery has a welcoming feel to it. The food is outstanding, though reasonably priced, and you can choose from a menu or a specials board. Dishes include such things as Hungarian goulash, chicken and mushroom pie, steak and ale pie, a seafood platter and lemon sole. It's juicy steaks are famous in the area. Children are more than welcome. Bar snacks are also served.

Wine, of course, is available, as is a wide selection of drinks at the bar. You can choose from five real ales, plus a selection of draught lagers, cider and stout. Not only that - the Scotch bar stocks over 600 malt whiskies, and practically every distilled drink on earth, from Aquavit to Zytnia.

This is a family run hotel, with a fine reputation in the area. Mike and Karen have years of experience in the hotel and licensing trade, and know exactly what people expect in the way of hospitality, a warm welcome and value for money.

Opening times: Open every lunchtime and evening

Food: Served 12.00-14.00 and 18.30-21.30 seven days

Credit cards: All major cards accepted

Accommodation: 7 en suite rooms, 3 of which are on the ground floor; breakfast is included in the price

Facilities: Car park; beer garden; function room

Local Places of Interest/Activities: Lincoln (historic cathedral city) 12 miles; Sleaford (historic town) 8 miles; Newark-on-Trent (historic town)10 miles

180   The Lincoln Green

*Lincoln Road,
North Hykeham,
near Lincoln,
Lincolnshire
LN6 8DL
Tel: 01522 688258*

Directions:

North Hykeham is
on the A46, 4 miles
south of Lincoln
city centre

Mick and Avril Pickard have been leaseholders of **The Lincoln Green** since 1999, and have a wealth of experience in the trade. They were managers of the place up until early 1998, so know the inn well. It was formerly part of the Home Brewery, and is a generous and handsome brick building set well off the road, and with a car park and small beer garden to the front.

They have great plans for The Lincoln Green, and want to enhance its reputation as a popular place for locals and visitors alike. It has recently undergone a complete refurbishment, creating an inn that has more than its fair share of character. In fact, for a building that is comparatively recent, it far outshines some older inns for comfort, warmth and that feeling of tradition and hospitality that is the hallmark of English pubs.

The bar and lounge areas have woodwork that is dark and rich, and the furniture is comfortable and welcoming, giving you plenty of room to stretch your legs while you have a quiet drink or enjoy a meal. The bar offers three real ales - John Smith Cask, Theakston Best, and a rotating guest ale. Plus there is John Smith Smooth, Guinness, Fosters, Kronenberg and Strongbow.

Children are welcome if you're eating, and you can choose from a menu or the daily specials board. On offer is a range of dishes and options, such as full meals, jacket potatoes, sandwiches and light bites. Vegetarian meals are also available, and everything is prepared on the premises from good, fresh ingredients. The Sunday roast is very popular, though you would be advised to book in advance.

Opening times: Open all day, every day

Food: Lunchtimes only at present from 12.00-15.00 Monday to Thursday and 12.00-16.30 from Friday to Sunday

Credit cards: Cash and cheque only at present

Accommodation: None

Entertainment: Quiz night every Thursday at 12.30

Facilities: Car park; beer garden

Local Places of Interest/Activities: Lincoln (historic cathedral city) 4 miles; Newark-on-Trent (historic town) 11 miles; Southwell Minster 16 miles

Monks Abbey Hotel 181

85 Monks Road, Lincoln,
Lincolnshire LN2 5HR
Tel: 01522 544416

Directions:
The Monks Abbey Hotel is situated in
Monks Road, a short walk from the city
centre and cathedral

Lincoln is one of the most fascinating cities in Britain. It's three towered cathedral – the third largest in Britain – rises majestically above a jumble of roofs and streets, and is a perfect backdrop to a place that cries out to be explored. And while you're there, why not pay a visit to one of the city's best inns, the **Monks Abbey Hotel?** It's a sturdy, yet picturesque, three storey building of warm red brick with inviting bay windows on the first floor. It dates from the 19th century, and is a popular place for locals and visitors, who find that the food and drink is excellent.

Peter Dunn has been at the inn for four years, first as manager and now as tenant. He has created an inn that is full of character. The whole place was recently refurbished to an exceptionally high standard, while still retaining all the feel and atmosphere of bygone days. God, honest pub grub is available, and everything is cooked to perfection on the premises, using produce that is is always fresh and sourced locally wherever possible. The portions are hearty, and represent amazing value for money. You can eat throughout the inn, and choose from an extensive printed menu or from the daily changing specials board. Children over 14 years of age are very welcome.

You'll want something to drink as well, no doubt, and the Monks Abbey Hotel offers wine by the bottle or glass. Or why not try one of the ales and beers available at the bar? There's Tetley cask – an excellent real ale – or you can choose from Tetley Smooth, Ansell Mild, Carling, Stella, Scrumpy Jack cider or Guinness. And, of course, if you're driving, you can order a low alcohol or soft drink.

Opening times: Mon-Thu: 16.30-23.00; Fri-Sat: 12.00-23.00; Sun: 12.00-22.30

Food: Available during opening hours

Credit cards: Cash and cheques only at present

Accommodation: None

Entertainment: Karaoke, quiz nights and other forms of entertainment on Saturday evenings from 20.00 (ring for details); happy hour: Monday to Friday 17.00-19.00

Facilities: On-street parking

Local Places of Interest/Activities: All the attractions of Lincoln are within easy walking distance

182

The Nags Head

*2 The Green, Helpringham,
near Sleaford,
Lincolnshire NE34 0RJ
Tel: 01529 421274*

Directions:

Take the A17 east from
Sleaford for 4 miles and turn
into village of Heckington;
in the centre of the village,
turn south onto the B1394
and follow this road for 2
miles until you reach
Helpringham; the inn is
across from the village green

What a lovely little inn **The Nags Head** is! With it's whitewashed walls, hanging baskets and window boxes full of bright flowers in summer, it looks exactly like a village pub should look - inviting, cozy and full of character. It sits opposite the village green in the delightful village of Helpringham, and make a welcome stop. The building dates from the early 19th century, and has a fine, well proportioned front, with black framed windows that contrast perfectly with the walls.

In charge are Paul Breese and Fran Horrocks, who, though they've only been at the Nags Head for a short while, have lots of experience in running a village pub. The Nag's Head has a warm and welcoming interior, though it still retains many delightful period features, such as the low beams and the dark wood. The bar is cozy and neat, with masses of pewter pint pots hanging from the beams and soft wall lighting. Particularly welcoming are the staff - Pat, Sarah, Jan, Davina, Sue Kirsty and Michelle. All live in the village, and all seem to have the interests of the customers at heart.

The restaurant is well appointed and spotless, with carpeting on the floor and comfortable furnishings. It can seat 34 in comfort, and diners can choose from a printed menu or a specials board. If you want to eat on a Friday, Saturday or Sunday evening, you should book at least a week beforehand to avoid disappointment. There's also a bar lunch menu, which contains such favourites as lamb chop and mint sauce, roast chicken and sausages and onion gravy. Or why not try one of the famous Nags Head toasties?

Wine is available either by the bottle or glass, and you can choose from three real ales - Adnams, Theakstons and a rotating guest ale. Also available are John Smith Smooth, Chestnut Mild, Guinness, Fosters, Stella and Strongbow.

Opening times: Open every lunchtime and evening, except in the winter months, when it is closed on Monday lunchtime

Food: Served 12.00-14.00 and 18.00-21.30 (no food on Monday or Sunday evenings except on bank holidays)

Credit cards: All major cards accepted

Accommodation: None

Entertainment: Themed food nights on

Tuesday, Wednesday and Friday; Topical quiz every Friday evening from 21.30; pub games

Facilities: Beer garden; car park; barbecue area

Local Places of Interest/Activities: Heckington Windmill within village; Pearoom (centre for contemporary craft) within village; Boston (historic town) 12 miles; Sleaford (historic town) 5 miles

The Old Farmhouse Hotel **183**

Immingham Road,
Stallingborough,
Lincolnshire
DN41 8BP
Tel: 01469 560159

Directions:

Stallingborough is on the A1173, 3 miles south of Immingham

Between the bustling port of Immingham and the fishing port of Grimsby you'll find Stallingborough, a quiet village that contains a delightful inn called the **Old Farmhouse Hotel**. In its time it has been called "Little London" and "Rosie Malone's", and in 1911 was a house. But it is obvious that the building is much older than that, and contains a lot of history. In charge of the inn is Sue and Andrew King who, with their son Paul and daughter Kimberley, want to preserve the olde worlde character of the place. The bar and lounge area are especially attractive, with low ceilings, stout beams, country style furniture and thick carpeting. Bright horse brasses adorn the beams, and the walls have been painted a dark shade of orange to blend in with the wood. At the well stocked bar you can choose from a weekly rotating real ale, John Smith Smooth, Theakston Mild, Kronenberg, Fosters, Guinness, Strongbow and Red C. If of course, if you're eating, you can buy wine by the bottle or glass.

Children are allowed in the no smoking restaurant area, which seats 45 people in comfort, and is bright and spotlessly clean. The food is excellent, and best be described as "traditional English" with one or two foreign influences! You can choose from a bar menu and a specials blackboard, or from the restaurant carvery. Whatever you do, you'll be eating food that is beautifully cooked, well presented and represents great value for money. The Old Farmhouse Hotel is a popular place for Sunday lunch, so you are advised to book on that day to avoid disappointment. The inn boasts seven rooms, so this is an ideal base from which to explore the area. All are en suite, and if you wish to stay for a few nights, special terms are available.

Opening times: Open all day, every day

Food: Served Tuesday to Thursday 12.00-14.00 and 17.30-21.30; Friday and Saturday: 12.00-14.00 and 17.30-2.00; Sunday: 12.00-14.00; no food served on Monday

Credit cards: All cards except American Express

Accommodation: 7 en suite rooms, all upstairs; doubles, twins, family and single available; special rates for longer stays

Entertainment: Happy hours Monday 17.00-19.00; solo/duo artists Thursday evenings at 21.15; Karaoke and happy hours 19.30-2.00 Friday evening; bands on Saturday evening from 21.30; pub games

Facilities: Car park; children's play area; beer garden; barbecues and live music outside in summer months

Local Places of Interest/Activities: Grimsby (historic town) 4 miles; Cleethorpes (holiday resort) 7 miles; Pleasure Island (Theme Park) 8 miles; Thornton Abbey (ruin) 7 miles 0-21.00; Saturday and Sunday: 12.00-14.30 and 18.00-22.00

184 Plough Inn

4 Spring Lane, Horbling,
near Sleaford,
Lincolnshire NG34 0PF
Tel: 01529 240263

Directions:

Horbling is on the B1177, 2 miles south of its junction with the A52 and 7 miles south east of Sleaford

To the west of the pleasant village of Horbling in Lincolnshire you'll find the Horbling Line Nature Reserve. This stretch of former railway line is home to such bird species as whitethroat and lesser whitethroat, spotted flycatcher, nightingale and tree sparrow, and, if you enjoy nature, you could spend a delightful couple of hours here.

And while you're in the village, why not pay a visit to the delightful **Plough Inn**, and have a relaxing drink or a delicious meal? Even if you're not a bird watcher or nature lover, it is still the perfect stopping off point if you're in this part of the county. It's made of old, warm brick, and is a truly picturesque building dating back to at least 1750. The frontage is well proportioned, with a lovely, Georgian entrance and wonderful small-paned windows.

When you step over the threshold you could almost be stepping back in time. Under the careful management of Ruth and Terry Light since 1993, it has retained many of its period features. There are old beams, open fires, gleaming brass and comfortable furniture. And as the inn has well appointed accommodation, it is the ideal base from which to explore the area. There is an airy, 28 seater dining area where children are welcome, though you can eat through the inn. The food is excellent, with juicy steaks being the most popular dish. You can choose from a menu or the specials board, and everything is beautifully cooked on the premises. At the bar, you can choose from a rotating guest ale, draught bitter and mild, as well as Heineken, Stella, Guinness , draught ciders and soft drinks.

Opening times: Open at lunchtimes and in the evenings

Food: Served 12.00-14.30 and 19.00-22.00; advance booking is required at weekends

Credit cards: All major credit cards accepted

Accommodation: 1 double en suite room; one twin room and one single room, both with wash hand basins; breakfast included in price; weekend break deals available

Entertainment: Occasional entertainment (ring for details)

Facilities: Good off-road parking; monthly gourmet evenings (booking required - ring for details)

Local Places of Interest/Activities: Boston (historic town) 14 miles; Sleaford (historic town) 7 miles; Grantham (historic town) 12 miles

Thorold Arms

185

High Street,
Harmston,
Lincolnshire
LN5 9SN
Tel/Fax: 01522 720358

Directions:

Take the A15 south from Lincoln, then turn off onto the A607, 3 miles out from the city centre. Harmston is just off this road, 3 miles along.

This picturesque old inn is situated in the heart of the village of Harmston, and is made of warm old stone. It has small paned windows on the upper floor, thick walls and a slated roof, and you can tell just by looking at it that the building is very old indeed. In fact, it was built in 17th century, when things ran at a more leisurely pace. It's name is derived from a one time lord of the manor in these parts, so even here it preserves a lot of history and tradition, And still today, when you step over the threshold, you know you are leaving the modern hurly burly of the world behind. **Thorold Arms** is owned and run by Mr and Mrs Davidson, and inside you can feel the happy family atmosphere. They have completely refurbished the place, while still retaining many of its lovely period features. The bar and lounge has soft lighting and comfortable furniture, while the 28 seat dining area, with its linen, cutlery and sparkling glasses, looks more like an upmarket restaurant than an inn.

The food is wonderful. The menu is chalked up on a daily changing blackboard, and you can chose from many wonderful dishes created by the inn's own chef. Fish dishes are the inn's speciality, and they're popular with locals and visitors alike. Children are welcome if eating, and there is a small selection of vegetarian dishes. If you want to eat at weekends, you are advised to book. Every month, there is a themed food night.

You can choose wine to accompany your meal by the glass or by the bottle, or you can choose from one of the four real ales on offer at the bar - John Smith Cask, Theakston Supercool and two rotating guest ales. You can also have Guinness, John Smith Smooth, Kronenberg, Fosters or Stamford Press. On special occasions, the inn hosts wine tasting evenings.

Opening times: Open at lunchtimes and in the evening, except for Monday lunchtime, though it is open at this time on bank holidays

Food: Served 12.00-14.00 and 18.00-121.30; no food served on Monday or Sunday evenings, though free cheeseboard is available on Sunday

Credit cards: All major cards except American Express and Diners

Accommodation: B&B -ring for details

Entertainment: Quiz night every Tuesday at 20.30

Facilities: Car park

Local Places of Interest/Activities: Lincoln (historic cathedral city) 3 miles; Sleaford (historic town) 11 miles; RAF Waddington (viewing area) 1 mile

186 Wheatsheaf Hotel

Market Place,
Swineshead,
near Boston,
Lincolnshire PE20 3LJ
Tel: 01205 820349

Directions:

The village of Swinehead is off the A17, 6 miles west of Boston

It was in an abbey near Swineshead that King John and his entourage lodged in 1216 when his baggage was lost in the Wash. In his play King John, Shakespeare had the monks of the abbey poison the King before he met his end at Newark, but there is no truth in the story whatsoever. In fact, he enjoyed the best of hospitality while there. Today, regulars and visitors alike get the best of hospitality at **The Wheatsheaf Hotel** in the heart of the village. It is managed by Philip Baker, who has been in the trade for over 27 years, and is a solid, well proportioned building of three storeys, with whitewashed walls and black window frames and quoins. It was built over 300 years ago, and was at one time a coaching inn.

The interior is charming, and reflects the sturdiness found on the outside. Philip makes sure that the place is well maintained, and has retained some period features which impart an air of tradition and history to the inn. It is full of character, and can truly be described as "olde worlde". There is a bar, a 40 seater lounge, and a restaurant which can take 36 people in comfort. The cuisine can best be described as good, honest traditional English with some foreign influences, with excellent fish dishes, tasty sauces and wonderful juicy steaks being the highlights. Children are welcome if you're eating, giving the place has a cheery, family atmosphere. If you want to eat on Sunday, however, you are advised to book. You can choose form a menu, or from a daily specials board. "Lite bites" are also available at lunchtime if you feel you can't handle the main menu's generous portions.

To accompany you meal, the inn offers three real ales, one of which is always Bateman XB. In addition you can order from a range of three draught lagers, or Tetley Smooth, Guinness, and Dry Blackthorn. This is the ideal place to have that quiet drink or meal. It's popular with visitors and locals alike, and you'll get a warm Lincolnshire welcome from Philip if you call.

Opening times: Sunday to Friday: open lunchtimes and evenings; Saturday: open all day

Food: Tuesday to Sunday: 12.00-14.00 and 19.00-21.30; no food served on Mondays except bank holidays

Credit cards: All major cards accepted except American Express and Diners

Accommodation: 4 rooms available (no en suite); breakfast included in price

Entertainment: Themed food evenings each Thursday from 19.00; occasional music and quizzes (ring for details)

Facilities: Car park

Local Places of Interest/Activities: Boston (historic town) 6 miles; Spalding (historic town and bulb fields) 11 miles

White Hart Hotel   187

96 High Street,
Crowle,
near Scunthorpe
Lincolnshire
DN17 4LB
Tel: 01724 710333

Directions:
Crowle is on the
A161 west of
Scunthorpe, 8 miles
from its town centre

Crowle is in that area of Lincolnshire known as the Isle of Axholme, which was formerly fenland before being drained in the 17th century. It is a place full of history, as it was in Epworth, a few miles to the south, that John and Charles Wesley were born. The oldest pub on the Isle is **The White Hart Hotel** in Crowle. It dates from the early part of the 17th century, and contains a wealth of period features which makes it the ideal place to have a drink or meal. It sits near the heart of this small town, and is a picturesque, whitewashed building with a roof of old red tiles. and quaint windows.

Inside is even better. There are beamed ceilings old, dark wood panelling throughout, and open fireplaces that give a warming glow on the coldest of winter days. Mine hosts Trevor and Carole Cole have only been here for a short while, but they are determined to keep the inn's period features, while offering a service that is up to date and always represents good value for money. At the bar you can order from a wide selection of drinks, including John Smith Cask, John Smith Magnet, Chestnut Dark Mild, Worthington Creamflow, Carlsberg, Fosters, Carlsberg, Scrumpy Jack and Guinness. Of course, if you want to eat, you can also order wine by the glass or bottle. The food represents all that is best about good, honest English cuisine, and can be ordered from the menu or the daily specials board. The portions are generous, and everything is tasty and beautifully cooked. Try the steak and mushroom pie - it's a firm favourite with the locals.

This is one in which really could be described as "olde worlde". Pay it a visit - you won't be disappointed!

Opening times: Open every lunchtime and evening

Food: Served seven days 12.00-14.00 and 18.00-21.00

Credit cards: Cash and cheques only at present

Accommodation: None

Entertainment: Phone for details

Facilities: Car park; function room

Local Places of Interest/Activities: Epworth (birthplace of John and Charles Wesley) 6 miles; Scunthorpe 8 miles; Goole 7 miles

188 White Horse Inn

Dunston Fen,
Metheringham,
Lincolnshire
LN4 3AP
Tel: 01526 398341

Directions:

Take the turn into
Metheringham from
the B1188, 8 miles
south of Lincoln; from
the village, follow the
signs for Dunston Fen
(not Dunston) which is
5 miles along a narrow
country road

This is a real gem of a hidden inn. It sits at the end of a long lane which strikes out across the flat Lincolnshire countryside, with a caravan site attached. It is a whitewashed building and sits complacently beside the River Witham. **The White Horse Inn** is a free house, under the personal supervision of Carol and Steve Whitmore and son and daughter- in-law, Paul and Joanne Carlsen, who have only been owners since April 2001. They have great plans for the place, though it is already cozy and inviting. The bar is especially attractive, with old casks holding up the bar top, a cheery open fire, low, beamed ceilings and gleaming brass.

The food can best be described as English traditional, with one of two foreign influences. It is always beautifully cooked on the premises, with generous portions, and the produce used is sourced locally if possible. So much so that if it's good, home cooking you're after, this is the place. The no smoking restaurant has dark, polished wood furniture, and is spotlessly clean. It can seat up to 30 in comfort, and children are more than welcome. It's an ideal place to have a leisurely meal, though so popular is it at weekends that you should book to make sure of a table. You can order wine by the bottle or glass, and if you prefer beer or ale, the bar offers a fine range. You can choose from real ales - Batemans and guest ales, or from a selection of draught beers. lagers stouts and cider.

If you're touring with a caravan, then there's a caravan site on the doorstep, with electrical hookups and on site toilets etc. It is open eleven months of the year, and the facilities of the inn are available to those staying on the site. The inn also has 110 metres of frontage of the River Witham,where there is a pontoon, moorings and fishing available.

Opening times: Thurs-Sat 12.00-14.00; Mon-Sat 19.00-23.00; Sun 12.00-22.30

Food: Served Thurs-Sun lunchtimes and Tues-Sun evenings

Credit cards: Cash and cheque only at present

Accommodation: caravan park; ring for details

Entertainment: ring for details

Facilities: Car park; fishing; moorings on river

Local Places of Interest/Activities: Lincoln (historic cathedral city) 11 miles; River Welland (boating); Sleaford (historic town) 12 miles; Tattershall Castle 8 miles

7 South Derbyshire

PLACES OF INTEREST:

PUBS AND INNS:

The Hidden Inns of the Heart of England

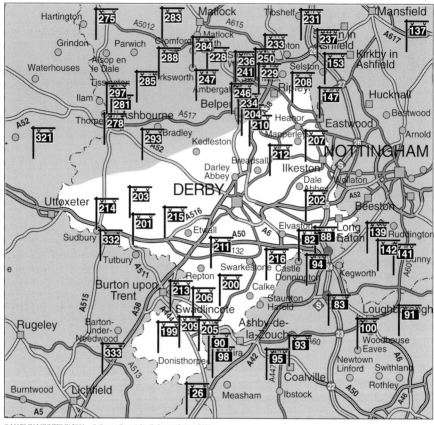

© MAPS IN MINUTES ™ 2001   © Crown Copyright, Ordnance Survey 2001

199	**Black Horse Inn & Restaurant**, Coton in the Elms
200	**The Bulls Head**, Hartshorne
201	**The Castle Hotel**, Hatton
202	**The Coach and Horses**, Draycott
203	**The Holly Bush Inn**, Church Broughton
204	**The Hollybush Inn**, Makeny
205	**Navigation Inn**, Overseal
206	**New Inn**, Woodville
207	**The Punchbowl**, West Hallam

208	**The Red Admiral**, Codnor
209	**Red Lion**, Linton
210	**Spotted Cow Inn**, Holbrook
211	**The Swan Inn**, Milton
212	**The Three Horseshoes**, Morley Smithey
213	**The Traveller's Rest**, Church Gresley
214	**Vernon Arms**, Sudbury
215	**The White Swan**, Hilton
216	**Ye Old Packhorse Inn**, Kings Newton

Please note all references refer to page numbers

South Derbyshire encompasses the regions of the county going by the picturesque names of the Amber Valley and the eastern part of the area known as Erewash. These two regions cover the eastern and southeastern parts of Derbyshire respectively. The Rivers Amber, Derwent and Trent run through this part of the county. Though the scenery is perhaps less dramatic than the popular Peak District, in which most of north Derbyshire lies, there are ample opportunities to enjoy pleasant walks in the extensive grounds of many of the estates.

The southeast area of Derbyshire has been heavily influenced by the two towns of Derby and Nottingham. Originally, small farming communities many of the villages grew at the time of the Industrial Revolution and they can, in many cases, be characterised by rows of workers' cottages. However, notwithstanding this there are some interesting and unique buildings to be found in this corner of Derbyshire. Whilst a lot of the area did not escape from the growth of Derby and Nottingham, several villages remain, their centres almost intact. Unlike the area to the west, there are no great stately mansions, except for one, Elvaston Castle, which, along with its extensive grounds, is an interesting and delightful place to explore. Dale Abbey is another of the region's attractions, a now ruined abbey founded here by Augustinian monks in the 13th century.

In the valley of the River Trent, which runs through the southern part of the county, can be found many splendid stately homes, including Kedleston Hall and the eccentric Calke Abbey. The scenery affords ample opportunities to enjoy pleasant walks. This chapter also includes the western side of the region known as Erewash.

Derbyshire was at the forefront of modern thinking at the beginning of the Industrial Revolution. The chief inheritor of this legacy was Derby, and this city is still a busy industrial centre and home to the Industrial Museum. There are plenty of other places to visit in Derby, which is not, as is often supposed, the county town (that honour goes to Matlock).

PLACES OF INTEREST

BREADSALL

Breadsall began life as a small hamlet clustered around its Norman church. It is now known primarily as a residential suburb of Derby, with new estates that have sprung up around the original centre. The parish **Church of All Saints** possesses one of the most elegant steeples in the country, dating from the early 1300s. The south doorway is Norman and the tower and chancel date back to the 1200s. The church was burnt down by suffragettes in 1914 and carefully restored over the next two years. Inside there is a touching pieta from the late 1300s. This beautiful alabaster depiction of the Virgin Mary with the crucified Christ lying across her

knees was found under the floor of the church after another fire, and was restored to its present position by W D Caroe.

Opposite the west end of the church can be found **The Old Hall**, which has been part of village life for over 600 years. It was originally the manor house when the village was divided into the wards of Overhall and Netherhall. In later years it has been employed as a school, farmhouse, hunting box, public house, shop, joiner's shop and post office. It currently serves as a parish hall and is used by various village organisations.

As its name suggests, **Breadsall Priory** stands on the site of an Augustinian Priory

The Hidden Inns of the Heart of England

which was founded in the 13th century. The only part of the original building extant is an arch in the basement. Most of what stands today dates back to the Jacobean period, with many early 19th century additions and embellishments. Breadsall Priory was home to Erasmus Darwin (born in 1731) in his later years. A poet, physician and philosopher, he is better known as grandfather of Charles Darwin. He died in Breadsall in 1802, and there is a memorial to him in All Saints Church. The Priory is now a private hotel with golf course.

CALKE

In 1985 the National Trust bought **Calke Abbey**, a large Baroque-style mansion built in 1701 on the site of an Augustinian priory founded in 1133. However, it was not until 1989 that the Trust were able to open the house to the public, for this was no ordinary house at all. Dubbed "the house that time forgot" since the death of the owner, Sir Vauncy Harpur-Crewe in 1924 nothing had been altered in the mansion! In fact, the seclusion of the house and also the rather bizarre lifestyle of its inhabitants had left many rooms and objects untouched for over 100 years. There was even a spectacular 18th century Chinese silk state bed that had never been unpacked.

Today, the Trust has repaired the house and returned all 13,000 items to their original positions so that the Abbey now looks just as it did when it was bought in 1981. The attention to detail has been so great that none of the rooms has been redecorated. Visitors can enjoy the silver display and trace the route of 18th century

Calke Abbey

servants along the brewhouse tunnel to the house cellars. Calke Abbey stands in its own large park with gardens, a chapel and stables that are also open to the public. There are three walled gardens with their glasshouses, a restored orangery, vegetable garden, pheasant aviaries and the summer flower display within the unusual "auricular" theatre. Calke is home to lots of wildlife including Fallow Deer, weasels, stoats, Barn, Little and Tawny Owls, woodpeckers, Common Toads, butterflies and beetles.

DALE ABBEY

The village takes its name from the now ruined abbey that was founded here by Augustinian monks in the 13th century. Beginning life in a very humble manner, local legend has it that a Derbyshire baker came to the area in 1130, carved himself a niche in the sandstone and devoted himself to the way of the hermit. The owner of the land, Ralph FitzGeremunde, discovered the baker and was so impressed by the man's devotion that he bestowed on him the land and tithe rights to his mill in Borrowash. The sandstone cave and the romantic ruined 40 foot high window archway (all that now remains of the original abbey) are popular attractions locally and a walk around the village is both an interesting and pleasurable experience. Nearby **Hermit's Wood** is an ancient area of woodland with beech, ash, oak and lime trees. It is wonderful at any time of year, but particularly in the spring when the woodland floor is covered with a sea of bluebells.

The village **Church of All Saints**, which dates back to the mid 12th century, must be the only church in England which shares its roof with a farm. At one time the farm was also an inn; the adjoining door was blocked up in the 1820s to prevent swift transition from salvation to damnation. To the north of the village is the **Cat and Fiddle Windmill**, built in the 18th century and a fine example of the oldest type of mill. The stone roundhouse is capped with a box-like wooden structure which houses the machinery and which is fitted onto an upright post round which it can rotate to catch the wind.

DARLEY ABBEY

The Augustinian **Abbey of St Mary** was founded in 1137 and grew to become the most powerful abbey in Derbyshire and possibly in the whole of the Midlands. In 1538 the Abbey was surrendered as part of the Dissolution of the Monasteries. Sadly, few monasteries could have been so completely obliterated, so much so that what is now known as The Abbey public house is the only building remaining. The layout is of a simple medieval hall house and is thought to have been used as the Abbey's guest house for travellers and pilgrims during the 13th century.

DERBY

Essentially a commercial and industrial city, Derby's position, historically and geographically, has ensured that is has remained one of the most important and interesting cities in the area and, consequently, there is much for the visitor to see, whether from an architectural or historical point of view. There are, however, two things almost everyone, whether they have been to the city before or not, know of Derby: Rolls-Royce engines and **Royal Crown Derby** porcelain. When in 1906 Sir Henry Royce and the Hon C S Rolls joined forces and built the first Rolls-Royce (a Silver Ghost) at Derby, they built much more than just a motor car. Considered by many to be the best cars in the world, it is often said that the noisiest moving part in any Rolls-Royce is the dashboard clock! The home of Royal Crown Derby, any visit to the city would not be complete without a trip to

Derby Cathedral

the factory and its museum and shop. The guided tours offer an intriguing insight into the high level of skill required to create the delicate flower petals, hand gild the plates and to hand paint the Derby Dwarves.

The city's **Cathedral of All Saints** possesses a fine 16th century tower, the second highest perpendicular tower in England. The airy building was actually built in the 1720s by James Gibbs. Inside is a beautiful wrought-iron screen by Robert Bakewell and, among the splendid monuments, lies the tomb of Bess of Hardwick Hall. Originally Derby's Parish Church, it was given cathedral status in 1927. In the late 1960s the building was extended eastwards and the retrochoir, baldacchino and sacristy were added along with the screen.

One of Derby's most interesting museums is **Pickford House**, situated on the city's finest Georgian street at number 41. It is a Grade I listed building, erected in 1770 by the architect Joseph Pickford as a combined family home

Pickford House Museum, Derby

and place of work. Pickford House differs from the majority of grand stately homes; unlike most it does not have a wealth of priceless furniture and works or art. Instead, visitors are able to gain an insight into everyday middle-class life during the 1830s. Pickford House is the epitome of a late Georgian professional man's residence. There is an exciting programme of temporary exhibitions as well as other displays which deal with the history of the Friargate area and the importance of Joseph Pickford as a Midlands architect. The displays include a late

194

18th century dining room, breakfast rooms and an early 19th century kitchen and scullery. One special feature of Pickford House is the excellent collection of costumes, some dating back to the mid 1700s. A period 18th century garden is also laid out at the rear of the house.

Just a short walk from Pickford House is the **Industrial Museum**. What better place to house a museum devoted to the preservation of Derby's industrial heritage than the beautiful old **Silk Mill**; a building which stands on one of the most interesting sites in the country and which preceded Richard Arkwright's first cotton mill by over 50 years. The Silk Mill was badly damaged by fire in 1910 and had to be substantially rebuilt, however it still gives an impression of Lombe's original mill and tower. The whole of the ground floor galleries are devoted to the Rolls-Royce aero engine collection and illustrate the importance played by the aeronautical industrial in the city's history.

Since 1915 Derby has been involved with the manufacture of engines, and this section of the Museum displays model aircraft and sectioned engines demonstrating how aircraft fly. A specially designed annexe houses a complete RB211 Turbo-fan engine. On the first floor of the building there is an introduction to other Derbyshire industries with displays of lead and coal mining, iron founding, limestone quarrying, ceramics and brick making. There is also a railway engineering gallery complete with a signal box and displays on the growth of the railway works in Derby since the 1840s. Since the coming of the railways in 1839, the railway industry has also played a large part in the life of the City. Along with Rolls Royce, British Rail Engineering Ltd (BREL) is one of the largest employers in Derby and its development is well documented within the Museum and allows visitors to broaden their knowledge.

The **City Museum and Art Gallery** is also well worth visiting. Opened in 1879, it is the oldest of Derby's museums and the displays include natural history, archaeology and social history exhibits. One section of the museum is devoted to a Military Gallery and relates to Derby's local historical regiments. The walk-in First World War trench scene attempts to capture the experience of a night at the front. A ground floor gallery houses the city's superb collection of fine porcelain, manufactured in

Derby from the mid 18th century. The museum is also home to a collection of portraits, landscapes, scientific and industrial scenes by the local painter Joseph Wright, ARA. On the second floor of the Museum are temporary exhibition galleries. These change every three or four weeks and cover not only the museum's own collection but also travelling exhibitions representing an exciting range of arts and crafts both modern and traditional in a variety of styles and techniques. The **Derby Heritage Centre** has local history displays, tea room and souvenir shop housed in one of the city's oldest buildings. Another of the city's treats is the **Derbyshire Constabulary Memorabilia Museum**, which has a display of uniforms and weapons dating from the mid 17th century to the present day.

The ancient custom of well-dressing, more commonly associated with the villages and towns of northern Derbyshire and the Peak District, has found expression here in Derby (in Chester Green, at Mansfield Street Chapel) since 1982, on the Saturday before the late Spring Bank Holiday (Whitsun).

ELVASTON

Elvaston is gathered around the edge of the **Elvaston Castle** estate, home of the Earls of Harrington. The magnificent Gothic castle seen today replaced a 17th century brick and gabled manor house; part of the original structure can be seen on the end of the south front. Designed by James Wyatt, the castle was finished in the early 19th century but, unfortunately, the 3rd Earl died in 1829 and had little time to enjoy his new home.

It is, perhaps, the grounds which make Elvaston Castle famous today. They were originally laid out and designed for the 4th Earl by William Barron. Barron, who was born in Berwickshire in 1805, started work in 1830 on what, at first, appeared to be an impossible task. The 4th Earl wanted a garden 'second to none', but the land available, which had never been landscaped, was flat, water-logged and uninspiring with just two avenues of trees and a walled kitchen garden (but no greenhouses or hot houses). First draining the land, Barron then planted trees to offer shelter to more tender plants. From there the project grew. In order to stock the gardens, Barron began a programme of propagation of rarer tree species and, along with the tree-planting methods he developed specially to deal with Elvaston's problems, his fame spread. The gardens became a showcase of rare and interesting trees, many to be found nowhere else in Britain. Barron contined to work for the 5th Earl, but resigned in 1865 to live in nearby Barrowash and set up his own nursery. Now owned by Derby County Council, the gardens, after years of neglect, have been completely restored and the delights of the formal gardens, with their fine topiary, the avenues and the kitchen garden can be enjoyed by all visitors to the grounds, which are now a Country Park.

As well as fine formal gardens and the walled kitchen garden, there are gentle woodland walks and, of course, the man-made lake. However, no visit to Elvaston would be complete without a walk down to the Golden Gates. Erected in 1819 at the southern end of the formal gardens, the gates were brought from the Palace of Versailles by the 3rd Earl of Harrington. Little is known of the Gates' history, but they remain a fine monument and are the symbol of Elvaston. Around the courtyard of the castle can be found a restarant as well as an information centre and well-stocked gift shop. All manner of activities take place from the castle which can provide details.

ETWALL

This charming place has a fine range of Georgian buildings including some 17th century almshouses built by Sir John Port, the founder of nearby Repton College. The original site of **Etwall Hall**, where Sir John lived, is now the home of a large comprehensive school which bears his name. For a village that derived its name from "Eata's Well", it seems strange that Etwall only took up the custom of well-dressing recently and by chance. To mark the centenary of the village primary school, the teachers dressed a token well while the Women's Institute, with the help of people from two villages within the Peak District, dressed the only true well in Etwall, Town Well. This was in 1970 and the event, in mid May, was so successful that it is now an annual occasion and a total of eight wells are decorated.

As there is no long-standing tradition of well-dressing in the village the themes for the dressings are not the more usual Biblical subjects but have covered a wide range of stories and ideas including racial unity and the life and times of Sir John Port. Etwall is also the most southerly village to take part in the custom of well-dressing and its position, well below the harsh uplands of Derbyshire's Peak District, has ensured that there is always a good supply of flowers even though the dressing takes place late in spring.

HEANOR

The hub of this busy town centres on the market place, where the annual fair is held, as well as the twice weekly market (Fridays and Saturdays). Away from the bustle of the market are the **Memorial Gardens**. This peaceful setting always promises a magnificent spread of floral arrangements, herbaceous borders and shrubberies.

To the south of Heanor is the **Shipley Country Park**, on the estate of the now demolished Shipley Hall. In addition to its magnificent lake, the Country Park boasts over 600 acres of beautiful countryside which should keep even the most enthusiastic walker busy. Well known as both an educational and holiday centre, there are facilities for horse riding, cycling and fishing. This medieval estate was mentioned in the Domesday Book and, under the auspices of the

Shipley Country Park

Miller-Mundy family it became a centre for farming and coal-mining production during the 18th century. Restoration over the years has transformed former railways into wooded paths, reservoirs into peaceful lakes, and has re-established the once-flowering meadows and rolling hills, which had been destroyed by the colliery pits.

ILKESTON

The third largest town in Derbyshire, Ilkeston received its royal charter for a market and fair in 1252; both have continued to the present day. The history of the town, however, goes back to the days when it was an Anglo-Saxon hilltop settlement known as Tilchestune. Once a mining and lace-making centre, its history is told in the **Erewash Museum**, housed in a fine Georgian house on the High Street. Other fine examples of elegant 18th century houses can be found in East Street whilst, in Wharncliffe Road, there are period houses with art nouveau features.

Ilkeston commands fine wide views from the hillside above the valley of the **Erewash**, which here bounds the county. The town's church-crowned hilltop is a landmark that can be seen from far afield. This textile-manufacturing town in a colliery district has a fine church, which has undergon many changes since it was first erected in the 1300s. It is particularly notable for its window tracery, especially in the six windows in the older part of the church. A former tower and elegant spire were destroyed by storm in 1714; the tower only was rebuilt, to be succeeded by another on the old foundations in 1855. This tower was then moved westwards in 1907, at which time the nave was doubled in length. One intriguing feature it has retained throughout all these changes is its 13th century archway. The organ is also distinguished, in that it was built from one which came from a London church and is known to have been played by the great Mendelssohn himself.

KEDLESTON

Kedleston Hall has been the family seat of the Curzon family since the 12th century and, until it was taken over the by National Trust, it had the longest continuous male line in Derbyshire and one of the longest in the country. Nothing remains of the original medieval structure and little is known about it other than details recorded in a survey of 1657 which state that one of the doorways was over 500 years old and that there was also a large hall and a buttery. The present elegant mansion was built between 1759 and 1765 by Robert Adam and it remains one of the finest examples of his work. Since taking over the property, the National Trust have embarked on a major restoration programme and many of the stately home's rooms have been beautifully furnished with contemporary pieces; modern photographs of the family can be seen mingled with priceless paintings and other treasures such as Blue John

Kedleston Hall

vases. The three-mile Long Walk was created in 1776. Along with the house itself, there is the park with its lakes, boat house and fishing pavilion to explore.

One member of the family, George Nathaniel Curzon, was the Viceroy of India from 1899 to 1905. When he returned to England he brought back numerous works of art, carvings and ivories that can be seen on display in the **Indian Museum**. Though he was out in India for some time, George would not have missed his family home, as Government House in Calcutta is a copy of Kedleston Hall. Once back in England, George did not have much time to enjoy his lands: he became a member of Lloyd George's inner War Cabinet, which met over 500 times during the First World War.

Nearby All Saints' Church, the only part of the village that was allowed to remain when the rest was moved in 1765 to make way for the landscaped park around the Hall, dates from the 12th century. It is of an unusual design for Derbyshire in that it is cruciform in shape and the tower is placed in the centre. Inside are Curzon monuments dating from 1275 to the present day; the only brass in the church is to Richard Curzon, who died in 1496.

MAPPERLEY

This historic village was first granted a market charter in 1267 and, though its old church was demolished due to mining subsidence, the modern church has some interesting stained glass windows. In the heart of Derbyshire mining country, any stroll from the village centre will take the walker past industrial remains.

To the south of Mapperley is the former branch line of the Midland Railway which served Mapperley Colliery as well as the old raised track which is all that remains of an old tramway which ran from the Blue Fly Shaft of

West Hallam Pit to the **Nutbrook Canal** further east. The Canal, which opened in 1796, carried coal from the pits at Shipley to the ironworks at Stanton and beyond. Only just over 4 miles long, the Canal had some 13 locks but it fell into disuse after the Second World War.

REPTON

This village, by the tranquil waters of the River Trent, is steeped in history. The first mention of Repton came in the 7th century when it was established as the capital of the Saxon kingdom of Mercia. A monastery, housing both monks and nuns, was founded here sometime after 653 but the building was sacked by the Danes in 874. A battleaxe, now on display in the school museum, was excavated a little distance from the church. It had apparently lain undisturbed for well over 1,000 years.

The parish **Church of St Wystan** is famous for its Anglo-Saxon chancel and crypt, but it also contains many of the major styles of medieval architecture. When the chancel and part of the nave were enlarged in 1854, the original Anglo-Saxon columns were moved to the 14th century porch. The crypt claims to be one of the oldest intact Anglo-Saxon buildings in England. The burial place of the Kings of Mercia, including St Wystan in 850, the crypt was rediscovered by chance in 1779 by a workman who was digging a hole for a grave in the chancel floor.

The ancient **Cross**, still at the central crossroads in the village, has been the focal point of life here for centuries and it has also stood at the heart of the Wednesday market. Right up until the late 19th century a Statutes Fair, for the hiring of farm labourers and domestics, was also held here at Michaelmas.

Parts of an Augustinian priory, founded in 1170, are incorporated in the buildings of **Repton College**, itself founded in 1557. Sir John Port had specifically intended the College to be a grammar school for the local poor children of Etwall, Repton and Burnaston. These intentions have somewhat deviated over the passing years and now Repton stands as one of the foremost public schools in the country. Interestingly, two of its headmasters, Dr Temple and Dr Fisher, went on to become Archbishops of Canterbury, while Dr Ramsey was a pupil at the school under Dr Fisher's guiding light. Film buffs will recognise the 14th century gatehouse and causeway, as they featured in both film

versions of the popular story *Goodbye, Mr Chips.*

Just to the west of the village is **Foremark Hall**, built by Robert Adam in the 1762 for the Burdett family. It is now a preparatory school for Repton College.

RIPLEY

Once a typical small market town, Ripley expanded dramatically during the Industrial Revolution when great use was made of the iron, clay and coal deposits found nearby. The town's Butterley ironworks, founded in 1792 by a group of men which included renowned engineer Benjamin Outram, created the roof for London's St Pancras station. Outram's even more famous son Sir James enjoyed an illustrious career that saw him claimed Bayard of India, and earned him a resting place in Westminster Abbey.

The village church was erected in 1820 the stem to tide of rebellion and "irreligion" that swept the area in the hard years after the Battle of Waterloo, when the local weavers and stockingers rebelled against their harsh living conditions. The insurrection saw three rebels brought to the scaffold and drove some into exile, and became a *cause celebre* throughout the nation.

SUDBURY

This is the estate village to **Sudbury Hall**, the late 17th century mansion and home of a branch of the Vernon family who lived at Haddon Hall. The house is intriguing, the garden restful. Gifted to the National Trust in 1967, the Hall is an unexpected mixture of architectural styles. A splendid example of a house of Charles II's time, inside Sudbury Hall contains elaborate plasterwork and murals throughout, wood carvings by Grinling Gibbons, and some fine examples of mythological paintings by

Sudbury Hall

Laguerre. Of particular interest is the **Museum of Childhood** which is situated in the servants' wing and provides a fascinating insight into the lives of children down the ages. Fascinating displays range from a wealthy family's nursery and an Edwardian schoolroom to a "chimney climb" and coal tunnel for the adventurous. The formal gardens and meadows lead to the tree-fringed lake. Wildlife abounds, including Kestrels, Grey Herons, Grass Snakes, dragonflies, newts, frogs, toads, Little and Tawny Owls and woodpeckers. Special events are held throughout the year.

SWARKESTONE

Excavations in the village of Swarkestone, at Lowes Farm, led to the discovery that the district was occupied in the Bronze Age and also in Saxon times. This small village has also been, quite literally, a turning point in history. The **Swarkestone Bridge**, with its seven arches and three-quarter-mile long causeway, crosses the River Trent. In 1745, during the second Jacobite Rebellion, the advance guard of Bonnie Prince Charlie reached the Bridge and, had they managed to cross the River at this point, they would have faced no other natural barriers on their 120-mile march to London. As it transpired, the army retreated and fled north, Bonnie Prince Charlie managed to escape and the Jacobite Rebellion was no more.

Legend has it that the original bridge at Swarkestone was built by two daughters of the Harpur family in the early 13th century. The girls were celebrating their joint betrothals when their fiancés were summoned to a barons' meeting across the river. While they were away torrential rain fell, flooding the river, and the two young men drowned as they attempted to ford the raging torrent on their return. The girls built the bridge as a memorial to their lovers. Both girls later died impoverished and unmarried.

Black Horse Inn & Restaurant | 199

Burton Road,
Coton in the Elms,
Swadlincote,
Derbyshire
DE12 8HJ
Tel: 01283 763614

Directions:

Coton in the Elms
is 5 miles south of
Burton on Trent,
on an unmarked
road which can be
reached either from
the A444 or the
A38

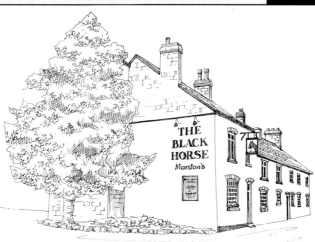

Step inside the **Black Horse Inn and Restaurant**, and you'll be greeted with a warm, welcoming interior which is spotlessly clean and gleaming. Within the pub area, the furniture is dark and comfortable, and the ceiling has stout beams. The walls are half panelled in dark, attractive wood, while above, they are cream coloured and half timbered. In addition, the beamed ceilings are low and the copper and brass ornaments positively sparkle! If you think this means good old English tradition and good service, then you're not far wrong!

The inn is set in the picturesque village of Coton in the Elms, in the heart of some lovely countryside. Opposite runs a small stream, where ducks swim or parade along the banks. It is a red brick building set at the end of a short terrace dating from the early 19th century. Craig Marsland has been running the place for a few months now, though he has had over four years's experience in the trade. He has great plans for the inn, hoping to add to its many attractions and making it a comfortable, welcoming inn which is popular with both locals and visitors. There's a dining area which seats 32, and the food is excellent. It is only available at lunchtime on Sunday at present, though this will change in the future. With its roasts and choice of other meats, it is especially recommended, though you may have to book. The bar is well stocked, and you can have Marston's Pedigree (a real ale), plus Bank's Smooth, Carlsberg, Kronenberg, Strongbow and Guinness.

There's a no-smoking area, a beer garden, and children are welcome. There's a function suite which can be hired, and behind the inn is a substantial car park.

Opening hours: 15.00-23.00 Monday-Thursday and 12.00-23.00 Friday-Sunday

Food: Sunday lunches from 12.00-16.00 only at present; there is a choice of roasts and meats

Credit cards: Cash only at present

Accommodation: None

Entertainment: Occasionally; ring for details

Facilities: Car parking; beer garden; no-smoking area

Local Places of Interest/Activities: Calke Abbey (NT) 9 miles; Staffordshire Regiment Museum 7 miles; Staunton Harold Church (NT)

Internet/Website:
www:midlandspubs.co.uk/derbyshire
www:blackhousecoton@aol.com

200

The Bulls Head

1 Woodville Road,
Hartshorne, Swadlincote,
Derbyshire DE11 7ET
Tel: 01283 215299
Fax: 01283 221380

Directions:

Take the A514 north from its junction with the A511, near Swadlincote. Hartshorne is a mile along this road

The village of Hartshorne is a small village nestling in some delightful country-side. Near its centre is **The Bulls Head**, an old inn that is housed in a building full of history and character. The elegant and well proportioned frontage is Georgian, while some of the ground floor at the rear is Elizabethan, dating from about 1570-1600. Christine and Clive Powis have been mine hosts since 1988, and have created a delightful inn which is full of character and warmth. It's a friendly place, and the interior is every bit as attractive as the outside. It brims over with character. Think of low, dark-beamed ceilings, exposed brick walls, country style furniture, and a wealth of shining brass and old prints adorning the walls. Think of subdued lighting, soft carpeting and leaded windows.

Think also of good food, which uses local fresh produce wherever possible, and which is keenly priced. The Bulls Head serves lunches and evening meals, and so popular is the place that you are advised to book if you want to eat on Friday or Saturday evenings or Sunday lunchtime. The menu carries a wide range of dishes, from succulent fillet and rum steaks to salads, chicken curry and grilled trout. Plus there are great starters, wonderful sweets and a good selection of vegetarian dishes. There's also a specials board that changes daily. The bar carries a good selection of drinks, from real ales such as Top Hat (and a rotating guest ale) to Burtonwood Smooth, lager, stout and cider. And if it's wine you're after, you're sure to find a suitable bottle of something from the small but comprehensive wine list. This is an inn that is renowned for its hospitality and friendliness. It's popular with locals, and people come from miles around to sample the food. The reason? It's simple - it offers good food, good drink, and a traditional English welcome within a traditional English pub!

Opening hours: 11.00-15.00 and 18.30-23.00 Monday to Saturday; 12.00-16.00 and 18.30-22.30 on Sunday

Food: Lunches are served from 12.00-14.00 every day except Sunday, when it is 12.00-16.00; evening meals are served from 18.30-21.00 seven days a week

Credit cards: All credit cards except American Express

Accommodation: Four en suite rooms at reasonable rates; a traditional English breakfast is included in the price

Facilities: Car park

Local Places of Interest/Activities: Calke Abbey (NT) 3 miles; Staunton Harold Church (NT) 3 miles; Donnington Park (motor racing) 7 miles

The Castle Hotel | 201

Station Road,
Hatton,
Derbyshire
DE65 5DW
Tel: 01283 813396
Fax: 01283 520649

Directions:

The village of
Hatton is on the
A511, one mile
south of its junction
with the A50 and 8
miles east of
Uttoxeter

Just north of historic Tutbury, with its castle and Norman church, you'll find the village of Hatton. And on its the southern edge, and next to the bridge across the scenic River Dove, is a fine hostelry, **The Castle Hotel**. It's a substantial building in old brick which dates from about 1870, and offers a warm welcome to anyone who calls in for a quiet drink, a meal or a place to stay. It was built as a hotel, and retains many of the original features, though the whole place has been modernised to reflect today's demand for high standards of comfort and service.

This is a family run inn, and under its owner Mike Freeman, it has established a fine reputation in the area. The main lounge is especially comfortable and welcoming, having been recently refurbished to an exceptionally high standard. The eight en suite rooms have also been refurbished, and are fully equipped with TVs and tea and coffee making facilities. Two of them even have a swirl pool bath in the bathroom! There's also a bar, and a spacious restaurant which serves delicious and beautifully cooked meals. This restaurant has an extensive a la carte menu which includes everything from tasty steaks to catfish. If it's a lunch or bar snack you're after, there's a popular specials board in the bar. Wine is available, as is a fine range of drinks at the bar. Choose from 4 real ales, or a selection of draught bitters, mild, stout, lager and cider.

In 1831, a hoard of 100,000 coins was discovered in the field between the hotel and the River Dove. You won't find any ancient coins nowadays - what you'll find instead is a great inn that offers everyone a warm and friendly welcome!

Opening times: Open lunchtimes and evenings

Food: Served lunchtimes and evenings; a la carte menu in restaurant in the evening

Credit cards: All the major cards

Accommodation: 8 en-suite rooms

Entertainment: Occasional quizzes (ring for details)

Facilities: Car park; beer garden with occasional barbecues in summer

Local Places of Interest/Activities: Tutbury within walking distance; Burton-upon-Trent (historic town) 5 miles; Sudbury Hall (NT) 4 miles; Uttoxeter (historic town with horse racing) 8 miles

202 The Coach and Horses

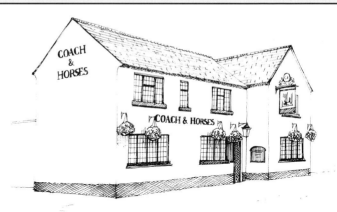

1 Victoria Road,
Draycott,
Derbyshire
DE72 3PS
Tel: 01332 872483

Directions:

Draycott is on the A6005, halfway between Derby and Long Eaton

Draycott is a former lace making village. Draycott Mill, with its green capped clock tower, was built in 1888, and dominates the place. It is now an electrical component factory. Also in Draycott is **The Coach and Horses**, a former coaching inn which dates from around 1736. It is a fine old building, with many period features, and in charge for over four years are husband and wife team Paul and Caroline Bainbridge. Running the inn is their first venture in the licensing trade, and they've managed to turn the inn into one of the most popular in the area.

The interior is welcoming and cozy. The old, thick walls means that it's warm in winter and cool in summer, making it an excellent place for a meal or drink. The bar offers two real ales - Marston's Pedigree and a rotating guest ale, plus beers, stout and cider. There's Caffrey's, Boddington's, Whitbread Best Scotch, Heineken and Heineken Export, Stella, Labatt's, Guinness and Strongbow. No one could possibly be disappointed with that impressive range! And, of course, there's a fine choice of spirits and wines.

The food can best be described as traditional and nutritious, with all the dishes being cooked on the premises. There's no fast food here - just honest to goodness value for money and fresh ingredients! You can choose from the printed menu, or from the specials blackboard. There are also tea time specials, and in the summer months there are occasional barbecues in the beer garden. But beware - the Coach and Horses is a popular place, so if you want to eat on a Sunday, you should book in advance.

Opening times: Open all day, every day

Food: Good, honest tasty food is served from 12.00-15.00 and 17.00-20.00 Monday to Thursday; 12.00-20.00 on Saturday; 12.00-16.00 on Sunday; there are also tea time specials

Credit cards: Most credit cards accepted except American Express

Accommodation: None

Entertainment: Karaoke and a live artist alternating every Saturday at 21.00; Sunday: national jumbo quiz; phone for further details

Facilities: Beer garden; skittle alley (open in summer months); children's play area; large screen TV; small pet's corner

Local Places of Interest/Activities: American Adventure (theme park) 7 miles; Shipley Country Park 8 miles; Derby (historic city) 5 miles; Nottingham (historic city) 9 miles; Elvaston Castle Country Park 2 miles

The Holly Bush Inn | 203

Main Street,
Church Broughton,
Derbyshire
DE6 5AS
Tel: 01283 585345

Directions:

Take the A50 east from Uttoxeter for 7 miles, then turn north onto the minor road for Church Broughton

Husband and wife Brian and Jean James have been tenants of **The Holly Bush Inn** for the last 17 years, and have 40 years experience in the trade. It sits in the picturesque village of Church Broughton, which has the beautiful 14th century church of St Michael as its main feature. The inn is a substantial red brick building with gables that are half timbered near the top. At one time it housed three cottages, and became an inn over 200 years ago.

Over the years, Brian and Jean have worked hard to make the Holly Bush Inn one of the best in the area it is popular with both locals and visitors alike, and offers a real Derbyshire welcome to anyone who steps over its threshold. The inside is smartly decorated, and has a warm, handsome bar where a quiet drink can be savoured and appreciated in comfort. The dining room area has country style furniture, subdued lighting and deep carpeting. It can seat up to 40 people in comfort.

There's a full and varied menu of traditional food on offer, and you can order dishes such as delicious home made steak pie and lasagna. Everything cooked on the premises, using ingredients that are fresh and, wherever possible, local. Or you could go along on a Sunday, and have a traditional three course lunch for a set price. For evening meals and the Sunday roast, you should book to avoid disappointment. The bar offers Marston's pedigree (a real ale) as well as Banks Bitter, Stella, Carlsberg, Guinness and Scrumpy Jack Cider.

The Holly Bush is the hub of village life in Church Broughton, and is a friendly and extremely pleasant hostelry, popular with both the locals visitors. If you pay a visit for a drink or meal, you won't be disappointed.

Opening times: Open every lunchtime and evening

Food: Served Monday to Saturday 12.00-13.45 and 18.30-21.15; Sunday: 12.00-13.45 (no food served on Sunday evening)

Credit cards: Cash and cheques only at present

Accommodation: None

Entertainment: Occasional entertainment; phone for details

Facilities: Car park; beer garden; patio

Local Places of Interest/Activities: Sudbury Hall (NT) 3 miles; Darley Moor (motor cycle racing) 6 miles; Kedleston Hall (NT) 8 miles

204 The Hollybush Inn

Hollybush Lane,
Makeney, Milford,
Derbyshire DE56 0RX
Tel: 01332 841729

Directions:

Take the A6 south from Belper and as you enter the village of Milford, turn left before a right hand bend onto a road signposted Makeney; follow the signs for the Hollybush Inn

A lovely name for a lovely old inn. **The Hollybush Inn** is one of the best known hostelries in the whole of Derbyshire, and is housed in a sturdy yet captivating stone built building, parts of which date from the 18th century. However, it has a timeless quality about it, and looks as if it has been part of the landscape for centuries. At one time it formed part of a farm owned by the Strutt family, who were lords of the manor. Now, thank goodness, it is a pub, sitting peacefully by the roadside ready to offer a warm, traditional welcome to traveller and local alike.

The inside looks as if it came from a film set. Nothing could be this picturesque, surely? But everything about it is real - the solid beams, the bare stone walls, the open log fire, the original blackened range and the gleaming horse brasses. The landlord is John Bilbie, and he has presided over the place since June 1979, making sure it loses none of its olde worlde atmosphere or period fittings. This is a real ale pub, with at least eight real ales on offer, including Ruddles County, Marston's pedigree, and Brain's Mild. And if that's not all, there are five rotating guest ales from all over. You can also order lagers, Guinness, Dry Blackthorn and Scrumpy Old Rosie, a cider which is still served from a container in the old way. Twice a year, the Hollybush Inn has a beer festival, when no less than 12 real ales can be sampled. Good, traditional English fare is served at lunchtime, including roasts, fish, pork pies and so on. You can chose from the blackboard, and children are welcome.

Think of an English inn that is steeped in history and tradition, and you could be thinking of the Hollybush Inn. It has a charm and a timelessness that will appeal to everyone, and if you pay it a visit, one thing's for certain - you'll be back!

Opening times: Open at lunchtimes and evenings Monday to Thursday, and all day Friday to Sunday

Food: Good, honest traditional food served every lunchtime

Credit cards: Cash and cheque only at present

Accommodation: None

Entertainment: Twice yearly beer festival;

phone for dates

Facilities: Car park

Local Places of Interest/Activities: American Adventure (theme park) 6 miles; Belper North Mill 2 miles; Shipley Country Park 6 miles; Kedleston Hall (NT) 3 miles; Denby Potteries 4 miles

Navigation Inn

116 Spring Cottage,
Overseal,
Derbyshire DE12 6ND
Tel: 01283 760493

Directions:
Leave the M42 at
Junction 11 and travel
north west along the
A44 for three miles. The
inn is on the B5003, on
the outskirts of Overseal

The Navigation Inn
stands close to a canal,
on the outskirts of a
small, scenic village. Built
of warm red brick , it
dates back to the late
18th century, and is a popular place both for visitors and locals. Under the personal supervision of local husband and wife team Wayne and Stephanie Granger for over two years, it
has gained a great reputation as a place where customers can enjoy a quiet drink, snack, or
meal. This is no company-owned inn, but a real family run establishment that offers traditional service, coupled with efficiency and friendliness.

Inside is warm and cozy, with old style furniture and beamed ceilings. The place is
immaculate, with subdued lighting and upholstered benches which are soft and inviting.
The purpose built restaurant, with its half timbered walls painted a soft cream, can seat up
to 90 people (with high chairs available), and there's an extensive Á la carte menu offering
a range of traditional dishes made on the premises from fresh ingredients. Portions are
ample, and represent good, old fashioned value for money. A carvery is available on Tuesday, Wednesday, Thursday and Sunday lunchtime. And so popular are meals on Saturday
and Sunday evenings that you're well advised to book in advance. To accompany your
meal, there's a small but lively wine list, or you can sample one of the three real ales that are
always on offer, or the rotating guest ales. There are also two draught lagers and draught
ciders to choose from, plus Guinness Mansfield Smooth. There's a special no smoking area,
and children are welcome. Outside there's even a play area for them, plus a beer garden and
a car park which can accommodate up to 100 cars.

Opening hours: Open all day

Food: Served up until 21.00; extensive Á la
carte menu, plus a lunchtime carvery on
Tuesday-Thursday and Sunday; no food served
on Monday.

Credit cards: All credit cards

Accommodation: None

Facilities: Car parking; beer garden; childrens'
play area

Local Places of Interest/Activities:
Donnington Park (motor racing) 10 miles;
Burton upon Trent (historic town) 6 miles;
Twycross Zoo 6 miles; Donnington le Heath
(13th century manor house) 8 miles

Internet/Website:
www.the-navigation-inn.co.uk
e-mail: enquiries@the-navigation-inn.co.uk

206

New Inn

2 High Street,
Woodville, Swadlincote,
Derbyshire DE11 7EH
Tel: 01283 217553

Directions:

On the A511, between
Burton on Trent and
Ashby de la Zouch and
two miles from
Swadlincote

This inn is a substantial
building right on
Woodville's main street,
built from old, warm
bricks that seem just right
for this small village. It dates from the late 18th century, and was the first pub bought by the
brewers Bass in 1843. The windows are leaded, there's a small, wooden porch, and altogether
it has a pleasing, welcoming aspect. The locals already know of charms of **The New Inn**, and
many visitors are now discovering them as well. Inside is beautifully laid out, with a carpeted
dining area that has flowers on the tables, a soft carpet on the floor and curtained windows
that add to the cozy atmosphere. It will soon be extended to seat up to 85 people.

Here you'll find the traditional English inn - warm in winter and cool in summer, with a
friendly clientele and a spotlessly clean interior. The place has been in the hands of the
Rogers family for over 26 years, so there is a feeling of continuity about it. The present
licensees, Glen and Michelle Rogers, have only been in charge for under two years now, and
already they're making their mark. The bar stocks a wide range of beers, spirits and wines.
There's Bass real ale, Worthington, Tetley's Smooth, Guinness, a range of lagers and two
ciders on offer. If you're looking for a bar lunch, or an evening meal, then there's a comprehensive menu that offers reasonably priced dishes with good honest portions.There's also a
Sunday carvery, and so popular is it that you should book for it (and for a Saturday evening
meal as well) in advance. Children are welcome if you are eating. When the new dining area
is ready, food will be served all day.

The New Inn has one unusual feature - it's own bowling green, and there is nothing
nicer on a summer evening than, glass in hand, watching a bowl rolling towards the jack. If
you play a bit yourself, you could even get a game!

Opening hours: 12.00-15.30 and 18.00-23.00
Monday to Thursday; 12.00-16.00 and 18-
23.00 on Friday; 12.00-23.00 on Saturday;
12.00-16.00 and 19.00-22.30 on Sunday

Food: Wednesday to Sunday (private
functions only on Monday and Tuesday); bar
lunches: 12.00-14.30; evening meals: 18.30-
22.00; Sunday carvery: two sittings, at 12.00
and 14.00

Credit cards: All credit cards

Accommodation: None

Entertainment: Quiz machine; darts; crib;
dominoes

Facilities: Bowling green; beer garden; patio
area

Local Places of Interest/Activities: Calke
Abbey (NT) 9 miles; Staffordshire Regiment
Museum 10 miles; Staunton Harold Church
(NT) 6 miles Donnington Park (motor racing)
10 miles

The Punchbowl 207

43 The Village,
West Hallam,
near Ilkeston,
Derbyshire
DE7 6ER
Tel: 0115 932 0050

Directions:

Take the A609 west
from Ilkeston for two
miles, then turn
south onto an
unmarked road for
West Hallam, which
is just under a mile
along the road

Stephen and Michele Gascoigne have been mine hosts at **The Punchbowl** since 1998, and have turned the hostelry into a charming and welcoming establishment that is popular with both locals and visitors alike. Originally a farmhouse dating from 1754, it later became a coaching inn. The former cow sheds were converted into a comfortable dining area in 1989.

The interior is clean and welcoming, with walls painted a restful peach and turquoise, and a ceiling that has picturesque exposed beams. This is the kind of inn where it is a positive pleasure to stretch out your legs and enjoy a relaxing drink, or sit down to a well cooked and presented meal. It's also an inn that is child friendly

The food is marvellous - tasty, beautifully cooked on the premises and well presented, with ample and filling portions. There are bar meals at lunchtime or in the evenings, and full meals in the dining room from 19.00-21.00. The speciality of the house is home made steak and kidney pie, and you can also choose from fish, chicken, beef or pork. If you want something a bit spicier, you can order chilli or rogan josh! If you want to eat in the restaurant, it's as well to book in advance to avoid disappointment. The Punchbowl is renowned for the range of real ales behind its well stocked bar. You can have Marston's Pedigree, Burton, Tetley or a rotating guest ale, plus a full range of beers, cider and stout such as Tetley Smooth, Carlsberg, Stella, Dry Blackthorn, Guinness, Murphy's or Ansell's mild. Plus, of course, there is a good range of wines and spirits.

The Punchbowl is an inn that combines the best of traditional values with friendly service and value for money. If you visit the place, you'll get a warm welcome from Stephen and Michele.

Opening times: Open every day at lunchtimes and in the evenings

Food: Bar meals are served between 12.00-14.00 and 18-20.30; the restaurant opens at 19.00 and closes at 21.00

Credit cards: Most credit cards accepted

Accommodation: None

Facilities: Beer garden; children's play area

Local Places of Interest/Activities: American Adventure (theme park) 1 mile; Shipley Country Park 1 mile; Kedleston Hall (NT) 7 miles; Ilkeston (historic town) 3 miles

208

The Red Admiral

Alfreton Road,
Codnor,
Derbyshire
DE5 9QY
Tel: 01773 745873

Directions:

Take the A38 north out of Derby, then after 8 miles turn right at a roundabout onto the A610. Codnor is three miles along this road.

You can't miss **The Red Admiral**. It sits within the village of Codnor, and has a striking exterior. Built in 1873, it is a fine mixture of Tudor and Victorian, with a red tiled roof, and baskets and window boxes of colourful flowers everywhere. Under the personal supervision of mother and daughter team of Anne Greensmith and Julie Walker, it has earned the reputation of being the inn to visit in Codnor.

Inside, a definite effort has been made to create a snug and cozy ambience, though there is still plenty of space to stretch out and relax as you enjoy a well-earned drink. The floors are carpeted, the tables are of oak, and the seating is well-upholstered and comfortable. All in all, it is a lovely example of a semi-rural English pub that puts its clientele first.

There is an excellent range of beers, including cask-conditioned, and an extensive and excellent wine list. There is a popular beer garden, and a conservatory restaurant. The food is locally sourced wherever possible, and beautifully cooked and presented. From quick bar snacks to imaginative dishes on the extensive evening menu, there's something for everyone. In fact, it's the Red Admiral's proud boast that it tries to give a dining experience to remember.

The inn sits close to both Derby and Nottingham, which can easily be reached by car within twenty minutes, and the historic towns of Mansfield and Chesterfield (with its crooked -spired church) are a short distance to the north.

Opening Hours: 12.00-23.00 Monday to Saturday and 12.00-22.30 on Sunday

Food: Lunches are served from 12.00-1500 in the bar and conservatory.

Credit Cards: All major cards with the exception of Amex.

Accommodation: None

Facilities: Beer garden; conservatory restau-

rant; upstairs restaurant (evenings only).

Entertainment: Regular quiz nights; live music every month on a Saturday evening.

Local Places of Interest: Midlands Railway Centre: 2 miles; Newstead Abbey 8 miles; Denby Pottery Visitors Centre 2 miles; Kedleston Hall (NT) 8 miles; Shipley Country Park 4 miles; American Adventure Theme Park 5 miles.

Red Lion | 209

28 Main Street,
Linton,
Derbyshire
DE12 6PZ
Tel: 01283 761396

Directions:

Linton sits off the
A444 on a minor
road, half way
between Burton on
Trent and Junction
11 on the M42

This is a lovely old inn, set well back from the road, with whitewashed walls and hanging baskets which, during the summer, overflow with colour. It dates from the mid 1700s, and was once three (some say four) old cottages. It's a popular place, not just with the locals, but with walkers and ramblers, who come to this part of Derbyshire to enjoy the open country-side and beautiful scenery. Philip and Caroline Shipley took over in 1999, and set about creating an inn that brims with character and friendliness.

The Red Lion serves food which is honest, good and traditional. There's a comprehensive menu, plus a daily specials board. The meals are always tasty, keenly priced, well cooked and presented. Nearly everything is prepared on the premises, and wherever possible, Philip and Caroline have gone for fresh, local produce. You can eat at lunchtime or in the evenings, plus there's a traditional Sunday lunch (not served in the evenings), and there's a wide range of drinks to accompany your meal. There's a good selection of real ales such as Bass and Pedigree, plus mild, Worthington's Creamflow, Stella and Carling lager, Strongbow cider and Guinness. The wine list is small but select, and all have been carefully chosen to complement the dishes on the menu.

The Red lion is one of those English pubs that has managed to keep its traditional atmosphere and character. But Philip and Caroline have also made sure that modern concepts such as efficiency, good service and value for money haven't been sacrificed! It is snug, warm and friendly in winter, and cool and welcoming in the summer months. You can have a quiet drink in the comfortable bar, or, when the temperatures rise, you can take your drink out into the large beer garden or attached patio.

Opening hours: Monday to Thursday: 11.30-15.30 and 18.00-23.00; Friday and Saturday: 11.30-23.00; Sunday: 12.00-15.30 and 18.30-22.30

Food: Served is served from 12.00-14.30 and from 18.00-21.30; Sunday lunches are only served between 12.00-14.30

Credit cards: most cards accepted

Accommodation: None

Facilities: Car parking; beer garden; patio

Local Places of Interest/Activities: Calke Abbey (NT) 7 miles; Ashby de la Zouch (historic town) 5 miles; Twycross Zoo 7 miles

210 Spotted Cow Inn

12 Town Street,
Holbrook,
Derbyshire
DE56 0TA
Tel: 01332 881200
Fax: 01332 881936

Directions:

Holbrook is 5 miles north of Derby city centre on a minor off the A38

The picturesque **Spotted Cow Inn** lies at the heart of the village of Holbrook, north of Derby. It's built of stone and red brick and dates from the 18th century. The layout of the inn gives it a sort of courtyard effect, and it blends in well with the rest of the village, which is very old and picturesque. The interior has recently been refurbished, but the place has lost none of its period charm. There are stone floors, reclaimed timber beams and a wealth of gleaming brass and copper to add those finishing touches. In the winter months, open fires throw a cozy glow around the place, and in summer it remains cool and comfortable, no matter what the temperatures are outside.

It is run by Graham Thomas and Donna Coombes, and together they have created the perfect English pub – a cozy place where you can escape from the pressures of modern living while enjoying a drink or a meal. There's a full à la carte menu and a Sunday carvery, and the recently modernised restaurant seats 96 in absolute comfort. The chef has a great reputation in the surrounding area, and the menu he has put together reflect this, with many dishes that are sure to please, such as fillet steak, rack of lamb, pork medallions with black pudding, and even ostrich medallions.

There is a superb wine list, of course, with something to suit everyone, and altogether this is the perfect spot for a superb lunch or a celebratory dinner. And why not treat yourself to a drink form the bar as well? You can choose from no less than four real ales – two resident and two guest, plus draught bitter, cider, stout, lager or mild. If you fancy a brandy after your meal, there's a fine selection of spirits, or you can stick to soft drinks if you're driving.

Opening times: Monday to Saturday 11.30-15.00 and 18.00-23.00; Sunday: 12.00-16.00 and 19.00-22.30

Food: Lunches served between 12.00-14.00 and dinners served between 18.30 and 21.00

Credit cards: All major cards accepted except American Express and Diners

Accommodation: None

Entertainment: Quiz every Tuesday evening

with a cash jackpot

Facilities: Car park; beautiful gardens; beer garden and summer barbecues

Local Places of Interest/Activities: Derby (historic city) 6 miles; American Adventure (theme park) 5 miles; Shipley Country Park 5 miles; Kedleston Hall (NT) 4 miles

Internet/website:
e-mail: reservations@spottedcowinn.co.uk
website: www.spottedcowinn.co.uk

The Swan Inn

211

49 Main Street, Milton,
Derbyshire DE65 6EF
Tel: 01283 703188

Directions:

Take the B5008 north from its junction with the A511, near Burton on Trent; Milton is one mile beyond Repton

This is a well proportioned red brick inn, painted white, with wonderful shutters on the ground floor that give it an almost continental air. The hamlet of Milton sits in one of the most historical areas in the Midlands. Close by is the picturesque village of Repton, which at one time was the capital of the Saxon kingdom of Mercia, and it was here that King Penda first introduced Christianity to his people. Nowadays it is best known for its public school, and the place is well worth exploring. Stella and Roger Salt took over as tenants a few months ago. It was a real love affair for them, as they lived across the road from **The Swan Inn**, and used it as their local for 30 years. They sadly watched as it became run down, until eventually they decided to take over the place themselves. Now, in their first venture in the licensing trade, they've set it back on an even keel, though they admit that there's still a lot of work to be done. Inside is spick and span, with subdued wall lighting, white walls, and highly polished, comfortable furniture. It's a real village hostelry where children are welcome, popular with both locals and visitors, and Stella and Roger are determined to keep it that way. No inappropriate "improvements" for them; instead there's a commitment to tradition (framed prints on the wall, open fires, etc.) and old style hospitality.

The bar has a railway theme, and two real ales are on offer - Marston's Pedigree and a rotating guest ale. There's also lager, Guinness and Strongbow, plus the usual wines and spirits. No food is served at present, though Stella and Roger have plans to introduce meals at lunchtime and in the evenings. At present, afternoon teas and ice cream etc. is available, though you should ring for details. And if you need a conversation opener during your visit, ask about the "Milton Scud", a piece of modern folklore dating from the Gulf War! It's commemorated within a frame behind the bar.

Opening times: Open lunchtimes and evenings, with occasional all day opening (ring for details)

Food: No food at present, though it will be introduced in the near future; tea, coffee and ice creams available occasionally in the afternoon; ring for details

Credit cards: Cash and cheque only at present

Accommodation: None

Entertainment: Occasional entertainment; pub games such as pool, darts, crib and chess (ring for details)

Facilities: Car park; beer garden; children's play area

Local Places of Interest/Activities: Repton 1 mile; Sudbury Hall 11 miles; Tutbury Castle 7 miles; Derby 6 miles; Melbourne 4 miles; Calke Abbey, Ticknal 3½ miles; Foremark Resevoir 1 mile

212 The Three Horseshoes

Morley Smithy,
Derbyshire
DE7 6DF
Tel: 01332 831294

Directions:

Take the A608 north from Derby to Heanor; the inn sits adjacent to the road about 4 miles from the city centre

This is a clean, attractive roadside establishment that is popular with both locals and tourists, and welcomes children. It's a lovely inn, compact and warm in winter and cool and welcoming in summer, with whitewashed walls and a charming porch over the door. Though it looks much older, the present building dates from only 1914. It was built on the site of a much older alehouse and smithy, and the 18th century cellars can still be seen. This alehouse provided lodgings, and had a picturesque thatched roof and attached brewhouse.

Ann and Mike Gwinnut have been in charge of **The Three Horseshoes** for the last eight years, and have been in the licensed trade since 1972. The decor is firmly traditional, with beamed ceilings and furniture in dark, highly polished wood. Brasses adorn the beams, there are ornaments and memorabilia on the shelves, framed prints on the cream walls, and a roaring open fire in the winter months. Some of the floor is carpeted, and some is tiled, and altogether it has a cozy yet surprisingly airy feel to it.

The dining area seats 32 in comfort, and the food wholesome, traditional and always well presented. It is cooked on the premises from ingredients that are fresh and bought locally wherever possible. You can choose from such dishes as juicy steaks, breaded king prawns, battered cod, filled Yorkshire puddings, steak and onion pie, chicken Kiev or scampi tails. On Sunday lunchtime, the inn only serves traditional roasts, with a choice of meats. You are advised to book if you want a table on a Friday night or a Sunday lunchtime. To accompany your meal, the bar has an excellent selection of drinks. on offer are real ales such as Marston's Pedigree and Mansfield, as well as Banks Smooth, Guinness, Heineken, Stella and Strongbow.

Opening times: Open lunchtimes and evenings, with all day opening on Saturday

Food: Good, popular, value for money meals are served Tuesday to Friday from 12.00-14.00 and 18.00-20.30; Saturday and Sunday:12.00-14.00; no food served on Mondays

Credit cards: Most credit cards accepted

Accommodation: None

Entertainment: Occasional entertainment

(ring for details); pub games such as pool, darts, crib and chess

Facilities: Car park; secluded beer garden; children's play area; nearby golf course

Local Places of Interest/Activities: Kedleston Hall (NT) 6 miles; American Adventure (theme park) 4 miles; Derby (historic city) 4 miles; Shipley Country Park 4 miles

The Traveller's Rest   213

2 New Street,
Church Gresley,
Swadlincote,
Derbyshire
DE11 9PS
Tel: 01283 216813

Directions:
Church Gresley is on the A444, two miles south east of Burton on Trent and two miles west of Swadlincote

Church Gresley is a former mining village close to Swadlincote. In 1790 a pottery was established here by Thomas Goodwin Green, and the first mine was sunk in 1829. However, the history of the village goes back into the mists of time. It was named after the great Derbyshire family of Gresley, which has owned land in the area since before the Domesday Book. A priory once stood here, as did a castle in the nearby village of Castle Gresley. Nothing remains of the priory, though the site of the castle - now called Castle Knob - can still be seen. The church dates partly from the 12th century, and has one tangible reminder of the Gresleys – a monument to Sir Thomas, which shows the marriages of his ancestors right back to the Norman Conquest.

In the village, you'll find the delightful **Traveller's Rest**, owned and run by Barbara Bent and Stephen Thompson. It is a handsome, white washed building dating back to 1864, with a cozy and welcoming interior that has been refurbished to an extremely high standard. Its food is renowned and you can choose from a printed menu or a specials board. On offer are such things as juicy steaks, fish, gammon, chilli con carne, curries or chicken. If you prefer something lighter, there are also jacket potatoes, sandwiches, filled baguettes, salads and so on. All the food represents amazing value for money, and is prepared on the premises from only the freshest produce. On Wednesday there is an ever popular "themed food night", where you can eat as much as you like for a fixed price. If you want something to drink with your meal, the bar offers real ales such as Bass and Marston's Pedigree, plus Carling, Fosters, Worthington Smooth and Strongbow. The Traveller's Rest is a friendly, family run inn that puts the comfort of the customer first. Children are allowed up until 20.00, and if you visit, you're sure of a very warm welcome from Barbara and Stephen.

Opening hours: Monday 17.00-23.00; Tuesday-Friday 12-14.30 and 17.00-23.00; Saturday 12.00-16.00 and 19.00-23.00; Sunday 12.00-15.00 and 19.00-23.00

Food: Lunchtimes only, with "eat as much as you like like" special on Wednesday evenings from 19.00-21.30

Credit cards: Cash and cheque only at present

Accommodation: None

Entertainment: Occasional live entertainers on Saturday evenings; ring for details; pool; darts; fruit machine, quiz machine

Facilities: No-smoking area

Local Places of Interest/Activities: Calke Abbey (NT) 9 miles; Staffordshire Regiment Museum 10 miles; Staunton Harold Church (NT) 6 miles Donnington Park (motor racing) 10 miles; National Forest Visitor Centre, Moira 3 miles

214

Vernon Arms

Main Road,
Sudbury,
Derbyshire
DE6 5HS
Tel: 01283 585329
Fax: 01283 585098

Directions:

Sudbury is just south of the A50, near its junction with the A515 and 4 miles from Uttoxeter town centre

Close to the lovely little village of Sudbury is Sudbury Hall, built in the 17th century for the Vernon family, and now under the care of the National Trust. But even older is the **Vernon Arms**, a coaching inn that stands in the main street of the village, and originally dates from the 16th century.

It was named after the local lords of the manor, of course, and is a substantial building made if the local stone, on a link road that is one of the oldest in England. Sandra Hipperson is mine host, and she invites you to pay a visit to one of the best inns in the area.

The interior has recently been completely refurbished to an extremely high standard, while still retaining many of the period features that make the inn such a pleasant place to visit. There are open fires, for instance, and the original old oak floors. The inn boasts two bars, which are friendly and full of atmosphere. This is a pub that is a favourite with the locals, which is an advertisement in itself!

Food is ordered from a chalked specials board, and the dishes on offer are hearty and filling. All the produce used is as fresh as possible, and the inn has a great reputation for its fish and steak dishes with all the trimmings. Not only that – the inn has a clear view kitchen, and you can actually see your food being prepared!

The bar has a great range of drinks. There are two real ales, plus bitter, mild, lager, cider and stout. Soft drinks are also available, plus a range of spirits and wines.

Opening times: Monday and Tuesday: 12.00-15.00 and 18.30-23.00 (summer months only); Wednesday to Saturday: open all day until 23.00; Sunday: open all day until 22.30

Food: Lunches are served between 12.00-14.30 and evening meals are served between 18.30 and 21.00 except Sunday and Monday.

Credit cards: All major cards accepted except American Express and diners

Accommodation: None

Entertainment: Salmon and champagne theme nights; occasional entertainment (ring for details)

Local Places of Interest/Activities: Sudbury Hall (NT) 1 mile; Uttoxeter (historic town and horse racing) 5 miles; Darley Moor (motor cycle racing) 6 miles; Alton Towers (theme park) 9 miles

The White Swan 215

Eggington Road,
Hilton,
Derbyshire
DE65 5FJ
Tel: 01283 732305

Directions:
Travel 10 miles east
from Uttoxeter on
the A50 and turn off
south at the A516.
Once in Hilton,
look for the
Eggington Road,
and go along it for
just under a mile.
The inn is on your
right

Set well back from the road, **The White Swan** is a building of mellow red brick surrounded by some wonderful scenery. Andrew and Sabrina Pickering took over as leaseholders in September 2000. This is their first venture into the licensing trade, and they have great plans for the inn. They want to preserve all that is good about the place while at the same time introducing the concept of efficient, friendly service and real value for money.

This is a real hidden gem of an inn, with an interior that speaks of olde worlde charm and tradition. The whole place is spotlessly clean, with country style furnishings, carpeted floors, cheery curtains and a wealth of brass and memorabilia dotted about. There's a solid, brick built fireplace that offers a warm, glowing welcome in the winter months, and low, dark beams. If you're eating, children are welcome, and the food is beautifully cooked on the premises from fresh ingredients wherever possible. You can choose from a printed menu or the specials blackboard. So popular is the White Swan on a Sunday that if you want to eat, you're well advised to book in advance. There's a comprehensive wine list to complement your meal, or you can choose from a fine selection of ales and beers at the bar. There are two real ales - Bass and Marston's pedigree - plus lager, Guinness, Murphy's and Blackthorn cider.

Opening times: Open all day, every day

Food: Served 12.00-14.30 and 18.00-21.00 Tuesday to Sunday; 12.00-14.30 on Monday

Credit cards: Most credit cards accepted

Accommodation: None

Entertainment: Quiz night on Monday, starting 21.00; regular events such as disco, cheaper drinks or curry nights are available on Tuesday, Wednesday and Thursday

evenings; phone for details

Facilities: Car park; huge beer garden; no smoking area; bouncy castle and secure adventure playground for kids

Local Places of Interest/Activities: Sudbury Hall (NT) 6 miles; Uttoxeter (horse racing) 9 miles; Tutbury Castle (ruined) 3 miles; Derby (historic city) 8 miles

216 | Ye Old Packhorse Inn

Pack Horse Road,
Kings Newton,
Melbourne,
Derbyshire
DE73 1BZ
Tel: 01332 862767
Fax: 01332 865766

Directions:

The inn is short walk or drive from the centre of Melbourne

What a splendid looking inn **Ye Old Packhorse** is! Warm, mellow brick, old, small paned windows, red tiled roof, a colourful sign, dormer windows, and, just to complete the picture, the addition of an old bow window that somehow adds character to an already charming building. It dates from the late 17th century, and was formerly a coaching inn and alehouse on the pack horse route between Nottingham and Burton on Trent. Now it is managed by Wendy and Terry Sowerby, who have been there for eight years, though they've had 19 years in the trade. They've turned the place into everyone's idea of a warm, snug inn, with dark panelled walls, a wealth of polished copper and brass, potted plants, country style furniture, and wall lighting that adds that special air of coziness to it all. As soon as you enter Ye Old Pack Horse, you know you're in a well run and popular establishment that appeals to locals and tourists alike.

There is seating for at least 55 diners, and food is served every day. The menu has a range of mouth watering and tasty dishes that are beautifully prepared and presented, and always represent good value for money. Most of them are home made on the premises, using produce that is always fresh and nutritious. You can order such dishes as steaks, grills, salads, salmon fillet, as well as chicken Kiev, half roast chickens, pasta, or even delights from the East such as chicken tikka masala, Thai chicken curry and lamb balti. There's a seven day carvery plus a selection of vegetarian dishes, but beware - so popular is the place with diners that there may be a waiting list in operation.

Three real ales are available - Burtonwood, Top Hat and a brewery guest ale, plus a wide range of lagers, stout and cider. In the summer months, you could carry your drink or bar meal out into the beer garden behind the inn, where there's a secure play area for children. Here you can relax and while away a pleasant hour or two over good, honest food and a pint of the establishment's best!

Opening times: Open lunchtimes and evenings

Food: Served Monday 11.30-14.00 and 18.00-21.00; Tuesday to Saturday 11.30-14.00 and 18.00-21.30; Sunday: 12.00-14.00 and 19.00-21.00

Credit cards: Cash and cheques only at present

Accommodation: None

Facilities: Beer garden; children's play area

Local Places of Interest/Activities:
Donington Park (motor racing) 2 miles; Calke Abbey (NT) 2 miles; East Midlands Airport 5 miles; Staunton Harold Church (NT) 3 miles; Melbourne Hall & Pool ¾ mile

8 Northeast Derbyshire & the Amber Valley

PLACES OF INTEREST:

PUBS AND INNS:

The Hidden Inns of the Heart of England

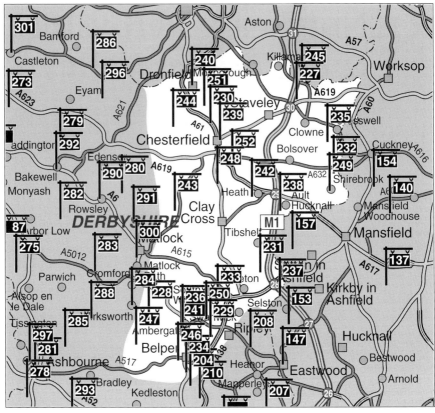

© MAPS IN MINUTES ™ 2001   © Crown Copyright, Ordnance Survey 2001

227	The Apollo Inn, Balborough	240	Hearts of Oak, Dronfield Woodhouse
228	The Bear Inn and Hotel, Alderwasely	241	The Hurt Arms, Ambergate
229	The Black Boy, Heage	242	Jolly Farmers, Holmewood
230	Bulls Head, Old Whittington	243	Kelstedge Inn, Kelstedge
231	The Clock Inn, South Normanton	244	The Peacock, Barlow
232	The Devonshire Arms, Upper Langwith	245	The Pebley Inn, Balborough
233	The Dog Inn, Pentich	246	The Railway, Belper
234	The Duke of Devonshire, Belper	247	The Railway, Shottle
235	The Elm Tree Inn, Elmton	248	The Royal Oak Inn, Old Tupton
236	The Excavator, Buckland Hollow	249	The Summit, Shirebrook
237	The Greyhound Inn, Pinxton	250	The White Hart Inn, Heage
238	Hardwick Inn, Hardwick Park	251	White Horse , Old Whittington
239	Hare and Hounds, Stone Gravels	252	Winsick Arms, Hasland

Please note all references refer to page numbers

Northeast Derbyshire and the District of Bolsover, with the Peak District to the west, South Yorkshire to the north and Nottinghamshire to the east, centres around Chesterfield. This was the heart of the county's coal-mining area, and many of the towns and villages reflect the prosperity the mines brought in Victorian times. Sadly, the vast majority of the collieries are now closed; there was for a while a period of decline, but visitors today will be surprised at the wealth of history and fine architecture to be seen throughout the region.

East Derbyshire encompasses the regions of the county going by the picturesque names of the Amber Valley and the eastern part of the area known as Erewash. These two regions cover the eastern and southeastern parts of Derbyshire respectively. The Rivers Amber, Derwent and Trent run through this part of the county. Though the scenery is perhaps less dramatic than the popular Peak District, in which most of north Derbyshire lies, there are ample opportunities to enjoy pleasant walks in the extensive grounds of many of the estates.

PLACES OF INTEREST

ALFRETON

This historic town dates back to Saxon times and, despite obvious appearances, Alfred the Great was not immortalised in the naming of the place. This attractive former coal-mining town stands on a hill close to the Nottinghamshire border. Along the charming High Street can be found the George Hotel, a fine Georgian building that looks down the length of the High Street. There are also a number of other 18th century stonebuilt houses. The parish church of St Martin is large and has an impressive fine western tower. The ground floor of the church dates back to the 1200s.

Among the many splendid old buildings in Alfreton, the most impressive is **Alfreton Hall** (private), the centrepiece of an attractive public park. In soft mellow stone, the Hall was built around 1730, with 19th century additions. Owned until fairly recently by the Palmer Morewood family, owners of the local coal mines, it is now used as an Arts and Adult Education Centre. The park is quite extensive, boasting its own cricket ground and a horse-riding track around its perimeters. In **King Street** there is a house of confinement, or Lock-up, which was built to house lawbreakers and catered mainly for the local drunkards. The close confines of the prison with its two cells, minute windows and thick outer walls must have been a very effective deterrent.

AMBERGATE

Where the River Amber joins the mighty Derwent, Ambergate is one of the main gateways to the Peak District for travellers going north on the A6. A marvellous bridge crosses the Derwent. The village itself is surrounded by deciduous woodland, including the fine Shining Cliff Woods, an important refuge for wildlife. The railway, road and canal here are all squeezed into the tight river valley, and the railway station, standing 100 feet above the road, was one of the few triangular stations in Britain. Built in the late 19th century, the church of St Anne was a gift to the village from the Johnson family of the Ambergate Wire Works, now known as the business concern Richard Johnson and Nephew. Inside the church there is a marble figure depicting angel protecting a child from a serpent; this was the creation of a Belgian sculptor who sought refuge in Ambergate during the First World War.

220 | AULT HUCKNALL

The strange name of this village probably means 'Hucca's high nook of land', and this pleasant place, standing on a ridge close to the Nottinghamshire border, is home to the magnificent Tudor house, **Hardwick Hall**. "More glass than wall", it is one of Derbyshire's Big Three stately homes alongside Chatsworth and Haddon, all three glorious monuments to the great land-owning families who played so great a role in shaping the history of the county. Set in rolling parkland, the house, with its glittering tiers of windows and crowned turrets, offers quite a spellbinding sight. Inside, the silence of the chambers strewn with rush matting, combined with the simplicity of the white-washed walls, gives a feeling of almost overwhelming peace. The letters E S can be seen carved in stone on the outside of the house: E S, or Elizabeth of Shrewsbury, was perhaps better known as Bess of Hardwick. This larger-than-life figure had attachments with many places in Derbyshire, and the story of her life makes for fascinating reading.

She was born in the manor house at Hardwick in 1520. The house stood only a little distance from the present-day Hall and was then not much more than a farmhouse. The young Bess married her neighbour's son, Robert Barlow, when she was only 12. When her young husband, himself only 14, died a few months later she naturally inherited a great deal of property. Some 15 years later she married Sir William Cavendish and, when he died in 1557, she was bequeathed his entire fortune. By this time she was the richest woman in England, save for one, Elizabeth, the Queen.

The Gallery at Hardwick Hall, with its gorgeous lavender-hued tapestries, has, in pride of place, a portrait of this formidable woman. The portrait depicts a personage who could be mistaken for Elizabeth R, and it seems only right to compare the two. First the "Virgin" Queen who commanded so forcibly the men around her yet never married, and then Bess, who married and survived four husbands. Bess began the building of the house in 1590, towards the end of her life and after her fourth lucrative marriage to George Talbot, sixth Earl of Shrewsbury. It stands as a monument to her wealth and good taste, and is justly famous for its magnificent needlework and tapestries, carved fire-places and friezes, which are considered as among the finest in Britain.

Though Bess is the first person that springs to mind with regard to Hardwick Hall, it was the 6th Duke of Devonshire who was responsible for the Hall's antiquarian atmosphere. He inherited the property in 1811 and, as well as promoting the legend that Mary, Queen of Scots stayed here, he filled the house with furniture, paintings and tapestries from his other houses and from Chatsworth in particular.

As well as viewing the Hall, there are some wonderful grounds to explore. To the south are the formal gardens, laid out in the 19th century and separated by long walks lined with yew. One area has been planted as a Tudor herb garden and is stocked with both culinary and medicinal plants used at that time. Down in the southeastern corner of the garden is the small Elizabethan banqueting hall used as a smoking room by the 6th Duke's orchestra, as they were not allowed to smoke in the Hall. There is also, to the back of the house, a lake and lime avenue. Owned by the National Trust, Hardwick Hall is a must for any visitor to Derbyshire and is certainly a place not to be missed. The parkland, which overlooks the valley of the Doe Lea and the M1, is home to an impressive herd of Longhorn cattle among the stag-headed oaks. The ruins of **Hardwick Old Hall** (English Heritage) also stand in the grounds, and are the interesting remains of Bess' former Tudor mansion.

The village **Church of St John the Baptist**, situated on a back lane, is one of the finest in Derbyshire. Overlooking Hardwick Hall's beautiful parklands, with the square towers of Bess of Hardwick's great house in the distance, the battlemented church exterior does not prepare visitors for its dark, mysterious interior, which reveals the church's much earlier origins. There are many Norman features, including the north arcade, nave and the narrow arches holding up the rare crossing tower. There is more Norman work in the plain capitals of the north arcade.

There are several interesting tombs in the church, such as the large and detailed wall monument just below the east window to the first Countess of Devonshire, dating from 1627. On the floor in front is a simple black slab commemorating the influential and renowned philosopher Thomas Hobbes - author of *The Leviathan* and *De Mirabilibus Pecci: Concerning the Wonders of the Peak* (the latter being one of the first accounts of the Seven Wonders of the Peak) - who died at Hardwick. A much simpler table in the north aisle commemorates Robert Hackett, a keeper of Hardwick Park who died n 1703. It reads: "Long has he chas'd/The red and fallow deer/But death's cold dart/At last has fix'd him here."

BELPER

Famous for its cotton mills, the town is situated alongside the **River Derwent** on the floor of the valley. In 1776, Jedediah Strutt, the wheelwright son of a South Normanton famer, set up one of the earliest water-powered cotton mills here to harness the natural powers of the river to run his mills. With the river providing the power and fuel coming from the nearby South Derbyshire coalfield, the valley has a good claim to be one of the cradles of the Industrial Revolution. Earlier, in 1771 Strutt had gone into profitable partnership with Richard Arkwright, to establish the world's first water-powered cotton mill at Cromford. Strutt and his son, William, retained the North Mill at Belper in 1872 when the partnership with Arkwright was dissolved, having added another at Milford in 1780. Great benefactors to Belper for 150 years, the Strutt family provided housing, work, education and even food - from the model farms they established in the surrounding countryside. Many parts of the town still reflect their influence.

Three hundred years later the mills are still standing and, along with them, are some unique mill-workers' cottages. To discover more about the cotton industry, the influence of the Strutt

Derwent Valley, Belper

family on the town and of Samuel Slater, Strutt's apprentice who emigrated to America in 1789, built a mill there and went on to become "the Father of American manufacturers", a visit to the **Derwent Valley Visitor Centre** is a must. The oldest mill still surviving is the two-storey **North Mill** at Bridgefoot, near the magnificent crescent-shaped weir in the Derwent and the town's main bridge. Built in 1876, the mill has cast-iron columns and beams, and hollow tile floors which provided a warm-air central heating system. It is now the visitor centre. The massive, neighbouring redbrick **East Mill** was constructed in 1912, but now is largely empty. A Jubilee Tower in terracotta was erected on the mill site in 1897 to mark Queen Victoria's 60th anniversary on the throne.

Train travellers through Belper are among those treated to a glimpse of George Stephenson's mile-long cutting, walled in gritstone throughout and spanned by no fewer than 10 bridges. When completed in 1840 it was considered an engineering wonder of its day. In addition to all its industrial history the town goes back to well before the Industrial Revolution. Not only was it mentioned in the Domesday Book (as *Beau Repaire* - the beautiful retreat), but in 1964 the remains of a Roman kiln were found here.

There are also some lovely waterside walks in this bustling little town. Among Belper's other interesting buildings are the **Christ Church**, a lofty, spacious house of worship built in 1849, the parish **Church of St Peter** with its pinnacled west tower (1824) and **Chapel of St John the Baptist** in The Butts, dating from 1683. A monument to George Brettle can be seen in St Peter's Church - **George Brettle's Warehouse**, in Chapel Street, is a distinctive and elegant building created in 1834.

The **River Gardens** were established in 1905 and today they are a pleasant place for a stroll among the beautifully tended gardens. Rowing boats can be hired for a trip along the Derwent. The Gardens are a favourite with the film industry, having been used in Ken Russell's Women in Love, as well as television's Sounding Brass and In the Shadow of the Noose. The riverside walk through the meadows is particularly rich in bird life.

222 | BOLSOVER

The approach to Bolsover from the north and east is dominated by the splendid, sandstone structure of **Bolsover Castle**, which sits high on a limestone ridge. A castle has stood here since the 12th century, though the present building is a fairytale "folly" built for Sir Charles Cavendish during the early 1600s on the site of a ruined

Bolsover Castle

castle. By the mid 18th century much of the building had been reduced to the ruins seen today, though thankfully the splendid keep has withstood the test of time.

Pevsner remarked that not many large houses in England occupy such an impressive position as Bolsover Castle, as it stands on the brow of a hill overlooking the valley of the River Rother and Doe Lea. The first castle at Bolsover was built by William Peverel, illegitimate son of William the Conqueror, as part of his vast Derbyshire estates. Nothing remains of that Norman building. Now owned by English Heritage, visitors can explore the Little Castle, or Keep, which is decorated in an elaborate Jacobean celebration with wonderful fireplaces, panelling and wall paintings. The series of remarkable rooms includes the Vaulted Hall, the Pillar Room, the Star Chamber, the Elysium and the Heaven Room. Sir Charles' son, William, was responsible for the eastern range of buildings known as the Riding School, an impressive indoor area built in the 17th century, and the roofless but still impressive western terrace. The ruins of the state apartments are also here to be discovered. The whole building later descended to the Dukes of Portland, and it remains a strangely impressive place, though even now it is threatened by its industrial surroundings and the legacy of centuries of coal-mining beneath its walls: subsidence.

The Hudson Bay public house across the road from the castle recalls in its name the fact that it was originally built by Peter Fidler, a Bolsover man who was a distinguished surveyor with the Hudson Bay Company in Canada during the 18th century. A Peter Fidler Society exists in Canada to this day. Bolsover's oldest public house is probably The White Swan, and is said to have served as the moot hall from the Middle Ages to the early 19th century. Bolsover was granted its market charter by Henry III in 1225.

Naturally, the parish **Church of St Mary's** in Bolsover holds many monuments to the Cavendish family, but it seems amazing that the Church has survived when its recent history is revealed. Dating from the 13th century, the church's monuments include two magnificent tombs to Charles Cavendish, who died in 1617, and Henry Cavendish, who died in 1727. Destroyed by fire in 1897, except for the Cavendish Chapel, St Mary's was rebuilt, only to be damaged again by fire in 1960. It has since been restored. Buried in the churchyard are John Smythson and Huntingdon Smythson, the 17th century architects probably responsible for the design of the rebuilt Bolsover Castle.

CHESTERFIELD

This friendly, bustling town on the edge of the **Peak District National Park** grew up around its open-air market which was established over 800 years ago and claims to be England's largest. As the town lies at the crossroads of England, the hub of trade routes from all points of the compass, the town's claim seems easily justified. Life in Chesterfield has revolved around this market since the town's earliest days. It was earning Royal revenue in 1165, as the Sheriff of Derbyshire recorded in the Pipe Rolls and, in that year, the market earned the princely sum of £1 2s 7d for the Crown. The Pipe Roll of 1182 also mentions a fair in Chesterfield. Such fairs were large markets, usually lasting for several days and drawing traders and buyers from a much wider area. Chesterfield's formal charter, however, was not granted until 1204, and this charter made the town one of the first eight free boroughs in the country. Escaping the prospect of redevelopment in the 1970s, the markets are as popular as ever and are held every Monday, Friday and Saturday, with a flea market each Thursday.

The town centre has been conserved for future generations by a far-sighted council, and many buildings have been saved, including the Victorian **Market Hall** built in 1857. The traditional cobbled paving was restored in the Market Place, and New Square was given a complete facelift. There are several Tudor buildings in the heart of Chesterfield, most notably the former Peacock inn which is now home to the **Peacock Heritage Centre** and the tourist information office - built in 1500 for the wealthy Revell family, who later moved to Carnfield Hall near Alfreton. The black-and-white timbering in Knifesmithgate, however, was built only in the 1930s, to resemble the famous rows in Chester.

Visitors to the town are drawn to a peculiarly graceful spire reaching high into the skyline; twisting and leaning, it is totally confusing to the eye. Recognised as one of Chesterfield's landmarks, the **Crooked Spire of St Mary & All Saints' Church** has dominated the skyline for so long that local folk have ceased to notice its unusual shape. Superstition surrounds it, and sadly the real story to its unusual appearance has been lost over the years. The truth probably lies in the wake of the Black Death during the 14th century, when the people of Chesterfield were building their beautiful new church

St Mary & All Saints' Church

and awe-inspiring steeple. Many must have fallen to the plague and, among them, skilled craftsmen who knew how to season wood. The survivors built the spire out of green timber which, over the years, has distorted under the heavy lead covering. However, some stories say it was the Devil, who, pausing for a rest during one of his flights, clung to the spire for a moment or two. Incense from the Church drifted upwards and the Devil sneezed, causing the spire to twist out of shape.

This magnificent spire rises to 228 feet and leans 9 feet 4 inches from its true centrepoint. It is eight-sided, but the herringbone pattern of the lead slates trick the eye into seeing 16 sides from the ground. The Crooked Spire is open most Bank Holidays and at advertised times; the church is open all year, Monday to Saturday 9 a.m. to 5 p.m. (9 a.m. to 3 p.m. January and February), and Sundays at service times only.

Opposite the Church is **Chesterfield Museum and Art Gallery**, home to exhibitions depicting the story of the town, from the arrival of the Romans to the first days of the market town, the industry of the 18th century and the coming of the "Father of the Railways", George Stephenson. The Art Gallery displays paintings by local artists such as Joseph Syddall (who lived at nearby Whittington).

Chesterfield owes much of its prosperity during the industrial age to the great railway engineer George Stephenson. His home, Tapton House, lies just outside the town and it was to here that he retired and carried out his experiments in horticulture. Buried in Holy Trinity Church, where one of the windows was created in his memory, his death, in 1848, was announced by one local newspaper with the headline "Inventor of Straight Cucumber Dies".

Perhaps surprisingly, Chesterfield is home to one of the earliest canals in the country, the **Chesterfield Canal**. After seeing the success of the Bridgewater Canal in 1763, the businessmen of Chesterfield, which was at the start of its rapid expansion, looked to link the town with the River Trent via Worksop and Retford in Nottinghamshire. Construction work began in 1771, just a year before its builder, James Brindley, died whilst surveying the Caldon Canal. The biggest engineering project along the length of the new canal was the Norwood Tunnel; at some 2,850 yards long, it took four years to build. Opened in 1775, on one of the first sections of the canal to carry traffic, the Tunnel was closed in 1908 after some of the roof had collapsed. The whole length of the Canal is open to walkers and, though some sections border onto busy roads, much of the waterway runs through quiet and secluded countryside.

Finally, although the custom of tap-dressing took place in Chesterfield in the 19th century, it was not until 1991 that the tradition, this time of well-dressing, was revived. Initially with help from local experts from Holymoorside, the Chesterfield dressers are developing their own styles and customs and, while the well-dressing at the Peacock Centre takes its inspiration from buildings, their colleagues at St Mary and All Saints Church follow the theme of the stained glass windows within the church.

CRESWELL

Once a sleepy hamlet nestling amid peaceful farming country, the character of Creswell was irreversibly changed at the end of the 19th century. It was then that Creswell Colliery was opened, and now the village is one of the biggest in the county. There is also a village within a village here as, between 1896 and 1900 a model village of houses and cottages was built.

Lying close to the Derbyshire-Nottinghamshire border, the limestone gorge of the **Creswell Crags** are well worth seeing. Formed thousands of years ago by the erosion of a river which cut through the limestone, this rock, which is porous and subject to erosion underground as well as on the surface, contributes by its very nature to the forming of natural chambers. The subterranean movement of water created a vast network of caves, which were subsequently exposed. Used by Neanderthal man as shelters while out hunting, tours can be taken from the visitor centre, where there is also a display of artefacts found in the area. Testimony to the artistry of the later inhabitants of these caves was the discovery of a bone carved with the head of a horse, which is about 13,000 years old, and can now be seen in the British Museum. The largest cavern, Church Hole Cave, extends some 170 feet up the side of the gorge; it was here that hand tools were found.

Not far from the village and close to the county border with Nottinghamshire is **Steetley**

Chapel, thought by many to be the most perfect specimen of Norman architecture in Europe. Whether this is so or not, the elaborate chapel has a rare and unique beauty. Having laid derelict for many years after being desecrated during the Commonwealth, the Chapel of All Saints was restored in the 1880s and at this time some of the wonderful carvings to be seen in the porchway were re-created. Luckily much of the interior remains intact, having survived the test of time. It remains a mystery as to why such a small building should be given such elaborate decoration in the mid 12th century.

HEATH

To the north of Heath, overlooking the M1, are the ruins of what was one of the grandest mansions in Derbyshire, **Sutton Scarsdale**. Built in 1724 for the 4th Earl of Scarsdale, to the designs of Francis Smith, the stonework of the previous Tudor manor house was completely hidden behind the Baroque splendour of the new hall. The magnificent Italian plasterwork can now be seen at the Philadelphia Museum, in Pennsylvania, and demolition of the back of the house has revealed some Tudor brickwork. At the beginning of the 20th century Sutton Scarsdale was owned by a descendent of Sir Richard Arkwright, the famous industrialist. It is this gentleman that D H Lawrence is supposed to chosen as the inspiration for his character of

Sutton Scarsdale

The village church was erected in 1820 the stem to tide of rebellion and "irreligion" that swept the area in

225

the hard years after the Battle of Waterloo, when the local weavers and stockingers rebelled against their harsh living conditions. The insurrection saw three rebels brought to the scaffold and drove some into exile, and became a *cause celebre* throughout the nation.

SOUTH WINGFIELD

Above the village, on the rise of a hill, stand the graceful ruins of the 15th century **Wingfield Manor**. Built by Ralph Lord Cromwell, the manor house was used as Mary Queen of Scots' prison on two separate occasions in 1569 and 1584 when she was held under the care of the Earl of Shrewsbury. The local squire, Anthony Babington, attempted to rescue the Queen and

Stainsby Mill

Sir Clifford Chatterley in the novel *Lady Chatterley's Lover*.

Also close to Heath is the National Trust-owned **Stainsby Mill**. With its machinery now restored to illustrate the workings of a 19th century water-powered corn mill, Stainsby is well worth a visit. Though there has been a mill here since medieval times, the buildings seen today date from 1849 when the then new machinery was first fitted. The large, 17 foot cast-iron waterwheel, which because of its particular design is known as a high breast shot, not only provided power to turn the millstones but also for lifting sacks, cleaning the grain and sieving the flour. Open between the end of March and the end of October, visitors can watch the operations from a viewing gallery.

RIPLEY

Once a typical small market town, Ripley expanded dramatically during the Industrial Revolution when great use was made of the iron, clay and coal deposits found nearby. The town's Butterley ironworks, founded in 1792 by a group of men which included renowned engineer Benjamin Outram, created the roof for London's St Pancras station. Outram's even more famous son Sir James enjoyed an illustrious career that saw him claimed Bayard of India, and earned him a resting place in Westminster Abbey.

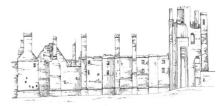

Wingfield Manor

lead her to safety but the plot failed and, instead, lead to them both being beheaded. One of the less well-known of Derbyshire's many manor houses and mansions, the history and architectural interest provided by the ruins make it one of the more fascinating homes in the area. A wander around the remains reveals the large banqueting hall with its unusual oriel window and a crypt which was probably used to store food and wine. Whatever its use, it is a particularly fine example and rivals a similar structure at Fountains Abbey. High up in the tower can also be seen a single archer's slit, built the opposite way round so that only one archer was needed to defend the whole tower.

TIBSHELF

Stretching from here north, to Grassmoor, the **Five Pits Trail** is a scenic route which passes the old collieries at Tibshelf, Pilsley, Alameda, Williamthorpe and Grassmoor. At first the idea of exploring these old coal workings may not

226

appeal, but since their reclamation by Derbyshire County Council this is now an interesting and entertaining seven-mile walk. Suitable for walkers, cyclists and horse riders, the Trail is quite lovely, and offers some splendid views.

With the closure of the pits, which had been largely developed since the middle of the 19th century, the land had fallen into disuse. With the help of the Countryside Ranger Service, Derbyshire County Council manages the Trail and there is also a great deal of support from local groups who have contributed much time and effort to bring this land back to life. The clearing of paths and the addition of plantations, ponds and meadows has ensured that many species of wildlife have been encouraged to return here. Wild plants to look out for include the bush vetch, meadowsweet and the corn poppy. At one time these lovely wild flowers could be seen in abundance in many of Derbyshire's fields and hedgerows.

The Apollo Inn

227

High Street,
Barlborough,
near Chesterfield,
Derbyshire S43 4EY
Tel: 01246 810346
Fax: 01246 819128

Directions:

Barlborough is just
east of the M1, on
the A619

Situated in the heart of the pleasant village of Barlborough, **The Apollo Inn** is an imposing, Georgian building with a well proportioned facade that looks out onto the street. It dates form 1827, though an inn wasn't established here until the end of the 19th century. In charge is Rory Hallam and Barbara Huntington, who have created an interior that is cozy and inviting. There's a snug public bar, a comfortable lounge, a games room and a no smoking restaurant that sets 24 people in absolute comfort. The restaurant is especially charming, with its open fire, framed prints, shining brass and comfortably upholstered seating.

At the bar you can order from a range of three real ales, one of them being Cameron's Strong Ale, plus you can have draught mild, bitter, stout, cider and lager. The cuisine is traditional English, with many dishes on the menu that are sure to please everyone. You can order such old time favourites as bangers and mash (always piping hot, and always tasty!), juicy steaks with all the trimmings, and fresh fish. If you'd like a real treat, order the beef and Guinness pie – its a firm favourite with the locals. The ingredients that go into the dishes are always as fresh as possible, and the portions are generous, and represent amazing value for money. In the summer months, there are also occasional barbecues in the beer garden.

This is an inn that is a firm favourite with the locals, which is always a good sign. If you pay it a visit, it's sure to become a firm favourite of your as well!

Opening times: Monday to Saturday: 11.00-23.00; Sunday: 12.00-22.30

Food: Monday to Saturday: 12.00-14.30 and 17.00-20.00; Sunday: 12.00-14.30

Credit cards: Cash only at present

Accommodation: None

Entertainment: Thursday evening: quiz; Friday evening: live music; Sunday evening: disco

Facilities: Car park; beer garden; children's play area; barbecues in summer

Local Places of Interest/Activities: Sheffield (historic city) 12 miles; Chesterfield (historic town) 7 miles; Sutton Scarsdale Hall 6 miles; Stainsby Mill (NT) 7 miles; Hardwick Hall (NT) 8 miles

228 The Bear Inn and Hotel

Alderwasley,
near Belper,
Derbyshire
DE56 2RD
Tel: 01629 822585
Fax: 01629 826676

Directions:

Take the A6 north from Belper towards Matlock. After 4 miles turn west at Whatstandwell onto a minor road signposted for Alderwasley

When you cross the threshold of this old Inn, you could be forgiven for thinking that you're stepping into someone's home, so cozy is it. It has a beautiful interior, with plenty of ornaments on the shelves, framed prints on the walls, and comfortable furniture. The ceilings are low and beamed, and the walls rugged and rustic. Over part of the ceiling there even seems to be a vine growing, and against a wall a homely Welsh dresser groans with willow pattern plates, bowls and knick knacks. On cold winter evenings, the open fires cast a warm glow over everything. But **The Bear Inn** isn't wholly trapped in the past as it is the only hostelry in Derbyshire that boasts a helicopter pad!

The Inn dates partly from the 17th century, and was once a farmhouse. It is a well proportioned, thick walled, white washed building with a rustic charm that is homely and inviting. Nicky and Tim Fletcher-Musgrave are the owners, and they've tried to keep the traditional look of the place as far as possible while offering the modern concepts of good, friendly service and value for money. The inn is famous in the area for its food, which is traditional English fare with some continental dishes thrown in. There's no menu - you order from the blackboard which changes daily, and everything arrives delicately arranged, piping hot and beautifully cooked. Food is not allowed in the bar, but there is a spacious dining area known as the "Bear Hall" which has been painted in a 17th century design dotted with wild birds. There's another small area known as "Oberon's Keep" which seats up to ten in comfort. Four real ales are available at the bar - Bass, Marston's Pedigree and two rotating guest ales, plus a good range of beers, lagers, stout and cider. There is an extensive wine list with wine being available by the bottle or glass(awarded Golden Goblet award 2001).The Bear Inn also offers accommodation in eight en-suite rooms, all of which are extremely comfortable and welcoming.

Opening times: Open all day every day

Food: Served 12.00-21.00 from Monday to Sunday

Credit cards: Most credit cards except American Express

Accommodation: Eight comfortable en-suite rooms

Facilities: Large car park; helicopter pad; children over 14 welcome

Local Places of Interest/Activities: Peak District National Park 3 miles; Carsington Water and Visitor's Centre (fishing) 4 miles; Wirksworth Heritage Centre 1 mile; National Stone Centre, Wirksworth 1 mile; National Tramway Museum, Crich 3 miles

The Black Boy

229

Old Road,
Heage,
near Belper,
Derbyshire
DE56 2BN
Tel: 01773 856799

Directions:

Heage is on the
B6013, 2 miles west
of Ripley

Take an old stone building dating from the mid 1800s, add masses of climbing plants and tubs of flowers, season with a lovely small porch and small paned windows, and what do you have? **The Black Boy** in Heage, of course! It's a lovely inn, standing well off the road and with benches and seating placed in front of it. The village is picturesque, and the inn blends in beautifully with the old houses and the quiet charm.

Inside there's plenty of genuine atmosphere, and you feel – quite rightly – that this is a real village pub, popular with the locals and with people passing through who fancy a relaxing drink or a meal. The bar is especially attractive, and has a semi circular look to it, giving the place a great atmosphere. The furniture is comfortable, and there's loads of leather, and old brass and copper ornaments and plates which have been polished until they shine. Two cask ales are on offer at the bar, plus draught bitter, stout, cider, lager and mild. There's also a good range of soft drinks for those who are driving. Colin and Lesley Gregory, an experienced husband and wife team, are in charge, and they take great pride, not just in the ales, but in the great food that's available. This is home cooking at its best – tasty, well presented and cooked to perfection. There are good, hearty portions that will satisfy the largest of hungers, and the fayre is traditional. All the produce that goes into the tasty dishes is fresh – Colin and Lesley see to that!

This is an area of Derbyshire which is truly rural, with old, winding country lanes, green meadows and rich woodland. It cries out to be explored, and The Black boy is the ideal stopping off point for a drink or meal.

Opening times: Monday to Friday: 11.30-15.00 and 18.00-23.00; Saturday: 11.00-15.00 and 18.00-23.00; Sunday 12.00-16.30 and 19.00-22.30

Food: Lunches are served every day between 12.00-14.00 and evening meals are served between 18.00-20.00 Mon-Thurs and18.00-21.00 Fri-Sat.. Closed Sunday

Credit cards: All major cards accepted except American Express and diners

Accommodation: None

Entertainment: Quiz every Wednesday evening

Facilities: Car park; beer garden with summer barbecues

Local Places of Interest/Activities: National Tramway Museum, Crich 3 miles; Heights of Abraham (cable car) at Matlock Bath 6 miles; Belper (historic town) 2 miles

230

Bulls Head

Old Whittington,
near Chesterfield,
Derbyshire
S41 9DB
Tel: 01246 456305

Directions:

Old Whittington is on the B6052, off the A6, 3 miles north of Chesterfield town centre

The Bulls Head is a real Derbyshire pub. The original building, which dated from 1728, is long gone, but the husband and wife team of Joan and Martin Shaw, who are in charge of the present pub, have maintained the long traditions of hospitality and a warm welcome that you find in Derbyshire. This is an inn that is lively and friendly, and welcomes sporty types, be they golfers, footballers, rugby players or those who find their pleasures in the sound of hooves on turf. Joan and Martin have great plans for the place, and by the end of the summer of 2001 the inn's kitchen will have been completely refurbished, so that they can introduce a fine menu that contains many traditional and hearty English dishes, plus a few that owe more to Italy and India, such as lasagna and curry. The food will all be cooked on the premises, and represent good value for money.

The interior is spotlessly clean, with a great atmosphere and plenty of space to relax and stretch you legs as you enjoy a quiet drink. You can choose from John Smith's cask ale (which is a real ale) or from a range of draught bitters, mild, stout, lager and cider. If you're driving, there's also a fine selection of soft drinks, so you'll never be disappointed!

Even if you're not a great sporting person, you'll still get a hearty Derbyshire welcome at the Bulls Head. Joan and Martin plan on being at the inn for a long time, and they want to make it one of the best hostelries in the area, popular with locals and visitors alike.

Opening times: Seven days from 12.00-23.00

Food: Will be served from the end of summer 2001

Credit cards: Cash only at present

Accommodation: None

Entertainment: Thursday and Saturday evenings: karaoke; a varied programme of live music on Friday, Saturday and Sunday (ring for details)

Facilities: Car park

Local Places of Interest/Activities: Revolution House (within village); Chesterfield (historic town) 3 miles; Sheffield (historic city) 8 miles; Longshore Estate (NT) 7 miles; Chatsworth 8 miles

The Clock Inn   **231**

107 Market Street,
South Normanton,
Derbyshire
DE55 2AA
Tel: 01773 811396
Fax: 01773 784580

Directions:

Leave the M1 at Junction 28 and follow the signs for South Normanton. At the BP Service Station turn right, and The Clock is about 400 metres along on the left.

Never judge a book by its covers - or an inn by its exterior! The unpretentious exterior of this pub, housed in a building which dates from the 1850s, conceals a warm and charming atmosphere. The pine and tile floors in the bar and lounge are original, and the ambience of the place speaks of a well maintained and spotlessly clean establishment. Run by the father and son team of Bob and Edward Skinner, **The Clock** is a true family local, used by the people of South Normanton who are looking for a relaxed atmosphere and good food at reasonable prices.

There's almost an "Irish" feel to the inn, with its congenial ambience and friendly yet efficient staff. It has a neat, welcoming bar area and a comfortable lounge where the clientele can sample the cask conditioned beers and ales from Marston and Shepherds Neame. There are also regular guest beers, and the inn has even started a guest beer mailing list, sent via email, to lovers of real ale everywhere. The wines on offer are from Sutter Home and Blossom Hill.

The food is cooked by Bob Skinner, and is honest, ample and unpretentious. It is always reasonably priced, and always tasty - so much so that people who have already discovered the inn regularly make the short detour from the M1 to enjoy a break from their journey, plus a meal. It even serves a breakfast which costs from £2.55.

Bob and Edward have big plans for The Clock. They've already established musical evenings, featuring jazz, rock n' roll and music from the 60s to the 80s, and they want to smarten the whole place up. This is a pub to watch!

Opening Hours: 11.00-23.00 Monday-Saturday, 12.00-22.30 Sunday. Food: 12.00-14.30 Monday-Friday, all day Saturday and 12.00-16.30 on Sunday

Food: Wholesome, unpretentious, reasonably priced and always good.

Credit Cards: Cash & cheques at present

Accommodation: None

Facilities: Small patio/garden area.

Entertainment: Tuesday evenings: live trad jazz; Occasional music at weekend; South Normanton Folk Club last Friday of the month

Local Places of Interest: Newstead Abbey 6 miles; Midlands Railway Centre 4 miles; Hardwick Hall (NT) 5 miles; Stainsby Mill (NT) 6 miles.

Internet/Website:
www.theclockinn.co.uk
e-mail: thebar@theclockinn.co.uk

232 | The Devonshire Arms

Upper Langwith, near Mansfield,
Nottinghamshire NG20 9RF
Tel: 01623 742209

Directions:
Upper Langwith is just south of the A632,
3 miles west of Bolsover town centre

Upper Langwith is one of the Derbyshire villages that takes part each July in the ancient custom of well dressing. It's a custom that predates Christianity, and at one time the church tried to stamp it out, but to no avail. Now it is a colourful reminder of our past, and attracts many visitors who come to view the beautiful floral displays that adorn the wells and springs. Within the village you'll find **The Devonshire Arms**, an inn that isn't quite as old as well dressing, but does date from the 17th century.

It sits on a corner site, and is a whitewashed building that is full of character and old world charm. The interior has bare stone walls, old beams, comfortable furnishings and lots of polished brass – in fact, everything you could wish for in a friendly inn. There's a snug and cozy bar, a lounge and a cheery dining room that seats 36 people. In charge are the husband and wife team of Bob and Carol Shanks, who have tried to make a visit to the pub – whether for a drink or a meal – an enjoyable experience. The bar is well stocked, with two real ales including Mansfield Cask, plus Mansfield Smooth and Original, Heineken, Kronenbourg, Guinness, Strongbow and Woodpecker.

If it's food you're after, you've come to the right place. Children are welcome, and although there's a dining area, you can eat throughout the pub. There's a printed menu and a daily specials board that offer a range of delicious dishes. Treat yourself to the pub's steak and kidney pie or lasagna – both are famous in the area! So to is the inn's ambience, value for money and friendly service. Try it for yourself, and you're bound to agree.

Opening times: Open lunchtime and evenings all week

Food: Served 12.00-14.00 and 19.00-21.00 seven days; it is advisable to book for meals on a Sunday

Credit cards: Cash and cheques only at present

Accommodation: None

Entertainment: Monday evening quiz;

occasional entertainment on other evenings; ring for details

Facilities: Car park, Beer Garden, children's play area

Local Places of Interest/Activities: Hardwick Hall (NT) 5 miles; Stainsby Mill (NT) 5 miles; Mansfield (historic town) 5 miles; Sherwood Forest Country Park and Visitor Centre 6 miles

The Dog Inn

233

Main Road,
Pentrich,
near Ripley,
Derbyshire
DE5 3RE
Tel: 01773 742781

Directions:

Take the A610 west from Ripley, then turn north onto the the B6013. Pentrich is one mile along this road

Pentrich is a stone built village that is full of history. It was here that the Pentrich Revolution - England's last uprising - took place in 1817. There was much poverty and hardship in the land, and groups were forming which demanded political reform. Thomas Bacon was a Pentrich man who was active in the movement all over the Midlands and the North. In 1817 he reported back to the village that an insurrection was imminent, and that organised groups of men would be marching on London. By this time unrest had died down, but Oliver still persuaded Pentrich men to march. Oliver subsequently went into hiding, but the men did set out for London, led by someone called Jeremiah Brandreth. They got as far as Nottinghamshire, where they were confronted by the King's Hussars, who broke up the march. Three men were subsequently executed (including Jeremiah), 14 were transported and six were imprisoned. A well signposted trail takes you round the village, highlighting places associated with the Revolution.

The Dog Inn was built in 1611, so witnessed the events. Up until 1984 it was owned by the Dukes of Devonshire, but was then sold to Peter and Anne Edwards, who have been in charge ever since. It's a four square, handsome stone building in the heart of the village, and now proudly claims to keep alive the memory of the revolutionaries. Peter and Anne are even founder members of the inn's Revolution Club.

The inside looks exactly like a traditional English inn should - low, stout beams, leaded windows, prints on the walls, roaring fires and wall lighting that throw a cozy glow onto the dark polished wood. On offer are two rotating real ales, one of which is usually Bass, plus Kimberley Smooth and Kimberley Mild, Stones, lager, stout and cider. The food is prepared on the premises, and is good, hearty traditional fare, with tasty hot and cold snacks at reasonable prices. So popular is the place that if you want a meal you're advised to book. In the summer months, there are occasional barbecues serving steaks and seafood. When you step over the door of the Dog Inn, you know you're stepping straight into English history!

Opening hours: 11.30-15.00 and 19.00-23.00 seven days

Food: The food is served daily from 11.30-14.30 and 19.00 until late. No food served on Sunday.

Credit cards: Cash only at present

Accommodation: None

Facilities: Car park; beer garden; patio

Local Places of Interest/Activities: National Tramway Museum, Crich: 3 miles; Newstead Abbey 9 miles; Denby Potteries 3 miles; Cromford Mill 6 miles

234 The Duke of Devonshire

71 Bridge Street,
Belper,
Derbyshire
DE56 1BA
Tel: 01773 822324

Directions:

Take the A6 north from Derby for 7 miles until you come to Belper. Bridge Street is in the centre of the town.

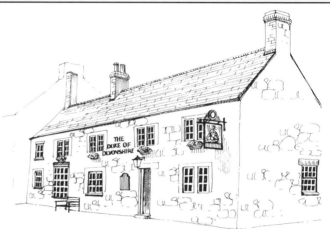

Belper is a former mill town situated in the Amber Valley District of Derbyshire, and it still retains much of its Georgian and Victorian architecture. **The Duke of Devonshire** itself is a handsome 19th century building, stone-built and sturdy, with a nononsense slate roof and a frontage directly onto the main street. But it also has a charm that reminds you of more leisurely days, with its small windows and picturesque pub sign which features - obviously enough - a former Duke of Devonshire.

It's a typical town centre inn with a faithful clientele and - an absolute must in bustling Belper! - a large car park. Inside is spacious and comfortable. The bar gleams with highly polished brass, and the tables and floors are spotless. There's a cozy snug, a lounge, a public bar and a games room where pool is a favourite pastime.

Its food is ample, unpretentious, but always beautifully cooked. The menu consists of traditional Derbyshire dishes plus some old favourites from around the country, and all can be washed down with a glass of the inn's Pedigree cask ales, or one of its frequent guest beers. The place is run by Lisa Simmons, who has just taken it over. Every year, Lisa promises, it will be smartened up and improved to maintain its position as one of the best pubs in Belper.

This is a lovely old pub in a town that deserves to be explored, and it's sure to get even better in the future, as the new owners' plans for it are brought to fruition.

Opening Hours: Open all day

Food: Traditional menu, with the dishes all beautifully cooked

Credit Cards: Cash only at present

Accommodation: None

Facilities: Large car park; beer garden; games room; children's play area

Entertainment: Regular quiz nights; Thu & Sat: karaoke night; Fri: live music

Local Places of Interest/Activities: Kedleston Hall (NT) 5 miles; American Adventure Theme Park 6 miles; Shipley Country Park 5 miles; National Tramway Museum 4 miles; Midlands Railway Centre 4 miles

Internet\Website: e-mail: duke.of.Devonshire@barbox.com

The Elm Tree Inn | 235

Elmton,
near Creswell,
Worksop,
Nottinghamshire
S80 4LS
Tel: 01909 721261

Directions:

Elmton is on a minor road, 1 mile south of the A616 and 3 miles east of the B6417 which connects Bolsover with Clowne or take J30 from the M1

The Elm Tree Inn is one of the most picturesque inns in Derbyshire. The building dates back over 500 years, and with its warm stone and its hanging baskets, it is everything a country inn should be. The interior brims with character and period details, which owners Gwen and Tony Robinson have lovingly preserved. There are low beamed ceilings, subdued wall lighting, comfortable furniture, and a wealth of framed prints, memorabilia and brass ware which sets everything off beautifully.

The food is outstanding. The Old Barn Owl Restaurant is housed in a barn behind the main building, and is open on Friday and Saturday evenings as well as Sunday lunchtimes. The menu for this restaurant includes dishes such as salmon in filo pastry, lamb steak with minted gravy, grilled sirloin steak, tenderloin of pork and griddle chicken breast, plus a selection of vegetarian dishes. Everything is prepared by the inn's own chef, who prides himself on using only the freshest of produce. The Sunday lunches include a range of roasts, with chicken or fish if you prefer.

You can still eat within the inn itself for the rest of the week, and there is also a snack menu and an ever changing specials board that is sure to contain something for everyone. Choose from such things as beef and ale pie, mixed grills, and the amazing "Almighty Cod"! To accompany your meal, wine is available by the bottle or glass. Tony is a former brewer, so as you can imagine, he keeps a good cellar. Four reals ales – Black Sheep, Black Sheep Special, Old Speckled Hen and Tetley – are on offer at the bar, plus Tetley Smooth, Calders, Guinness, Carlsberg, Stella, Holsten, Scrumpy Jack and Strongbow.

Opening times: Open lunchtimes and evenings from Mons to Tues; all day opening Weds to Suns and Bank Holidays

Food: The restaurant is open 19.00-21.30 on Fri and Sat, and 12.00-14.30 on Sun; booking for the restaurant is essential; Food is served in the inn on Mon and Tue between 12.00-14.30 and 18.00-21.30, and all day from Wed to Sun and Bank Holidays

Credit cards: All major cards except Amex

Accommodation: None

Facilities: Car park; large beer garden which is ideal for children

Local Places of Interest/Activities: Worksop (historic town) 9 miles; Chesterfield (historic town) 8 miles; Sutton Scarsdale Hall (ruin) 5 miles; Creswell Craggs 2 miles; Bolsover Castle 3 miles

Internet/website:
robinsons@elmtreeinnelmton.freeserve.co.uk

236 The Excavator

Buckland Hollow,
Ambergate,
Belper,
Derbyshire
DE56 2HS
Tel: 01773 744400

Directions:

Take the A610 east
from Ambergate for
1 mile; The inn
stands just off the
road

In the past, the building occupied by **The Excavator** has been an ice cream parlour and a transport café. Now it is an inn with a strange name - but not so strange when you consider that a past owner actually had a full sized JCB displayed on the roof! Nowadays the locals refer to the inn simply as "The Digger". The building, however, is quite old, with parts dating from the 19th century, when it was an old canal house on the Cromford Canal called Ladybank House. It is a well proportioned, stone building set well off the road, with a finely proportioned frontage and small paned windows.

Ian and Julie Atkinson have been tenants for over two years, and during that time they have made The Excavator one of the most popular inns in the area. There is a warm, cozy bar, a lounge and a restaurant that can comfortably seat 100 people. All are immaculately clean, with pine furniture, rose-coloured walls covered in framed prints, and carpeted floors. Both Ian and Julie are qualified chefs, so the food, naturally enough, is beautifully cooked and presented. There is a varied menu to choose from, or you can order from a specials board. There's everything from a sandwich to a plump, juicy steak, complete with vegetables and chips or potatoes, plus a fine selection of starters and sweets. Children are welcome if they're eating as well. There's also a well stocked bar, with a good range of real ales, keg bitters, ciders, lagers and spirits. Plus, of course, there is a wine list.

The fact that the Excavator has been given an affectionate nickname by the locals tells you this is is a popular and well patronised inn. Ian and Julie have done themselves proud by the high standards they have set and maintained. They have created an inn that offers great value for money, and is both welcoming and friendly.

Opening times: All day, every day in season

Food: High quality food is served from 12.00-21.00 Sunday to Wednesday, 12.00-21.30 on Thursday and Friday, and 12.00-22.00 on Saturday

Credit cards: All major credit cards accepted

Accommodation: None

Facilities: Car park, disabled access at rear,

smoking and non-smoking areas

Local Places of Interest/Activities: National Tramway Museum, Crich: 3 miles; Cromford Mill 5 miles; Golden Valley Light Railway 2 miles; Wirksworth Heritage Centre 5 miles; National Stone Centre, Wirksworth 5 miles; Belper North Mill, Belper 3 miles

The Greyhound Inn 237

Town Street,
Pinxton,
Derbyshire
NG16 6JP
Tel: 01773 810548

Directions:

Pinxton is close to Junction 28 on the M1, 7 miles south west of Mansfield town centre

Anyone visiting the former mining community of Pinxton in Derbyshire shouldn't miss the John King Museum. In the 19th century, King invented a mechanism that made travel in pit cage much safer. Now the museum not only celebrates his name, but displays a wealth of equipment and tools from the days when mining was the main employer in the area.

Not to be missed also is **The Greyhound Inn**. It is renowned for its good food, drink and friendly service, and is housed in a grade 2 listed building that, in the summer months, is a riot of colour thanks to the hanging baskets that adorn its front. It is under the personal management of Les and Irene Stevens, who have 30 years experience in the trade. So you can imagine that the inn is immaculate and well kept, with a snug lounge bar and a 26 seat dining area that is bright and airy.

You can order from a range of ales, including Banks Smooth, Mansfield Original, Smooth and Dark Mild, Fosters, Strongbow, Woodpecker and Guinness. The food is cooked on the premises by Irene and Les's son Peter, who is a trained chef. There's a daily specials board or a printed menu that contains such favourites as lasagna, steak and kidney pie, Lincolnshire sausage, cod fillet in batter and chilli con carne, plus a range of steaks with all the trimmings. If it's just a snack you're after, then there's a range of tasty filled baked potatoes, sandwiches and so on. Vegetarians are catered for, and there is a selection of great starters and sweets. There's also a special Sunday lunch menu, though if you wish to eat then you should book in advance. Every dish at The Greyhound Inn represents outstanding value for money, so you can't go far wrong if you pay it a visit!

Opening times: Open all day, every day

Food: Served every day between 12.00-14.00 and 17.30-21.00; there are lots of special food offers, especially at lunchtime

Credit cards: Cash and cheques only at present

Accommodation; None

Entertainment: Wednesday and Friday evening quiz at 21.00; live entertainment on Saturday evening from 21.00

Facilities: Car park; large beer garden which is safe for children

Local Places of Interest/Activities: John King Museum in the village; Hardwick Hall (NT) 5 miles; Stainsby Mill (NT) 6 miles; Mansfield (historic town) 6 miles; Newstead Abbey 5 miles

238 Hardwick Inn

Hardwick Park,
near Chesterfield
Derbyshire
S44 5QJ
Tel: 01246 850245
Fax: 01246 850365

Directions:

Leave the M1 at
Junction 29. The
inn is at Hardwick
Park, which is well
signposted

This is one of the most historic inns in Derbyshire. So much so that it belongs to the National Trust, and someone has even written a book about its history! It dates from the late 16th century, and was probably founded by Elizabeth Talbot, Countess of Shrewsbury, better known as Bess of Hardwick. It's a mellow, large building of dark, local stone, with leaded windows, gables and an area of grass in front of it that houses a large beer garden. When you step over the threshold of **The Hardwick Inn**, you seem to be stepping back into history. There are two bars, three family rooms, meeting rooms, and roaring coal fires in the winter months. But there are two things the inn lacks, thank goodness - slot machines and juke boxes. Tradition is important here, though the present landlords, Peter and Pauline Batty, haven't sacrificed modern service and efficiency to preserve it.

The range of ales and wines is first class. There are five ales available, including such favourites as "Old Speckled Hen" and "Old Peck". Over 150 malt whiskies and wines galore are also on offer. People come from miles around to sample the food. Bar meals are served, and there's a carvery restaurant with dishes such as roast beef (popular for Sunday lunches), steak and kidney pies (for which the inn is famous), casseroles and fish. There's also a grill, and a changing specials board, though booking in advance is advisable.

The Hardwick Inn is a special place, as it is steeped in history and tradition. Children are welcome, and there's nowhere better for a family meal or quiet, relaxing drink!

Opening hours: Open all day

Food: Bar meals and full meals. Bar meals are served from 11.30-21.30 Monday to Saturday, and 12.00- 21.00 on Sunday. The carvery restaurant is open from 12.00-13.45 and 19.00-21.00 Tuesday to Saturday, and 12.00- 13.45 on a Sunday. It is closed on Monday. Booking for the carvery is advisable.

Credit cards: All credit cards

Accommodation: None

Facilities: Car parking; beer garden

Local Places of Interest/Activities: Stainsby Mill (NT) 1 mile; Hardwick Hall (NT) 1 mile; Sherwood Forest 10 miles; Sutton Scarsdale Hall 3 miles; Newstead Abbey 8 miles

Internet/Website:
website: www.hardwickinn.co.uk
email: batty@hardwickinn.co.uk

Hare And Hounds

239

Sheffield Road, Stonegravels,
Chesterfield, Derbyshire S41 7JH
Tel: 01246 234579

Directions:

The Hare and Hounds is near the centre of Chesterfield

Chesterfield has one of the largest markets in the whole of England, and is open on Monday, Friday and Saturday. It is world famous for its parish church of St Mary and All Saints, which has a crooked spire. It's other clam to fame is that, with its cathedral-like size, it is the largest church in Derbyshire. And not far from this landmark, close to the town centre, is the **Hare and Hounds**, a friendly pub that is managed by husband and wife team Josephine and Steven Lawrence. It is a long building of great charm, built in 1966 to replace an earlier inn which stood where the car park now is. Josephine and Steven have been here since 1998, and have created an inn that is full of character and warmth, making it one of the most popular in the town.

Inside is equally as charming, with a large lounge, a bar and a dining area. This is the kind of place that would appeal greatly to families, as it all tastefully laid out, with plenty of space in which to relax and have a drink or meal. At the bar you can order from a fine selection of draught beers, including John Smith Extra Smooth, Stones, Webster and Chestnut Mild. There are also three lagers, two ciders and Guinness. And if you're driving, of course, there's a good range of soft drinks. Josephine is in charge of the food, and a great job she makes of it. She prepares pub lunches and early evening bar meals that are imaginative, well presented and always value for money. On Friday evening there's a themed food night, which features dishes from all over the world! So popular is it that if you wish to attend you should book in advance to avoid disappointment.

Opening times: Friday to Saturday: 11.00-23.00; Sunday: 12.00-22.30

Food: Served 12.00-14.00 and 17.30-19.30 Mon-Fri (until 21.00 on Friday); Sun 12.00-16.00; Sat - bar snacks only

Credit cards: Cash only at present

Accommodation: None

Entertainment: Monday evening: jamming session; Tuesday evening: pool night; Wednesday evening: quiz night; Thursday evening: music; Friday evening: themed food night, Saturday evening : live music; Sunday evening: quiz night.

Facilities: Car park

Local Places of Interest/Activities: Chesterfield crooked spire in the town; Chesterfield Museum in the town; Sutton Scarsdale Hall 4 miles; the Cuckoo Way, a footpath along the Chesterfield Canal, starts in the town; Revolution House 3 miles

240

Hearts of Oak

22 Northern Common,
Dronfield Woodhouse,
near Chesterfield,
Derbyshire S18 8XJ
Tel: 0114 289 0210
Fax: 0114 254 7058

Directions:

Dronfield Woodhouse
is on the A61, 5 miles
north of Chesterfield

At one time a there was a great forest where the **Hearts of Oak** now stands - hence the pub name. Now the area is semi-suburban, with the pub being one of the most popular in the district. The current building dates from 1931, though an inn has stood on the site since at least the late 17th century. The present building is handsome and impressive, with an interior where you would imagine no expense has been spared to create the perfect ambience. The tables and chairs are of heavy, well polished wood, the floors are thickly carpeted and the wall seating is well upholstered and comfortable. All in all, this is an inn that deserves to be visited for that quiet drink or meal.

Graham and Sharron Hodgkinson have been in charge since December 2000, and are well on their way to creating a pub that has a great atmosphere and offers good service and value for money. Sharon is in charge of cooking, and the chalk board menu has many dishes that are sure to please. You can order dishes that owe their origins to such places as Italy, India, Mexico, Thailand and good old England! The place seats 104 people in comfort, and you can eat throughout the inn.

Wine is available by the glass or bottle, or you can have Stones cask ale. There is also a great range of draught bitter, mild, stout, cider and lager. Why not pay the Hearts of Oak a visit? The drink is excellent, the atmosphere is relaxing, and the food is superb!

Opening times: 12.00-23.00 over 7 days

Food: Served 12.00-15.00 and 17.00—20.00 Monday to Thursday; 12.00-20.00 Friday and Saturday; 12.00-16.00 on Sunday

Credit cards: All major cards accepted except American Express and Diners

Accommodation: None

Entertainment: Quiz and "Play Your Cards Right" on Wednesday evening; karaoke on Friday evenings; live music on Saturday evenings

Facilities: Car park; function room

Local Places of Interest/Activities: Sheffield (historic city) 6 miles; Longshore Estate (NT) 6 miles; Revolution House 3 miles; Chesterfield (historic town) 5 miles

Internet/Website:
e-mail: heartsofoak@ic24.net

The Hurt Arms 241

Derby Road,
Ambergate,
Derbyshire
DE56 2EJ
Tel:01773 852006
Fax: 01773 852372

Directions:
Ambergate is on the
A6, 3 miles west of
Ripley and 3 miles
north of Belper

This is a splendid inn, standing right on the A6. It is a tall, imposing three-storeyed building of golden stone, and was originally a post house with livery and stables. There are fields and a cricket pitch to the side of it and fields and a river to the back, so it occupies a picturesque position. If you're lucky, you might even see a balloon flight, as the field to the back is a popular taking off point! And if you're wondering about the curious name, it comes from the then lord of the manor when the place was built in 1876. In charge since 1998 is Eamonn O'Donoghue, who has been in the trade for over 33 years, and has a wealth of experience in running and maintaining an establishment as prestigious as **The Hurt Arms**.

The place has undergone a recent refurbishment to the highest standards, and is now a popular place, not just for people driving past on the A6, but with the locals as well, which is always a good sign. Eamonn has gone out of his way to create a roadside inn that offers a warm, traditional welcome, In the bar you have the choice of real ales, which include Marston's Pedigree and Mansfield Cask, plus John Smith's Smooth, Budweiser, Fosters, Guinness and Strongbow. You can buy wine by the glass or bottle, and there is a well thought out and reasonably priced wine list (including some fine Champagnes!) if you fancy something special with your meal.

The Hurt Arms restaurant seats 50, and the food is excellent. You can have a bar lunch (which you can also eat in the comfortable lounge), by choosing from the menu or a specials board, or a full meal in the dining room. On Monday, Wednesday and Friday evenings there are "steak nights", which are always popular. So too are the roast lunches on Sunday. In fact, you'd be well advised to book on a Friday, Saturday or Sunday. The Hurt Arms is the sort of inn where you'll always get a warm welcome. Eamonn and his staff will see to that!

Opening times: All day, every day

Food: High quality food is served from 12.00-21.00 every day; there are special "steak nights" every Mon, Wed, Fri

Credit cards: All major credit cards accepted

Accommodation: None

Entertainment: Quiz night every Friday

starting around 21.15-21.30; sometimes watching balloons take off from the field behind the inn!

Facilities: Car park; children's area; patio

Local Places of Interest/Activities: National Tramway Museum, Crich: 2 miles; Cromford Mill 4 miles; Golden Valley Light Railway 3 miles; Wirksworth Heritage Centre 4 miles

242

Jolly Farmers

Heath Road,
Holmewood,
Derbyshire
S42 5RB
Tel: 01246 855608

Directions:

Leave the M1 at Junction 29 and follow the A615 west for 1 mile

The Jolly Farmers is a friendly inn set in the pleasant Derbyshire village of Holmewood. At one time it was a hotel and country club before being converted into an inn by a former pit owner. But for all its origins, the place looks exactly how a country inn should look, even though it must be the only pub in Britain with its own belfry!

Under the guidance of husband and wife team Mick and Karen Revill, it has earned an enviable reputation in the area as a place that offers not only a warm welcome to its visitors – be they locals or people passing through – but great value for money when it comes to food and drink. The interior is comfortable and cozy, with carpeted floors, oak fittings, gleaming brass and copper, and superb lighting that adds the right touch of ambience and class to the place. As soon as you step over the threshold you know – this is the kind of inn where you can really relax and enjoy a drink or meal!

Try its steak and ale pie, which is a living legend in the area. In fact, all its food is beautifully cooked and presented. Karen is in charge of the kitchen, and prides herself in using only the freshest ingredient, which are bought locally if possible. The cuisine is wide ranging, and you can have dishes that are traditionally English, or you can go for something with a hint of Italian of Greek about it. This isn't surprising – they used to run two pubs on a Greek island! You can buy wine by the bottle or glass, or why not try one of the two real ales on offer at the bar? There's also a range of draught bitters, mild, lager, stout and cider, and , of course, soft drinks if you're behind the wheel. And one more thing – if you're a computer buff, seek out Mick. He owns his own software business!

Opening times: 12.00-23.00 seven days

Food: Monday to Saturday: 12.00-15.00 and 17.30-21.30; Sunday (carvery) 12.00-15.00

Credit cards: All major cards accepted except American Express and Diners

Accommodation: None

Entertainment: Saturday evenings: live music; Thursday evenings: quiz; occasional theme nights (phone for details)

Facilities: Car park; beer garden; children's play area; barbecues in summer

Local Places of Interest/Activities: Chesterfield (historic town) 4 miles; Mansfield (historic town) 7 miles; Sutton Scarsdale Hall 2 miles

Internet/Website:
e-mail: micknevill@totalise.uk

Kelstedge Inn 243

Matlock Road,
Kelstedge,
near Chesterfield
Derbyshire
S43 0DX
Tel:01246 590448

Directions:
The village of
Kelstedge is on
the A632, 6 miles
south west of
Chesterfield town
centre

Within the pleasant village of Kelstedge you'll find the **Kelstedge Inn**. It dates form 1759, and has all the appeal of a traditional country pub. It sits on a corner site at the brow of a steep hill, and is an attractive building of local stone, with an old barn attached, creating a small courtyard to the front. The walls are thick, the windows are small paned and quaint, and it is everything an English pub should be – warm and cozy in winter, and cool and welcoming in summer. The range of fine ales at its bar will also keep you cool when temperatures rise. There are three real ales on offer – two resident and a rotating guest ale, plus draught mild, bitter, stout, lager and cider.

In charge is Mandy Goodlad, and under her care, the inn has gained an enviable reputation in the local area as the place for a drink or a meal. The interior is every bit as attractive as the exterior, with open fires, highly polished wood and comfortable furniture. Just off the main bar is the 25 seat restaurant, which has a roomy feel to it. Here, you feel as you enter, is the ideal place to eat! The inn has its own highly experienced chef, who has put together a menu that features many classic country dishes. If you want a real treat, try his steak and mushroom pie, which is very popular with the regulars. He prides himself in sourcing only the finest local produce for his dishes, and everything must be as fresh as possible.

This is an inn that offers real value for money. The barn will soon be converted into comfortable accommodation, offering three double and three twin rooms, all en suite, and these too will be competitively priced.

Opening times: Monday to Friday: 11.00-15.00 and 18.00-23.00; Saturday and Sunday: all day

Food: 12.00-14.30 and 18.00-21.00 every day

Credit cards: None

Accommodation: 3 double rooms and 3 twin rooms, all on the ground floor, and all en suite. with TV and tea and coffee making facilities

Entertainment: Quiz night every 4th Tuesday

Facilities: Car park; beer garden; children's play area

Local Places of Interest/Activities: Chesterfield (historic town) 6 miles; Mansfield (historic town) 12 miles; Peak Railway 4 miles; Chatsworth 7 miles; Heights of Abraham 4 miles

244

The Peacock

Hackney Lane,
Barlow,
near Chesterfield,
Derbyshire
S18 7TD
Tel: 01142 890296

Directions:

Barlow is on the
B6051 4 miles north
west of Chesterfield
town centre

Barlow is a pleasant little village nestling in the hills that edge the Peak District National Park. And within it you'll find **The Peacock**, a quaint yet sturdy inn built of local stone. One look tells you that it is steeped in history and tradition. It dates from the 17th century, and with its thick walls, picturesque porch and white framed windows, it is everything an English inn should be. Mine host Dave Burgess takes a great pride in the look and atmosphere of the place, and he has created an interior that is every bit as attractive as the outside. As you step over the threshold, you are greeted in winter by roaring log fires, gleaming wood and brass, and an old world atmosphere that speaks of comfort and hospitality.

The small bar is especially inviting, and is a favourite place for locals and visitors alike to meet and relax. You can order from a wide range of drinks, including Pedigree cask ale, draught bitter, mild, lager, stout and cider, plus, of course, soft drinks if you're driving. You can also eat here, and the food is traditional English, with some European and Indian influences, and many old favourites are on the menu or the daily specials board. The dishes are always beautifully cooked and presented, and all use the freshest of ingredients. There's also a popular Sunday carvery, with a choice of two roast meats. There is one en suite family room to let, and the price includes a hearty English breakfast.

David is a man who loves both his village and his pub. So much so, that in a village with no bank, he even offers a cash-back service to his customers! If you visit his inn, he'll offer you a warm Derbyshire welcome.

Opening times: Monday to Friday: 12.00-15.00 and 18.00-23.00; Saturday and Sunday: all day

Food: Served 12.00-14.30 and 18.00-20.30; Sunday lunch served from 12.00-15.00

Credit cards: All major cards accepted (with cash back facilities)

Accommodation: 1 en suite family room with fridge , colour TV and tea and coffee making facilities

Entertainment: Occasional murder/mystery evenings; phone for details

Facilities: Car park; beer garden with summer barbecues

Local Places of Interest/Activities: Chesterfield (historic town) 3 miles; Sheffield (historic city) 8 miles; Longshore Estate (NT) 5 miles; Chatsworth 6 miles

Internet/Website:
e-mail: Davidburgess89@freeserve.co.uk

The Pebley Inn

Rotherham Road,
Barlborough,
Chesterfield
S43 4TH
Tel and Fax:
  01246 810327

Directions:

Leave the M1 at
Junction 30. The Pebley
Inn is on the A618
between Barlborough
and Killamarsh

This is one of those wayside inns that England does so well - smart, whitewashed walls, bay windows, hanging baskets and an attractive red-tiled roof. It's been given a recent makeover, and the owners, Chris Dennis and Andrea Godfrey Cooke, who have only recently taken over, are planning great things for it, without sacrificing any of its traditional atmosphere.

Inside is cozy, welcoming and spotlessly clean. There's a large snug and lounge, and the walls are covered with framed colliery awards. The seating is especially comfortable, and there is no assault on the ears, as a juke box is conspicuous by its absence! Instead there is background music (not too loud!) which both relaxes and soothes as you stretch your feet out and enjoy a quiet drink or a bar meal.

If you're after good, traditional home cooking, then **The Pebley Inn** is for you. The meals are made from fresh, local home grown produce, and are always reasonably priced and tasty. Try the fisherman's breakfast, which is one of the inn's specialities. If you're a walker, then there's hot tasty soups, tea and coffee. Drinks on offer include cask conditioned beers, guest ales, and the usual wines and spirits.

Chris and Andrea are working hard to make this one of the best inns in the district, and judging by what they've achieved so far, they're well on the way to succeeding. Children and dogs are welcome, and they're eager to extend a warm welcome to regulars and newcomers as well.

Opening hours: 12.00-23.00 from Monday to Saturday and 12.00-22.30 on Sunday

Food: Traditional, honest and tasty.

Credit cards: Visa, Access and Switch

Accommodation: Phone for a list of the nearest guest houses

Entertainment: Local live music on special days (such as St Patrick's Day); darts and other pub games; regular fun quiz nights

Facilities: Large car park

Local Places of Interest/Activities: Pebley Reservoir close to inn (fishing); good walking country; Bolsover Castle 4 miles; Hardwick Hall 8 miles; Clumber Park (NT) 9 miles; Sherwood Forest 11 miles

246

The Railway

King Street,
Belper,
Derbyshire
DE56 1PW
Tel: 01773 822223

Directions:

Belper is on the A6, 7 miles north of derby. The inn is on one of the town's main streets

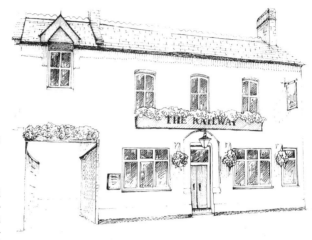

Belper is an ex mill town with many Victorian and Georgian buildings from its industrial past. Located on one of the town's main streets near the railway station, is **The Railway**, an inn that has a traditional look - brick built, whitewashed, colourful and full of character. It was once part of a hotel dating from the early 19th century, and is now run by Geoff and Gill Fisher, who both left professional occupations a few months ago to take it over.

The interior is smart and airy, yet with a homely feel. It has a wonderful mixture of old and new, the predominant features being dark wood, papered walls and thick carpets throughout. This is very much a town inn, popular with locals, passersby and visitors alike who want a friendly welcome, cheery surroundings and good company. The inn is open all day, and stocks a wide selection of drinks. There are rotating real ales, plus John Smith's Smooth, Younger's Scotch, Theakston's Mild, Fosters, Kronenberg, draught Budweiser, Strongbow and Guinness. The food is best described as "traditional pub", and you can order from a menu or specials board. The dishes include such dishes as rump steaks, an all day breakfast, battered fish, beef and ale pie and lasagna, all served with crispy, piping hot chips. Plus you can order extra portions of onion rings, breaded mushrooms, garlic bread and so on. There's also a vegetarian and children's menu, and a range of desserts. Sunday lunches - which are roasts only - are always popular, and you can choose from a choice of meats. This is an "eat anywhere" pub, and children are welcome if you're having a meal.

Opening times: Open all day every day

Food: Served Monday to Saturday 11.30-14.00 and 16.30-19.00; Sunday: (roasts only) 12.30-14.30; no food served on a Sunday evening

Credit cards: Cash and cheques only at present

Accommodation: None

Entertainment: Karaoke every Thursday

evening at 20.00; vocalist/guitarist once a month on Wednesday or Sunday - phone for details

Local Places of Interest/Activities: Belper North Mill within the town; Kedelston Hall (NT) 5 miles; American Adventure (theme park) 6 miles; Shipley Country Park 6 miles; National Tramway Museum, Crich 5 miles

The Railway

Cowens Lane,
Shottle,
Derbyshire
DE56 2LF
Tel: 01773 550271
Fax: 01773 550832

Directions:

The village of Shottle is on a minor road 3 miles north west of Belper

The Railway at Shottle sits on a busy crossroads controlled by traffic lights, but is miles away from the hustle and bustle of life lived in the fast lane. It is a clean, whitewashed building that dates from the 1800s, and seems to hark back to a simpler time when people had time to relax and put their feet up. In the summer months, the exterior positively froths with hanging baskets, adding lots of bright colour to an already enchanting inn.

Shottle itself is a picturesque hamlet in the midst of many country lanes, and it has kept its unspoiled look. It was here that Samuel Slater, apprentice to Jedediah Strutt, who built the first water powered cotton mill in the USA, was born.

Under the guidance of John Uttley for the last 30 years or so, the inn has become the hostelry in the area if you want to eat or drink. Its food, in fact, is famous throughout the district. Both John and his wife cook, and they've put together a wonderful menu that includes many delicious and popular dishes. The cuisine can best be described as good, old fashioned English fayre, and both John and his wife pride themselves in the quality and freshness of the produce that goes into every dish. The large restaurant can seat up to 100 people in absolute comfort, and the inn's Sunday lunches and carvery are a legend. In fact, there are two carveries a week just to keep up with the demand!

The interior manages to combine a sense of space with a cozy, warm atmosphere. The tables are of oak, there are carpets on the floor, and the lighting is subdued – the ideal place in which to relax over a quiet drink. You can choose from Marston Pedigree, Banks or Mansfield real ales, or there's a selection of draught bitters, mild, stout, cider and lager. There's also a wide range of spirits, and, if you're driving, soft drinks.

Opening times: Open 11.30-23.00 seven days

Food: Served whenever open

Credit cards: Most major credit cards accepted except American Express and Diners

Accommodation: None

Facilities: Car park; beer garden with occasional barbecues in summer; children's play area

Local Places of Interest/Activities: Belper (historic town) 3 miles; Carsington Water (fishing) 4 miles; Wirksworth Heritage Centre 3 miles; National Tramway Museum, Crich 4 miles

248   The Royal Oak Inn

Derby Road,
Old Tupton,
near Chesterfield,
Derbyshire S42 6LA
Tel: 01246 862180

Directions:

Old Tupton is on the A61, 3 miles south of Chesterfield town centre

The Royal Oak is famous for its real ales. No less than nine varieties are on offer at its bar, something that the husband and wife team of Karen and John Angus is extremely proud of. They've been mine hosts for some time now, and have created an inn that is a pleasure to visit. It dates from 1830, and is a handsome, well proportioned building that sits on a roundabout. With its old, mellow red brick, its small paned windows and jaunty pub sign, it represents everything that is traditional and good about the English inn. The interior continues this theme. There is a snug, cozy bar and a comfortably furnished lounge with carpeted floor and sparkling woodwork, as well as a games room with pool table, dart board, giant Jenga and skittles. It's all spotlessly clean and welcoming, meaning that any visit to this inn is a pleasure.

Apart from the nine real ales served in oversized glasses, you can also order from a fine selection of lagers, stout and cider, and, of course, there are soft drinks if you're driving. Wine is available by the glass or bottle, and they complement the food perfectly. It is John that does the cooking, and a great job he makes of it. The cuisine is traditional English, with many old favourites on the menu. The most popular dish, according to the regulars, is liver and onions with mashed potatoes and peas, and they would recommend it to anyone. All the meals are cooked to perfection, using fresh produce wherever possible, and the portions are generous.

The Royal Oak is an inn that sets great store by value for money. Karen and John want to make any visit to their hostelry an enjoyable experience, and in this they succeed admirably. Voted CAMRA pub of the Season, it also has the Cask Marque (Certificate of Excellence).

Opening times: Monday to Saturday 12.00-23.00; Sunday 12.00-22.30

Food: Monday to Saturday 12.00-14.30; Thursday to Saturday 18.00-20.00(steak nights)

Credit cards: Cash or cheques only

Accommodation: None

Entertainment: Thursday and Sunday: quiz nights

Facilities: Car park; children's play area; skittle alley; pétanque court; games room

Local Places of Interest/Activities: Chesterfield (historic town) 3 miles; Mansfield (historic town) 10 miles; Sutton Scarsdale Hall 4 miles; Stainsby Mill (NT) 4; Hardwick Hall (NT) 5 miles

The Summit 249

Carter Lane,
Shirebrook,
near Mansfield,
Nottinghamshire
NG20 8NA
Tel: 01623 742375

Directions:

Shirebrook is 4 miles north of Mansfield, on the B6407; the inn is situated a short walk from the town centre

Shirebrook is a large colliery village whose last pit closed in 1993, ending a long tradition of coal mining in the area that stretched back well over 100 years. And within the village you'll find an attractive inn called **The Summit**, which, though it dates only from the 1950s, continues another long tradition – that of hospitality and a warm welcome. It is built of warm, red brick, with an attractive gable at the front and window frames painted in a contrasting white.

Stephen and Donna Barrowcliffe have been mine hosts since 2000. Stephen is local – in fact, he was born in the next street to the inn – and he has over 15 year's experience in the licensed trade. For this reason, The Summit is dear to his heart. There's a snug bar, a well appointed lounge, a 40 seat restaurant where children are welcome, and all are spotlessly clean.

Here you can have a lunchtime meal of a drink in complete comfort. At the bar, there's a choice of a hand pulled real ale, plus you can have John Smith Smooth, Theakston bitter and mild, Fosters, McEwans lager or Strongbow and Woodpecker cider. The food is good, honest pub grub, and none the worse for that! The portions are hearty, the ingredients are always as fresh as possible, and they represent great value for money. Every Sunday there's a traditional roast carvery, and so popular is it that to avoid disappointment you should book a table. In the evenings, basket meals are also available.

This is an inn where you're sure of a warm welcome. It's a real "local" which is appreciated by regulars and visitors alike.

Opening times: Monday to Saturday: lunchtimes and evenings; Saturday and Sunday: all day

Food: Served 12.00-15.00; basket meals only in the evening

Credit cards: Cash and cheques only at present

Accommodation: None

Entertainment: Bingo on Tuesday at 21.30; quiz every Thursday at 21.30; live entertainment every Saturday and Sunday at 21.30

Facilities: Car park; beer garden to rear

Local Places of Interest/Activities: Hardwick Hall (NT) 4 miles; Stainsby Mill (NT) 4 miles; Mansfield (historic town) 4 miles; Sherwood Forest Country Park and Visitor Centre 6 miles

250 The White Hart Inn

2 Church Street,
Heage, Derbyshire
DE56 2BG
Tel: 01773 852302

Directions:

From the A38(Derby/
Mansfield Road) take
the A610 towards
Ambergate/Matlock.
After ¼ mile turn left
signed B6013 Heage/
Belper. The pub is at
the end of this road
as you enter Heage.

You can't miss the village of Heage. As soon as you see an impressive windmill standing proud in a field, you know you're there! It was restored in the 1960s, and was originally used to grind corn when a stream that drove a watermill dried up in summer. Standing in the middle of the village, and every bit as proud, is the 400 year old **White Hart Inn**. With its lower walls made of mellow stone, and the upper walls half timbered, it presents a picturesque sight. Since March 2000 Malcolm and Marian Hawley have personally run, as landlord and landlady, this freehouse village pub that brims over with character and warmth. The interior is comfortable and welcoming, with subdued lighting in the bar and dining area. This is a real ale pub with cask conditioned ales such as Marston's Pedigree, Bass, Courage Directors and a rotating guest ale. If you're driving, Kaliber is stocked as well.

The food is marvellous. You can choose from a large and varied menu, which includes bar lunches and snacks, full restaurant meals plus something for the kids. Home made meals include Steak & Ale pie, curry and chilli with many of the desserts also home made. In the main menu there's everything from deep fried scampi to steaks, mixed grills and chicken. The specialities menu includes giant filled Yorkshire puddings, pasta and tuna mix and the vegetarian menu is predominately home made. Sunday lunches are very popular, and you're advised to book. The White Hart hosts themed food nights on the last Wednesday of each month, and themes so far have included Mexico, Scottish, Medieval, Spanish and Cajun-Creole. If you want wine with your meal, you can buy it by the glass or bottle from a comprehensive wine list.

Opening times: Mon to Fri: 12.00-14.30, 17.00-23.00; Sat: 12.00-15.00,18.00-23.00; Sun: 12.00-15.00, 19.00-22.30

Food: Bar food ; Mon to Fri: 12.00-14.00, 18.00-19.00: Restaurant meals; every day until 21.00: the speciality menu available until 21.00 Mon to Sat; Sun lunch; 12.00-14.30.

Credit cards: all major credit cards accepted

Accommodation: None

Entertainment: themed food nights

Facilities: Games/childrens room; disabled facilities; car park; function room; patio and garden area

Local Places of Interest/Activities: Heage Windmill on edge of village; Village Carnival & Fete annually in June; National Tramway Museum, Crich: 3 miles; Cromford Mill 4 miles; Golden Valley Light Railway 2 miles

Internet/website:
website: www.white-hart-heage.co.uk
e-mail: whitehart@heage.fsbusiness.co.uk

White Horse

251

High Street,
Old Whittington,
near Chesterfield,
Derbyshire
S41 9LQ
Tel: 01246 450414

Directions:

Old Whittington is on the B6052, off the A6, 3 miles north of Chester-field town centre

The White Horse is an inn that is famous for its real ale. No less that four are available at its bar – two permanent and two rotating guest ales. The building itself dates from 1726, though, of course, there have been additions to it throughout the years. It is well situated, and is popular with the locals and those passing through. In addition to the real ales, you can also order from a fine selection of draught bitters, mild, stout, cider and lager, plus of course, there's a range of soft drinks as well.

The inn is run by the husband and wife team of Martin and Hazel Smith, who take a great pride in its appearance and the service it offers. The interior is spotless, with a comfortable lounge, bar and a small dining area. The whole place is cozy and snug, while at the same offering plenty of space in which to relax. It's a real family pub where children are welcome, and it makes the ideal stopping off point if you're exploring an area that is rich in history and attractions. The food can best be described as traditional pub food – beautifully cooked on the premises, and hearty portions on the plate! All the ingredients are as fresh as possible, and source locally wherever possible.Try the speciality of the house, steak and kidney pie. It's a local legend! There's a printed à la carte menu and a daily specials board, and for those who just want a bar snack, these can be provided as well.

Martin, as anyone local will tell you, is the star turn in the White Horse! Both he and Hazel will give you the warmest of welcomes should you visit.

Opening times: Monday to Saturday: 11.45-15.00 and 17.00-23.00; open all day Sunday until 22.30

Food: Served 12.00-14.00 and 17.00-21.00 Monday to Saturday and 12.00-20.00 on Sunday

Credit cards: All major cards accepted

Accommodation: None

Entertainment: Make your own!

Facilities: Car park

Local Places of Interest/Activities: Revolution House (within village); Chesterfield (historic town) 3 miles; Sheffield (historic city) 8 miles; Longshore Estate (NT) 7 miles; Chatsworth 8 miles

Internet/Website:
e-mail: martinwhitehorse@tiny-co.uk

252   Winsick Arms

Mansfield Road, Hasland,
near Chesterfield,
Derbyshire S41 0JH
Tel: 01246 206847 Fax: 012246 221204

Directions:

The Winsick Arms is next to the village of Hasland, which is on the A617, 2 miles south east of Chesterfield town centre

Though it is on the outskirts of Chesterfield, the hamlet of Winsick still retains a feeling of rural calm. Within the hamlet you will find the **Winsick Arms**, a handsome and rambling inn that has, as its core, an old farm house. As we are in a former coal mining area, it will come as no surprise to find that it has mining associations – it was once the local pit manager's house. It sits close to Junction 29 of the M1, so it makes the ideal stopping off point for a drink or meal.

In charge of the inn is the Owen family – Rosemarie, Glyn and son Jonathan. They've been there since 1996, and in that time have completely changed the place, both in character and atmosphere. Now it is a warm, friendly place, and popular with the local population. The interior is spotlessly clean, with lots of nooks, crannies and comfortable corners where you can sample the range of ales on offer at the bar. The real ale here is Theakston, though you can also order Tetley, Boddington and two guest ales, as well as cider, stout and lager. You can order from a printed menu or from a specials board which changes daily. The inn takes great care with the food it serves, and dishes such as steak and kidney pie, grilled gammon and fish of the day are much in demand by the regular customers. From Monday to Saturday 18.00-21.00, you can even get a free starter and sweet with every main course you order. On Sunday, the Winsick Arms offers a three course special lunch, for which it is advisable to book, and it represents amazing value for money.

Opening times: Monday to Saturday: 12.00-23.00; Sunday 12.00-22.30

Food: Served 12.00-21.00 seven days

Credit cards: All except Amex and Diners

Accommodation: None

Entertainment: Quiz night on Tuesday and Thursday; occasional theme nights (ring for details)

Facilities: Car park; beer garden; children's play area; occasional barbecues in the summer

Local Places of Interest/Activities: Chesterfield (historic town) 2 miles; Sutton Scarsdale Hall 3 miles; Hardwick Hall (NT) 6 miles; Stainsby Mill(NT) 5 miles

9 The Peak District and Derbyshire Dales

PLACES OF INTEREST:

PUBS AND INNS:

The Hidden Inns of the Heart of England

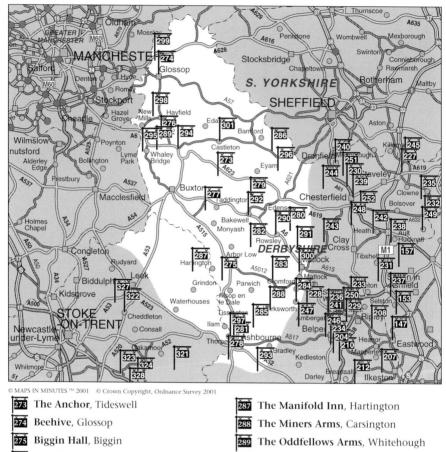

© MAPS IN MINUTES ™ 2001   © Crown Copyright, Ordnance Survey 2001

273 The Anchor, Tideswell

274 Beehive, Glossop

275 Biggin Hall, Biggin

276 Chinley Lodge, Chinley

277 Church Inn, Chelmorton

278 The Cock Inn, Clifton

279 Croft Country House Hotel, Great Longstone

280 The Devonshire Arms, Beeley

281 The George and Dragon, Ashbourne

282 The George Hotel, Youlgreave

283 The Hollybush Inn, Grangemill

284 The Hope and Anchor, Wirksworth

285 The Ketch, Kniverton

286 The Little John, Hathersage

287 The Manifold Inn, Hartington

288 The Miners Arms, Carsington

289 The Oddfellows Arms, Whitehough

290 The Peacock Hotel, Rowsley

291 Plough Inn, Two Dales

292 The Red Lion, Bakewell

293 The Red Lion Inn, Hollington

294 The Roebuck, Chapel-en-le-Frith

295 The Shepherds Arms, Whaley Bridge

296 Sir William Hotel, Grindleford

297 Smiths Tavern, Ashbourne

298 The Sycamore, Birch Vale

299 The Victoria Inn, Hadfield

300 The White Lion, Starkholmes

301 Ye Old Cheshire Cheese Inn, Castleton

Please note all references refer to page numbers

The Peak District and
Derbyshire Dales

Most of north Derbyshire has come to be synonymous with The Peak District. The first of Britain's National Parks, The Peak District covers an area of 540 square miles. Its situation, close to the large industrial conurbations of Manchester, Sheffield, Derby, Nottingham and Staffordshire, have meant that this region of high, windswept moorland and charming river valleys has always been popular. From the time of the first railways into the area, in the mid 19th century, the Peak District has been a mecca for walkers and those wishing to discover its many secrets. The National Park is scattered with the remains of ancient settlements. The origin of the word 'peak' probably comes from the Pecsaetans, or hill people, a primitive tribe who are thought to have settled here in around the 7th century. At most of the crossings into the Park there are millstones standing on stone plinths at the side of the road. These are used as boundary markers by the Park Authority, which has also adopted the millstone symbol as its logo.

Referred to as the Dark Peak as well as the High Peak, the northern area of the Peak District National Park is not as foreboding as it names might suggest. These high moors are ripe for exploring on foot, and a walk from the Kinder Reservoir will lead to the western edge of Kinder Scout. This whole area is really a series of plateaux, rather than mountains and valleys, with the highest point on Kinder Scout some 2,088 feet above sea level. In this remote and wild area the walker can feel a real sense of freedom - however, it is worth remembering that the moors, with their treacherous peat bogs and unpredictable mists which can rise quickly even in summer, should not be dismissed as places for a casual ramble.

The northern region of the Derbyshire Dales, sometimes also known as the Central Peaks and occupying the central area of the Peak District National Park, is less wild and isolated than the remote High Peak area. The two main rivers, the Wye and the Derwent, which both have their source further north, are, in this region, at a more gentle stage of their course. Over the centuries, the fast-flowing waters were harnessed to provide power to drive the mills situated on the riverbanks; any walk taken along these riverbanks will not only give the opportutnity to discover a wide range of plant and animal life, but also provide the opportunity to see the remains of buildings that once played an important part in the economy of north Derbyshire.

The southern section of the Peak District is probably best known for the beautiful Dovedale. The wonderful valley, just a few hundred yards from the large carpark at Thorpe, is well worth experiencing. It is also the place to have a go at crossing a river on stepping stones, something that has delighted children for many, many years, though, particularly when the water level is high, there is a bridge just downstream which ensures that the crossing can be made with dry feet.

The River Dove is also a mecca for keen fishermen. It was a favourite spot for Izaak Walton, who wrote his famous book, *The Compleat Angler* (first published in 1653) in the area, and his influence is impossible to escape. Nor is Dovedale the only dale worth exploring. The River Manifold offers some equally wonderful scenery and, in particular, there is Ilam. A beautifully preserved estate village, with a well established youth hostel, this is also a popular starting point from which to explore the Manifold Valley.

The ancient custom of well-dressing is almost exclusively confined to the limestone areas of the county. The porous rock, through which rainfall seeped leaving the surface completely dry just a few hours after heavy rainfall, meant that, for the people of these closeknit communities, the well or spring was of utmost importance. If this dried up, the lives of the whole community were at risk. There are plenty of theories as to why well dressing began or was revived at Tissington. One centres on the purity of the Tissington wells during the Black Death which swept through the country in the mid-1300s. During this time some 77 of the 100 clergy in Derbyshire died and the surviving villagers simply returned to the pagan custom of well dressing. Another plausible theory dates back only as far as the great drought of 1615, when the Tissington wells kept flowing though water everywhere was in very short supply. Whichever theory is true, one thing is certain, that in the last 50 years or so many villages who had not dressed a well for centuries, if ever, are now joining in the colourful tradition.

PLACES OF INTEREST

ALSOP-EN-LE-DALE

The old station on the Ashbourne-Buxton line which once served this tiny hamlet is today a car park on the Tissington Trail. The tranquil hamlet itself is on a narrow lane east of the main road towards Parwich, just a mile from Dovedale. Alsop-en-le-Dale's parish church of St Michael is Norman, though it was rebuilt substantially during Victorian times. The nave retains Norman features, with impressive double zigzag mouldings in the arches, but the west tower is only imitation Norman, and dates from 1883. One unusual feature which dominates this small church is its extraordinary 19th century, square mock-Gothic pulpit.

Opposite the church is the graceful and slender building known as **Alsop Hall**, constructed in the early 1600s. Though privately owned, it is worth seeing even for its exterior, as it is built in a handsome pre-classical style with stone-mullioned windows.

Alsop makes a good base for exploring the White Peak. It is also convenient for Dovedale. The renowned **Viator's Bridge** at Milldale is only a mile away to the west, as immortalised in Izaak Walton's The Compleat Angler in a scene in which the character Viator complains to another about the size of the tiny, two-arched packhorse bridge, deeming it "not two fingers broad".

ARBOR LOW

This remote stone circle is often referred to as the "**Stonehenge of the Peaks**", and although many of the stones now lie on the ground it is still an impressive sight. There are several stone circles in the Peak District but none offer the same atmosphere as Arbor Low, nor the same splendid views. Built around 4,000 years ago by the early Bronze Age people, there are a total of 40 stones each weighing no less than 8 tonnes. Probably used as an observatory and also a festival site, it is likely that the stones, which have been placed in pairs, never actually stood up. The circular mound to the south of the stone circle, which originally rose some 20 feet above the ditch, offers some protection against the weather and this is from which Arbor Low got its name - "sheltered heap".

ASHBOURNE

Featuring as "Esseburn" (ash tree stream) in the Domesday Book, Ashbourne was originally a small settlement lying on the northern bank of Henmore Brook, which already had a church. It was a 13th century lord of the manor who laid out the new town to the east around its unusual shaped market place. Many of the town's traders, in order to continue to enjoy the benefits without paying the town's tolls, built themselves houses on the south side of the Brook. The area became known as Compton and it was slowly absorbed into the town. When writing *Adam Bede*, George Eliot based "Oakbourne" in "Stonyshire" on the town.

Often called The Gateway to the North, today this is one of Derbyshire's finest old towns, with a wealth of wonderful Georgian architecture. It is a pleasure to visit, with plenty of shop-filled streets to potter up and down. The triangular cobbled **Market Square**, in the heart of Ashbourne, was part of the new development begun in the 13th century that shifted the town to the east, away from the Church. Weekly markets have been held in the square since 1296, and now take place every Saturday. It was from this market place, that used to be lined with ale houses, that Bonnie Prince Charlie proclaimed his father to be King James III, and so started the Jacobite Rebellions. Though the old bull ring no longer exists, the town boasts many fine examples of 18th century architecture as well as some older buildings, notably the Gingerbread Shop which is timber framed and probably dates from the 15th century. Traditional Ashbourne gingerbread is said to be made from a recipe that was acquired from French prisoners of war who were kept in the town during the Napoleonic Wars.

Also worthy of a second glance is the **Green Man and Black's Head Royal Hotel**. The inn sign stretches over the St John's Street and was put up when the Blackamoor Inn joined with the Green Man in 1825. Though the Blackamoor is no more, the sign remains and it claims to be the longest hotel name in the country. Of Georgian origin, the amalgamated Hotel has played host to James Boswell, Dr Johnson and the young Princess Victoria. Ashbourne was, in fact, one of Dr Johnson's favourite places; he came to the town on several occasions between 1737 and 1784. He also visited the hotel so often that he had his own chair with his name on it! The chair can still be seen at the Green Man.

A stroll down Church Street, described by Pevsner as one of the finest streets in Derbyshire, takes the walker past many interesting Georgian houses - including the **Grey House** which stands next to the **Grammar School**. Founded by Sir Thomas Cockayne on behalf of Elizabeth I in 1585, the school was visited on its 400th anniversary by the present Queen. Almost opposite the Grey House is **The Mansion**, the late 17th century home of the Reverend Dr John Taylor, oldest friend of Dr Johnson. In 1764, a domed, octagonal drawing room was added to the house, and a new brick facade built facing the street. Next to The Mansion are two of the many almshouses established in Ashbourne during the 17th and 18th centuries. Ashbourne also retains many of its narrow alleyways and, in particular, there is Lovatt's Yard where the town lock-up can be seen.

In **St Oswald's Parish Church** Ashbourne has one of the most impressive and elegant churches in the country, described by George Eliot as "the finest mere parish church in England". James Boswell said that the church was "one of the largest and most luminous that I have seen in any town of the same size". St Oswald's stands on the site of a minster church mentioned in the Domesday Book, though most of what stands today dates from rebuilding work in the 13th century. There is a dedication brass in the south transept dated 1241. The south doorway, with its dog-toothed decoration and ribbed moulding, reflects the church's classic Early English style. St Oswald's has chapels to its transepts, adding to the spacious feeling that is more reminiscent of a small cathedral than a parish church.

The alabaster tombs and monuments to the Bradbourne and Cockane families in the north transept chapel are justly famous. Perhaps the best-known monument is that to Penelope Boothby, who died in 1791 at the tender age of five. Thomas Banks' white Carrara marble figure of the sleeping child is so lifelike that she still appears to be only sleeping. The moving epitaph reads: "She was in form and intellect most exquisite; The unfortunate parents ventured their all on this frail bark, and the wreck was total." It is said that Penelope's parents separated at the child's grave and never spoke to each other again. The tower and gracious 212 foot spire of the church were erected between 1330 and 1350, at the crossing of the nave and transepts.

Ashbourne is home, too, to the famous Shrovetide football game played on Shrove Tuesday and Ash Wednesday. The two teams, the "Up'ards" (those born north of the Henmore Brook) and the "Down'ards" (those born south of it) begin their match at 2 p.m. behind the Green Man Hotel. The game continues until well into the evening. The two goals are situated three miles apart, along the Brook, on the site of the old mills at Clifton and Sturston. It is rare for more than one goal to be scored in this slow-moving game.

BAKEWELL

The only true town in the Peak District National Park, Bakewell attracts many day-trippers, walkers and campers as well as locals who come to take advantage of its many amenities. The beautiful medieval five-arched bridge spanning the River Wye is still in use today as the main cross-

258

ing point for traffic. A stonebuilt town set along the banks of the River Wye, Bakewell enjoys a picturesque setting among well-wooded hills. With only 4,000 inhabitants it is nevertheless generally acknowledged as the capital of the Peak District National Park.

However, for most people it is a dessert that has made the name of Bakewell so famous, but please remember it is referred to locally as a *pudding* and most definitely not as a tart! Its invention is said to have been an accident when what was supposed to have been a strawberry tart turned into something altogether different. The cooking mishap took place in the kitchens of the Rutland Arms Hotel, which was built in 1804 on the site of a coaching inn. One of the hotel's more famous guests was the novelist Jane Austen, who stayed there in 1811. The Rutland Arms featured in her book *Pride and Prejudice*, while Bakewell itself appears as the town of Lambton.

Bakewell's situation has always made it the ideal place for a settlement and, as well as being home to the Romans, an Iron Age fort has been discovered close by. Another reason for the popularity of the town was the existence of 12 fresh water springs and they also gave the town its name - Bad kwell means bath spring. This Old English name means "Badeca's spring" or "well", and is a reference to the warm, iron-bearing springs which rise in and around the town.

The market town for this whole central area of the Peak District, markets were held here well before the granting of a charter in 1330. In fact, its importance during the 11th century was such

that, as recorded in the Domesday Book of 1086, Bakewell had two priests. Monday is now Bakewell's market day and the cattle market, one of the largest in Derbyshire, is an important part of the area's farming life. The annual Bakewell Show, held every summer, started in 1819 and has gone on to become one of the foremost agricultural shows in the country. Across the River Wye stands the enormous, new Agricultural and Business Centre, where the livestock market takes place.

The large parish **Church of All Saints** was founded in Saxon times, as revealed by the ancient preaching crosses and stonework. Its graceful spire, with its octagonal tower, can be seen for miles around. One of the few places in Derbyshire in the Domesday book to record two priests and a church, the churchyard and church itself contain a wonderful variety of headstones and coffin slabs and, near the porch, a most unusual cross. Over 1,200 years old, it stands an impressive 8 feet high. On one side it depicts the Crucifixion, on the other are the Norse gods Odin and Loki.

Behind the church is the lovely **Old House Museum**, housed in a building on Cunningham Place which dates back to 1534. It is thought to be the oldest house in Bakewell. This beautiful building escaped demolition and has been lovingly restored by the Bakewell Historical Society and now displays its original wattle and daub interior walls. It was extended during the early 17th century and, at one time, the building was converted into tenements by the industrialist Richard Arkwright for his mill-workers. Now established as a folk museum, it houses a fascinating collection of rural bygones.

The town is full of delightful, mellow stone buildings, many of which date from the early 17th century and are still in use today. The **Old Town Hall**, famous as the scene of the Bakewell riots, is now the Tourist Information Centre of the Peak District. Few buildings remain from the days when Bakewell was a minor spa town, but the **Bath House**, on Bath Street, is one such building. Built in 1697 for the Duke of Rutland, it contained a large bath which was filled with the spa water and kept at a constant temperature of 59 degrees Fahrenheit. At the nearby Bath Gardens a Roman bath was discovered near the British Legion's Garden of Remembrance.

Traditionally well-dressing flourished in the town in the 18th century, when Bakewell had aspirations to become a fashionable spa. How-

River at Bakewell

ever, the recent revival dates back only to the 1970s, when the British Legion - with the help of the well-dressers of Ashford in the Water - dressed the warm well at Bath House. Today, all five wells - all in the same room - are dressed on the last Saturday in June.

Only a mile to the south of Bakewell down the Matlock Road, on a bluff overlooking the Wye, the romantic **Haddon Hall** stands hidden from the road by a beech hedge. The Hall is thought by many to have been the first fortified house in the country, although the turrets and battlements were actually put on purely for show. The home of the Dukes of Rutland for over 800 years, the Hall has enjoyed a fairly peaceful existence, in part no doubt because it stood empty and neglected for neary 300 years after 1640, when the family chose Belvoir Cas-

Haddon Hall, Bakewell

tle in Leicestershire as their main home. Examples of work from every century from the 12th to the 17th are here in this treasure trove. As with all good ancestral homes, it has a family legend. In this case the story dates from the 16th century when Lady Dorothy Vernon eloped with Sir John Manners. Although there is no historical evidence to back the claim that Dorothy Vernon eloped with John Manners during a ball - many feel this legend was invented by the Victorians, in part because neither the steps nor the pretty little packhorse bridge across the Wye, over which Dorothy is supposed to have escaped, existed during her time - a small museum by the gatehouse tells of their romantic journey, as well as the history of the Hall.

Little construction work has been carried out on the Hall since the days of Henry VIII and it

remains one of the best examples of a medieval and Tudor manor house. The 16th century terraced gardens are one of the chief delights of the Hall and are thought by many to be the most romantic in England. The Hall's splendour and charm have led it to be used as a backdrop to television and film productions including *Jane Eyre*, *Moll Flanders* and *The Prince and the Pauper*. Nikolaus Pevsner described the Hall as "The English castle par excellence, not the forbidding fortress on an unassailable crag, but the large, rambling, safe, grey, loveable house of knights and their ladies, the unreasonable dream-castle of those who think of the Middle Ages as a time of chivalry and valour and noble feelings. None other in England is so complete and convincing."

BAMFORD

This charming village situated between the Hope Valley and Ladybower Reservoir, stands at the heart of the Dark Peak below Bamford Edge and close to the Upper Derwent Valley Dams. When the Derwent and Howden Dams were built in the early years of the 20th century, the valley of the Upper Derwent was flooded, submerging many farms under the rising waters. The 1,000 or so navvies and their families were housed at Birchinlee, a temporary village which came to be known locally as 'Tin Town', for its plethora of corrugated iron shacks. During the Second World War the third and largest reservoir, the Ladybower, was built. This involved the inundating of two villages — Derwent and Ashopton. The dead from Derwent's church were re-interred in the churchyard of St John the Baptist in Bamford. The living were rehoused in Yorkshire Bridge, a purpose-built hamlet located below the embankment of the Ladybower Dam. There is a Visitor Centre at **Fairholmes** (in the Upper Derwent Valley) which tells the story of these 'drowned villages'.

The **Derwent Dam**, built in 1935, was the practice site for the Dambusters, who tested dropping their bouncing bombs here.

Bamford's **Church of St John the Baptist** is unlike any other in Derbyshire. Designed in 1861 by famous church architect William Butterfield, it has a slender tower and an extra-sharp spire. Also worthy of note, particularly to lovers of industrial architecture, is **Bamford**

260

Mill, just across the road by the river. This cotton mill was built in 1820; it retains its huge waterwheel and also has a 1907 tandem-compound steam engine. Like many cotton mills of its time, the original mill burnt to the ground just 10 years after it was erected; the mill standing today was its replacement.

Along the A57 towards Sheffield, the road dips and crosses the gory-sounding **Cutthroat Bridge**. The present bridge dates back to 1830, but its name comes from the late 16th century, when the body of a man with his throat cut was discovered under the bridge which then stood here.

BRADLEY

A regular visitor to the Georgian **Bradley Hall** (private) was Dr Johnson, who would visit the Meynell family here when he was staying in Ashbourne with his friend, Dr John Taylor. The Meynells had come to Bradley in 1655 and bought the hall from Sir Andrew Kniveton, who had been financially ruined by the Civil War.

The archway crossing the formerly gated road between cottages at Moorend is known locally as "The Hole in the Wall". The village pub has the distinction, common in Derbyshire, of having two official names, The Jinglers and the Fox and Hounds. Nearby **Bradley Wood** was given to the people of Ashbourne in 1935 by Captain Fitzherbert Wright.

BUXTON

Referred to as the heart of the Peak District, Buxton, England's highest market town at 1,000 feet above sea level, provides a wealth of things to do. The current popularity of the town can be attributed to the 5th Duke of Devonshire, however it was the Romans who first discovered the waters here and named the place *Aquae Arnemetiae* - The Spa of the Goddess of the Grove. With waters maintained at a constant temperature of 82 degrees F (28 degrees C), Buxton soon became a place of pilgrimage, particularly for sufferers of rheumatism. Among the pilgrims from all over Britain was Mary Queen of Scots, held at Chatsworth for many years. **St Anne's Well** still provides water and many people coming to the town make a point of trying the tepid waters. The people of Buxton also say that it makes the best cup of tea possible, and collect bottles of it to take home.

In the 18th century, the 5th Duke of Devonshire, with the intention that Buxton would rival Bath as a spa town, commissioned the building of **The Crescent** to ensure that visitors would flock here. Designed by John Carr of York, the building is similar to the architecture found in Bath and, after suffering from neglect, underwent a huge restoration programme. As with many places, the coming of the railway to Buxton in 1863 marked the height of popularity of the town. Nothing, however, could be done to alter the harsh climate, and the incessant rainfall meant that the Duke's dream of making Buxton the 'Bath of the North', was never truly realised.

Originally built in 1905, the attractive **Opera House** was restored, in 1979, to its grand Edwardian style. After being used as a cinema for many years, it is once again the host of live performances and, as well as offering a comprehensive and popular programme throughout the year, also has one of the largest stages in England.

The attractive **Pavilion Gardens** have a conservatory and octagon within the grounds - antique markets and arts shows are often held here, and it is a very pleasant place to walk any time of year. Laid out in 1871 by Edward Milner, with money donated by the Dukes of Devonshire, the 23 acres include formal gardens, serpentine walks and decorative iron bridges across the River Wye. The conservatory was reopened in 1982 following extensive renovation; there is also a swimming pool filled with warm spa water.

It is not known for certain whether well-dressing took place in Buxton before 1840, though there are stories that Henry VIII put a stop to the practice, but it has certainly been a part of Buxton's cultural calendar since the Duke of Devonshire provided the townsfolk with their first public water supply at **Market Place Fountain**. From then on, High Buxton Well (as the fountain came to be called) and St Anne's Well were decorated sporadically. In 1923, the Town Council set about organising a well-dressing festival and carnival that continues to this day. Every year on the second Wednesday in July, this delightful tradition is enacted.

Buxton is surrounded by some of the most glorious of the Peak District countryside. These moorlands also provide one of the town's specialities - heather honey. Several varieties of heather grow on the moors: there is *ling*, or common heather which turns the land purple in late summer; there is bell-heather which grows on dry rocky slopes; and there is cross-leaved heather which can be found on wet, boggy ground.

The town is also the starting point for both the **Brindley Trail** and the **Monsal Trail**. Covering some 61 miles, the Brindley Trail, which takes its name from the famous canal engineer, leads southwest to Stoke-on-Trent, while the Monsal Trail, beginning just outside Buxton at Blackwell Mill Junction, finishes as Coombs Viaduct near Bakewell, some 8 miles away.

To the west of the town lies **Axe Edge**, the highest point of which rises to 1,807 feet above sea level. From this spot on a clear day (and the weather here is notoriously changeable) the panoramic views of Derbyshire are overwhelming. Just beyond, at 1,690 feet above sea level, the **Cat and Fiddle Inn** is the second highest pub in England. Axe Edge Moor, which receives an average annual rainfall of over 4 feet, is strictly for hardened walkers. It should come as no surprise that this Moor is the source of several rivers which play important roles in the life of the Peak District. The **River Dove** and the **River Manifold**, which join at Ilam, rise not far from one another; the **River Wye** rises above Buxton to join the Derwent further south; the **River Goyt**, a major source of the Mersey, rises to the west of Axe Edge.

Those who venture to **Errwood Reservoir** will be surprised to see rhododendrons growing near the banks of a man-made lake. They once stood in the grounds of Errwood Hall, which was built in the 1830s for the Grimshawe family. The house was demolished before the Reservoir was flooded, but the gardens were left to grow wild. Not far away can be seen the strange-looking Spanish Shrine. Built by the Grimshawes in memory of their Spanish governess, it is a small stone building with an unusual beehive roof.

The highest point in this area is **Shining Tor**, overlooking Errwood Reservoir and standing some 1,834 feet above sea level. To the north is Pym Chair, the point at which an old packhorse road running east to west crosses this gritstone ridge. An old salters' route, it was used for transporting salt from the Cheshire plains across the Peak District moorlands to the industrial and well-populated areas of south and west Yorkshire.

Also to the west of town, **Poole's Cavern** on Green Lane is a natural limestone cave which was used by tribes from the Neolithic period onwards. Visited by Mary, Queen of Scots (the 'chair' she used is still in evidence, and pointed out during the regular tours of the cave on offer) evidence of prehistoric remains have been found near the

261

Poole's Cavern, Buxton

cave entrance. Above the cavern and about 20 minutes' walk away is Grin Low Country Park and the prominent folly and scenic viewpoint, built in 1896, known as Solomon's Temple.

CASTLETON

Situated at the head of the Hope Valley, Castleton is sheltered by the Norman ruin of **Peveril Castle** (built by Henry II in the 1170s) and is overlooked by Mam Tor. Approaching Castleton from the west along the A625, the road runs through the **Winnats Pass**, a narrow limestone gorge. Thought to have been formed under the sea, from currents eroding the seabed, the gorge has been used as a road for centuries and is still the only direct route to the village from the west.

Originally laid out as a planned town below its castle, the shape of the village has changed little over the years and it has become a popu-

262

lar tourist centre. The mainly 17th century church of St Edmund was heavily restored in 1837, but retains its box pews and a fine Norman arch, as well as a Breeches Bible dated 1611.

The hills to the west of Castleton are famous for their caves. The **Blue John Mine and Caverns**, which have been in the hands of the Ollerenshaw family for many years, are probably one of Derbyshire's most popular attractions. Amazing trips down into the caves themselves can be made. During these trips, as well as seeing the incredible natural beauty of the caverns and the unique rock formations, there are collections of original 19th century mining tools.

At the bottom of Winnats Pass lies **Speedwell Cavern**, a former lead mine which used boats on an underground canal to ferry the miners and iron ore to and from the rockface. Visitors can follow the same boat journey underground in the company of a guide. The mine had a short life: it started up in 1771 and, following an investment of £14,000, closed in 1790 after only £3,000 worth of iron ore had been extracted.

Peak Cavern, reached by a delightful riverside walk, has the widest opening of any cave in Europe. Up until the 17th century, little cottages used to stand within the entrance. The ropemakers who lived in these tiny dwellings used the cave entrance, dry in all weathers, for making rope: the ropewalk, which dates back some 400 years, can still be seen. Guides re-enact the process of making rope, and one ropemaker's cottage is still extant. Recently the cave was used by the BBC, who filmed an episode of *The Chronicles of Narnia* series here. Over the years successive Kings and Queens would entertain deep within the belly of the cave, which would be festooned with candles and other open flames - visitors can see the ledge on which the Royal musicians would perch. Peak Cavern was originally known as The Devil's Arse, though the Victorians - ever fastidious - felt this was 'inappropriate' and changed it to the name it carries today.

No description of Castleton would be complete without a mention of **Mam Tor**. The name means 'Mother Hill', and locally the Tor is referred to as Shivering Mountain, because the immense cliff face near the summit is constantly on the move owing to water seepage. A climb to the top of the ridge is well worth while, as the views are splendid - in particular of the two diverse rock formations which can be made out and which separate the White (limestone) Peak from the northern Dark (gritstone) Peak.

CROMFORD

Cromford is a model village known the world over, which was developed by Richard Arkwright into one of the first industrial towns. In addition to housing, he also provided his workers with a market place and a village Lock-Up. Born in Lancashire in 1732, Arkwright was the inventor of the waterframe, a machine for spinning cotton that was powered by water. He built his first mill at Cromford in 1771, the project taking a further 20 years to complete. It was the world's first successful water-powered cotton spinning mill. The area he had chosen proved to be perfect: the River Derwent, described by Daniel Defoe as "a fury of a river", provided an ample power supply; there was an unorganised but very willing workforce, as the lead-mining industry was experiencing a decline, and probably most importantly, Cromford was away from the prying eyes of Arkwright's competitors. In 1792, Arkwright commissioned the building of the village church, where he now lies. The Mill proved to be a great success and became the model for others both in Britain and abroad, earning Arkwright the accolade "Father of the Factory System". His pioneering work and contributions to the great Industrial Age resulted in a knighthood in 1786, and one year later he became High Sheriff of Derbyshire.

Cromford Mill and the associated buildings are now an International World Heritage site. Tours of the mill and Cromford village are available throughout the year. Continuing refurbishment and conservation by The Arkwright Society, who bought the site in 1979, ensures that future visitors will be able follow the fascinating history behind this pioneering establishment. It is sponsored by Derbyshire County Council and the Derbyshire Dales District Council. Within the complex of the mill site there are a range of craft workshops and also the Mill Restaurant with its excellent home-cooked refreshment including a wide selection of wholefood dishes.

Cromford has a rather odd 15th century bridge, which has rounded arches on one side and pointed arches on the other. It was from this bridge, in 1697, so local folklore has it, that a horse and rider took a flying leap from the parapet, plunged into the river 20 feet below and lived to tell the tale. The **Cromford Venture Centre** is an ideal base for study visits, holidays, training and self-development courses. It offers self-catering accommodation for parties of up to 24 young people and four staff. It is run by the Arkwright Sociey in association with the Prince's Trust.

For lovers of waterways, there is an opportunity at **Cromford Canal** to potter along the five-mile stretch of towpath to Ambergate, or better still, to take a peaceful canal boat ride. The Cromford Canal Society, which organises the boat trips along the canal, also maintains the **Cromford Wharf Steam Museum**. Its exhibits include the 1902 Robey horizontal engine donated by Friden Brickworks from nearby Hartington. The Museum is open by arrangement for private steamings and working demonstrations. The old **Leawood Pumping Station**, which transferred water from the River Derwent to the Cromford Canal, has been fully restored. Inside the engine house is a preserved Cornish-type beam engine which is occasionally steamed up. Close by the Pump House is the **Wigwell aqueduct**, which carries the Canal high over the River Derwent.

The **High Peak Trail**, which stretches some 17 miles up to Dowlow near Buxton, starts at Cromford and follows the trackbed of the Cromford and High Peak Railway. First opened in 1880, the railway was built to connect the Cromford Canal with the Peak Forest Canal and is somewhat reminiscent of a canal as it has long level sections interspersed with sharp inclines (instead of locks) and many of the stations are known as wharfs. After walking the trail it is not surprising to learn that its chief engineer was really a canal builder! The railway was finally closed in 1967; the old stations are now car parks and picnic areas; there is an information office in the former Hartington station signal box. Surfaced with clinker rather than limestone, the trail is suitable for walkers, cyclists and horses.

EDALE

In the valley of the River Noe, Edale marks the start of the **Pennine Way**. Opened in 1965, this long-distance footpath follows the line of the backbone of Britain for some 270 miles from here to Kirk Yetholm, just over the Scottish border. Though the footpath begins in the lush meadows of this secluded valley, it is not long before walkers find themselves crossing the wild and bleak moorland of featherbed Moss before heading further north to Bleaklow. Many travellers have spoken of Derbyshire as a county of contrasts, and nowhere is this more apparent than at Edale. Not only does the landscape change dramatically within a short distance from the heart of the village, but the weather - as all serious walkers will know - can alter from brilliant sunshine to snowstorms in the space of a couple of hours.

The village, in the heart of dairy-farming and stock-rearing country, began as a series of scattered settlements that had grown around the shepherds' shelters or bothies. The true name of the village is actually Grindsbrook Booth, but it is commonly known by the name of the valley. Tourism first came to Edale with the completion of the Manchester to Sheffield railway in 1894, though at that time there was little in the way of hospitality for visitors. Today there are several hotels, camping sites, a large Youth Hostel and adventure and walking centres.

Not far from the village is the famous **Jacob's Ladder**, overlooking the River Noe. Nearby is the tumbledown remain of a hill farmer's cottage; this was the home of Jacob Marshall, who some 200 years ago cut the steps into the hillside leading up to Edale Cross.

EDENSOR

This model village (the name is pronouced Ensor) was built by the 6th Duke of Devonshire between 1838 and 1842 after the original village had been demolished because it spoilt the view from Chatsworth House. Unable to decide on a specific design for the buildings, as suggested by his architect Paxton, the Duke had the cottages and houses in the new village built in a fascinating variety of styles. The village church was built by Sir George Gilbert Scott; in the churchyard is buried the late President Kennedy's sister Kathleen, who had married into the Cavendish family. Both she and her husband, the eldest son of the 10th Duke, were killed during the Second World War. The original village of Edensor lay nearer to the gates of Chatsworth House; only Park Cottage remains there now.

The home of the Dukes of Devonshire, **Chatsworth House**, known as the "Palace of

264

the Peak", is without doubt one of the finest of the great houses in Britain. The origins of the House as a great showpiece must be attributable to the redoubtable Bess of Hardwick, whose marriage into the Cavendish family helped to secure the future of the palace.

Bess' husband, Sir William Cavendish, bought the estate for £600 in 1549. It was Bess who completed the new House after his death. Over the years, the Cavendish fortune continued to pour into Chatsworth, making it an almost unparalleled showcase for art treasures. Every aspect of the fine arts is here, ranging from old masterpieces, furniture, tapestries, porcelain and some magnificent alabaster carvings.

The gardens of this stately home also have some marvellous features, including the Emperor Fountain, which dominates the Canal Pond and is said to reach a height of 290 feet. There is a maze and a Laburnum Tunnel and, behind the house, the famous Cascades. The overall appearance of the park as it is seen today is chiefly due to the talents of "Capability" Brown, who was first consulted in 1761. However, the name perhaps most strongly associated with Chatsworth is Joseph Paxton. His experiments in glasshouse design led him eventually to his masterpiece, the Crystal Palace, built to house the Great Exhibition of 1851.

Plague Cottages, Eyam

The village itself is quite large and self-contained, and typical of a mining and quarrying settlement. An interesting place to stroll around, there are many information plaques documenting events where they took place. The **Church of St Lawrence** houses an excellent exhibition of Eyam's history. Also inside the Church are two ancient coffin lids; the top of one of the lids is known as St Helen's Cross.

Born in Derbyshire, St Helen was the daughter of a Romano-British chief and the mother of Emperor Constantine. She is said to have found a fragment of the cross on which Jesus was crucified. In the churchyard is the best preserved Saxon cross to be found in the Peak District, along with an unusual sundial which dates from 1775.

The home of the Wright family for over 300 years, **Eyam Hall** is a wonderful, unspoilt 17th century manor house that is now open to the public. As well as touring the house and seeing the impressive stone-flagged hall, tapestry room and the magnificent tester bed, there is also a cafe and gift shop. The Eyam Hall Crafts Centre, housed in the farm building, contains several individual units which specialise in a variety of unusual and skilfully-fashioned crafts.

EYAM

Pronounced "Eem", this village will forever be known as the **Plague Village**. In 1666, a local tailor received a bundle of plague-infected clothing from London. Within a short time the infection had spread and the terrified inhabitants prepared to flee the village. However, the local rector, William Mompesson, persuaded the villagers to stay put and, thanks to his intervention, most neighbouring villages escaped the disease. Eyam was quarantined for over a year, relying on outside help for supplies of food which were left on the village boundary. Out of a total of 350 inhabitants, only 83 survived.

An open-air service is held each August at Cucklet Delf to commemorate the villagers' brave self-sacrifice, and the well-dressings are also a thanksgiving for the pureness of the water. Taking place on the last Sunday in August, known as Plague Sunday, this also commemorates the climax of the plague and the death of the rector's wife, Catherine Mompesson.

GLOSSOP

At the foot of the Snake Pass, Glossop is an interesting mix of styles: the industrial town of the 19th century with its towering Victorian mills and the 17th century village with its charming old cottages standing in the cobble streets. Further back in time, the Romans came here and established a fort now known as **Melandra Castle**, but probably then called Zerdotalia (or Ardotalia). Built to guard the entrance to Longdendale, little survives today but

Old Glossop

queror", Grindon is reputed to have been visited by Bonnie Prince Charlie on his way to Derby.

The splendid isolation in which this village, like others nearby, has always stood is confirmed by a look around the churchyard. The names on the epitaphs and graves reflect the closeknit nature of the communities. The Salt family, for instance, are to be seen everywhere, followed closely by the Stubbs, Cantrells, Hambletons and, to a lesser extent, the Mycocks.

In the church can also be found a memorial to six RAF men who were killed in 1947 when their Halifax aircraft crash landed during a blizzard on Grindon Moor when trying to parachute in food packages to the surrounding villages which had been totally cut off by the excessive snowfall.

the stone foundations. The settlement developed further, as part of the monastic estates of Basingwerk Abbey in north Wales and the village received its market charter in 1290 but, subsequently, there was a decline in its importance. Little remains of Old Glossop except the medieval parish Church of All Saints.

Planned as a new town in the 19th century by the Duke of Norfolk, the original village stood on the banks of the Glossop Brook at the crossing point of three turnpike roads. The brook had already been harnessed to provide power for the cotton mills, as this was one of the most easterly towns of the booming Lancashire cotton industry. Many still refer to the older Glossop as Old Glossop and the Victorian settlement as Howard Town, named after the Duke, Bernard Edward Howard.

From Glossop, the A57 East is an exhilarating stretch of road, with hair-pin bends, known as the **Snake Pass**. The road is frequently made impassable by landslides, heavy mist and massive snowfalls in winter but, weather permitting, it is an experience not to be missed. For much of the length of the turnpike road that Thomas Telford built across Snake Pass in 1821, the route follows the line of an ancient Roman road, known as **Doctor's Gate**, which ran between Glossop and a fort at Brough. The route was so named after it was rediscovered, in the 16th century, by Dr Talbot, a vicar from Glossop.

GRINDON

This unique moorland hill village stands over 1,000 feet above sea level and overlooks the beautiful Manifold Valley. Recorded in the Domesday Book as "an ancient manor in the 20th year of the reign of William the Con-

HARTINGTON

This charming limestone village was granted a market charter in 1203 and it is likely that its spacious market place was once the village green. Now a Youth Hostel (the oldest in the Peak District, opening in 1934), **Hartington Hall**, built in the 17th century and enlarged in the 19th century, is typical of many Peak District manor houses and a fine example of a Derbyshire yeoman's house and farm. The village is also the home to the only cheese factory remaining in Derbyshire. From the dairy, not far from the village mere, Stilton, veined, plain or flavoured, is still made and can be bought at the dairy shop.

The village is very much on the tourist route and, though it is popular, Hartington has retained much of its village appeal. As well as the famous cheese shop, there are two old coaching inns left over from the days when this was an important market centre, which still serve refreshments to visitors. One of these goes by the rather unusual name of The Charles Cotton; named after the friend of Izaak Walton.

Situated in the valley of the River Dove, Hartington is an excellent place from which to explore both the Dove and the Manifold valleys. To the south lies Beresford Dale, the upper valley of the River Dove that was immortalised by Izaak Walton and Charles Cotton when *The Compleat Angler* was published in 1653. Telling of their fishing experiences on this famous trout river, it is not surprising that the pair chose this

266

Dale as their favourite site. Cotton was born, and lived, at Beresford Hall and, though it is no more, the Dale is easily as pretty as its more famous neighbour Dovedale.

HAYFIELD

This small town below the exposed moorland of **Kinder Scout** is a popular centre for exploring the area and offers many amenities for hillwalkers. Like its neighbour New Mills, Hayfield grew up around the textile industry, in this case wool weaving and calico printing. Many of the houses seen today were originally weavers' cottages. A curious building can be found in **Market Street** on the left of a small square known as **Dungeon Brow**. Built in 1799, this was the town's lock-up and was referred to as the New Prison. However, the stocks in front of the building appear to be somewhat newer than the prison itself.

At the other end of the Sett Valley Trail, the old station site has been turned into a picnic area and information centre. The elegant Georgian parish **Church of St Matthew** is a reminder of this Pennine town's former prosperity.

Three miles northeast of the town is **Kinder Downfall**, the highest waterfall in the county, found where the River Kinder flows off the edge of Kinder Scout. In low temperatures the fall freezes solid - a sight to be seen. It is also renowned for its blow-back effect: when the wind blows, the fall's water is forced back against the rock and the water appears to run uphill! There are not many natural waterfalls in Derbyshire, so Kinder Downfall appears on most visitors' itineraries. Not far from the bottom of the fall is a small lake known as Mermaid's Pool. Legend has it that those who go to the pool at midnight on the night before Easter Sunday will see a mermaid swimming in the dark waters.

ILAM

Now a model village of great charm, Ilam was originally an important settlement belonging to Burton Abbey. Following the Reformation in the 16th century, the estate was broken up and Ilam came into the hands of the Port family. In the early 19th century the family sold the property to Jesse Watts Russell, a weathly industrialist. As well as building a fine mansion, **Ilam Hall**, for himself, Russell also spent a great deal

of money refurbishing the attractive cottages. Obviously devoted to his wife, he had the Hall built in a romantic Gothic style and, in the centre of the village, he had the Eleanor Cross erected in her memory. No longer a family home, Ilam Hall is now a Youth Hostel.

The ancient parish **Church of the Holy Cross**, with its saddleback tower, was largely rebuilt in 1855, and again the family are not forgotten as there is an enormous Watts Russell mausoleum dominating the north side. Opposite, on the south side, there is a little chapel which was rebuilt in 1618 and contains the shrine of a much-loved Staffordshire saint and local Saxon prince, Bertelin. The chapel became the object of many pilgrimages in medieval times. Another important Saxon item inside the church is the font in the nave whilst outside in the churchyard there are several Saxon cross shafts. As with many other churches in Derbyshire, it was the custom for garlands to be hung in the Church on the death of a young girl in the parish. The sad, faded "virgin crants", referred to by Shakespeare at the death of Ophelia, can still be seen.

Many places in the Peak District have provided the inspiration for writers over the years and Ilam is no exception. The peace and quiet found here helped William Congreve create his bawdy play *The Old Bachelor*, whilst Dr Johnson wrote *Rasselas* whilst staying at the Hall. In the valley of the River Manifold, and a much-used starting point for walks along this beautiful stretch of river, in summer the Manifold disappears underground north of the village to reappear below Ilam Hall. The village is the place where the Rivers Manifold and Dove merge. Though Dovedale is, and probably deservedly so, the most scenic of the Peak District valleys, the Manifold Valley is very similar and whilst being marginally less beautiful it is often much less crowded. The two rivers rise close together, on Axe Edge, and for much of their course follow a parallel path, so it is fitting that they should also come together.

LYME PARK

Lyme Park is an ancient estate, now in the hands of the National Trust, was given to Sir Thomas Danyers in 1346 by a grateful King Edward III after a battle at Caen. Danyers then passed the estate to his son-in-law, Sir Piers Legh, in 1388. It remained in the family until 1946, when it was given to the Trust. Not much remains of the original Elizabethan manor house; today's visitors are instead treated to the sight of a fantastic Palladian mansion, the work of Venetial architect Giacomo Leoni. Not daunted by the bleak landscape and climate of the surrounding Peak District, Leoni built a corner of Italy here in this much harsher countryside. Inside the mansion there is a mixture of styles: the elegant Leoni-designed rooms with rich rococo ceilings, the panelled Tudor drawing room, and two surviving Elizabethan rooms. Much of the three-dimensional internal carving is attributed to Grinling Gibbons, though a lot of the work was also undertaken by local craftsmen.

As well as the fantastic splendour of the mansion, the estate includes a late 19th century formal garden and a medieval deer park. The grounds now form a country park administered by the local Borough Council. Though close to the Manchester suburb of Stockport, the estate lies wholly within the Peak District National Park.

MATLOCK

Matlock is a bustling town nestling in the lower valley of the River Derwent, and is the administrative centre of Derbyshire as well as being a busy tourist centre bordering the Peak District National Park. There are actually eight Matlocks which make up the town, along with several other hamlets. Most have simply been engulfed and have lost their identity as the town grew, but Matlock Bath, the site of the spa, still maintains some individuality.

Matlock itself is famed as, at one time, having the steepest-gradient (a 1-in-5½) tramway

Peak Rail, Matlock

in the world; it was also the only tram system in the Peak District. Opened in 1893, the tramcars ran until 1927 and the Depot can still be seen at the top of Bank Street. The old Ticket Office and Waiting Room at Matlock station have been taken over by the Peak Rail Society and here can be found not only their shop, but also exhibitions explaining the history and aims of the society. The Peak Rail has its southernmost terminus just a few minutes' walk from the mainline station.

Peak Rail is a rebuilt, refurbished and now preserved railway running between Matlock Riverside station (just a five-minute walk from the mainline station at Matlock) through the charming rural station of Darley Dale to the terminus Rowsley South. In future it is hoped that the line can be extended to Bakewell.

Inside Matlock's **Church of St Giles** can be seen the faded and preserved funeral garlands or "virgin crants" that were once common all over Derbyshire. Bell-shaped, decorated with rosettes and ribbons and usually containing a personal item, the garlands were made in memory of a deceased young girl of the parish. At her funeral the garland was carried by the dead girl's friends and, after the service, it would be suspended from the church rafters above the pew she had normally occupied.

High up on the hill behind the town is the brooding ruin of **Riber Castle**. The castle was built between 1862 and 1868 and is often linked with the McCaig folly which overlooks Oban on the west coast of Scotland. The castle's creator, John Smedley, a local hosiery manufacturer who became interested in the hydropathic qualities of Matlock, drew up the designs for the building himself. Lavishly decorated inside, Smedley constructed his own gas-producing plant to provide lighting for the Castle and it even had its own well.

Following the death of first Smedley and then his wife, the castle was sold and for a number of years it was boys' school. During the Second World War, the school having closed, the castle was used as a food store before it was left to become a ruined shell. Today the building and surrounding grounds are home to a sanctuary for rare breeds and endangered species; the **Wildlife Park** has been particular successful at breeding lynx, and boasts the world's largest collection of this magnificent animal.

268

To the west of Matlock, down a no-through road, can be found one of Derbyshire's few Grade I listed buildings, the secluded and well-hidden **Snitterton Hall.** Little is known of the history of this fine Elizabethan manor house, though it is believed to have been built by John Milward in 1631, around the same time that he purchased half the manor of Snitterton.

MATLOCK BATH

It is not known whether the Romans discovered the hot springs here, but by the late 17th century the waters were being used for medicinal purposes and the Old Bath Hotel was built. Like many other spa towns up and down the country, it was not until the Regency period that Matlock Bath reached its peak. As well as offering cures for many of the ills of the day, Matlock Bath and the surrounding area had much to offer the visitor and, by 1818, it was being described as a favourite summer resort. The spa town was compared to Switzerland by Byron and it has also been much admired by the Scottish philosopher, Dr Thomas Chalmers, and Ruskin, who stayed at the New Bath Hotel in 1829. Many famous people have visited the town, including the young Victoria before she succeeded to the throne.

The coming of the railways, in 1849, brought Matlock Bath within easy reach, at small cost, to many more people and it became a popular destination for day excursions. Rather than being a town for the gentility, it became a place for the genteel. Today, it is still essentially a holiday resort and manages to possesses an air of Victorian charm left over from the days when the puritanical Victorians descended on the town looking for a "cure".

One of the great attractions of the town is **The Aquarium**, which occupies what was once the old **Matlock Bath Hydro** that was established in 1833. The original splendour of the Bath Hydro can still be seen, in the fine stone staircase and also in the thermal large pool which now is without its roof. The pool, maintained at a constant temperature of 68 degrees Fahrenheit, was where the rheumatic patients came to immerse themselves in the waters and relieve their symptoms. Today, the pool is home to a large collection of Large Mirror, Common and Koi Carp whilst the upstairs consulting rooms now house tanks full of native, tropical

and marine fish. Visitors are welcome to feed the fish with food obtainable from the Aquarium. Also at The Aquarium is the **Hologram Gallery** a mind-boggling exhibition of three dimensional pictures made using the latest laser technology, the **Petrifying Well** - where visitors can see the petrifying process taking place as the famous Matlock Bath thermal water is sprayed onto objects, gradually turning them to stone - and the beautiful **Gemstone and Fossil Collection.**

Down by the riverbank and housed in the old Pavilion can be found the **Peak District Mining Museum** and **Temple Mine**, the only one of its kind in the world. Opened in 1978 and run by the Peak District Mines Historical Society, the Museum tells the story of lead mining in the surrounding area from as far back as Roman times to the 20th century. As well as the more usual displays of artefacts and implements used by the miners over the years, one of the Museum's most popular features are the climbing shafts and tunnels which allow the whole family to get a real feel for the life of a working lead miner. The Museum also houses a huge engine, dating from 1819, which was recovered from a mine near Winster. A unique survivor in Britain, the engine used water instead of steam to provide it with pressure. Adjacent to the Museum can be found the restored workings of Temple Mine.

For many, model railways are an interesting and absorbing hobby that friends and family find hard to understand, but **The Model Railway** on show in Temple Road is more a work of art than just another model railway. The brainchild of David White, this is a reconstruction of the Midland Railway Company's track through some of the most scenic areas of the Peak District. Combining magnificent dioramas with locomotives and carriages based on the designs of 1906, the trains, slowed down to a speed in scale with the models, travel the realistic route. This is a fascinating place for young and old, as well as a mecca for railway enthusiasts.

Being a relatively new town, Matlock Bath has no ancient place of worship, but the Church of the Holy Trinity is a fine early Victorian building which was added to in 1873 to accommodate the growing congregation. Of greater architectural merit is, however, the **Chapel of St John the Baptist,** found on the road between Matlock and Matlock Bath. Built in 1897, it was designed to be a chapel-of-ease for those finding it difficult to attend St Giles' in Matlock, but it also became a place of worship for those who preferred a High Church service.

Though on the edge of the splendid countryside of the Peak District National Park, Matlock Bath is surrounded by equally beautiful scenery. Found in the Victorian Railway Station buildings is the **Whistlestop Countryside Centre**, which aims to inform and educate the public on the wildlife of the county as well as manage wildlife conservation. Set up by the Derbyshire Wildlife Trust and run by volunteers, the Centre has an interesting and informative exhibition and a gift shop and the staff are qualified to lead a range of environmental activities.

For spectacular views of Matlock Bath, nothing beats a walk on **High Tor Grounds**. There are 60 acres of nature trails to wander around, while some 400 feet below the River Derwent appears like a silver thread through the gorge. A popular viewing point for Victorian visitors to the town, today rock climbers practise their skills climbing the precipitous crags of the Tor. For the less energetic, the walk to the top is rewarded by the views and the chance of a cup of tea and slice of home-made cake from the summit cafe.

On the opposite side of the valley are the beautiful wooded slopes of Masson Hill, the southern face of which has become known as the **Heights of Abraham**; this particular name was chosen after the inhabitants of Matlock had shown great enthusiasm for General Wolfe's victory in Quebec, this part of the Derwent valley being seen to resemble the gorge of the St Lawrence River and the original Heights of Abraham lying a mile north of Quebec. Today it is a well-known viewing point, reached on foot or, more easily, by cable car. The Heights of Abraham have a long history. For many years the slope was mined for lead but, in 1780, it was first developed as a Pleasure Garden and since then trees and shrubs have been planted to make it a pleasing attraction for those visiting the town to take the waters. In 1812, the **Great Rutland Show Cavern**, on the slope, was opened to the public, a new experience for tourists of the time, and it was visited by many including the Grand Duke Michael of Russia and Princess Victoria. Following this success, in 1844, the **Great Masson Cavern** was opened and construction of the Victoria Prospect Tower

was begun. Built by redundant lead miners, the Tower became a new landmark for the area and today still provides a bird's eye view over Derbyshire. The Heights of Abraham are today as popular as ever and provide all the amenities of a good country park.

269

Matlock Bath's Illumination and Venetian Nights are held annually from the end of August to the end of October.

MONYASH

This village was once at the centre of the Peak District's lead mining industry and had its own weekly market (the charter being granted in 1340); the old market cross still stands on the village green. Due to its isolated position, Monyash had for many years to support itself and this led to a great many industries within the village. As far back as prehistoric times there was a flint-tool "factory" here and, as well as mining, candle-making and rope-making, mere-building was a village speciality.

Today, Monyash, which is situated at the start of **Lathkill Dale**, is busy, during the season, with walkers keen to discover the surrounding countryside. The valley of the **River Lathkill**, Lathkill Dale is a road-free beauty spot with ash and elm woods that was designated a National Nature Reserve in 1972. The River Lathkill, like others in the limestone area of the Peak District, disappears underground for parts of its course. In this case the river rises, in winter, from a large cave above Monyash, known as Lathkill Head Cave. In summer, the river emerges further downstream at Over Haddon. In the valley can be found the remains of the area's lead-mining activities and, in particular, there is an old engine house at **Mandale Mine** that was built in 1847. Further upstream from the mine are the stone pillars of an aqueduct, built in 1840, which carried water down to the engine house.

NEW MILLS

Situated by the River Sett, New Mills takes its name from the Tudor corn mills that once stood on the riverbanks. Later, in the 18th and 19th centuries water power was used to drive several cotton-spinning mills in the town and, as New Mills grew, the textile industry was joined by engineering industries and the confectionery trade.

The town is also the start of the **Sett Valley Trail** which follows the line of the old branch railway to Hayfield some three miles away. Opened in 1868, the single track line carried passengers and freight for over 100 years. However, by the late 1960s much of the trade had ceased and the line closed soon afterwards. In 1973, the line was reopened as a trail and is still well used by walkers, cyclists and horse riders and it takes in the remains of buildings that were once part of the prosperous textile industry.

PARWICH

This typical Peak District village is delightful, with stone houses and an 1870s church around the village green. Conspicuous amongst the stonebuilt houses is **Parwich Hall**, constructed of brick and finished in 1747. The wonderful gardens at the Hall were created at the turn of the 20th century and it remains today a family home though, over the years, it has changed hands on several occasions.

Parwich Moor, above the village, is home to many mysterious Bronze Age circles, which vary in size. Though their function is unknown, it is unlikely that they were used as burial chambers. Close to Parwich is Roystone Grange, an important archaeological site where, to the north of the farmhouse, the remains of a Roman farmhouse have been excavated and, to the south, are an old engine house and the remains of the old medieval monastic grange. Both Roystone Grange and Parwich lie on an interesting and informative **Roystone Grange Archaeological Trail** which starts at Minniglow car park. Some 11 miles long, the circular trail follows, in part, the old railway line that was built to connect the Cromford and the Peak Forest Canals in the 1820s before taking in some of the Tissington Trail.

ROWSLEY

This small village, at the confluence of the Rivers Wye and Derwent, is home to the impressive Peacock Hotel. Built originally as a private house, it is aptly named, as the carved peacock over the porch is actually part of the family crest of the Manners family, whose descendents still live at nearby Haddon Hall.

On the banks of the River Wye lies **Caudwell's Mill**, a unique Grade II listed historic roller flour mill. A mill has stood on this

Caudwell's Mill, Rowsley

site for at least 400 years; the present mill was built in 1874, powered by water from the River Wye, and was run as a family business for over a century up until 1978. Since then the Mill has undergone extensive restoration by a group of dedicated volunteers and, using machinery that was installed at the beginning of this century, the Mill is once again producing wholemeal flour. Other mill buildings on the site have been converted to house a variety of craft workshops, shops and a restaurant.

On Chatsworth Road near the terminus of the Peak Rail line, **Peak Village** is an extensive factory outlet shopping centre offering a range of ladies' and men's fashion, sports and outdoor wear, home furnishings, jewellery, toys and books, and eateries. Also on-site is the charming **Wind in the Willows** attraction, created by an award-winning team of craftsmen and designers to bring the adventures of Ratty, Mole, Badger and Mr Toad to life.

TADDINGTON

Now lying just off the main Bakewell to Buxton road, Taddington was one of the first places to be bypassed. A small village and one of the highest in England, the cottages here are simple but the church is rather grand. Like many churches in the Peak District, it was rebuilt in the 14th century with money gained from the then-booming woollen and lead industries in the area.

Taddington Hall, one of the smaller of the Peak District manor houses, dates back to the 16th century though much of the building seen today was constructed in the 18th century. As with all good halls, Taddington has its share of ghost stories. One in particular concerns two brothers. The pair ran a hessian factory from the Hall and one day they quarrelled. The next day one of the brothers, named Isaac, was found dead. The other brother was found guilty of the act. It is said that Isaac has been heard wandering around the passages of the Hall from time to time.

Up on Taddington Moor can be found **Five Wells** tumulus, the highest megalithic tomb in England. The harsh moorland weather has eroded the earth away to reveal two limestone slabs, the burial chambers of 12 people. Flint tools and scraps of pottery were also found in the chambers.

THORPE

Thorpe lies at the confluence of the Rivers Manifold and Dove, and is dominated by the conical hill of **Thorpe Cloud**, which guards the entrance to **Dovedale**. Although the Dale becomes over-crowded at times, there is always plenty of open space to explore on the hill as well as excellent walking. For much of its 45 mile course from Axe Edge to its confluence with the River Trent, the **River Dove** is a walker's river as it is mostly inaccessible by car. The steep sides to its valley, the fast-flowing water and the magnificent white rock formations all give Dovedale a special charm. Dovedale, however, is only a short section of the valley; above Viator Bridge it becomes **Mill Dale** and further upstream again are **Wolfscote Dale** and **Beresford Dale**. The temptation to provide every possible amenity for visitors, at the expense of the scenery, has been avoided and the village of Thorpe, while providing some accommodation, remains an unspoilt and unsophisticated limestone village. The Norman village Church, with its early 14th century nave, has walls of limestone rubble which give the curious impression that the building is leaning outwards. If on horseback it is possible to read the curious sundial at the Church, but otherwise it is too high up!

Close by the River Dove, not far from the village, is the 17th century farmhouse that has been sympathetically transformed into the Izaak Walton Hotel. The delights of trout fishing along this stretch of the river have been much written about, and most famously in *The Compleat Angler*, by Sir Izaak. His fishing house, which he shared with his friend Charles Cot-

ton, is preserved and can be seen in Beresford Dale. At this point along the river there is also a public car park, complete with other amenities useful to the walker and sightseer.

The Victorians delighted in visiting Dovedale, it was praised by the such writers as Byron and Tennyson and soon became as popular as Switzerland. However, their enthusiasm for the Dale also had a down side and, as well as providing donkey rides up the Dale, in the late 19th century sycamore trees were planted along the sides of the Dale. Not native to this area, they overshadow the native ash and obscure many of the rock formations that make this such a special place. The National Trust are keeping the trees in check and encouraging the ash to grow. On higher, more windswept ground, the story would have been different as sycamore trees are ideal for providing a natural wind break.

The **Stepping Stones**, a delight for children, are the first point of interest, though for those who do not want to cross the river at this point there is a foot bridge closer to the carpark just below Thorpe Cloud. Further up the Dale is the limestone crag known as Dovedale Castle and, on the opposite bank, the higher hill known as Lover's Leap after a failed lover's suicide. Other interesting natural features with romantic names found along the way include the Twelve Apostles and the Tissington Spires.

TISSINGTON

Sitting at the foothills of the Pennines, Tissington is, perhaps, most famous for its ancient festival of well-dressing, a ceremony which dates back to 1350, or earlier. Today this takes place in the middle of May and draws many crowds who come to see the spectacular folk art created by the local people. The significance of the event in Tissington may have been to commemorate those who survived the ravages of the Black Death when it raged throughout the villages of Derbyshire. This was attributed to the purity and plentitude of the local spring waters, and the villagers were extremely lucky to have no fewer than five wells to choose from. A total of six wells are dressed at Tissington, the Hall, the Town, the Yew Tree, the Hands, the Coffin and the Children's Wells; each depicts a separate scene, usually one from the Bible. Visitors should follow the signs in the village or ask at the Old Coach House.

The Hidden Inns of the Heart of England

Very much on the tourist route, particularly in the early summer, Tissington has plenty of tea rooms and ice cream shop to satisfy the hot and thirsty visitor. The village, though often overlooked in favour of the colourful well-dressings, has some interesting buildings. The **Church of St Mary**, situated on a rise overlooking Tissington, has an unusual tub-shaped font which dates back to the time of the original Norman Church. The pulpit too is unusual; converted from a double-decker type, it once had a set of steps leading out from the priest's stall below.

Following the old Ashbourne to Parsley Hay railway line, the **Tissington Trail** is a popular walk which can be combined with other old railway trails in the area or country lanes to make an enjoyable circular country walk. The Tissington Trail passes through some lovely countryside and, with a reasonable surface, it is also popular with cyclists. Along the route can also be found many of the old railway line buildings and junction boxes and, in particular, the old Hartington station, which is now a picnic site with an information centre in the old signal box.

WATERHOUSES

Between here and Hulme End, the Leek and Manifold Valley Light Railway, a picturesque narrow-gauge line, used to follow the valleys of the Manifold and the Hamps, crisscrossing the latter on little bridges. Sadly trains no longer run but its track bed has been made into the **Hamps-Manifold Track**, a marvellous walk which is ideal for small children and people in wheelchairs, since its surface is level and tarred throughout its eight miles. The Track can be reached from car parks at Hulme End, Waterhouses, Weags Bridge near Grindon, and Wetton.

The **River Hamps** is similar to the River Manifold and, indeed, other rivers which pass over limestone plateaux, in that it too for some of its course disappears underground: in the case of the Hamps, at Waterhouses; it then re-appears again near Ilam before it merges with the River Manifold.

WIRKSWORTH

Nestling in the lush green foothills of the Peak District where north meets south, Wirksworth is home to a distinctive **Heritage Centre** which

takes visitors through time from the Romans in Wirksworth to the present day. Quarrying, lead-mining and local customs such as clypping the church (a ceremony in which the parish church is encircled by the congregation holding hands around it) and well-dressing are explored with interactive and fascinating exhibits. One of the town's most interesting sights is the jumble of cottages linked by a maze of jitties on the hillside between The Dale and Greenhill, in particular the area known locally as "The Puzzle Gardens".

Wirksworth's well-dressing takes place during the last few days May/first week of June.

The **National Stone Centre** tells "the story of stone", with a wealth of exhibits, activities such as gem-panning and fossil-casting, and outdoor trails tailored to introduce topics such as the geology, ecology and history of the dramatic Peak District landscape. Nearby, the **Steeple Grange Light Railway** runs along a short line over the High Peak Trail between Steeplehouse Station and Dark Lane Quarry. The former quarry is now overgrown with shrubs, trees and a profusion of wildflowers and birds. Power is provided by a battery-electirc locomotive; passengers are carried in a manrider salvaged from Bevercotes Colliery in Nottinghamshire.

Carsington Water just outside Wirksworth is one of Britain's newest reservoirs. This 741 acre expanse of water is a beauty spot that has

Carsington Water, Wirksworth

attracted over a million visitors a year since it was opened by Queen Elizabeth in 1992. It can be reached on foot from Wirksworth along a series of footpaths. Sailing, windsurfing, fishing and canoeing can be enjoyed here, as well as just quiet strolls or bike rides. The Visitor Centre on the west bank offers visitors the opportunity to learn about Severn Trent Water and all aspects of water supply.

The Anchor   **273**

Tideswell, near Buxton,
Derbyshire SK17 8RB
Tel/Fax: 01298 871371

Directions:
Tideswell is 5 miles north east of Buxton,
just south of the A623 on the B6049

One of the oldest villages in the Peak District is Tideswell, and with its magnificent parish church, sometimes called "the cathedral of the Peak", it is certainly well worth a visit. While you're there, why not have a drink or meal at **The Anchor**, a charming inn in this charming village? It dates from 1830, and is a former coaching inn. However, it has changed little over the years, and still evokes earlier times when life was lived at a slower pace.

Step over the threshold and you'll discover that this theme is continued in the interior. Many delightful period features have been retained, such as open fires, thick, dark beams, original oak floorboards and sturdy flagstones. There's a definite old world atmosphere about The Anchor that makes any visit a pleasure. The inn is run by Bill Sniffin and Graham Peddie, and they have created a pub that is popular both with the locals and those visiting the village. The food – cooked by Bill – is excellent. All the ingredients are as fresh as possible, and there's a wide range of dishes to choose from. The cuisine covers the globe, though the specialities of the house are char grilled cuts of meat, and juicy steaks with all the trimmings. Everything is prepared to order, and to your taste, so don't expect fast food here!

And to accompany your meal, you can order from the inn's excellent wine list. Or you can choose from one of the two real ales on offer at the bar, plus the range of draught bitter, mild, stout, cider and lager. If you're behind the wheel, then the bar also carries a large selection of soft drinks to suit all tastes.

Opening times: 11.00-23.00 7 days

Food: Served Monday to Saturday: 12.00-14.30 and 18.00-21.00; Sunday: lunchtimes only 12.00-15.00

Credit cards: All major cards accepted except American Express and Diners

Accommodation: None

Entertainment: Ring for details

Facilities: Car park; beer garden; children's play area

Local Places of Interest/Activities: Eyam (Great Plague associations) 4 miles; Buxton (historic town) 6 miles; Chatsworth 8 miles; Bakewell (historic town) 6 miles

Beehive

Hague Street,
Glossop,
Derbyshire
SK13 8NR
Tel: 01457 852108
Fax: 01457 857207

Directions:

Glossop is on the
A57, 12 miles west
of Manchester city
centre; the Beehive
is a short drive from
Glossop town centre

Glossop sits on the western edge of the Peak District National Park, at the foot of the Snake Pass. It's a former mill town with, at its heart, a 17th century village with old, quaint, cottages. If you visit the place, you should seek out the **Beehive**, a solid, well built inn of warm, local stone not far from the centre of town. Here you're sure of a warm welcome and a range of drinks and food that represents wonderful value for money. The building has changed little since it was built in the early 1800s, and today it has retained the many period features that make it a popular stopping point for both regulars and visitors. The interior is spotless, and its soft lighting, dark oak furniture and carpeted floors add a welcoming ambience to the place.

Lisa Harrop and Richard Parker have been the owners since March 1999, and during that time have created a warm and welcoming inn out of one that at one time was ailing and threatened with closure. Richard is local, and knows the area well, and if you're looking for places to visit, he's the man to ask! The Beehive has its own chef, and he has put together a menu that calls upon all the traditions of good pub food but with an added twist. Many of the dishes are specialities, and only the finest local produce is used in their preparation.

Quality and value for money are the watch words at the Beehive, and this includes the drinks. Two cask ales are on offer (one being Pedigree) plus draught bitter, mild, stout, cider and lager. You can also order wine by the glass or bottle, and there's always a fine range of soft drinks.

Opening times: Monday to Friday: 17.00-23.00; Saturday and Sunday: all day

Food: Weekdays -evening meals only; Thurs-Sun 13.00-21.00

Credit cards: Accepted for food orders

Accommodation: None

Entertainment: Occasional quiz nights and live music (ring for details)

Facilities: Parking to rear: patio to the front

Local Places of Interest/Activities: Walking on the Peak District National Park; Manchester (historic city) 12 miles; Pennine Way (national footpath) 3 miles; Etherow Country Park 4 miles; Buxton,Castleton,Eyam - all within easy reach

Internet/website:
Please call for details

Biggin Hall

275

*Biggin Country
   House Hotel,*
Biggin,
near Buxton,
Derbyshire
SK17 0DH
Tel: 01298 84451
Fax: 01298 84681

Directions:
Biggin is 1 mile
west of the A515
and 11 miles south
of Buxton

Biggin Hall is an historic house of 17th century origin, centrally situated in the Peak District National Park, in peaceful open countryside, 1000 feet above sea level. Insomniacs and asthma sufferers have commented on the beneficial effect of the Biggin air. The diverse nature of the Derbyshire landscape with its dry stone walling, deep wooded valleys, heather clad moorlands, timeless market towns and villages provides the perfect setting for a relaxing holiday.

Biggin Hall stands in its own spacious grounds of 8 acres and is a protected building of historic interest, Grade II* listed. The present owner has completely renovated it in keeping with its original character. Many of the stone mullioned leaded windows have only recently seen daylight again after their obliteration during the window taxes of the 1790's. The rooms are spacious and individually furnished with antiques. Visitors have a choice of two sitting rooms, one with a library, the other with a large open stone fireplace, and there is a spacious dining room. Biggin Hall is also ideal is ideal for small private functions and conferences where delegates are guaranteed a no pressure hassle-free environment.

Dinner at Biggin Hall is one of the highlights of your stay, when the open fire, excellent food, and a good selection of wines all combine to create a convivial atmosphere for an enjoyable meal. Much of the food is of local origin with the accent on free range wholefoods and natural flavours, together with the seasonal selection of vegetables. The menu, featuring a set main course with vegetarian alternative, is changed daily to give a variety of country house fare through the week. We are always happy to assist with any special dietary requests given prior notice.

The Peak District has a special appeal in the autumn and winter. Why not take advantage of a budget winter break?

Opening Times: Open all year

Food: One sitting for dinner - 7.00 pm

Credit Cards: All major cards except Diners

Accommodation: 19 en suite rooms in main house and outbuildings.

Facilities: Car park, conference facilities

Local Places of Interest/Activities: Excellent walking and cycling from grounds, Chatsworth, Haddon Hall, Keddleston, Prehistoric Arbor Low, etc are all within easy reach

Internet/website:
http://www.bimjzinhall.co.uk
e-mail: bigginhall@compuserve.co.uk

276 Chinley Lodge

1 Green Lane,
Chinley,
High Peak,
Derbyshire SK 23 6AA
Tel: 01663 751200
Fax: 01663 750210

Directions:

Chinley is 2 miles north
west of Chapel-en-le-
Frith, just off the A6 on
the B6062

At one time, Chinley station was a major interchange on the main Manchester to London railway line, and had the Flying Scotsman pass though it many times. Nowadays the line connects Manchester with Sheffield, and the main line passes south of the village. But one building remains of Chinley's great days – **The Chinley Lodge**. This proud, solid hostelry was built in 1903 as a railway hotel, and given the name Princes Hotel. Now it is a listed building, and was recently bought by Jane and Nick McArdle, who want to restore it to its former "steam days" glory. It will be a mammoth task, but one well worth the effort. Some parts have already been restored, and they have turned the inn into a supremely comfortable place, with a bar that is both warm and welcoming. There's a fine range of cask ales, draught bitter, mild, cider, lager and stout on offer, plus a wine list that is sure to please everyone.

The inn has always been renowned for its food, and both Jane and Nick are determined to continue this tradition. The regular chef, Jen, has put together an excellent menu that draws on the best of English, European and Asian food, plus there's a Sunday roast that has become a must with the locals. Try the knuckles of lamb marinated in wine and served with grain mustard – delicious! There's also a children's and a vegetarian menu.

The Chinley Lodge is the ideal venue for a business or social function, and has a large function suite. It also offers first class accommodation, and makes the ideal base for exploring the surrounding countryside. There are seven comfortable and extremely well appointed en suite rooms, all with TV and tea and coffee making facilities. Thanks to Jane and Nick, the glory days are returning to Chinley Lodge!

Opening times: Monday: 17.00-23.00 Tuesday to Saturday: 12.00-15.00 and 17.00-23.00; 12.00-23.00 on Sunday and bank holidays

Food: Served whenever the inn is open

Credit cards: All major cards accepted except American Express and Diners

Accommodation: 7 en suite rooms

Entertainment: Thursday evening: jazz;

Sunday evening: live music and karaoke; Saturday evening: dinner dance

Facilities: Car park; beer garden; decked patio with al fresco dining

Local Places of Interest/Activities: Chapel-en-le-Frith (historic town) 2 miles; Manchester (historic city) 16 miles; Lyme Park (NT) 4 miles

Internet/Website: www.chinleylodge.co.uk

Church Inn 277

Main Street,
Chelmorton,
near Buxton,
Derbyshire SK17 9SL
Tel/Fax: 01298 85319

Directions:

Take the A515 south east from Buxton and turn east onto the A5270; turn south onto a minor road signposted for Chelmorton

Right in the heart of the Peak District, famous as the setting for the TV programme "Peak Practise", you'll find the attractive village of Chelmorton. It has all the look and feel of a true upland village, and surrounding it are signs of ancient field patterns that may date back to Saxon times. It has the reputation of being the highest village in Derbyshire. Not only that – it has the highest church in the county, and, in the **Church Inn**, the highest inn. This charming hostelry dates from the early 1800s, and is a solid, stone building of great charm, which has been lovingly preserved throughout the ages.

The interior has retained many of its period features, thanks to Julie Hadfield and Justin Satur, who take a great pride in the place. Though it has all been recently refurbished, the original oak beams are still there, and the walls are covered in a wealth of old prints and photos of the village. There's a long through lounge, a cozy bar and comfortable dining area which served the very best in food. Both Julie and Justin cook, and the menu is traditional, with dishes that use only the freshest vegetables, meats, poultry and fish. For a special treat, order the thick, juicy gammon steaks!

Wine is available by the glass or bottle, and at the bar there's a great selection of cask ales, draught bitter, mild, stout, cider and lager. Next to the inn is a small self catering cottage with all mod cons which you can hire. It sleeps five, plus there is a child's cot.

This is a truly delightful inn, where you can escape from the hustle and bustle of modern life. Julie and Justin will offer you a warm welcome if you pay them a visit.

Opening times: 12.00-15.30 and 19.00-23.00, though these times may change in the summer months

Food: Served whenever the inn is open

Credit cards: Cash/cheques only at present

Accommodation: 1 self catering cottage with all mod cons

Facilities: Beer garden

Local Places of Interest/Activities: Walking on the Peak District National Park; Buxton (historic town) 4 miles; Magpie Mine (old lead mine) 4 miles; Eyam (plague associations) 7 miles

Internet/Website:
e-mail: justinsatur@hotmail.com

278   The Cock Inn

Clifton,
near Ashbourne,
Derbyshire
DE6 2GJ
Tel: 01335 342654

Directions:
Clifton is on the
A515, 2 miles south
of Ashbourne town
centre

The Cock Inn at Clifton dates originally from the 17th century, so is a hostelry that is full of history and character. It was originally a roadside coaching inn which, or course, has been added to and altered over the years. But it still manages to retain the look and feel of those earlier times, when a coach and horses would draw up at the entrance, and life was lived at a less hectic pace. It is a solid, whitewashed building of local stone, with good proportions and many period features.

And just as it was a staging point long ago when coaches were the preferred mode of transport, so it remains today the perfect stopping off point for a drink or a delicious meal when the car has taken over. The inside is well maintained and friendly, and everything is spotlessly clean. Here, you feel as you enter, you can relax and stretch your legs. The bar is well stocked, and carries no less than three real ales, two resident and a guest, as well draught bitter, mild, lager stout and cider. And being a roadside inn, there's a great selection of soft and alcohol free drinks if you're behind the wheel.

The food is good, honest pub fayre, with a selection of simple but beautifully cooked dishes which are all prepared on the premises using ingredients that are as fresh and full of flavour as possible. The portions are hearty and filling, and each dish on the menu is realistically priced to suit you pocket.

The Cock Inn is owned by Delphe Sadsby, who is very hands on. She works hard to provide an atmosphere that combines a sense of tradition and history with the thoroughly modern concepts of friendly service, efficiency and value for money.

Opening times: Monday: 18.30-23.00 (closed lunchtime); Tuesday to Friday: 12.00-14.30 and 18.30-23.00; Saturday and Sunday: open all day

Food: Lunches are served every day (except Monday) between 12.00-14.30 and evening meals are served between 18.30 and 21.00

Credit cards: All major cards accepted except American Express and diners

Accommodation: None

Entertainment: Monthly quiz nights; themed food nights; darts games (ring for details)

Facilities: Car park; beer garden; children's play areas

Local Places of Interest/Activities: Ashbourne (historic town) 2 miles; Darley Moor (motor cycle racing) 2 miles; Derby (historic city) 13 miles; Alton Towers (theme park) 6 miles

Croft Country House Hotel 279

Great Longstone, near Bakewell,
Derbyshire DE45 1TF
Tel: 01629 640278
Fax: 01629 640369

Directions:
Great Longstone is on a minor
road off the A6020, 2 miles north
west of the centre of Bakewell

The village of Great Longstone nestles under Longstone Edge in the heart of the Peak District National Park. It has a charming church dating from the 13th century, and a medieval market cross. Not so old, but every bit as picturesque, is the fabulous **Croft Country House Hotel,** standing in three acres of ground. It was converted to a hotel in 1984, and had previously been a 19th century farmhouse. This is very much a hotel for the discerning traveller. The gardens could almost have been taken from the pages of Country Life, and the standards of comfort and luxury are second to none. So much so that in 1996 it was awarded the WHICH? Hotel Guide Derbyshire Hotel of the Year award.

The house boasts a spectacular main hall with a lanterned ceiling and a galleried landing, and from this lead nine fully en suite bedrooms, all with colour TV, tea and coffee making facilities and independently controlled central heating. And the food is spectacular. The comfortable restaurant offers a table d'hôte menu which contains many wonderful dishes, such as carrot and cumin soup, fruit compote with Grand Marnier sauce, roast cod with garlic pomme puree, fillet of beef with braised oxtails and beer sauce, duck with balsamic vinegar, and a sweet called "chocolate heaven", which says it all! This is cooking at its best, and the chef uses only the freshest of ingredients in season, most of them sourced locally

There's a select wine list, of course, and a great range of drinks at the bar. The hotel is the perfect base from which to explore the beautiful Peak District, or to hold a wedding, business conference private dinner party or family weekend. If you decide to make it your base, you'll be pampered all the way. John and Pat Thursby, who own the hotel, will even welcome you to your room with a pot of tea and sherry!

Opening times: All day, every day except in January and the first two weeks in February

Food: Served evenings in the restaurant

Credit cards: All major cards accepted

Accommodation; 9 en-suite rooms

Entertainment: John, the owner, is a magician, and will entertain his guests each Saturday evening!

Facilities: Car park; function suite; lift; one bedroom is wheelchair friendly

Local Places of Interest/Activities: Walking on peak District National Park; Bakewell (historic town) 2 miles; Magpie Miner (lead mine) 3 miles; Chatsworth 4 miles

Internet/website:
e-mail: jthursby@ukonline.co.uk
website: www.croftcountryhouse.co.uk

280 The Devonshire Arms

Beeley,
near Matlock,
Derbyshire
DE4 2NR
Tel/Fax:
* 01629 733259*

Directions:

Take the A6 north
west from Matlock
for 4 miles, then
turn north onto the
B6012. Beeley is one
mile along this road

Situated in the lovely
conservation village
of Beeley, this is one of the most picturesque and historic inns in Derbyshire. It sits almost
at the gates of Chatsworth House, one of the most magnificent mansions in Britain, and
home to the Duke and Duchess of Devonshire. The inn is actually owned by the Duke, and
is within a building dating from 1726 that was originally three cottages. However, it was in
1747 than the three cottages were combined to form the inn.

The Devonshire Arms is built of warm, mellow local stone, and, with its small windows and tall chimneys, fits snugly into the landscape. The inside is equally as attractive.
Low, beamed ceilings and dark wood combine to create a welcoming atmosphere, and in
the winter the crackle of log fires adds a warmth to this welcome. The inn has been managed by the Grosvenor family since 1962, and is now managed by John Grosvenor, who
took over in 1988. The inn is renowned for its food - especially fish dishes - and ranges from
simple sandwiches and salads to something just that bit more special. For starters, for instance, you could have soup of the day, and for a main course steak and ale pie. Or you
could go for avocado pear and prawn cocktail followed by venison in plum sauce. All the
dishes are individually cooked from good, local produce wherever possible, and all are reasonably priced. There's a comprehensive range of drinks available, including Theakston's
Old Peculier and XB, plus rotating ales as well as lager, stout and cider. There is a small but
select wine list which fully complements the dishes on the menu.

In July 1872 there was a tremendous flood in Beeley, and the nearby brook burst its
banks and flooded the Devonshire Arms. The same thing happened in in August 1997, and
the height of the water is recorded on a beam in the bar.

Opening hours: All day, every day

Food: A good, comprehensive menu, with
food being served from 12.00-21.30 every day,
with Victorian breakfasts being served every
Sunday from 10.00-12.00. The restaurant is
non smoking, and booking is advisable

Credit cards: All credit cards except American
Express

Accommodation: None

Facilities: Small beer garden to the front;
parking

Local Places of Interest/Activities:
Chatsworth House 1 mile; Peak Railway 2
miles; Haddon Hall 2 miles; Riber Castle
Wildlife Park 5 miles; Hob Hurst's House
(tumulus)1 mile

The George and Dragon   281

43 Market Place, Ashbourne,
Derbyshire DE6 1EU
Tel: 01335 343199

Directions:

The town of Ashbourne is just off the
A52, 13 miles north west of Derby

This handsome, well proportioned inn
sits overlooking the market place of the
old, historic town of Ashbourne. Surrounded by buildings in red brick, it is
a whitewashed, bow-windowed affair
dating to the mid 18th century, with a
large colourful carving of St George
killing the dragon set high on the front
wall. It is no surprise to learn that this
popular hostelry was once a coaching
inn, and it still retains the atmosphere
and charm of times gone by.

Tracey and Jim Quigley have been tenants now for several months, and have managed
to create an establishment that speaks of quality and comfort. The bar is richly carpeted and
scrupulously clean, with lots of dark wood to give the place a warm, homely feel. Subdued
wall lighting, a roaring fire in the winter months and comfortable seating completes the
picture. This is the kind of place where you want to relax, stretch out, and enjoy a quiet
drink or bar meal! There's a wide variety of choices on the menu or the specials board, and
everything is freshly prepared on the premises using local produce wherever possible. Food
is only served from Tuesday to Sunday at lunchtime at present, except for bank holidays,
when it is available on Mondays as well. The bar boasts two or three rotating real ales at any
one time, plus a range of beers, lagers, stout and - a real treat that must be tried - hand
pulled Scrumpy cider.

The George and Dragon has five well appointed en suite guest rooms - three double
and two twins. This makes it the ideal base for exploring the Peak District National Park as
well as the counties of Derbyshire and Staffordshire. Ashbourne itself, with its high-spired
parish church of St Oswald, is also well worth exploring. If you visit on Shrove Tuesday,
you'll see the well known football match played between the Up'ards and the Down'ards of
the town, with the goals three miles apart!

Opening times: Open lunchtimes and
evenings, and all day in the summer months

Food: Good, honest traditional food served
Tuesday to Friday 12.00-14.30 and Saturday-
Sunday 12.00-15.30; no food served on a
Monday, apart form bank holidays

Credit cards: Cash and cheque only at
present

Accommodation: 5 superb en suite rooms - 2

double and 3 twin; you can book B&B or
room only; children welcome

Entertainment: Saturday evening disco from
20.00; occasional live entertainment on
Friday evenings; phone for details

Local Places of Interest/Activities: Peak
District National Park: 2 miles; Ilam Park (NT)
4 miles; Alton Towers 7 miles; Darley Moor
(motor cycle racing) 3 miles; Carsington
Water and Visitor's Centre (fishing) 5 miles

282
The George Hotel

Church Street,
Youlgreave,
near Bakewell,
Derbyshire
DE45 1VW
Tel: 01629 636292

Directions:

Youlgreave sits on
an unmarked road
a couple of miles
south west of the
A6

This is a friendly, village pub situated in a small, attractive village which nestles in the Peak District National Park, close to Lathkill and Bradford Dales, where there is good walking and rambling. Opposite the inn is one of the most imposing churches in the Peak District, parts of which date from Norman times. **The George Hotel** itself dates from the 17th century, and was once a coaching inn called the Pigg Lead, a name that comes from the lead mining once carried out in the area. With its bow windows, overflowing flower baskets and window boxes, it is a colourful and attractive site, just right for that quiet drink or bar lunch.

George and Sandra Marsh have been mine hosts for over eight years now, and thanks to them and their son Stephen, the place has earned an enviable reputation in the area for good service, a friendly welcome and value for money. This is a real village inn, where children are welcome, and where you can eat all day throughout the premises. The inside is comfortable and smart, yet still manages to retain that sense of tradition and history that turns a good pub into an great one. The place is spotlessly clean, and the woodwork positively gleams, so well polished is it.

There are four real ales on offer, including John Smith's Cask and rotating ales, plus Theakston's mild, McEwans, lagers such as Fosters and Kronenberg, Guiness and Strongbow cider. Plus there's the usual range of spirits and a small selection of quality wines. The food is beautifully cooked on the premises, and you can chose from the blackboard menu. Try the rabbit casserole - it's very popular with the locals! You don't have to book, unless you're part of a larger party, and a children's menu is available.

Opening hours: Open all day

Food: The food is beautifully cooked, wholesome and filling. From Monday to Friday it is served from 12.00-14.00 and 18.30-21.00; On Saturday it is served from 12.00-20.45, and on Sunday from 12.00-19.45

Credit cards: Cash and cheques only at present

Accommodation: Three rooms, one double en suite, a family en suite and a standard double; Prices include breakfast

Facilities: Car park

Local Places of Interest/Activities: Lathkill and Bradford Dales 1 mile; Bakewell (historic town) 2 miles; Chatsworth House 5 miles; Haddon Hall 2 miles; Magpie Mine (lead mine) 3 miles; Peak Railway 4 miles; Nine Ladies (stone circle on Stanton Moor) 3 miles

The Hollybush

283

Grangemill,
near Matlock,
Derbyshire
DE4 4HU
Tel: 01629 650300

Directions:
The hamlet of
Grangemill sits just
off the A5012 near
its junction with
the B5056, 4 miles
south west of
Matlock

Standing beside a small crossroads in the quiet hamlet of Grangemill stands an early 16th century coaching inn called **The Hollybush**. It has remained unchanged over the years, and while it cannot be said to be particularly beautiful or picturesque, it does have a quaint charm that soon endears you to the place. We're on the edge of the lovely Peak District here, and hiker and walkers often stop at this spot for a meal or a refreshing drink after their exertions. In fact, they are allowed to keep their muddy boots on if they want to!

That's not to say that the interior isn't well maintained or clean. In fact, it is spotless, and full of old fashioned character. There are bare stone walls, open fires, a mix of flagstones and carpets on the floors, and comfortable furniture that invites you to sit down and stretch your legs. The husband and wife team of Dawn and Keith Jacklin have been mine hosts since the year 2000, and they have created a great pub that puts comfort before fashionable and fancy fittings and good food and drink at the top of the agenda. It's a family friendly place, and children are welcome. The cuisine is traditional, with many popular dishes on the menu, such as juicy steaks or – the local's favourite – steak and kidney pie, with all the trimmings. Choose from a menu of a daily changing specials board. You get great value for money, and the helpings are ample and filling. All the food is delicious, and beautifully cooked on the premises by Dawn.

If it's a drink you're after, there's a great range available at the bar. There are two real ales (one resident and a guest) and draught bitter, mild, cider, stout and lager. Plus, of course, there's a fine selection of wines, spirits and soft drinks.

Opening times: 11.00-23.00 Mon-Sat; 12.00-22.30 Sun

Food: Served when the inn is open

Credit cards: Cash only at present

Accommodation: None

Entertainment: Occasional charity nights and fortnightly theme nights (ring for details)

Facilities: Car park; beer garden; children's play room with pool table and darts, non-smoking dining room

Local Places of Interest/Activities: Walking on peak District National Park; Bakewell (historic town) 2 miles; Magpie Miner (lead mine) 3 miles; Chatsworth 4 miles, Matlock Bath (Heights of Abraham) 5 miles

284 The Hope and Anchor

Market Place,
Wirksworth,
Derbyshire DE4 4ET
Tel: 01629 824620

Directions:

Wirksworth is a small
market town on the
B5023, four miles
south of Matlock off
the A6; the inn is is
the centre of the
town

This is a solid, three storeyed building next to the old market place in the small town of Wirksworth. It stands right on the pavement, and is built from local stone. Looking substantial and strong, it still manages to look welcoming at the same time. Originally three buildings, it has long history, with parts dating back as far as 1590. The interior is lovely - old dark wood, low beams, carpeted floors, polished brass and country style furniture that is both comfortable and attractive, and Note the magnificent wooden fireplace surround, which dates from 1610.

Beth and Graham Betts have been landlords here for three years, and have six years in the trade. Their combined experience has paid off in this lovely old inn, and it is a truly warm, cozy place, a firm favourite with locals and visitors alike. Here you can stretch out, enjoy a relaxing drink in friendly company, and forget about the problems of the world world for a short while. There are always at least four real ales on offer, including Marston's Pedigree, Home bitter and two rotating guest ales. You can also order John Smith's bitter, Chestnut mild, Guinness. two kinds of lager (Stella and Kronenberg), and Strongbow cider.

The food is good, honest, traditional fare (lunchtimes only) which Beth cooks on the premises from local produce as far as possible. Her steak pie is one of the specialities of the house, though such dishes as lasagna are also available. On Sunday there is a Sunday lunch of roast meats, which is so popular that you should book in advance.

The Hope and Anchor Hotel is a relaxing, friendly place, where you're sure to get a warm welcome!

Opening hours: Monday to Saturday: 12.00-15.00 and 19.00-23.00; Sunday: 12.00-15.00 and 19.00-22.30

Food: Lunchtimes only from 12.0-14.30

Credit cards: Cash only at present

Accommodation: None

Facilities: Garden

Local Places of Interest/Activities:
Wirksworth Heritage Centre (at Crown Yard within the town); Heights of Abraham Country Park and Caverns 3 miles; Riber Castle Wildlife Park 3 miles; Cromford Mill 2 miles; National Tramway Museum, Crich: 4 miles

The Ketch

Kniveton,
Ashbourne,
Derbyshire
DE6 1JF
Tel: 01335 342341

Directions:

The inn sits on the outskirts of Kniveton, which is 3 miles north east of Ashbourne on the B5035

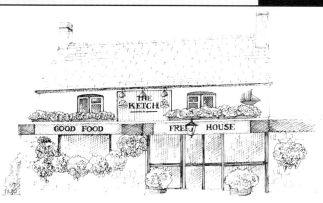

Seen on a warm summer's day, there is no finer sight than this inn Its many window boxes and tubs positively froth with flowers and greenery. In front of it is a good, long car park, so visitors gets a good view as they approach. The building was formerly a farmhouse before becoming a pub. In the past it has been called the Ketchum Inn and the Greyhound, but now it is firmly **The Ketch**, a popular place for locals and tourists alike.

It's a freehouse, owned and managed by husband and wife team Alan and Carol Fowler, who have been in the trade for 14 years, and who have been in charge at The Ketch for the last four. So they've brought a wealth of experience to the place, and it shows. The outside is neat and smart, with stone and whitewash lending the place a traditional look. Inside is spotless and beautifully maintained. The fittings and furniture are in pine, and the place is carpeted throughout. Framed prints hang on the walls and an open fire keeps the bar area cozy and warm on the coldest of days. The inn is all on one level, with no steps, so it is disabled-friendly. From the well stocked bar you can order Worthington Creamflow, Guinness, Carling, Stella, Bass Mild and Blackthorn cider. In addition, there are always two real ales on offer - Bass and Marston's pedigree. Plus, of course, there's a range of wines and spirits. Alan does the cooking, and there's a good menu and specials board. The speciality of the house are cuts from a "Lamb Henry" (a half shoulder of lamb), and the curries are always popular. Other dishes include Beef in ale pie, poached salmon, lemon chicken and prime steaks. The dining area can seat up to 60 in comfort. In front of the inn there's a small caravan park with five electric hook ups, which takes camper vans and caravans only, and there's a good sized car park. The Ketch is a peach of an inn, homely and warm, with a great ambience. It's what traditional English hospitality is all about.

Opening times: Open lunchtimes and evenings, and all day during the summer months

Food: Monday to Friday: 12.14.00 and 18.30-21.00; Saturday and Sunday: 12.00-14.30 and 18.30-21.00

Credit cards: All major cards except Amex and Diners

Accommodation: Small caravan park for towing caravans and camper vans only; water and waste disposal points on site

Facilities; No smoking areas; beer garden; car park; children's play area

Local Places of Interest/Activities: Peak District National Park 1 mile; Ilam Park (NT) 5 miles; Alton Towers 9 miles; Darley Moor (motor cycle racing) 5 miles; Carsington Water and Visitor's Centre (fishing) 2 miles

286

The Little John

Station Road,
Hathersage,
Hope Valley,
Derbyshire S32 1DD
Tel: 01433 650225
Fax: 0870 1684988

Directions:
Hathersage is on the
A625, 9 miles west of
Sheffield city centre

Hathersage is one of the most interesting and picturesque villages in the Peak District. Charlotte Brontë visited in 1845, and used it as the model for her "Norton" in Jane Eyre. She also gave Jane the same surname as the local lords of the manor. The place has associations with the legend of Robin Hood, and that is why you'll find an inn here called **The Little John**. It is run by Stephanie Bushell, who has created a hostelry of great character which is popular with both locals and visitors alike. It is a handsome stone building which dates from the 19th century, and inside many period features have been retained. There's a bar, a no smoking lounge and an excellent, roomy restaurant. The inn also has extensive accommodation available, from cottages and apartments to en suite rooms.

This is the place to have a relaxing drink or a meal after a day walking on the high moors. Stephanie is a qualified chef, so you know the food will be great. The cuisine is wide ranging, and only the finest, freshest ingredients go into each dish. If you have a real hunger, try the Robin Hood/Little John Mixed Grill, an enormous plateful which is every bit as much a legend in these parts as Robin himself! The inn has also won awards for its ale, and carries a good selection of real ales at the bar, plus draught bitter, stout, lager and cider.

Stephanie takes great pride in the fact that The Little John and some of its accommodation is wheelchair friendly. If you visit, she's sure to give you a warm welcome, and she'll dare you to order and finish that mixed grill!

Opening times: Open all day, every day

Food: Served 12.00-14.00 and 18.00-22.00 from Monday to Friday; served 12.00-22.00 on Saturday and 12.00-21.00 on Sunday

Credit cards: Cash or cheques only at present

Accommodation: 3 en suite rooms; 2 standard rooms (one with shower and sink); Loxley Cottage (sleeps 4 in double and twin); Squire's Cottage (sleeps 4 in two double); Sheriff's Cottage (sleeps two); Little John Cottage (luxurious cottage with balcony)

Entertainment: Quiz evening on Monday; Karaoke evening on Tuesday; promotional evenings on Thursday; "zany bingo"evening on Friday.

Facilities: Car park; outdoor heated swimming pool available April-September

Local Places of Interest/Activities: Longshaw Estate (NT) 2 miles; Eyam Museum (Great Plague associations) 4 miles; Sheffield (historic city) 9 miles

The Manifold Inn

287

Hulme End,
Hartington,
near Buxton,
Derbyshire
SK17 0EX
Tel: 01298 84537

Directions:
Hulme End is close
to Hartington, on
the B5054, 3 miles
west of the A515
and 10 miles south
of Buxton town
centre

The Manifold Inn takes its name from the River Manifold, on whose bank it sits. It is a picturesque and delightful building of old, mellow stone which is over 200 years old, and was one time a coaching inn. Hartington, which is close by, is a picturesque place, famous for its creamery and cheese shop, which is one of the few places in England that is allowed to make Stilton cheese.

This is the ideal base for exploring an area that has some breathtaking scenery. The inn boasts five well appointed en suite rooms (four double and one twin) in a converted black-smith's shop, and the nightly charge includes a full cooked breakfast. The twin room has been especially equipped for disabled guests. And if you can't bear to be parted from your dog, you can bring it as well, as there's a heated outhouse where it can stay!

Owners Bridgette and Frank Lipp have made sure that many period features have been retained in the outstanding interior. Guests have their own comfortable lounge, or they can join in the friendly atmosphere of the bar, where the locals will give them a warm Derbyshire welcome. Three real ales are on offer (one resident and two guest), and there's a range of draught bitters, mild, cider, lager and stout. If you want to eat, then wine is also available, either by the bottle or glass. The food is served in a cozy dining room, or you can eat in the wood-panelled bar, with its low beamed ceiling. The dishes are all cooked on the premises, and all are made from only the freshest of ingredients. The cuisine can best be described as good, honest "pub food" at sensible prices.

The Manifold Inn is a family run hostelry with a great reputation. people return it it again and again to sample the surrounding countryside ant the great hospitality it offers.

Opening times: 12.00-15.00 and 19.00-23.00 seven days

Food: Served 12.00-14.00 and 19.00-21.00 seven days

Credit cards: All major cards accepted except American Express and Diners

Accommodation: 5 en suite rooms – 4 double and 1 twin

Facilities: Car park; beer garden

Local Places of Interest/Activities: Dove Valley is on the doorstep; Buxton (historic town) 9 miles; Tissington (well dressing) 6 miles; Arbor Low Stone Circle 4 miles

Internet/website:
website: www.themanifoldinn.co.uk

288 | The Miners Arms

Mains Road,
Carsington,
Derbyshire
DE4 4DE
Tel: 01629 540207

Directions:

Take the B5035
from Wirksworth
to Ashbourne.
Carsington is on a
minor road half a
mile to the north,
about half way
between the two
towns

We're talking olde worlde here. **The Miners Arms** sits in the village of Carsington, close to Carsington Water, and dates from the 17th century. It is a solid, stone building which would defy anything the weather could throw at it., and sits just off the road, with a wooded slope behind. There are three storeys, the windows are small paned, and there's a welcoming porch with a lamp above.

The inside is a gem. Low ceilings, old, gnarled beams, stone walls, antiques and objets d'art dotted around, and old, stone fireplaces aglow with heat are timeless features that are a welcoming sight for anyone entering the inn on a cold winter's day. Everything is spotlessly clean, the brass ornaments gleam, and the wood of the country style furniture is polished to perfection. This is a wonderful place to enjoy a quiet drink, your legs stretched out on the carpeted floor and your back against a comfortably upholstered bench. There are usually a minimum of three real ales on offer, including Bass and rotating guest ales, as well as Worthington, Scrumpy, Guinness, Stella and Carling.

But it is also cool and welcoming in the summer, when you can sit out on one of the benches and watch the world go by. Vance Leahy only took over the Miners Arms in December 2000, and he's introducing some changes without compromising the feeling of history and tradition that the place conveys. There's a dining area that seats about 30 people, plus you can eat in the bar area as well. If you're looking for an evening meal on Friday or Saturday, you're well advised to book. The food is excellent, with the accent being on traditional cuisine. The favourite dish seems to be the steak pie, which is cooked to perfection. This is a real hidden gem of an inn.

Opening hours: 12.00-15.00 and 19.00-23.00 Saturday to Thursday; 12.00 and 18.00-23.00 on Friday

Food: 12.00-14.00 and 19.00-21.00 seven days

Credit cards: Cash only at present

Accommodation; None

Entertainment: Live music at weekends - ring for details

Facilities: Play area for kids; garden

Local Places of Interest/Activities: Good walking area with excellent scenery; Carsington Water Visitor Centre 1 mile; Winster Market House (NT) 4 miles; Ilam park (NT) 8 miles

The Oddfellows Arms | 289

Whitehough Head Lane,
Whitehough,
Chinley, High Peak,
Derbyshire SK23 6EJ
Tel: 01663 750306

Directions:

Take the A624 south from Glossop, and after 7 miles turn right onto the B6062. Go through Chinley towards Headlane. The inn is on the left hand side, about two miles from Whaley Bridge.

This sturdy, stone-built inn sits within the Peak District National Park. From the outside, it looks picturesque and welcoming , with its bow windows and tubs of bright flowers. It is proud of its traditional, homely atmosphere, and is much used by the locals - always a good sign! In fact, the interior has become something of a museum, because a lot of the ornaments and items you can see within the inn were donated by local people. Not only that - the inn furniture has been carefully restored, and there are excellent examples of craft work such as d'coupage.

The Oddfellows Arms is a family-run inn, under the personal supervision of Janice Newton, and this is reflected in its superb food, which is prepared on the premises by a fully qualified chef. There is a wide selection of bar snacks available, plus a full menu that contains such appetising dishes as home-made meat loaf, sirloin steak, filled baguettes and the traditional ploughman's lunch, all using fresh local produce whenever possible. The wine list is extensive, and along with Marston's ales (including hand pumped cask ales), there are usually two guest beers available each month.

There are occasional live entertainment nights, as well us Sunday quizzes, with the proceeds going to local charities. In the winter, there's always a welcoming log fire, and in the summer months you can sit out of doors and watch the world go by. This is a traditional, homely inn that will give the visitor a warm welcome.

Opening Hours: 11.00-2300 Monday to Saturday; 12.00-22.30 on Sunday;

Food: An extensive menu with traditional and more adventurous fare, available all day; full menu is available from 11.00-19.00 Monday to Saturday, and 12.00-17.00 on Sunday; a late breakfast is available from 11.00-14.00.

Credit Cards: Visa; Access; Delta; Switch

Accommodation: None

Facilities: Off street parking

Entertainment: Sunday night quiz; occasional garden entertainment; occasional live entertainment

Local Places of Interest/Activities: Good walking on the Peak District National Park; Kinder Scout, with its strange rock formations 3 miles; Lyme Park (NT) 3 miles; Hare Hill (NT) 10 miles; Peveril Castle 7 miles

290 The Peacock Hotel

Rowsley,
Matlock,
Derbyshire
DE4 2EB
Tel: 01629 733518
Fax: 01629 732671

Directions:
On the A6, four
miles north west of
Matlock.

The Peacock Hotel, built in 1652, is situated in what was the Dower House to Haddon Hall. It's a beautiful gabled building in warm, mellow local stone, with leaded windows and ivy clad walls. Now owned by the Jarvis Group, it is set in its own gardens leading down to the River Derwent, and has been a hotel since 1820. Inside is just as impressive, with antiques everywhere, deep carpets and warm, comfortable bars and lounges. Nothing can compare with the pampering and luxury of a top country hotel, and the Peacock has the lot. The food is justly famous, and it boasts a cellar of fine wines to accompany your meal. There's a lunch menu, or, in the evening you can sit in the well appointed Garden Restaurant and choose from the Á la carte or table d'hote menus. The food, prepared under the supervision of head chef Tony Jeanes, is quite superb. It consists of high quality English cuisine with French influences, using only the best ingredients available. But if it's just a quiet drink you're after, you can relax in the perfection of the Peacock Lounge, with its cozy nooks and crannies and roaring fire in winter.

There are sixteen fully equipped en suite rooms, two of them with four-poster beds, and all, of course, are fully equipped with tea and coffee making equipment, hair driers, and so on. It's a popular venue for weddings, and the staff go out of their way to make any event held there just that wee bit special! Dry fly fishing packages can be arranged on nearby rivers, and the chefs will be more than pleased to cook your catch. Or, if you prefer walking and rambling, the hotel can prepare picnic lunches to take with you.The Peacock is a favourite place for conferences, and it has all the usual amenities a businessman would expect. It offers the best in traditional, English hospitality, though it combines this with a friendly, unstuffy atmosphere.

Opening hours: Hotel is open all day; the bar is open11.00-15.00 and 18.00-23.30

Food: The food is superb, and is served in the restaurant from12.00-14.00 and 19.00-21.00

Credit cards: All major credit cards accepted

Accommodation: 16 fully equipped en suite rooms, two with a four poster bed

Facilities: Car park; conference facilities; large garden; fishing

Local Places of Interest/Activities: Haddon Hall close by; Bakewell (historic town) two miles; Matlock (historic town) 5 miles; Peak Railway 1 mile; Chatsworth 4 miles; Heights of Abraham Country Park and Caverns 5 miles

Plough Inn

291

Two Dales,
Matlock,
Derbyshire
DE4 2FF
01629 732260

Directions:

Take the A6 north west from Matlock for two miles, then turn north east onto the B5057. The village of Two Dales is just along this road

This old inn is full of character and atmosphere. Being 250 years old, it has a fine tradition to live up to, and offers a warm welcome to both locals and visitors. Karen Watson has only been in charge since January 2001, and such is her enthusiasm for the place that already she's redecorated and refurnished the place to an exceedingly high standard. But she's not finished yet, and has lots of plans for the future. She wants to turn it into a pub that is a firm favourite with the locals, and one which bring visitors back again and again.

The Plough Inn is a real ale inn, with at least seven real ales available at all times, including Abbots, Old Speckled Hen, Marston's Pedigree, Bass and Tetley's. There are also two rotating guest ales, plus a good range of lagers such as fosters and Stella, as well as Dry Blackthorn Cider and Guinness. The food is traditional and tasty, with good generous portions. On the menu is everything from a sandwich to a steak, and all the food is prepared and cooked by Karen herself on the premises. She tries to use good, fresh local produce whenever possible.

To the rear of the pub is a camping and trailer site which is open all year round, with its own toilets. There's also a children's play area, a boules pitch, and the local antique motor bike club meet here every second Tuesday - always a big crowd puller!

Karen has been in the trade for over 25 years, and has great plans for the Plough Inn. The potential is there to turn it into one of the best pubs in the area, and she extends a real Derbyshire welcome to both visitors and locals alike who come along to sample the hospitality of the Plough Inn!

Opening hours: Seven days a week: Easter to first week in October: 11.00-23.00; rest of year: 12.00-14.00 and 18.30-23.00

Food: Good, honest traditional food served between 12.00-14.30 and 18.00-20.30 Monday to Saturday

Credit cards: cash only at present

Accommodation: Camp site

Entertainment: Boules pitch; pool; darts; quiz night every Sunday evening from 21.30

Facilities: Childrens play area

Local Places of Interest/Activities: Peak Railway 1 mile; Winster Market House (NT) 3 miles: Riber Castle Wildlife Park 3 miles; Haddon Hall 4 miles; Heights of Abraham Country Park and Caverns 2 miles

292   The Red Lion

The Square,
Bakewell,
Derbyshire
DE45 1BT
Tel: 01629 812054
Fax: 01629 815842

Directions:

Bakewell is on the
A6, 7 miles north
west of Matlock and
eight miles south
east of Buxton

Bakewell is a small, stone built Derbyshire town famous for its Bakewell puddings. **The Red Lion** is also stone built, with sturdy, solid walls, and stands in the centre of the historic town. It has a picturesque, olde worlde look about it, and seems to welcome you in as you cross the threshold. The building dates from the 16th century, and thanks to Martin Zubertowski and Jennie Bradley, who only took over the running of the place in late 2000, it is fast earning a great reputation as somewhere to eat or have a quiet, relaxing drink. Inside, it is cozy and warm in winter and cool in summer, with low ceilings, dark wood, and a friendly atmosphere. The furnishings are smart and comfortable, and the whole place positively sparkles.

The excellent food is cooked by resident chef Neil Holmes, who has been with the Red Lion for twelve years. He uses fresh ingredients wherever possible, and most of the dishes on the menu are cooked on the premises. The place even sells breakfasts, which are popular with locals and visitors alike. The traditional Sunday lunches are also popular, as are the Saturday dinners, and you're well advised to book beforehand.

There's a good range of beers and ales, including real ales such as Tetley's, Speckled Hen, Directors and Theakston, plus John Smith's Smooth, Guiness, Carling. Kronenberg, Strongbow and Woodpecker. There's also a small but select wine list for that special occasion. This is a popular, traditional inn where the customer comes first. There's a no smoking area, for instance, and the whole place speaks of quality and value for money.

Opening hours: 9.00-23.00 seven days

Food: Breakfasts 9.00-11.30; full meals: 12.00-21.00

Credit cards: All except Diners

Accommodation: 5 rooms, 3 en suite, available all year except Christmas Eve and Christmas Day

Facilities: Car park

Local Places of Interest/Activities: Bakewell Pudding Shop in the town; Chatsworth House 3 miles; Haddon Hall 2 miles; Magpie Mine (lead mine) 3 miles; Peak Railway 4 miles

The Red Lion Inn 293

Hollington,
near Ashbourne,
Derbyshire DE6 3AG
Tel: 01335 360241

Directions:

Take the A52 west from Derby and turn south onto a minor road signposted for Hollington after Brailsford. The village is one mile along this road

If your looking for a hidden gem of an inn, then The Red Lion is for you. It sits in the small village of Hollington, a whitewashed building with a huge lawn in front of it and a path leading up to the front door. It looks very pretty, with its sleepy shutters and welcoming porch. Mine host, Robin Hunter, is the tenant, and has been in place for over a year. However, he brought a lot of experience with him when he took over, as he's been in the trade for 13 years.

The Red Lion was built in the early 19th century, and for the last 150 years has been an inn. The interior is carpeted and cozy, with a low, dark beamed roof, half panelled walls with white above and brick fireplaces that offer you a warm. roaring welcome in the cold winter months. The furniture is polished and smart, the walls are adorned with framed prints, and there are small ornaments, knick knacks and pieces of memorabilia on the shelves. This is the kind of place where any visitor would linger over a drink or meal, so comfortable is it. Two real ales are always on offer at the bar, Marston's Pedigree and and a rotating guest ale. Plus you can have Mansfield Smooth, Cameron's Dark Creamy, Stella, Heineken, Guiness and Strongbow.

There are always at least ten tasty and filling dishes on the blackboard, such as roast rack of lamb, fillet steak or pan fried hake fillet. The restaurant can seat up to 46 people, but so well known is the inn for its food that you are well advised to book in advance, especially if it's Sunday lunch you're after. The specialities of the house are the fish dishes, which are home made from good, fresh produce. Children are always welcome, and there are no smoking areas. This is an inn which is sure to please. Robin will give you a real, old fashioned welcome should you choose to visit.

Opening times: Open lunchtimes and evenings, and all day on Saturday and Sunday

Food: Lunches are served between 12.00-14.30, and evening meals between 18.30 and 21.00; the food is always excellent, and well presented

Credit cards: All major credit cards accepted

Accommodation: None

Entertainment: Occasional entertainment; phone for details

Facilities: Large, safe beer garden; no smoking areas

Local Places of Interest/Activities: Darley Moor (motor cycle racing) 4 miles; Kedleston Hall (NT) 5 miles; Denby Potteries 12 miles

294 | The Roebuck

Market Place,
Chapel-en-le-Frith,
Derbyshire
SK23 0EN
Tel: 01298 812274

THE ROEBUCK

Directions:
The Roebuck is off
Chapel-en-le-
Frith's main street

Under the careful management of Jackie Hearsum and Jill Davies, **The Roebuck** is rapidly becoming one of Chapel-en-le-Frith's most popular inns. It sits on a great site just off the main street, and is a handsome building that dates from the early 1800s. Both Jackie and Jill have many new ideas for the place, though they still want to retain that "traditional" look that says so much about the atmosphere and friendliness of a pub.

The traditional look is continued in the pub's interior. There's lots of floor space, and plenty of room to stretch out and relax over a drink or bar meal. There are old oak beams, low ceilings, delightful oak tables and chairs and upholstered wall seating, and all these combined make it a warm and welcoming place. The public bar and lounge are especially inviting, and there is a games room with a dart board.

The inn serves simple but delicious bar lunches – the kind for which England is justly famous. Everything is wonderfully cooked and presented, and the helpings are hearty and filling. Jackie and Jill reckon that using the freshest of ingredients wherever possible is the only way to keep customers happy, and entice them back again. You'll enjoy the inn's range of drinks as well. The bar boasts a wide range of cask ales, Tetley bitter, Tetley mild, lager, stout and cider, plus the usual soft drinks should you be driving.

The Roebuck is a cracking little inn, and well worth visiting. Its watchwords seem to be value for money and friendly service, and if you visit, you'll surely agree!

Opening times: Monday to Saturday 11.00-23.00; Sunday 11.00-22.30

Food: Served Monday to Saturday 12.00-14.00; Sunday 12.00-16.00

Credit cards: All major cards.

Accommodation: None

Entertainment: Occasional quizzes and theme nights; monthly entertainment (ring for details)

Facilities: Car parking opposite the inn

Local Places of Interest/Activities: Walking in the Peak District National Park; Peveril Castle 5 miles; Lyme Park (NT) 6 miles; Blue John Cavern 5 miles; Buxton (historic town) 5 miles

Internet/website:
e-mail: hearsun @sofine2.com

The Shepherds Arms   295

7 Old Road,
Whaley Bridge,
Derbyshire
SK23 7HR
Tel: 01663 732384

Directions:
Follow the A6
south east from
Stockport for nine
miles, then turn
south onto the
A5004 for Buxton.
Whaley Bridge is
one mile along this
road

This is a lovely little inn, set above the road in the small cotton town of Whaley Bridge. Seen on a summer's afternoon, when the beer garden is dotted with bright umbrellas, it presents a lovely aspect. The white rendered building dates from the 16th century, and is the second oldest in the town Under the personal supervision of husband and wife Graham and Monica Holland (helped by daughters Julie and Natalie), it has earned itself a reputation for having a lovely homely atmosphere, while at the same time offering modern and efficient service.

You really can't go wrong here. The seating is comfortable and welcoming, and there's a stone fireplace that heats you up on the coldest of winter days. The tap room still has the original stone flagged floors, giving the place a sense of continuity and history. A bar lunch within this inn is an experience not to be missed. You can choose from a substantial ploughman's lunch, black pudding with all the trimmings, home made soups and toasties or sandwiches. This is a Marston's pub, and you can wash your meal down with a selection of casked ales or one of the guest ales that are always on offer. There's also a good range of house wines at reasonable prices.

The Shepherds Arms is a traditional local, popular with cricketers, and as it's beside a canal, boat trips can be arranged. On the last Saturday in June, Whaley Bridge holds its annual carnival, so a visit then would be doubly enjoyable!

Opening hours: 12.00-23.00 from Monday to Saturday and 12.00-22.30 on Sunday

Food: Competitively priced and tasty, with good portions

Credit cards: Cash only at present

Accommodation: Phone for a list of the nearest guest houses

Entertainment: Local live music on special days (such as St Patrick's Day); darts and other

pub games; regular fun quiz nights

Facilities: Large car park

Local Places of Interest/Activities: Walking on the Peak District National Park; canal trips; walking through Todd Brooks and Goyt Valley; Lyme Park (NT) 3 miles; Tegg's Nose Country Park 6 miles; Peveril Castle 8 miles

296

Sir William Hotel

Grindleford,
Hope Valley,
Derbyshire
S32 2HS
Tel: 01433 630303
Fax: 01433 639753

Directions:

Grindlefor is on the B6001, 2 miles south of Hathersage on the A625

In the heart of the beautiful Peak district Peak District you'll find the pleasant village of Grindleford, on the banks of the Derwent. This is a great area for walks, especially up Padley Gorge and on the moorland around Burbage and Froggatt Edges. And close by are the ruins of Padley Hall, ancestral home of the Eyre family, from whom Charlotte Brontë got the surname for the heroine of her book.

Within Grindleford you'll find a lovely hotel called the **Sir William Hotel**, owned and run by Phil and Diana Cowe. Standing at a height of 1200 feet above sea level, it is an imposing building that overlooks the village, and is the ideal base if you wish to explore an area that is steeped in history. The interior of the hotel is as stunning as the exterior. There are seven beautifully appointed rooms, all en suite and all furnished to an extremely high standard, and most have beautiful views from their windows. With its fully equipped Jubilee Room, this is also the place to hold that away-from-it-all conference or function.

The cuisine at the hotel is English with Mediterranean influences, and whether you're a guest or someone who is passing through and wants a meal, you won't be disappointed. All the dishes are cooked with flair and imagination, using only the finest and freshest ingredients. There's an extensive wine list, and at the bar you'll discover an excellent range of temperature controlled real ales, plus a range of draught bitters, mild, stout, lager and cider.

Opening times: Open all day, every day

Food: Served all day

Credit cards: All major cards accepted except American Express and Diners

Accommodation: 1 family, 3 twin and 3 double rooms, all en suite and all with colour TV and tea and coffee making facilities

Entertainment: Live 60s music on Sunday evenings

Facilities: Car park; beer garden with summer barbecues; garden terrace

Local Places of Interest/Activities:
Longshore Estate (NT) 2 miles; Eyam Museum (Great Plague associations) 2 miles; Sheffield (historic city) 9 miles; Howden, Derwent and Ladybower Reservoirs (Dam Busters associations) 7 miles; Chatsworth 4 miles

Smiths Tavern

297

St John Street, Ashbourne,
Derbyshire DE6 1GL
Tel/Fax: 01335 342264
Directions:
The inn is on Ashbourne's main street,
right in the centre of town

If it's history you're after, the place to go is **Smiths Tavern** in the heart of Ashbourne. It dates from the 16th century, and at one time formed part of a monastery! The whole of Ashbourne is full of history, and it was here that Bonnie Prince Charlie proclaimed his father king of Great Britain in 1745. It also hosts the annual Royal Shrove Tuesday football match, where the goal are three miles apart.

The tavern is a beautiful building, with bags of character and many period features, and the interior is equally as charming. The walls are all at least 18 inches thick, which makes it warm and snug in winter and cool in summer. Over the cellar is a small bar with old oak beams, a small, comfortable lounge with a piano, and a restaurant that can seat 20 people in absolute comfort. At the bar you can order from a range of three real ales (two regulars and a guest ale), plus there is a great selection of draught bitters, mild, lager, stout and cider.

The cuisine comes from all over the globe, and the proprietor, Paul Mellor, takes a great pride in his kitchen. There's a printed menu, plus a daily specials board that is sure to contain something for everyone. If you're looking for a real treat, try the tavern's lamb shank marinated in garlic and rosemary, with garlic mash and a choice of vegetables in season. Delicious! Only the freshest of ingredients go into the dishes, and they are all prepared in the kitchen to your individual requirements. So don't expect fast food here!

Smiths tavern is a popular venue for the locals of Ashbourne, and this fact speaks volumes on the quality and value for money you can expect here.

Opening times: Monday to Saturday 11.00-15.00 and 17.00-23.00; Sunday 11.00-23.00

Food: Served 12.00-15.00 and 18.00-21.00 seven days

Credit cards: Cash only at present

Accommodation: None

Entertainment: Sunday evening quiz with a cash jackpot

Facilities: Street parking

Local Places of Interest/Activities: Ilam Park (NT) 4 miles; North Staffordshire Railway (steam) 12 miles; Darley Moor (motor cycle racing) 3 miles; Alton Towers (theme park) 7 miles

Internet/website:
e-mail: smithstavern@ talk21.com

298

The Sycamore

Sycamore Road,
Birch Vale,
near New Mills,
Derbyshire SK22 1AB
Tel: 01663 742715/747568
Fax: 01663 747382

Directions:

Birch Vale is on the A6015,
13 miles south east of
Manchester city centre

The Sycamore is a real hidden gem of an inn! It sits in the small village of Birch Vale, right on the edge of the Peak District National Park, but still close to Manchester and Stockport. It dates from the 19th century, and has thick stone walls and a look that speaks of a long tradition of hospitality and warmth. It's a family run inn, so the attention to detail is meticulous. There are seven en suite rooms, all well appointed and comfortable, with TVs, tea and coffee making facilities, central heating and trouser presses. It makes the ideal base to explore the surrounding area, which is outstandingly beautiful and steeped in history. For those who just wish to relax, then The Sycamore's riverside garden is the perfect place to while away a few hours. The grounds are a real haven for wildlife.

But if it's just a quiet drink or a meal you're after, the The Sycamore is still the place for you. There are two 60 seat restaurants, where you can order anything from an excellent dinner with wine to a tasty snack or an appetising bar lunch. The Sycamore has an excellent reputation for the quality of the home cooked food that it provides.Only the freshest of ingredients are used, and represents wonderful value for money. Choose from the 'Chef's Specials' or the printed menu – you'll never be disappointed!

There's a traditional, comfortable bar complete with log fire, where you can choose from a range of real ales. And if you have a special occasion coming up, be it a wedding, a party or a small business function, then the friendly and experienced staff at The Sycamore can take all the worry out of organising it. One of the inn's mottoes is "calm waters in the storm of life", and this accurately describes the atmosphere of what is a charming, sophisticated and yet immensely cheering place!

Opening times: Open every day from 11.00-23.00

Food: Served every day until 22.00

Credit cards: All major cards accepted except American Express and Diners

Accommodation: 7 en suite rooms, including single, double and family accommodation

Entertainment: Occasional live music and other events such as 60s nights (ring for details)

Facilities: Car park; beer garden; function/conference room; small children's zoo; children's adventure playground and trail; cocktail and music bar

Local Places of Interest/Activities: Manchester (historic city) 13 miles; Lyme Park (NT) 3 miles; Kinder Scout 2 miles; Peak National Park 1 mile; Eyam 14 miles; Castleton 8 miles; Chatsworth 18 miles.

Internet/Website: www.sycamoreinn.co.uk

The Victoria Inn

88 Broscroft, Hadfield,
Glossop, Derbyshire
SK13 1HE
Tel: 01457 855107

Directions:
From Manchester take the
M67 east from Junction 24
on the M60 until it joins the
A628; continue east along
the A628 for a mile, then
turn right onto the A57.
Hadfield sits just off this
road, on the left hand side.
The inn is in the centre of
the village.

Being right on the edge of the Peak District National Park, this is an excellent inn for walkers and motorists alike. It sits at the heart of Hadfield, on a corner opposite the village green, and is a welcoming, stone building that speaks of a long tradition of hospitality and good service. In fact, **The Victoria Inn** dates from 1838, and though it is no more than a mile from the busy A628 - one of the main trans-Pennine roads - it is situated in a village that is a haven of peace and quiet. Under the personal supervision of Beryl and Stuart McLaren, it has earned a reputation as being a favourite haunt of walkers visiting the National Park. It has a cozy, old-world interior and, in winter months, a roaring coal fire and comfortable seating is guaranteed to heat and cheer up the chilliest of hill walkers! Its afternoon teas (with home baked scones!) are legendary, and it has a fine range of ales, including Thwaites cask bitter and mild.

The food is reasonably priced, tasty and unpretentious. It is cooked on the premises using fresh produce, and the menu includes such favourites as steak, roast chicken, lasagna, breaded cod and gammon steaks. There's also a range of desserts, including a wonderful sticky toffee pudding. Vegetarian dishes and a children's menu are also available, as well as starters such as soup and a roll, prawn cocktail and garlic mushrooms. In the summer months, there are regular barbecues. There's also an added bonus - if you bring along a copy of "The Hidden Inns of the Heart of England", you'll be presented with a free glass of wine to accompany your meal!

Opening Hours: 11.00-23.00 Monday to Saturday; 12.00-22.30 on Sunday

Food: Small but comprehensive menu, plus superb afternoon teas; food is served all week between 12.00-20.00

Credit Cards: Visa; Access; Switch

Accommodation: Can be arranged -phone for details

Facilities: Children's play area; beer garden

Entertainment: Live music (various artists) on Saturday and Sunday evenings; quiz every Tuesday evening; various events in support of local charities.

Local Places of Interest/Activities: Walking on the Peak District National Park (Woodhead Pass, Snake Pass, etc.), plus aircraft memorial sites from the Second World War; Etherow Country Park 4 miles; Lyme Park (NT) 9 miles

300   The White Lion

*195 Starkholmes
Road,
Starkholmes,
Matlock,
Derbyshire
DE4 5JA
Tel: 01629 582511*

Directions:

Situated on the A6,
one mile south of
Matlock

This long, low inn sits hard against a beautiful wooded area of rising ground to the back, which provides a pleasing framework for its solid, stone built walls and tall chimneys, We're in former lead mining country here, and the inn was originally called the Buddles Inn, as local people used to "buddle", or wash, the lead in an adjacent barn. **The White Lion** is within a building which was once a farmhouse dating from the 18th century, and it still has that "rural" look about it. It sits well off the road, with a car park to the side and a small beer garden and boules pitch to the front which is a pleasant area to have a drink in the summer months and look at the stunning view. The interior is lovely. The bar has a low ceiling with old beams, dark, highly polished furniture and flagstones on the floor. The wall lighting is subdued, giving the place an olde worlde atmosphere which is cozy and welcoming. The small dining area is carpeted throughout, with bright cheerful table clothes and sparkling cutlery laid out ready for the many diners who want to sample the inn's good food.

Elaine Murray and Jim Parker took over the place in November 2000, and already their new ideas are beginning to bear fruit. The menu is wholly blackboard based, and contains many imaginative and upmarket dishes, such as sauteed fillet tail of monkfish, medallions of venison or breast of Gressingham duck, all keenly priced and all delicious. The bar is well stocked, with three real ales, including Home, Marston's pedigree and a rotating guest ale. Also available is John Smith's Smooth, Guinness, draught lagers and cider. If it's a bottle of wine you're after, then there's a choice of fine wines to accompany your meal. The White Lion offers traditional, friendly service, superb food and a great range of drinks. What more could you ask for?

Opening hours: Monday to Friday: 12.00-15.00 and 17.00-23.00; Saturday and Sunday: 12.00-22.30

Food: Excellent, imaginative cooking. Lunches are served from Monday to Saturday between 12.00-14.00 and Sundays 12.00-15.00; the Á la carte menu is available Monday to Saturday from 19.00-21.00

Credit cards: most cards accepted

Accommodation: Three guest rooms with private showers and toilets

Facilities: Car park: beer garden

Local Places of Interest/Activities: Wirksworth Heritage Centre: 3 miles; Heights of Abraham Country Park and Caverns 1 mile; Riber Castle Wildlife Park 1 mile; Cromford Mill 1 mile; National Tramway Museum, Crich: 3 miles

Internet/website:
website: www. whitelion-matlock.com
e-mail: e.murray@ntlworld.com;
elaine@whitelion-matlock.com

Ye Olde Cheshire Cheese Inn   **301**

How Lane,
Castleton,
Hope Valley,
Derbyshire
SS33 8WJ
Tel: 01433 620330
Fax: 01433 621847

Directions:
Castleton sits on the
A625, 6 miles east of
Chapel-en-le-Frith

Set deep in the heart of the Peak District National Park, Castleton is one of its most beautiful villages. It is famous for the caverns which are close by, such as Speedwell, Peak and Blue John Caverns. Perhaps its most striking building is Peveril Castle, whose ruins lie close to the Market Place.

Another striking building is **Ye Olde Cheshire Cheese Inn**, which dates back to 1660. It is a truly beautiful building, with half timbered walls and a myriad of flower-filled window boxes and hanging baskets. And inside you'll find log fires, black oak beams and a wealth of gleaming brass. But the inn is so much more than just a place to eat and drink. It also offers some of the best accommodation in the area, and if you want to explore the beautiful Peak District, this inn makes the ideal base. There are 10 beautifully appointed en suite rooms with TVs and tea and coffee making facilities, and the tariffs are competitively priced. All the rooms are individually styled, beautifully decorated and comfortable. Some even have four poster beds!

The restaurant seats 65 people, and over 30 dishes are available on the menu, from brewer's pie (for which the inn is famous!) to topside steak in real ale. The cuisine is English, with just a hint of the Orient or the Mediterranean thrown in. You can have wine with your meal, of course, or you can choose from a fine selection of beers and ales at the bar.

This is a real olde worlde inn, with some fabulous accommodation that just can't be bettered. Mine hosts Ken and Angie Slack will go out of their way to make your stay really enjoyable!

Opening times: Open all day, every day

Food: Served whenever the inn is open

Credit cards: All major cards except American Express and Diners

Local Places of Interest/Activities: Chapel-en-le-Frith (historic town) 7 miles; Buxton (historic town) 9 miles; Peveril Castle in village: walking on Peak District National Park and exploring caverns

Internet/Website:
e-mail: kslack@btconnect.com
www.peakland.com/cheshirecheese/

This page is left intentionally blank

10 Staffordshire

PLACES OF INTEREST:

PUBS AND INNS:

The Hidden Inns of the Heart of England

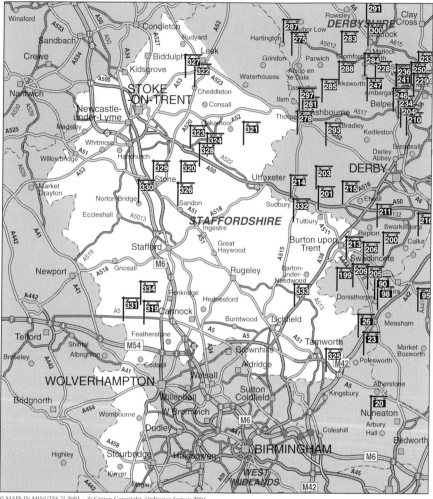

© MAPS IN MINUTES ™ 2001 © Crown Copyright, Ordnance Survey 2001

Please note all references refer to page numbers

Staffordshire

The southwest of Staffordshire encompasses many changing landscapes, from the busy, industrial towns of Stafford and Burton upon Trent to the peace and quiet of Cannock Chase. Along with the Hednesford Hills, the Chase provides a wonderful open area of woodland and moorland that is one of the county's great recreational centres. Well supported by an interesting and informative visitors' centre, the Chase is a must for anyone visiting this part of Staffordshire. The southeast of Staffordshire, although lying close to the Black Country - the depressing product of the heavy industrialisation of the 18th and 19th centuries - has managed to escape in the main. One legacy of the era and a feature throughout the whole of Staffordshire, however, is the canal network. Built to link Birmingham with the Trent & Mersey Canal, the less well known Coventry Canal and the Birmingham & Fazeley Canal pass through tiny villages and hamlets and the towpaths provide the opportunity to walk in some unexpectedly scenic countryside. The Industrial Revolution also left its mark on the landscape, though the two great reservoirs of Rudyard and Tittesworth, built to provide a water supply to the growing industry and population of the Midlands, now offer peaceful havens for a wide variety of plants, animals and birds as well as recreational facilities such as fishing and boating.

The area around Stoke-on-Trent is famous the world over for its pottery industry. Originally centred on the five towns of Stoke, Tunstall, Burslem, Hanley and Longton, The Potteries were at the heart of the Industrial Revolution. Both coal and clay were found locally, though imported clay from Cornwall was later used, which gave rise to the start of the industry but it was the foresight and ingenuity of men such as Wedgwood and Minton that really turned the cottage industry into production on a much larger scale. To support the industry in and around the centre, a network of canals, and later railways, was begun. The Trent & Mersey Canal, built by James Brindley with the support of Wedgwood and his friend the Duke of Bridgewater, was finally completed in 1777 and made possible navigation from coast to coast, between the busy ports of Liverpool and Hull. Together, the Trent & Mersey Canal, the Staffordshire & Worcester Canal, begun in the same year, the Shropshire Union Canal to the west and the Middlewich branch of the Llangollen Canal, form a wonderful four counties ring that can be undertaken wholly or partly by boat. These canals, with their accessible towpaths, run through the very heart of the towns as well as through the often delightful countryside.

PLACES OF INTEREST

BIDDULPH

John Wesley was a frequent visitor to this isolated moorland town but the history of Biddulph goes back to long before the days of Methodism. After the Norman Conquest the manor of Biddulph was granted by William the Conqueror to Robert the Forester, an overlord of what was then the extensively forested area of Lyme. The Biddulphs, a staunchly Catholic family, took control of the area. John Biddulph fought under the Royal flag during the Civil War and was killed at the Battle of Hopton Heath. His son entrusted the defence of Biddulph Hall to Lord Brereton, who withstood a determined siege until 1644, when he was finally subjected to heavy artillery. The Hall was then demolished to prevent its being regarrisoned.

Biddulph Grange belonged to the Cistercian monks of the Abbey at Hulton until the Dissolution and its garden is one of the most unusual and remarkable in the whole country. It was created by James Bateman in the mid-19th century as a series of connected parts to show specimens from his extensive collection, which was garnered from all parts of the globe. Highlights

Chinese Gardens, Biddulph

include the Egyptian Court and the Great Wall of China. The gardens are owned by the National Trust. Call 01782 517999 for visiting times.

BURTON UPON TRENT

The 'capital' of East Staffordshire, Burton upon Trent is famous for its brewing industry. It began many centuries ago, and even the monks of the Benedictine Abbey, founded here in 1100, were not the first to realise that the Burton well water was specially suited to brewing. William Bass began brewing in Burton in 1777, and by 1863 the brewery had grown to produce half a million barrels of beer each year on a 750-acre site. In 1998 Bass acquired the Burton premises of Carlsberg-Tetley, creating the biggest brewery site in the UK - 830 acres, brewing 5.5 million barrels yearly. The brewery is open for tours, and the entry fee includes a tour of the **Bass Museum of Brewing**, in Horninglow Street, and up to three pints of beer or lager. As well as being offered the opportunity of seeing, sniffing and sampling the traditionally brewed beer, visitors can tour the machinery, inspect the fleet of old vehicles (including the famous Daimler Worthington White Shield Bottle Car) and admire the famous Bass shire horses. During your visit, you will find out about bottom fermentation, dry hopping, kilning, mashing, pitching and sparging - but if you've downed your three pints you might have forgotten some of it by the end.

A Benedictine Abbey, founded by a Saxon earl called Wulfric Spot, was established on the banks of the River Trent, where the **Market Place** now stands. The focus of Burton, it was from here that the town grew and, in the 12th century, the monks constructed a large stone bridge of some 36 arches across the River Trent. Today's bridge replaced the medieval structure in 1864. The area along the banks of the Trent, between Burton Bridge and the later structure of Ferry Bridge, which opened in 1889, is known as the **Washlands**. Rich in native wildlife, the Washlands is a haven for all manner of birds, small mammals, trees and plants. This ancient area, now a wonderful, traditionally managed recreational centre for the town, has a history dating back beyond that of Burton itself. It was at Washlands that, in the 7th century, St Modwen is said to have built her chapel and settlement on Andresey Island. No evidence of the constructions remain and they were thought to have been destroyed in a Danish raid in 874. The site of the chapel is marked by a cherry orchard and some yew trees.

CANNOCK CHASE

Though close to areas of dense population, **Cannock Chase** is a surprisingly wild place of heath and woodland that has been designated an Area of Outstanding Natural Beauty. Covering some 20,000 acres, the Chase was once the hunting ground of Norman kings and, later, the Bishops of Lichfield and deer are still plentiful. Sherbrook Valley is a good starting point from which to find these timid creatures. Conifers now dominate, but it is still possible to find the remains of the ancient oak forest and, in the less well-walked marshy grounds, many rare species survive. A popular place for leisurely strolls, the Chase is also ideal for more strenuous walking and other outdoor recreational activities. Excellent view points can be found at **Coppice Hill** and **Brereton Spurs**, while **Castle Ring**, an impressive Iron Age hill fort, is well worth the effort to find.

Amid all this natural beauty, there are also reminders of the 20th century and, in particular, the unique military cemeteries near **Broadhurst Green**, where some 5,000 German soldiers from the First World War lie buried. Cannock Chase was used as a training ground during that war and was the last billet for many thousands of soldiers before they left for France. The remnants of the training area can still be seen, as can the prisoner of war camp. The use of the Chase as a training ground was not a new idea: in 1873, there were extensive manoeuvres here with one army base at Etching Hill and the other army at Hednesford Hills.

The **Museum of Cannock Chase** at the Valley Heritage Centre is only one of the many wonderful parts of Cannock Chase. Opened in May 1989, the Centre is set in the corn store of a former colliery where the pit ponies' feed was kept. Its galleries provide a variety of exhibitions, with rooms dedicated to the natural history of the Hednesford Hills and Castle Ring hill fort. Subjects covered in these galleries change every six months to deal with as many aspects of the area's history as possible. The colliery was a training pit where thousands of trainee miners worked in simulated underground conditions before beginning work in a real mine.

CHEDDLETON

The restored **Cheddleton Flint Mill**, in the rural surroundings of the Churnet valley, makes an interesting visit. The water-powered machinery was used to crush flint that had been brought in by canal and then transported, again by water, to Stoke where it was used in the hardening of pottery. The small museum includes a rare 18th-century 'haystack' boiler and a Robey steam engine and there are also collections of exhibits which relate to the preparation of raw materials for the pottery industry.

Cheddleton Flint Mill

Trips by narrow boats along the Caldon Canal can be taken from the mill.

The village of Cheddleton itself seems to perch dangerously on the side of a hill which is why it has such spectacular views. The parish **Church of St Edward** stands in open country and has some wonderful Morris windows as well as a lot of interesting Victorian decoration, the result of the restoration by George Gilbert Scott in the 1860s and a sight well worth seeing. The village station is home to the **Churnet Valley Railway and Museum**, which will give great delight to all railway enthusiasts. The Museum has a nostalgic collection of beautifully preserved locomotives and other railway memorabilia, and there are steam train rides to Leekbrook Junction and the lovely hamlet of Consall Forge. At present Cheddleton is the only point of vehicular access, but there are plans to extend the line beyond Consall to Froghall, where the main station and visitor facilities will be located. Call 01538 360522 for timetable and other details.

To the west of Cheddleton is **Deep Hayes Country Park**, which lies in a secluded valley by the Caldon Canal and Staffordshire Way. From the ridge there are breathtaking views but, for the less energetic, there is a very pleasant walk around two pools which has many offshoots into lovely countryside.

CONSALL

This is a beautiful spot hidden in a particularly deep section of the Churnet Valley downstream from Cheddleton. The little cottages keep in close company with the small bridges over the Caldon Canal. Originally known as Consall Forge, the hamlet took its name from an old iron forge that existed here in the first Elizabethan Age. As iron making became uneconomic here, the forge altered its operation and became one of the major lime making centres after the completion of the Caldon Canal.

Reached through **Consall village is Consall Nature Park**, an RSPB reserve that is a quiet and peaceful haven with much to delight the avid birdwatcher. Accessible only on foot or by canal, the village is very popular with walkers and boaters and has a pub to provide the necessary refreshment. Consall Forge Pottery produces hand-thrown stoneware ceramics - teapots a speciality.

308

ECCLESHALL

For over a thousand years Eccleshall Castle was the palace of the bishops of Lichfield but, at the beginning of this century, it became a family home when the Carter family moved from Yorkshire. The present simple sandstone house is typical of the best architecture of the William & Mary period and it incorporates part of the earlier 14th-century Castle. The interior of the

Eccleshall Castle

house has been augmented by successive members of the family, one of whom added a magnificent Victorian staircase and dome. Perhaps to remind them of the county from which they came, the Carters have collected a very interesting number of 19th-century paintings by Yorkshire artists. The library is full of superb books, among them many first editions, including a complete set of the works of Charles Dickens. The gardens have been created around the ruins of the old Castle and have a great deal of romantic appeal. The impressive parish church, standing at the end of the wide and open High Street, is a legacy from the days when Eccleshall was home to the Lichfield Bishops.

A little way north of Eccleshall, on the A519 at Cotes Heath, is **Mill Meece Pumping Station**, where two magnificent steam engines that once pumped more than three million gallons of water each day and three massive boilers that used 35 tons of coal each week are kept in pristine condition. The donkey work is done nowadays by powerful electric pumps which supply an average of 2.2 million gallons each day to Severn Trent customers. After being disinfected, the water is pumped five miles north to Hanchurch Reservoir, from where it is supplied to homes and businesses in the region. An exhibition tells the story of water and the history of the station, and during the summer there are steam weekends and special events.

FEATHERSTONE

Just to the south of the village is **Moseley Old Hall**, which visitors can be forgiven for thinking belongs to the 19th century; but it dates from the first Elizabethan Age and, inside, much of the original panelling and timber framing is still visible. The Hall once sheltered King Charles II for a short time following his defeat at the Battle of Worcester in 1651 and it is for this that the house is best remembered. Under cover of darkness the defeated King, disguised as a woodcutter, was escorted into the house by Thomas Whitgreave, the owner, and his chaplain, John Huddlestone. He rested here for two days and even evaded capture when Parliamentarians visited the house in search of the monarch before leaving, again in disguise, and fleeing to France. In 1940, the house was acquired by the Wiggin family and, in 1962, it became the property of the National Trust. At that time it had no garden to speak of, but fairly soon two experts recreated the garden in the style of the century. The outstanding feature is the knot garden with its box hedges and gravel beds. There is interest everywhere in this wonderful garden, which is full of rare 17th-century plants and herbs. In the barn is an exhibition showing the escape of King Charles.

GNOSALL

Some beautiful ash and sycamore trees form a delightful shaded arch over the road through this village (the name is pronounced 'Nawzell') and it also has its very own ghost! On the night of January 21st 1879 a man was attacked at Gnosall canal bridge by an alarming black monster with enormous white eyes. The police were quite sure it was the ghost of a man–monkey who had haunted the bridge for years after a man was drowned in the canal. It is worth staying a while in the village, ghost permitting, to have a look around the fine collegiate Church of St Lawrence. As well as containing some of the best Norman work to be seen in the county, the church, most of which dates from the 13th and 15th centuries, has a particularly ornate west crossing arch.

Despite its name, a large portion of the **Shropshire Union Canal**, some 23 miles, lies within the county of Staffordshire. Indeed, much of this southern section passes through wonderful countryside. Extending from Ellesmere Port, Cheshire, on the Manchester

Staffordshire

Ship Canal to Autherley junction near Wolverhampton, the Shroppie, as it is affectionately known, has a long history. Built by three separate companies, at three different times, the Canal was begun as early as 1772 and was finished in 1835, a few months after the death of Thomas Telford, who had worked on its construction.

In order to compete with the new railways, the canal had to be built as simply and economically as possible and so, unlike many canals before it, the Shropshire Union's route was short and straight, cutting deeply through hills and crossing lower ground on embankments rather than talking the longer route on level ground. The Canal's **Cowley Tunnel**, near the village, was originally intended to be longer than its actual 81 yards but, as it was being constructed, the rock towards the southern end, being softer, gave way. The dramatic fault, where the more solid sandstone of the northern end meets the soft marlstones, can still be seen by taking the towpath through the tunnel and cutting.

GREAT HAYWOOD

This ancient village is famous for having the longest packhorse bridge in England. Built in the 16th century, the Essex Bridge (named after the famous Elizabethan Earl who used nearby Shugborough Hall when hunting in the area) still has 14 of its original 40 arches spanning the River Trent. Here, too, is the interesting Roman Catholic Church of St John the Baptist. Built in 1828, in 1845 the whole church was moved from its original site at Tixall to Great Haywood by the local Roman Catholic community. With an ornate west front and Perpendicular windows, it is the richness of the west gallery that is the highlight of the building.

Most visitors to the village however, pass swiftly through it on their way to one of the most impressive attractions in the county, **Shugborough Hall**, the 17th-century seat of the

Shugborough Hall

Earls of Lichfield. This magnificent 900-acre estate includes Shugborough Park Farm, a Georgian farmstead built in 1805 for Thomas, Viscount Anson, and now home to rare breed animals and to demonstrations of traditional farming methods such as hand milking, butter and cheese making and shire horses at work. The former servants' quarters have been restored to the days of the 19th century and offer an insight into life below stairs. The mansion itself is a splendid piece of architecture, altered several times over its 300 years, but always retaining its distinct grandeur. The vast rooms, with their ornate plasterwork and cornicing, contain an impressive collection of paintings, ceramics and silverware as well as a wealth of elegant French furniture. Outside, in the beautiful parkland, can be found an outstanding collection of neoclassical monuments dotted around and the Lady Walk leads along the banks of the River Sow to the delightful terraced lawns and rose garden.

HANCHURCH

This tiny hamlet itself is unlikely to ring any bells with visitors as they pass by but the nearby gardens are world famous. The earliest reference to Trentham relates to a nunnery which was established by St Werburgh, daughter of the Anglo Saxon King of Mercia in AD 680, and later by the daughter of Alfred the Great in around 907. Ownership then passed, via Edward the Confessor and William the Conqueror, to William Rufus. After the Dissolution of the Monasteries, the estate was bought by James Leveson, a wealthy wool merchant who founded the dynasty of the Dukes of Sutherland, owners of the estate for over 300 years.

Trentham Gardens were landscaped by Capability Brown and given a more formal style by Sir Charles Barry, whose work can be observed in the lovely Italian gardens. Although the Hall was demolished in 1911, this style can still be recognised in such buildings as the orangery and sculpture gallery which remain today and form a framework for the outstanding conference, exhibition and banqueting centre that is Trentham. There is, normally, unrestricted access to 800 acres of woodland, lake and gardens, with opportunities for woodland walks, boating and jet skiing. There are first class facilities for trout and coarse fishing and clay pigeon shooting. Tuition in fishing and

310

shooting is available for the individual or for parties. The vast grounds and lake create a huge natural amphitheatre in which many sporting and other outdoor

Trentham Gardens

events take place in idyllic setting under a backdrop which is breathtakingly beautiful in all seasons.

HEDNESFORD

This former mining town lies on the edge of Cannock Chase and its oldest building, The Cross Keys Inn was built around 1746. The Anglesey Hotel, built in 1831 by Edmund Peel of Fazeley, was originally designed as a form of summerhouse in a Tudor style with stepped gables and this too lies on the heart of Hednesford.

Nearby, the **Hazel Slade Reserve** shows the adaptability of nature with an old-fashioned countryside of small fields, hedges, streams, marshes and woodland. In the 1960s the old broadleaf wood was felled for timber; hedges were planted and cattle grazed the cleared fields. However, a small area of the wood managed to recover and grew from the stumps and seeds that remained in the ground. Then, five years later, a pool and marsh started to form as the land began to subside as a result of the local mining activity. The Reserve is a popular place for fishermen as well as those interested in natural history.

Rising over 700 feet above sea level, the **Hednesford Hills** are a prominent local landmark which bring the countryside of Cannock Chase into the heart of Hednesford. Originally covered in oak and birch, these 300 acres of

heathland have been the scene of varied activities over the years. They have been quarried for sand and gravel, mined for coal and used for military training. The land is now a registered common and the hills are a tract of wild landscape with a plethora of heathland plants, abundant wildlife and the opportunity for recreation for the people who live nearby.

The hills have other sporting connections too. Cockfighting once took place at **Cockpit Hill** though the exact location of the old cockpit is unknown. In the last century prize fighters prepared themselves at the nearby Cross Keys Inn for boxing bouts on the hills and racehorses were trained on the land. Race meetings were held here regularly until 1840 when the racetrack at Etchinghill, near Rugeley, became more popular. In particular, three Grand National winners were stabled and trained on the Hednesford Hills: Jealousy won the race in 1861, Eremon in 1907 and Jenkinstown in 1910.

INGESTRE

The beautiful **Church of St Mary the Virgin**, in the small estate village, is something of a surprise. Standing close to the Jacobean Ingestre Hall, the sophisticated church was built in 1676 and has been attributed to Sir Christopher Wren. One of the few churches that Wren designed outside London, it has an elegant interior with a rich stucco nave ceiling and some of the earliest electrical installations in any church. The chancel, which is barrel vaulted, is home to some delightful garlanded reredos and there are many monuments to the Chetwynds and Talbots, who were Earls of Shrewsbury from 1856 and had their seat in the village.

Church of St Mary the Virgin

LEEK

Known as the 'Capital of the Moorlands', this is an attractive textile centre on the banks of the River Churnet. It was here that French Huguenots settled, after fleeing from religious oppression, and established the silk industry that thrived due to the abundance of soft water coming off the nearby moorland. Until the 19th century, this was a domestic industry with the workshops on the top storeys of the houses; many examples of these 'top shops' have survived to this day. Leek also became an important dyeing town, particularly after the death of Prince Albert, when 'Raven Black' was popularised by Queen Victoria, who remained in mourning for her beloved husband for many years.

William Morris, founder of the Arts and Crafts movement, lived and worked in Leek for many months between 1875 and 1878. Much of his time here was spent investigating new techniques of dyeing but he also revived the use of traditional dyes. His influence cannot only be seen in the art here but also in the architecture. Leek Art Gallery is also the place to go to find out more about the wonderful and intricate work of the famous Leek School of Embroidery that was founded by Lady Wardle in the 1870s.

Leek is by no means a recent town that grew up in the shadow of the Industrial Revolution. An ancient borough, granted its charter in 1214, Leek was a thriving market centre rivalling Macclesfield and Congleton. The Butter Cross, which now stands in the Market Place, was originally erected near the junction of Sheep Market and Stanley Street by the Joliffe family in 1671. Every road coming into the town seems to converge on the old cobbled Market Place and the road to the west leads down to the Parish Church. Dedicated to Edward the Confessor (the full name is St Edward's and All Saints' Church), the original Church was burnt down in 1297 and rebuilt some 20 years later though the building is now largely 17th century. The timber roof of the nave is well worth a second look and is the Church's pride and joy. It is boasted that each of the cross beams was hewn from a separate oak tree and, in the west part of the nave, an enormous 18th-century gallery rises up, tier on tier, giving the impression of a theatre's dress circle!

Although much has been altered inside the Church, most notably in 1865 when GE Street

rebuilt the chancel, reredos, sanctuary, pulpit and stalls, there still remains a rather unusual wooden chair. Traditionally this is believed to have been a ducking stool for scolds that was used in the nearby River Churnet. Outside, in the churchyard, can be found a rather curious inscription on a gravestone: "James Robinson interred February the 28th 1788 Aged 438"! To the north side of the Church is an area still known locally as 'Petty France', which holds the graves of many Napoleonic prisoners of war who lived nearby.

311

Another building worthy of a second glance is the imposing **Nicholson Institute**, with its copper dome. Completed in 1884 and funded by the local industrialist Joshua Nicholson, the Institute offered the people of Leek an opportunity to learn and also expand their cultural horizons. Many of the great Victorian literary giants, including George Bernard Shaw and Mark Twain, came here to admire the building. The town's **War Memorial**, built in Portland stone and with a clock tower, has a dedication to the youngest Nicholson son, who was killed in the First World War. Leek was the home of James Brindley, the 18th-century engineer who built much of the early canal network. A water-powered corn mill built by him in 1752 in Mill Street has been restored and now houses the **Brindley Water Museum**, which is devoted to his life and work. Visitors can see corn being ground and see displays of millwrighting skills. Leek has a traditional outdoor market every Wednesday, a craft and antiques market on Saturday and an indoor 'butter market' on Wednesday, Friday and Saturday.

The **River Churnet**, though little known outside Staffordshire, has a wealth of scenery and industrial archaeology and, being easily accessible to the walker, its valley deserves better recognition. The river rises to the west of Leek in rugged gritstone country, but for most of its length it flows through softer red sandstone countryside in a valley that was carved out during the Ice Age. Though there are few footpaths directly adjacent to the riverbank, most of the valley can be walked close to the river using a combination of canal towpaths and former railway tracks.

Four miles to the north of Leek on the A53 rise the dark, jagged gritstone outcrops of **The Roaches**, **Ramshaw Rocks** and **Hen Cloud**. Roaches is a corruption of the French word

312

'roches' or rocks and was reputedly given by Napoleonic prisoners: 'cloud' is a local word used for high hills. Just below The Roaches there is another delightful stretch of water, **Tittesworth Reservoir**, which is extremely popular with trout fishermen. It has some super trails, a visitor centre with an interactive exhibition, a restaurant and a gift shop.

LICHFIELD

Despite its 18th-century prominence Lichfield lagged behind other towns in extensive rebuilding programmes and consequently it still retains its medieval grid pattern streets with elegant Georgian houses and, mixed in among them, black and white Tudor cottages. First settled by the Celts and also close to the crossroads of the two great Roman roadways, Ryknild Street (now the A38) and Watling Street (now the A5), Lichfield was one of the most important towns of ancient days; the King of Mercia offered St Chad the seat of Lichfield and, on his death, the town became a place of pilgrimage and its subsequent importance as an ecclesiastical centre.

The first cathedral was built here in 669 but no traces of this building, or the later Norman structure, remain. The **Lichfield Cathedral** seen today dates from the 12th century and is particularly famous for the three magnificent spires which dominate the City skyline. Inside there are many treasures, including the beautiful 8th-century illuminated manuscript *The Lichfield Gospels* and Sir Francis Chantrey's famous sculpture *The Sleeping Children*.

The surrounding Cathedral Close is regarded by many as the most original and unspoilt in the country, and, being separated from the rest of the city by **Stowe and Minster Pools**, it is also a peaceful haven of calm. These two wonderful pools, Stowe and Minster, are used for fishing and sailing as well as being the site of the Festival fireworks display each July. The Minster Pool is particularly beautiful, it was landscaped in the late 18th century by Anna Seward and is now a haven for wildfowl.

At the very heart of Lichfield is the **Lichfield Heritage Centre**, part of St Mary's Centre in the Market Place. A church has stood on this site since the 12th century and the present building, the third, dates from 1868. As with many ecclesiastical buildings, the decline in the

Nave, Lichfield Cathedral

church-going population made St Mary's redundant and, to save it from being demolished altogether, the Centre was formed. A stroll round here is a fascinating experience and for the energetic, there are spectacular views across the city from the viewing platform on the spire. There are exhibitions on the history and everyday life of the city as seen through the eyes of its inhabitants over the centuries and it also includes the story of the siege of Lichfield Cathedral during the Civil War and displays of the city's silver, ancient charter and archives.

The City has been a place of pilgrims and travellers for centuries and, in 1135, **St John's Hospital** opened to offer shelter to those passing through Lichfield. One of the finest Tudor brick buildings in the country, the Hospital is now a home for the elderly. The **Hospital Chapel**, with its magnificent stained glass window by the designer of the celebrated east window at Coventry Cathedral, John Piper, is open daily.

The **Guildhall**, the meeting place of the city governors for over 600 years, has, at various times, also been the courthouse, a police station and a prison. Behind its Victorian façade, lie the remains of the city jail, complete with stocks and cells and the City Dungeons can be visited on Saturdays throughout the summer.

Lichfield's most famous son is Dr Samuel Johnson, the poet, novelist and author of the first comprehensive English dictionary. The son of a bookseller, Johnson was born in 1709 in Breadmarket Street, and the house is now home to the **Samuel Johnson Birthplace Museum**. Open every day except Sundays, the Museum, as well as exhibiting artefacts relating to his life and works, also has a series of tableaux showing how the house looked in the early 18th century. Dr Johnson was justly proud of his city:

'I lately took my friend Boswell (a Londoner) and showed him genuine civilised life in an English provincial town. I turned him loose in Lichfield, that he might see for once real civility.'

Here are a few more Johnson gems:

'A tavern chair is the throne of human felicity.'

'Depend on it sir, when a man knows he is to be hanged in a fortnight, it concentrates the mind wonderfully.'

'When two Englishman meet their first talk is of the weather.'

Memorials to Dr Johnson's stepdaughter Lucy Porter can be seen in the medieval St Chad's Church, which has a Norman tower. In the churchyard is a well in the place where St Chad used to baptise people in the 7th century. The ancient practice of well-dressing was revived at St Chad's in 1995 to celebrate the 50th anniversary of Christian Aid and is now an annual event.

Apart from the historic pleasure that Lichfield gives there is also plenty of parkland to enjoy and, in particular, the Beacon Park and Museum Gardens. The 75-acre Park encloses playing fields and a small boating lake and, in the Museum Gardens, can be found a statue of Commander John Smith, captain of the ill-fated Titanic, sculpted by Lady Katherine Scott, widow of Scott of the Antarctic.

Anna Seward, the landscaper of Minster Pool, is another of Lichfield's famous sons and daughters. She lived in the Bishop's Palace and was a poet and letter writer as well as being at the centre of a Lichfield-based literary circle in the late 18th century. Erasmus Darwin, the doctor, philosopher, inventor, botanist and poet, and the closest friend of Josiah Wedgwood, lived in a house in Beacon Street on the corner of The Close. The Erasmus Darwin centre, just three minutes from the Cathedral, is a fascinating place to visit, with touch-screen computers to access Darwin's writings and inventions and a garden where herbs and shrubs that would have been familiar to the doctor are grown. Erasmus was the grandfather of Charles Darwin, and had his own theories about evolution. David Garrick, probably the greatest actor-manager of the 18th-century theatre, had a home which stands opposite the west gate of the Cathedral.

Lichfield is a festival city, the premier event being the **Lichfield International Arts Festival** held in July.

MADELEY

Situated on an ancient packhorse route from Newcastle-under-Lyme, this village's name comes from the Anglo-Saxon 'maden lieg', which means 'clearing in the woods'. The focal point of this enchanting place, which has been designated a conservation area, is **The Pool**, formed by damming the River Lea to provide water power for the corn mill that still stands at its northern end. The pool is a haven for a variety of bird life. However, Madeley's grandest building is the **Old Hall**, an excellent

Madeley Old Hall

example of a 15th-century squire's timber framed residence. The village's large sandstone church can be seen through the trees from the mill pond. Standing in a raised churchyard, with ancient yew trees, All Saints Parish Church was originally Norman but was extensively enlarged in the 15th century; the chapel was rebuilt in 1872.

OAKAMOOR

This village was once the home of the Thomas Bolton & Sons copper works that produced some 20,000 miles of copper wire for the first transatlantic cable in 1856. Little now remains of the works, which were demolished in the 1960s, but the site of the mill has been turned into an attractive picnic site complete with the very large mill pond. Nearby **Hawksmoor Nature Reserve** and bird sanctuary covers some 300 acres of the Churnet Valley and is managed by a local committee. The trail through the Reserve includes glorious landscapes, abundant natural history and industrial architecture and it even goes over farmland to a riverside Victorian farm. A section of the 90-mile Staffordshire Way passes through the Reserve.

RUDYARD

In fond memory of the place where they first met in 1863, Mr and Mrs Kipling named their famous son, born in 1865, after this village. The nearby two mile long Rudyard Lake was built in 1831 by John Rennie to feed the Caldon Canal. With steeply wooded banks the lake is now a leisure centre where there are facilities for picnicking, walking, fishing and sailing. The west shore of the Reservoir is also a section of the Staffordshire Way, the long distance footpath which runs from Mow Cop to **Kinver Edge**, near Stourbridge This is a sandstone ridge covered in woodland and heath, and with several famous rock houses which were inhabited until the 1950s.

Back in Victorian days, Rudyard was a popular lakeside resort which developed after the construction of the North Staffordshire Railway in 1845. Its popularity became so great that, on one particular day in 1877, over 20,000 people came here to see Captain Webb, the first man to swim the English Channel, swim in the Reservoir.

SANDON

Near the village stands the ancestral home of the Earl of Harrowby, **Sandon Hall**. Rebuilt in 1850 after the earlier house had been damaged by fire, the Hall is surrounded by 400 acres of parkland which include a notable arboretum. The Hall is steeped in history and, along with the impressive interior, it makes an interesting and informative visit. The family too has led a fascinating life with no less than seven generations in parliament and three successive members of the family holding office in the Cabinet. The museum tells of their lives and also

includes costumes, toys and the duelling pistols of William Pitt the Younger. Open throughout the year, with many special events such as antiques fairs, craft shows and vintage car rallies, the Hall is also available for private events and functions.

SHALLOWFORD

Set in beautiful grounds in this tiny hamlet near Norton Bridge, **Izaak Walton's Cottage** is a pretty 17th-century half-timbered cottage which was once owned by Izaak Walton, famous biographer and author of *The Compleat Angler*. Walton bequeathed the cottage to Stafford Borough Council and it was subsequently transformed into the Museum found today. Fishing

Izaak Walton's Cottage

collections are on show, and there's a small souvenir shop. Within the grounds are an authentic 17th-century herb garden, a lovely picnic area and orchard. The Cottage is open daily Tuesday to Sunday and Bank Holidays from April to October. Shallowford Brook, which forms part of the River Meece, runs by Walton's Cottage and was a favourite angling haunt of the author.

STAFFORD

The Saxon origins of the county town of Staffordshire are still visible in the extensive earthworks close to the Castle and the foundations of a tiny chapel in the grounds of St Mary's Church. **Stafford Castle** is the impressive site of a Norman fortress, where visitors can follow the castle trail, wander around the medieval herb garden and explore the visitor centre built in the style of a Norman Guardhouse. The Castle grounds are often used for historical re-enactments by such groups as the Napoleonic Society and are the site for Sealed Knot battles as well as other outdoor entertainment. Stafford originally had a medieval town wall and evidence of it can still be seen today in the names of the town's main streets. However, only the **East Gate** remains of the structure. Stafford lies on the banks of the River Sow, and **Green Bridge** marks the site of the ancient ford across the river. There has been a bridge on this spot since the late 13th century but the gate in the town's medieval walls that was also at this point was demolished in 1777. Just to

Church Lane, Stafford

the east of the Bridge is **Victoria Park**, opened in 1908 and later extended to incorporate land reclaimed from the River Sow. There are many pleasant walks through the Park, which includes a mill pond and a weir, and, in particular, to the **Windmill at Broad Eye**. Built in 1796 by John Wright, the mill moved over to steam power in 1847 and continue to be used until 1880. Like many towns today, Stafford has its busy shopping streets and also an impressive shopping centre. However, many picturesque cobbled lanes still remain and provide the visitor with a quiet and relaxing contrast to the hurly burly of the 21st century. Of particular note are **Church Lane**, with its timbered buildings, and Mill Street with a varied array of shops, restaurants and pubs.

A place well worth visiting during any stay in Stafford is The **Ancient High House**, a beau-

tiful Elizabethan house built in 1595 that is in fact the largest timber-framed town house in England. Through

315

painstaking efforts over several years, Stafford Borough Council have restored this amazing piece of architecture to its former glory and, today, the building houses the Museum of Staffordshire Yeomanry and the Tourist Information Centre. The Ancient High House's varied history can be followed through the permanent displays in the period room settings taking the visitor through the 17th, 18th and 19th centuries and telling the stories of people who came to know this House so intimately. Not surprisingly, the house has royal connections, with both King Charles I and Prince Rupert having stayed here in 1642. The House also has a small heritage shop selling a variety of interesting and locally crafted gifts. The **Shire Hall Gallery** on the market square was the town courthouse and still retains the original panelled courtrooms. It is now a venue for contemporary exhibitions and children's workshops, and has a teashop and a workshop.

Close to the High House is the **Collegiate Church of St Mary**, an unusual building which dates, in part, from the late 12th century, but has received additions in the early English, Gothic and Victorian styles. The huge tower arches in the nave seem to divide the building into two, which is, in fact, exactly what they were intended to do, as St Mary's is two churches under one roof. The nave was the parish church of Stafford with its own altar while the chancel beyond was used by the Deans of the College of St Mary, whose duty it was to pray for deceased members of the Royal family. Although the College was abolished in 1548, the screens which divided the Church remained until 1841 and today the Church is still referred to as the Collegiate. Sir Izaak Walton was baptised here on 21st September 1593 and his bust can be seen on the north wall of the nave. Each year, at a civic service, a wreath is placed around the

Collegiate Church of St Mary

bust to commemorate his probable birthday (9th August). (Those interested in ecclesiastical architecture should also find time to visit the little Norman and medieval Church of St Chad.)

Best known today for his work *The Compleat Angler*, **Sir Izaak Walton** was famous throughout his lifetime as a writer of biographies. However, the story of his own life is somewhat obscure, though it is certain that he was born in Stafford in 1593. From humble origins, Walton became accepted in the intellectual and ecclesiastical circles of the day and, during the Civil War, he remained a staunch Royalist and stayed in the Stafford area. As might be expected Walton is associated with several buildings in the town though the house of his birth, in Eastgate Street, was demolished in 1888 and the site is now occupied by the Stafford Police Station.

In Staffordshire, as in many rural areas in the days before the first Divorce Court was established in 1857, the practice of selling a wife was the usual manner in which an unhappy marriage was ended. The practice followed a rigid pattern: the husband would accompany his wife to town, where he would pay a toll which gave him the right to sell merchandise, and he would parade his wife around the town extolling her virtues. An auction then followed and once a bid had been accepted, the husband would hand over the toll ticket as proof of ownership and the trio would retire to an inn to seal the deal. Prices ranged from a few old pence to as much as £1 and here, in 1800, it was recorded that a chimney sweep named Cupid Hodson sold his wife for 5 shillings and 6 pence (27½p).

St Mary's Mews dates back to the mid-19th century and is a Grade II listed building. The architect was the renowned Gilbert Scott, the famous church restorer of the 1850s. While visiting Stafford to do some work on St Mary's Church, Gilbert Scott was asked to design St Mary's schoolhouse.

STOKE-ON-TRENT

The city was established as late as 1910 when Fenton joined the five towns (Tunstall, Burslem, Hanley, Longton and Stoke) immortalised by the novels of Arnold Bennett. Once fiercely independent, the towns became progressively involved with each other as improvements in

roads, water supplies and other amenities forced them towards amalgamation. The new city's crest, of an ancient Egyptian potter at his wheel in one quarter, sums up the fortune on which the wealth of the area was created. Each of the old towns is also represented in the crest and the joint motto translates to "Strength is stronger for unity".

It was the presence of the essential raw materials for the manufacture and decoration of ceramics, in particular marl clay, coal and water, that led to the concentration of pottery manufacture in this area. Though production started in the 17th century it was the entrepreneurial skills of Josiah Wedgwood and Thomas Minton, who brought the individual potters together in factory-style workplaces, that caused the massive leap forward in production that took place in the 18th century. Their factories were large but there were also hundreds of small establishments producing a whole range of more utilitarian chinaware; production in The Potteries reached its height towards the end of the 19th century. For those interested in pottery and industrial architecture, Stoke-on-Trent is a wonderful place to visit, with many museums and factories open to the public to tell the story of the city. The **Spode Museum & Visitor Centre** in Church Street is one of several famous establishments open to visitors. For many, though, Stoke-on-Trent is best known for its football team, Stoke City, and for its local hero, the late Sir Stanley Matthews.

Hanley, one of the five towns of The Potteries, and part of the Stoke-on-Trent conurbation, was the birthplace of Arnold Bennett, Sir Stanley Matthews and John Smith (the captain of the ill-fated *Titanic*). The **Potteries Museum & Art Gallery** houses the world's finest collection of Staffordshire ceramics and offers many more attractions, including a natural history gallery and a lively programme of exhibitions, talks, tours and workshops. The Potteries shopping centre, situated in the heart of Hanley, is

The Potteries Museum & Art Gallery

317

every shopper's dream with a fantastic range of famous shops all brought together in a beautiful environment. Natural daylight cascades through the centre's many glazed roofs and plants, trees and water features create an outdoor feel.

Burslem, in the northern suburbs, is the home of the **Royal Doulton Visitor Centre**, which contains the world's largest display of Royal Doulton figures and many other treasures from the company's rich heritage. Factory tours, demonstrations, video-theatre, gallery, restaurant and shop. Another Burslem attraction is Ceramica, located in the Old Town Hall, with a huge kiln and an Arnold Bennett study area.

Etruria, to the west of the city centre, was created by Josiah Wedgwood in 1769 as a village for the workers at the pottery factory he built in this once rural valley. Though the factory has gone (it moved to Barlaston in the 1940s), Etruria Hall, Wedgwood's home, is still standing in what is now the National Garden Festival site. The pottery industry dominated the village, and the **Etruria Industrial Museum** displays a steam-powered potters' mill as well as other exhibits connected with the industry. Situated on the Trent and Mersey Canal, Etruria was also the point at which the Caldon Canal branches off to Froghall and Leek.

At Longton, two miles southeast of Stoke, the **Gladstone Working Pottery Museum** on Uttoxeter Road is a fascinating museum of the British pottery industry housed in a Victorian building. It tells visitors the story of how 19th-century potters worked, with the display of traditional skills, the original workshops, the cobbled yard and the huge bottle kilns creating a unique atmospheric time-warp. As the brochure proclaims: 'throwing, jiggering, fettling, saggar making, glazing, dipping, firing, painting, sponging, moulding, casting - it's all at Gladstone'. Aynsley China, John Tams and Staffordshire Enamels have their factory shops in Longton.

Three miles further southeast near Blythe Bridge station on the Stoke-Derby railway is a branch line built in 1893 to carry coal from Foxfield colliery. The colliery closed in 1965 but a section of the line was rescued by the Foxfield Light Railway Society. The delightful **Foxfield Steam Railway** is served by a number of ex-industrial tank engines hauling former British Railways carriages, including a bar and obser-

vation car called the Bass Belle.

A visit to The Potteries would not be complete without a visit to the **Wedgwood Visitor Centre and Museum**, five miles south of Stoke off the A34, set in a beautiful 500-acre country estate just outside Barlaston. The Museum traces the history of Wedgwood from the founding of the factory in 1759 to the present day through the displays of Queen's Ware, Jasper, Black Basalt and fine bone china. In rooms designed to recapture the style of specific periods there are hundreds of Wedgwood pieces from those eras. George Stubbs and Joshua Reynolds both painted portraits of the Wedgwood family which hang in the centre's art gallery. In the craft centre potters and decorators can be watched as they use traditional skills to create today's Wedgwood products. The centre is open every day.

TAMWORTH

A modern, busy town, Tamworth is actually much older than it first appears. Straddling the famous Roman Watling Street (now the A5), it has a fascinating and turbulent past. The first reference to the town dates back to the 8th century when it was the capital of the Kingdom of Mercia and the King, Offa, built his palace here. Raiding Danes managed to destroy the town

Tamworth Castle

twice and it was later invaded by the Scandinavians who left evidence of their visit in some of the street names such as Gungate.

Alfred's daughter, Ethelfleda, was busy here too and excavations in the town centre have revealed Saxon fortifications. Dominating Tamworth today is the fine Norman motte and bailey **Castle** set in the Pleasure Grounds which have truly magnificent floral terraces. The sandstone Castle, with its superb herringbone wall,

318

dates originally from the 1180s, having replaced a wooden tower on the present artificial mound constructed shortly after the Norman Conquest. A Saxon nun, Editha, is said to haunt Tamworth Castle. The story goes that when de Marmion took possession of his lands he expelled the nuns from a nearby convent. The order had been founded by Editha in the 9th century and the expelled nuns summoned her from her grave. Editha attacked de Marmion in his bedroom and, as a result of her severe beating, he restored the nuns to their home. The Parish Church of St Editha, founded in 963, is vast and was re-built after the Norman Conquest; then, again, after the Great Fire of Tamworth in 1345. The splendid 15th-century tower at the west end contains a most remarkable double staircase. The mixture of Victorian and modern stained glass found inside is surprisingly harmonious.

The **Town Hall**, built in 1701, is charming with open arches and Tuscan columns below. The building was paid for by Thomas Guy, the local Member of Parliament, who is probably more famous as the founder of the London hospital which bears his name. Thomas Guy also gave the town its 14 almshouses in Lower Gungate, which were rebuilt in 1913.

WESTON-UNDER-LIZARD

Sitated on the site of a medieval manor house, **Weston Park** has been the home of the Earls of Bradford for 300 years. Disraeli was a frequent visitor here and on one visit presented the house with a grotesque stuffed parrot. The parrot be-came famous when the present Earl, after leaving Cambridge, published a book entitled *My Private Parts and the Stuffed Parrot*. The stuffed parrot still enjoys the hospitality of Weston Park. The parkland at Weston has matured over several hundred years into a masterpiece of

Weston Park

unspoilt landscape. Many have left their mark, yet each successive generation has taken note of its predecessors. Disraeli loved the Park and, in one of his letters to Selina, 3rd Countess of Bradford, he refers to the 'stately woods of Weston'. There are some wonderful architectural features in the Park, including the Roman Bridge and the Temple of Diana, both designed and built by James Paine for Sir Henry Bridgeman in about 1760. Fallow deer and rare breeds of sheep roam the vast parklands and there are plenty of other interesting attractions for visitors of all ages including nature trails, a miniature railway and a Museum of Country Bygones.

WHITMORE

A delightful feudal village whose grandest building is **Whitmore Hall**, a splendid 17th-century country mansion built in rich red brickwork with stone dressings and a stone balustrade at the top. Whitmore has been the home of the Mainwaring family since Norman times and, strolling through the vast and ornately decorated rooms, visitors can trace the family's history from the portraits that have made the Hall famous. The Hall is open Tuesdays and Wednesdays from 2.00 pm–5.30 pm from May to August. The medieval **Church of St Mary and All Saints** is largely 12th-century, with extensive restoration in the 1880s. it is worth a visit just to see its unusual timber-framed clock tower, unique in this part of the county.

WILLOUGHBRIDGE

This remote hamlet, on the slopes of the Maer Hills, was once a fashionable spa after warm springs were discovered by Lady Gerard. Those days have long since gone but a trip to the **Dorothy Clive Garden** in the rolling countryside by the Shropshire border is well worth making. Designed in the 1930s by Colonel Harry Clive in memory of his wife, the original garden was a woodland garden created from a gravel pit that had become overgrown with all kinds of trees. The gardens have been extended considerably since and are a blaze of colour throughout the opening time of April to October. Among the different garden landscapes can be found many unusual and rare species, and a waterfall is among the many distinctive features.

The Admiral Rodney | 319

21 Dean Street,
Brewood,
Staffordshire
ST19 9BU
Tel: 01902 850583

Directions:

Take the A5 west
from Cannock
town centre for 5
miles, then turn
south at the
signpost for
Brewood

This old, picturesque inn was named after George Brydges Rodney, an admiral in the British Navy who became governor of Newfoundland between 1748 and 1751, and who later became an MP before being raised to the peerage. It is built of mellow red brick, with a handsome frontage that looks straight onto the street in the conservation village of Brewood (pronounced "Brood"). Terence and Anita Mellor have been tenants for over 14 years, and during that time have won many awards for the floral displays that adorn the frontage of **The Admiral Rodney** in the summer months.

The interior is charming, with open fires, attractive and comfortable furniture, and a wealth of brass and copper that positively gleams. Old oak beams adorn the ceilings, the floors are carpeted, and the whole place presents a charming picture of a bygone age when things moved at a less hectic pace. Here you can relax and stretch out as you enjoy a quiet drink in one of the best inns in this part of Staffordshire.

But why not have a meal as well? The Admiral Rodney has a roomy dining area that can seat 40, and the food is outstanding. There's a printed menu and a specials board that contain many popular dishes. The cuisine is good, honest traditional English, with hearty portions that are great value for money. And to accompany your meal you can have wine by the glass or bottle. Three real ales are available – Marston Pedigree, Abbot Ale and a rotating guest ale. You can also order Tetley Smoothflow, Stella, Carlsberg, Carlsberg Export, Guinness and Dry Blackthorn.

Opening times: Lunchtimes and evenings during the week, and all day on Saturday and Sunday

Food: Monday to Friday: 12.00-14.30 and 18.00-21.30; Saturday: 11.00-21.30; Sunday: 12.00-21.00 (booking is advisable for Sundays)

Credit cards: All major cards except American Express

Accommodation: None

Entertainment: Special themed food nights (ring for details)

Facilities: Car park; beer garden

Local Places of Interest/Activities: Stafford (historic town) 9 miles; Weston Park 5 miles; Cannock (historic town) 6 miles; Boscobel House 3 miles; Moseley Old Hall (NT) 4 miles

320 Bird In Hand Motel

Sandon Road,
Sharpley Heath,
near Hilderstone,
Staffordshire
ST15 8RG
Tel: 01889 505237

Directions:
The motel is at
Sharpley Heath,
close to Hilderstone

Nestling in some of the finest and most picturesque scenery in Staffordshire, but close to both Stafford and Stoke-on-Trent, you'll find the **Bird In Hand Motel**. It's the ideal base for exploring an area that is steeped in history, and it offers some of the best hospitality in the county. The building dates back to the 16th century, and was at one time a farmhouse and a brewery. It has been added to over the years, of course, and now one of its old barns has been converted into five beautifully appointed en suite rooms, with TVs and tea and coffee making facilities. Two of the rooms at at ground level.

The owners, Sharon and Ray D'Silva, make sure that the whole of the motel is just as welcoming and comfortable. There's a cozy bar and lounge, a restaurant that seats 76 people, a games room and a conservatory, and all are spotlessly clean and inviting. There's even a caravan and camping site adjoining the motel with six electric hook-ups, and a three acre lake, for which day and yearly fishing permits are available

Food can be ordered from the menu or from a daily specials board. Sharon does the cooking, and the cuisine varies from the traditionally English like steak pies and fish to curries and lasagnas. At Sunday lunchtime there's also a very popular carvery. Everything is cooked to order on the premises, and all the dishes represent astonishing value for money. At the bar, you can order from three real ales – Bass, Worthington and a locally brewed guest ale – as well as M&B Mild, Worthington Creamflow, Carling, Grosen, Scrumpy Jack and Guinness. Sharon and Ray have been in charge for only a short while, but already they've created a place that offers a warm welcome to everyone, including children. If you visit, you won't be disappointed.

Opening times: Monday to Saturday: 12.00-23.00; Sunday: 12.00-22.30

Food: Monday to Saturday: 12.00-15.00 and 18.00-20.30; Sunday: 12.00-15.00

Credit cards: All major cards accepted

Accommodation: 5 en suite rooms with TV and tea and coffee making facilities, and with a hearty breakfast included in the price

Entertainment: Live music every Friday and Saturday evening from 21.30, and once a month on Sunday evening from 19.30

Facilities: Car park; caravan and camping park; fishing lake; games room

Local Places of Interest/Activities: Stafford (historic town) 8 miles; Stoke-on-Trent (historic city) 8 miles; Shugborough Hall (NT) 9 miles; Izaak Walton's Cottage 6 miles; Wedgwood Visitors Centre 5 miles

Internet/website:
e-mail: sales@bird-in-handfsbusiness.co.uk
website: www.bird-in-hand.co.uk

The Blacksmiths Arms 321

Tythe Barn,
Alton,
Staffordshire
ST10 4AZ
Tel: 01538 702213
Fax: 01538 703225

Directions:
Alton is just off the
B5032, 4 miles east
of Cheadle

The Blacksmiths Arms is a substantial inn close to the famous Alton Towers Theme Park. One look at the building tells you it dates from many periods. In fact, some parts go right back to the 17th century, while others are no more than a few years old. It was once called the White Horse, and stood across the road from its present location. It's a mixture of modern brick and old stone, and sits off the road, with a large car park to the side of it.

It is owned and run by Dennis and Janet Power, who have been here for over twelve years. It was their first venture in the licensed trade, but so successful have they been that it is now a popular place for both locals and visitors to have a quiet drink or a meal. The inside has that traditional look about it - dark wood, solid beams and subdued lighting. The bar is warm and welcoming, with carpeted floors and a wealth of brass and copper. The large no smoking restaurant (the "Tythe Barn Restaurant") seats 80 in comfort, and is particularly attractive, with a large open fire and a tiled floor. The menu is wide ranging, with a selection of starters such as prawn cocktail and green shell mussels, and main courses such as steaks, venison, a mixed grill, salmon, scampi and chicken balti. Vegetarian dishes are available, and there's also a bar lunch menu, a children's menu and one for teens. All the food is freshly cooked to your liking, so don't expect fast food here! You can, of course, have wine with your meal, or, if you prefer, you can choose from one of the inn's three real ales, Bass, Worthington and a rotating guest ale. Or you can have Caffreys, lager, M&B Mild, Worthingtons Creamflow, Guinness and Strongbow.

Opening times: Tuesday to Friday: open lunchtimes and evenings; Monday: closed lunchtimes except during bank holidays; Saturday and Sunday: open all day

Food: Served Tuesday to Saturday 12.00-14.00 and 18.00-22.00; Monday: evenings only; Sunday: no food served after 21.30

Credit cards: All major cards accepted except American Express

Accommodation: None

Facilities: Car park; inn available for wedding receptions, parties etc.

Local Places of Interest/Activities: Alton Towers Theme Park 1 mile; Sudbury Hall (NT) 9 miles; Darley Moor (motor cycle racing) 6 miles; Croxden Abbey (ruins) 2 miles

Internet/Website:
www.theblacksmithsarmsalton.co.uk

322

The Boat Inn

170 Basford Bridge Lane,
Basford Bridge,
Cheddleton,
Staffordshire
ST13 7EQ
Tel: 01538 360683
*   or 01538 360035*

Directions:

Cheddleton is on the
A520, 7 miles north east
of Stoke-on-Trent

Think of a long, low building with stout walls of mellow stone. Think of small-paned windows, and hanging baskets and tubs that burst with colour in the summer months. Think also of the boat filled Calden Canal a few yards from its front door. That's **The Boat Inn**, a truly picturesque hostelry that speaks of a tradition of hospitality going back many years. It also has a charming setting, with a wooded area to the rear that frames it perfectly. The interior is equally as picturesque and inviting, with brick a fireplace, subdued lighting, comfortable furniture and a wealth of brass and copper ornaments dotting mantelpieces and shelves. Children are welcome, and under the personal supervision of Chris Massey and Andrew Monaghan, who have had many years's experience in the trade, it has become a popular place for a quiet, relaxing drink or a meal. In fact, it won the Restaurant Pub of the Year 2000 Award from the Sentinel newspaper, and has won other awards for its exterior.

Food is served in the 20 seat restaurant, in the bar, or in the summer months, outside in the beer garden. You can choose from a wide and varied menu. The dishes are all beautifully cooked on the premises, with the speciality of the house being juicy steaks with all the trimmings. Produce is sourced locally, and on Sunday there's a choice of roasts for your traditional Sunday lunch. You can have wine with your meal, or order a drink from the well stocked bar. Four real ales are available, Marstons Pedigree, Marstons bitter, Banks Original and a rotating guest ale. You can also order Mansfield Dark Mild, Fosters, Harp, Stella, Kronenberg, Guinness and Strongbow.

This is a lively and lovely canalside inn, popular with locals, motorists and those travelling on the water. If you visit, you'll get a real Staffordshire welcome from Chris and Andrew

Opening times: Open Monday to Friday at lunchtime and in the evening; open all day Saturday and Sunday

Food: Served Monday to Saturday 12.00-14.30 and 18.00-21.00; Sunday roasts are served 12.00-18.00, then reverting to main menu until 21.00

Credit Cards: All major cards accepted except American Express

Accommodation; None

Entertainment: Ring for details

Facilities: Car park; canalside beer garden

Local Places of Interest/Activities: North Staffordshire Railway 3 miles; Leek (historic town) 3 miles; Deep Hayes Country Park 1 mile; Flint Mill, Cheddleton 1 mile; Biddulph Grange (NT) 7 miles; Alton Towers 10 miles, Churnet Valley Railway Museum and Glencote Caravan Park both within walking distance.

The Butcher's Arms 323

Cheadle Road,
Forsbrook,
near Stoke-on-Trent
ST11 9AS
Tel: 01782 392531

Directions:
Forsbrook is just off
the A50 on the
A5212, 3 miles east
of Stoke-on-Trent
city centre

The Butcher's Arms is a picturesque inn which has all the looks of an ancient hostelry, with mock half timbering, bow windows and window boxes that are a riot of colour in the summer months. It sits right on the road, and turns many a passenger's head as cars drive past!

This is a real local - popular with both regulars and visitors alike. Gerry Hart and Chris Baines have been in charge for a number of years, and because they are local themselves, they take a great pride in ensuring that the inn is one of the best in the area. The bar and lounge are cozy, with oak beams, carpeted floors and comfortable furniture. Look out for one area in which you won't want to sit - the Old Git's Corner! The place boasts three real ales - Bass, Tetley and a rotating guest ale - plus Boddington, Bass Mild, Worthington Creamflow, Guinness, Carling Premier, Carling Black Label, Stella and Scrumpy Jack. There is also a good range of spirits, and if you fancy a meal, you can choose from a fine selection of wines.

The restaurant seats up to 38 people, and children are welcome. It is every bit as charming and cozy as the bar, and the food and the service are excellent - so much so that if you wish to eat here, you are well advised to book to avoid disappointment. You can choose from a printed menu or from a specials board, which changes daily. On offer are such dishes as steak and ale pie, braising steak in draught Bass, chicken pie, minted leg of lamb and rib eye steaks with all the trimmings. Everything is piping hot, the produce used is as fresh as possible, and it all represents astounding value for money.

Opening times: Open lunchtimes and evening from Monday to Friday, and all day Saturday and Sunday

Food: Served from 12.00-14.00 and 18.00-21.00 seven days a week, except Sunday, when no food is served in the evening

Credit Cards: Cash and cheques only at present

Accommodation; None

Entertainment: Live bands on Saturday evenings from 21.00; piano player and singer in the lounge on Sunday; quiz and "Open the Box" every Monday evening from 21.00

Facilities: Car park

Local Places of Interest/Activities: Croxden Abbey (ruins) 6 miles; Uttoxeter (historic town) 10 miles; Alton Towers Theme Park 7 miles; Stoke-on-Trent (historic city) 3 miles

324 The Draycott Arms

Cheadle Road,
Draycott-in
-the-Moors,
Staffordshire
ST11 9RQ
Tel: 01782 395595

Directions:

Take the A50 north west from Uttoxeter for 8 miles then turn north onto a minor road leading to Draycott-in-the-Moors

The Draycott Arms is a fine looking inn which occupies a corner site in the village. Made of neat, whitewashed brick, with full windows, it has an imposing presence, suggesting the best of hospitality. The building is old, with plenty of those period features which add just that touch of warmth and tradition to so many English inns.

Husband and wife team Sue and Michael Cunningham have been in charge for only a short time. However, they have lots of experience in the trade, and have great plans for the future. The interior is spotless, well decorated and comfortably furnished. There's bags of space, making this the kind of inn where you want to stretch out your legs and have a relaxing drink while the hurly and burly of modern life passes you by. The no smoking restaurant seats 26 people in absolute comfort, and is stylish and full of charm - the ideal place to have a leisurely meal. The inn's food is famous in the area, and it has a varied menu of home cooked, tasty dishes that are all prepared on the premises by the resident chef using fresh, local produce wherever possible. So popular is the place that for Friday and Saturday evening meals, booking is advisable to avoid disappointment. Wine is available to accompany your meal, of course, either by the bottle or glass, or you can choose from three real ales (Marston Pedigree, Martson Bitter or the rotating guest ale) that the bar offers. Or, if you prefer, you can have Mansfield Dark Mild, Guinness, lager, stout or cider.

Opening times: Open lunchtimes and evening 7 days of the week

Food: 12.00-14.00 and 18.00-21.30 six days. Sunday 12.00-20.30

Credit cards: All major cards accepted

Accommodation: None

Entertainment: Quiz night every Sunday at 20.30

Facilities: Car park

Local Places of Interest/Activities: Croxden Abbey (ruins) 5 miles; Uttoxeter (historic town) 8 miles; Alton Towers Theme Park 6 miles; Stoke-on-Trent (historic city) 7 miles

Internet/website:
www.draycottarms.co.uk
e-mail: draycottarms@hotmail.com

The Fox

325

105 High Street,
Dosthill,
Tamworth,
Staffordshire
B77 1LQ
Tel: 01827 280847

Directions:

Dosthill is a short drive from the centre of Tamworth on the A51 towards Coventry

This is an inn for real ale enthusiasts. It was voted CAMRA Pub of the Year in 1997, and has no less that seven real ales on offer - Tetleys and Ansells Mild, plus five rotating guest ales. It's a substantial, elegant building that dates from Victorian times, with a fine, well proportioned frontage that looks onto the road. Even if you're not a real ale enthusiast, **The Fox** has much to offer the discerning visitor. The inside is light and airy, with a carpeted lounge bar that is both comfortable and relaxing, and a restaurant at the rear that seats 40 in comfort. This restaurant is spacious, full of light and spotlessly clean, with gleaming cutlery, colourful serviettes on the tables and an atmosphere that speaks of friendly, efficient service. It welcomes children, and high chairs are available for toddlers.

The Fox has been managed for the last ten years by Sally Barrett and Ray Gwynne, and they've brought a standard of service and friendliness to the place that is hard to beat. Sally does the cooking, and you can choose from the printed menu or a daily specials board - all the dishes are freshly prepared on the premises. Sally likes to source good, fresh local produce wherever possible, which shows through in the quality of the inn's cuisine. Don't expect fast food at The Fox - Sally likes to ensure that every dish is cooked to perfection.

Apart from the range of real ales, The Fox also sells Tetley Smooth, Heineken, Carlsberg, Guinness and Stowford Press Cider. And if you wish to have wine with your meal, the comprehensive wine list is sure to please.

Opening times: 12.00-15.00 and 18.00-23.00(closed Monday lunchtime apart from bank holidays)

Food: Served Monday 18.30-21.30; Tuesday to Saturday 12.00-14.00 and 18.30-21.30; Sunday 12.00-14.00

Credit cards: All major credit cards accepted (except American Express)

Accommodation: None

Facilities: Car park

Local Places of Interest/Activities: Drayton Manor Theme Park 2 miles; Middleton Hall 4 miles; Ash End House Farm (children's farm) 4 miles; Lichfield (historic city) 7 miles; The Belfry(golf) 5 miles

326 | Greyhound Inn

Burston,
near Stafford,
Staffordshire
ST18 ODR
Tel: 01889 508263

Directions:

Burston is on the
A51, 3 miles south
of Stone

You can't go wrong if you pay a visit to the **Greyhound Inn** at Burston. This friendly inn is owned and run since 1973 by Alan and Joyce Jordan, who have created a hostelry full of old world charm that offers the best in English hospitality. It dates from the 17th century, when the building was two cottages, and only became an inn in the 19th century. It has been added to since, of course, and with its whitewashed walls and picturesque roadside setting, it is an ideal stopping off point for a relaxing drink or meal.

The interior is as appealing as the outside. There is a bar and lounge, and a spacious restaurant that can seat up to 75 people. The bar has three real ales on offer - Tetley, Bass and a rotating guest ale, plus you can choose from Tetley Smooth, Carlsberg, Stella, Guinness, Strongbow and Scrumpy Jack. Wine is also available, either by the glass or bottle.

If it's food you're after, you've come to the right place. There's a daily specials board, plus a printed menu that is outstanding. It contains many dishes that have become firm favourites with both locals and visitors alike, and everything is reasonably priced. You can choose from fish dishes, chicken, succulent steaks, Oriental food such as chicken tikka masala, Thai red chicken curry and lamb paitha, salads, pasta, and vegetarian. There's also a great selection of sweets, and a choice of coffees that will take your breath away! Traditional Sunday roasts are also served with all the trimmings, though you are advised to book a table at the weekends.

The inn is child friendly, and a separate menu is available for them, or you can just order smaller portions from the main menu.

Opening times: Open at lunchtimes and evenings and all day Sunday from 12.00

Food: Served Monday to Saturday from 12.00-14.30 and 18.30-22.00; served all day on Sunday

Credit cards: All cards accepted except Diners

Accommodation: None

Facilities: Car park; large beer garden

Local Places of Interest/Activities: Stafford (historic town) 5 miles; Stone (historic town) 3 miles; Shugborough Hall (NT) 7 miles; Izaak Walton's Cottage 3 miles

The Hollybush Inn — 327

Denford Road,
Denford,
near Leek,
Staffordshire
ST13 7JT
Tel: 01538 371819

Directions:

Take the A53 south from the centre of Leek for 2 miles, then turn left at Longsdon; Denford is signposted

What a lovely inn **The Hollybush Inn** is! It sits with the Caulden Canal to the front and the Leek branch of the canal to the rear, and is a favourite stopping point for people cruising the waters. Set in four acres of land, it was actually a cornmill before it became a pub. It is a whitewashed, picturesque building which dates originally from the early 17th century, with small-paned windows, a porch and an inn sign that incorporates a clock. The inside is delightful - everything an English inn should be. The floors are part quarry tiles, there are old oak beams, open fires, copper and brass ornaments, plenty of shire horse pottery on display, and comfortable seating. Children and pets are welcome. The restaurant area is roomy and well appointed, seating up to 20 people. You can also eat in the conservatory (which takes another 20 diners) plus you can eat elsewhere in the hostelry if you wish.

There is a printed menu and a specials board, and all the dishes are prepared in the inn's own kitchens from good fresh ingredients that are sourced locally if possible. Try the speciality of the house - home made beef and ale pie, or a dish that is famous in the area - the Hollybush grill. To accompany your meal, you can choose from a selection of wines, or you can order drinks from the bar. During the summer months, there are always six real ales on offer, and three in the winter, including Courage Best, Directors and Burton. Also available are John Smiths Smooth, Theakston's Mild, Fosters, Kronenberg, Strongbow and Guinness. The Hollybush Inn has been in the Prime family since 1979, and it has been owned by Steve and Linda since January 2000. A warm welcome awaits you if you visit their inn!

Opening times: Open all day, every day

Food: Served 7 days a week from 11.00-21.00 in the summer; 11.00-15.00 and 18.30-21.30 in winter

Credit Cards: Cash only at present; ring for updates

Accommodation: Two upstairs double rooms are available all year round, not en suite; breakfast is included in the tariff

Entertainment: Live entertainment every Thursday evening from 21.00

Facilities: Large car park; beer garden

Local Places of Interest/Activities: North Staffordshire Railway 2 miles; Leek (historic town) 3 miles; Deep Hayes Country Park 1 mile; Flint Mill, Cheddleton 2 miles; Biddulph Grange (NT) 6 miles

328 The Izaak Walton Inn

Cresswell Lane,
Cresswell,
near Stoke-on-Trent
ST11 9RE
Tel: 01782 392265

Directions:
Cresswell is 7 miles south east of Stoke-on-Trent city centre, just south of the A50

This is a picturesque inn, having a thatched roof, old, thick, whitewashed wall and a mass of hanging baskets, flower beds and window boxes. It is named, of course, after one of Staffordshire's most famous sons, Izaac Walton, who wrote "The Compleat Angler", and who was born in 1593.

The Izaak Walton Inn is a true hidden gem, and under the ownership of Anne and John Jenkinson, who have been here since December 2000, it has earned an enviable reputation as a place which offers a warm and friendly welcome, good food and good drink. The interior is warm and cozy in winter and cool in the summer, with a particularly appealing bar and lounge. There are also no smoking areas. The lighting is subdued, the woodwork gleams, there's an open fire, and pewter, brass and copper ornaments line the shelves. Downstairs there is seating for 50 people, while there are a further 25 places upstairs. You can choose a meal from a daily specials board or from the printed menu. Starters include soup, breaded mushrooms or prawn cocktail, and from the char grill you can have a mixed grill, a choice of steaks, fish, or chicken fillet. Other main courses include steak and mushrooms, Stilton and vegetable pie, chicken tikka masala or roast beef and Yorkshire pudding.

The wine list is sure to have something that appeals to you, or you can choose from a range of three real ales (Bass and two rotating ales), plus draught beer, lager, cider and stout. The inn also has a list of warm drinks which are available, such as decaffeinated coffee, mocha, cappuccino, café latte, espresso, tea or hot chocolate.

Opening times: Open all day, every day

Food: Available all day; On Monday and Tuesday 12.00-18.00 there are special meal deals

Credit Cards: All major cards accepted except American Express

Accommodation: None

Entertainment: Quiz night every Monday

evening from 20.30

Facilities: Car park

Local Places of Interest/Activities: Croxden Abbey (ruins) 5 miles; Uttoxeter (historic town) 8 miles; Alton Towers Theme Park 7 miles; Stoke-on-Trent (historic city) 7 miles

The Pheasant Inn 329

Old Road,
Stone,
Staffordshire
ST15 8HS
Tel: 01785 814603

Directions:

Stone is just off the
A34, 5 miles north
of Stafford; the inn
is north of the
main street

Stone is a small town that is filled with history. Monks established a priory here in the 12th century, though little of it now remains, and in 1771 the Trent and Mersey Canal reached the town, transforming its fortunes and making it one of the great Midlands canal towns. It still relies on the canal, though now it has been turned into a first class tourist amenity.

Just north of its main street, you'll find **The Pheasant Inn**, one of the most popular hostelries in the town. It is a handsome, well proportioned building that dates from the 18th century, and is in warm, red brick. Mine hosts are Simon and Lynn Burrell, who are local, and who know the area well. So if you're looking for places to visit, then they're the ones to ask! They took over the tenancy in early 2001, and have plans to improve the place even further. Simon does the cooking, and has put together a menu that contains many traditional English dishes that represent real value for money. You can choose from the main menu, a bar menu or from a selection of tasty snacks that range from sandwiches to jacket potatoes. Everything is beautifully prepared, and Simon takes a great pride in using only the freshest ingredients. He is also proud of the range of real ales on offer at the bar (so proud that he'll give you a tour of his cellar if you ask nicely). No less that five feature – Marston Pedigree, Banks Mild and three guest ales. You can also choose from a fine selection of beers, lagers, stout and cider.

The Pheasant Inn is a great place to have a meal or drink. It is comfortable and snug, and Simon and Lynn will give you a really warm welcome!

Opening times: Open all day, every day

Food: Served from 11.00-23.00, 7 days a week

Credit cards: Cash and cheques only at present

Accommodation: None

Entertainment: Occasional entertainment; ring for details; super league darts on a

Thursday evening

Facilities: Outdoor terrace; on-street parking

Local Places of Interest/Activities: Stafford (historic town) 7 miles; Shugborough Hall (NT) 9 miles; Izaak Walton's Cottage 4 miles; Wedgwood Visitors Centre 4 miles

330 | Railway Inn

Station Road,
Norton Bridge,
near Stone,
Staffordshire
ST15 0NT
Tel: 01785 760289

Directions:

Norton Bridge is 3 miles south west of Stone town centre, on the B5026

If you're looking for a charming inn that has great accommodation and good food and drink, then look no further than the **Railway Inn** at Norton Bridge. It sits in the midst of some lovely scenery, and is a four square, whitewashed building that dates from the 18th century. The front was added in the 19th century, and is well proportioned and handsome, with two large bay windows. The interior is equally as charming, with old, dark beams, low ceilings and open fires that throw a rosy glow over everything in the winter months. The whole place is cozy and inviting, and as soon as you step over the threshold you know that you'll get traditional hospitality coupled with friendly service and great value for money. The inn offers four rooms (2 doubles and two twins) all year round, and you can book in on a B&B or room only basis throughout the year.

Pamela Bebbington and Andrew Pearcey have been in charge since 2000, and they have created a place that strikes the right note with visitors and locals alike. If you want to eat, you can choose from a specials board or a printed menu, and you can have your meal in the no smoking restaurant or throughout the inn. The food is superb, and can best be described as traditional English. All the dishes are cooked on the premises using fresh produce that is sourced locally wherever possible. The Sunday lunches, where three roasts with all the trimmings are on offer, is especially popular, and you're advised to book for this. The bar stocks Marston Pedigree, Worthington cask and one other rotating guest ale, plus a selection of draught bitters, milds, ciders, lager and stout.

Opening times: Summer: all day, every day; winter: open from 15.30 Monday to Friday and all day Saturday and Sunday

Food: Served every day until 22.00

Credit cards: Cash and cheques only at present

Accommodation: 2 double and 2 twin rooms available all year; all are upstairs

Entertainment: Occasional entertainment at weekends; ring for details

Facilities: Car park; beer garden and play area; pub games

Local Places of Interest/Activities: Stafford (historic town) 6 miles; Stoke-on-Trent (historic city) 10 miles; Shugborough Hall (NT) 9 miles; Izaak Walton's Cottage 2 miles; Wedgwood Visitors Centre 6 miles

Royal Oak
331

Ivetsey Bank Road,
Bishop's Wood,
Staffordshire
ST19 9AE
Tel: 01785 840599

Directions:

Bishops Wood is 1 mile south of the A5, 9 miles west of Cannock

Within the pretty village of Bishop's Wood stands the **Royal Oak**. Mary Cochrane, who has lots of experience in the trade, has been mine host at this delightful hostelry since early 2001. Before taking over, she lived in the village for a number of years, so knows the inn well, and wants to turn it into one of the best hostelries in the area – a place renowned for its good food and drink and its cheerful atmosphere. She's well on the way to achieving this, and the place is well worth a visit if you fancy a relaxing drink or a meal.

The inn is housed in a charming whitewashed building that dates back to the mid 19th century. The bar offers three real ales, which are Marston Pedigree, Banks Bitter and a rotating guest ale. You can also order Mild, Carling, Fosters, Guinness and Scrumpy Jack.

The bar and snug are cozy and warm, with carpeted floors and comfortable, country style furniture. The non smoking restaurant area seats up to 32 in comfort, and is equally as picturesque as the rest of the inn, with prints on the walls and polished copper and brass ornaments hanging from the beams. Children under 14 are welcome in the restaurant, and diners can order from a menu which features many home made dishes and sweets that are sure to please. The cuisine is honest, traditional English fare, and the portions are hearty and amazing value for money. Sunday lunch is very popular and offers a variety of roasts, plus chicken, fish and a vegetarian dish, plus a range of starters and sweets.

Opening times: Lunchtimes and evenings, with some all day opening in summer; the inn is closed at lunchtimes on Monday, except for bank holidays

Food: Served 11.30-14.30 and 18.00-23.00

Credit cards: All major cards accepted

Accommodation: None

Entertainment: Special themed food nights once a month (usually Friday evenings); ring for details

Facilities: Car park

Local Places of Interest/Activities: Boscobel House 1 mile; White Ladies Priory 2 miles; Weston Park 2 miles

332

The Swan

Lichfield Road,
Draycott-in-
the-Clay,
near Ashbourne,
Staffordshire
DE6 5GZ
Tel: 01283 820031

Directions:

Take the A50 east
from Uttoxeter for
5 miles, then turn
south onto the
A515. The village is
two miles along
this road

A former coaching inn dating partly from the 16th century - solid walls - low, beamed ceilings - an open fireplace with logs stacked beside it - gleaming brass and ornaments - good food and drink - what more could you want? **The Swan** has the lot, and then some. Husband and wife team Paul and Wendy Weston have been managing the inn since October 2000, though they've been in the trade for over 17 years. They have created what must be one of the most delightful hostelries in the whole of Staffordshire – one that draws people from far and near.

Set in some wonderfully picturesque countryside, it speaks of history, tradition and a warm welcome to weary travellers. The place is floored in parquet and marble tiles, with carpeting in the restaurant, lounge and conservatory. The seating is comfortable, with plenty of room to stretch your legs. On offer at the bar are three real ales - Marston's Pedigree, Bass and a rotating guest ale. There's also Carling, Stella, Guinness and cider, plus a wide range of wines and spirits. The food, cooked on the premises by Paul, is an excellent mix of modern and traditional, which you choose from a comprehensive menu. In addition to starters such as soup, garlic mushrooms or a prawn and pineapple platter, there are all day breakfasts, juicy steaks, jacket potatoes, gammon steaks, lasagna, fish, burgers and omelettes. Cold platters are also available, as are vegetarian dishes and a selection of sweets. Meals can be served in a spacious conservatory, which has views across open countryside or down into the village, and behind the inn is a three acre field that can take caravans or tourers. Children are welcome.

Opening times: Open all day, every day

Food: Served between 12.00-21.00 every day; booking is advisable for Saturday evening and Sunday lunchtime; regular steak nights are planned; phone for details

Credit cards: Most credit cards except American Express

Accommodation: Field for caravans and tourers

Entertainment: Occasional quiz night or live entertainment; phone for details

Facilities: Car park; conservatory; three acre field for caravans and tourers

Local Places of Interest/Activities: Sudbury Hall (NT) 2 miles; Uttoxeter (horse racing) 5 miles; Tutbury Castle (ruined) 4 miles; Blithfield Reservoir (sailing and fishing) 6 miles

The Swan Inn

Fradley Junction,
Alrewas,
near Burton-
upon-Trent,
Staffordshire
DE13 7DN
Tel: 01283 790330

Directions:

Take the A38 south from Burton-upon-Trent for 7 miles. Alrewas is just off the road, to the west. Fradley Junction is 2 miles south of Alrewas

Two miles south of Alrewas, at Fradley Junction, where the Trent and Mersey Canal and the Coventry Canal meet, you'll find the **Swan Inn** (known affectionately as "The Mucky Duck" among the locals). It is a charming Grade 2 listed building of whitewashed, red brick, and was originally constructed to serve the workmen that dug the canals over 200 years ago. It sits in a conservation area, and is part of a picturesque row of buildings located only a few yards from the canal banks. The interior is snug and full of character, having vaulted, brick ceilings held up by pillars, comfortable furniture and subdued wall lighting.

Jacqueline Burton, the former assistant manager of the Swan Inn, is in charge, along with Jason Parker, the full time chef. Together they are working hard to create a warm and welcoming inn that serves good food and drink to locals and visitors alike. Three real ales are on offer at the bar - Ansells, Marstons Pedigree and Burton, and in the summer there's a fourth guest ale. Also on offer are Ansells mild, Carlsberg, Stella, Strongbow and Guinness. There is also a small wine list which is sure to contain something to your liking.The menu is wide ranging, and includes some excellent starters, fish dishes and vegetarian dishes, as well as main courses that include steak and kidney pie, sirloin, chicken Kiev, lasagna, gammon steaks and a superb mixed grill. You can also buy jacket potatoes, filled rolls and salad. Children are catered for in the children's menu. At Sunday lunchtime, the Sunday roast takes the place of the normal menu, though you are advised to book in advance for it.

Opening times: Open Monday to Saturday 11.00-15.00 and 18.00-23.00; open Sunday 12.00-14.30 and 19.00-22.30

Food: Served Monday to Saturday 12.00-14.00 and 18.30-21.00; served Sunday 12.00-14.00 and 19.00-21.00

Credit cards: All major credit cards accepted

Accommodation: None

Local Places of Interest/Activities: Burton-upon-Trent (historic town) 7 miles; Staffordshire Regimental Museum 5 miles; Lichfield (historic city) 5 miles

334 Vaughan Arms

Bickford Road,
Lapley,
near Stafford,
Staffordshire
ST19 9JU
Tel: 01785 840325

Directions:
Lapley is 7 miles
northwest of
Cannock and 1
mile north of the
A5

The food and drink at the **Vaughan Arms** is outstanding, and it is well worth seeking out the hidden inn for this alone. The cuisine can best be described as restaurant food at pub prices, and the inn has a menu that includes many favourite dishes, all of which are beautifully prepared and presented. You can have a choice of starters, followed by curries, chicken, fish, vegetarian, steak and kidney pies, salads, sandwiches, and a host of other dishes that are sure to make anyone's mouth water. The speciality of the house, however, is thick, juicy steaks with all the trimmings, and these are especially popular at Sunday lunchtime, when roasts are also served. The food is cooked to your own requirements, so this is no fast food outlet. This makes an eating experience at the Vaughan Arms something special! Children are welcome, though you are advised to book if you wish to eat on Saturday evening or Sunday lunchtime.

The inn itself is situated in a charming and picturesque village, and is a delightful building. The walls are whitewashed, and creepers grow up the walls and over the door. It dates from the early 1800s, and was formerly two cottages before becoming an inn in 1895, the name being taken from a former lord of the manor. In charge are Ray and Christine Bailey, and they have preserved many period details within the pub. There is snug, comfortable seating, open fires and polished brass, creating the ideal atmosphere in which to have a meal or a quiet drink.

No less than six real ales are available at the bar, three of which are rotating guest ales from all over the country. You can also choose from a range of draught lagers, stout and cider, plus wine is available by the glass or bottle.

Opening times: Open during lunchtimes and evenings seven days a week; closed Monday lunchtime, except on bank holidays

Food: Monday: 16.30-21.30; Tuesday to Friday: 12.00-14.00 and 16.30-21.30; Saturday: 12.00-14.00 and 19.00-21.00; Sunday: 12.00-14.00

Credit cards: Cash and cheques only at present

Accommodation: None

Entertainment: Jazz evening on the 1st Tuesday of the month; charity quiz on 2nd and 4th Tuesday evenings of the month

Facilities: Car park; small patio

Local Places of Interest/Activities: Stafford (historic town) 7 miles; Weston Park 4 miles; Cannock (historic town) 7 miles; Boscobel House 4 miles; Moseley Old Hall (NT) 7 miles

ALPHABETIC LIST OF INNS 335

ALPHABETIC LIST OF INNS

ALPHABETIC LIST OF INNS | 339

340 ACCOMMODATION

ACCOMMODATION

342

ALL DAY OPENING

ALL DAY OPENING

The Red Admiral	Codnor, Derbyshire	208
The White Swan	Hilton, Derbyshire	215

NORTHEAST DERBYSHIRE & THE AMBER VALLEY

The Apollo Inn	Balborough, Derbyshire	227
The Bear Inn and Hotel	Alderwasely, Derbyshire	228
Bulls Head	Old Whittington, Derbyshire	230
The Clock Inn	South Normanton, Derbyshire	231
The Duke of Devonshire	Belper, Derbyshire	234
The Excavator	Buckland Hollow, Derbyshire	236
The Greyhound Inn	Pinxton, Derbyshire	237
Hardwick Inn	Hardwick Park, Derbyshire	238
Hare and Hounds	Stone Gravels , Derbyshire	239
Hearts of Oak	Dronfield Woodhouse, Derbyshire	240
The Hurt Arms	Ambergate, Derbyshire	241
Jolly Farmers	Holmewood, Derbyshire	242
The Pebley Inn	Balborough, Derbyshire	245
The Railway	Belper, Derbyshire	246
The Railway	Shottle, Derbyshire	247
The Royal Oak Inn	Old Tupton, Derbyshire	248
Winsick Arms	Hasland, Derbyshire	252

THE PEAK DISTRICT AND DERBYSHIRE DALES

The Anchor	Tideswell, Derbyshire	273
Biggin Hall	Biggin, Derbyshire	275
Croft Country House Hotel	Great Longstone, Derbyshire	279
The Devonshire Arms	Beeley, Derbyshire	280
The George Hotel	Youlgreave, Derbyshire	282
The Hollybush Inn	Grangemill, Derbyshire	283
The Little John	Hathersage, Derbyshire	286
The Oddfellows Arms	Whitehough, Derbyshire	289
The Peacock Hotel	Rowsley, Derbyshire	290
Plough Inn	Two Dales, Derbyshire	291
The Red Lion	Bakewell, Derbyshire	292
The Roebuck	Chapel-en-le-Frith, Derbyshire	294
The Shepherds Arms	Whaley Bridge, Derbyshire	295
Sir William Hotel	Grindleford, Derbyshire	296
The Sycamore	Birch Vale, Derbyshire	298
The Victoria Inn	Hadfield, Derbyshire	299
Ye Old Cheshire Cheese Inn	Castleton, Derbyshire	301

STAFFORDSHIRE

Bird In Hand Motel	Sharpley Heath, Staffordshire	320
The Hollybush Inn	Denford, Staffordshire	327
The Izaak Walton Inn	Cresswell, Staffordshire	328
The Pheasant	Stone , Staffordshire	329
Railway Inn	Norton Bridge, Staffordshire	330
The Swan	Draycott-in-the-Clay, Staffordshire	332

CHILDRENS FACILITIES | 345

NORTHEAST DERBYSHIRE & THE AMBER VALLEY

The Apollo Inn	Balborough, Derbyshire	227
The Devonshire Arms	Upper Langwith, Derbyshire	232
The Duke of Devonshire	Belper, Derbyshire	234
The Hurt Arms	Ambergate, Derbyshire	241
Jolly Farmers	Holmewood, Derbyshire	242
Kelstedge Inn	Kelstedge, Derbyshire	243
The Railway	Shottle, Derbyshire	247
The Royal Oak Inn	Old Tupton, Derbyshire	248
The White Hart Inn	Heage, Derbyshire	250
Winsick Arms	Hasland, Derbyshire	252

THE PEAK DISTRICT AND DERBYSHIRE DALES

The Anchor	Tideswell, Derbyshire	273
The Cock Inn	Clifton, Derbyshire	278
The Hollybush Inn	Grangemill, Derbyshire	283
The Ketch	Kniverton, Derbyshire	285
The Miners Arms	Carsington, Derbyshire	288
Plough Inn	Two Dales, Derbyshire	291
The Sycamore	Birch Vale, Derbyshire	298
The Victoria Inn	Hadfield, Derbyshire	299

STAFFORDSHIRE

Railway Inn	Norton Bridge, Staffordshire	330

346   CREDIT CARDS ACCEPTED

CREDIT CARDS ACCEPTED | 347

RUTLAND

The Black Bull	Market Overton, Rutland	106
The Fox and Hounds	Kossington, Rutland	107
The Horse and Panniers	North Luffenham, Rutland	109
The Kingfisher	Preston, Rutland	110
The Noel Arms	Whitwell, Rutland	111
The Odd House	Oakham, Rutland	112
The Old Plough Inn	Braunston-in-Rutland, Rutland	113
The Sun Inn	Cottesmore, Rutland	114
The Wheatsheaf Inn	Longham, Rutland	116

NOTTINGHAMSHIRE

Angel Inn	Kneesall, Nottinghamshire	136
Brownlow Arms	High Marnham, Nottinghamshire	138
The Dog and Duck	Old Clipstone, Nottinghamshire	140
Three Horseshoes	East Leake, Nottinghamshire	142
The Manvers Arms	Radcliff-on-Trent, Nottinghamshire	143
The Manor Arms	Elton, Nottinghamshire	144
Martins Arms Inn	Colston Basset, Nottinghamshire	145
Plough Inn	Cropwell Butler, Nottinghamshire	148
The Red Hart Hotel	Blyth, Nottinghamshire	151
The Shepherds Rest	Lower Bagthorpe, Nottinghamshire	153
The Unicorns Head	Langar, Nottinghamshire	156
The White Lion	Huthwaite, Nottinghamshire	157

LINCOLNSHIRE

The Bird In The Barley	Messingham, Lincolnshire	174
The Five Bells	Claypole, Lincolnshire	178
The George Hotel	Leadenham, Lincolnshire	179
The Nags Head	Helpringham, Lincolnshire	182
The Old Farmhouse Hotel	Stallingborough, Lincolnshire	183
Plough Inn	Horbling, Lincolnshire	184
Thorold Arms	Harmston, Lincolnshire	185
Wheatsheaf Hotel	Swineshead, Lincolnshire	186

SOUTH DERBYSHIRE

The Bulls Head	Hartshorne, Derbyshire	200
The Castle Hotel	Hatton, Derbyshire	201
The Coach and Horses	Draycott, Derbyshire	202
Navigation Inn	Overseal, Derbyshire	205
New Inn	Woodville, Derbyshire	206
The Punchbowl	West Hallam, Derbyshire	207
The Red Admiral	Codnor, Derbyshire	208
Red Lion	Linton, Derbyshire	209
Spotted Cow Inn	Holbrook, Derbyshire	210
The Three Horseshoes	Morley Smithey, Derbyshire	212
Vernon Arms	Sudbury, Derbyshire	214
The White Swan	Hilton, Derbyshire	215

348 | CREDIT CARDS ACCEPTED

GARDEN, PATIO OR TERRACE 349

WARWICKSHIRE

The Bear	Long Lawford, Warwickshire	17
The Boot Inn	Ansley Village, Warwickshire	20
The Bridge	Napton, Warwickshire	21
The Cock Horse Inn	Rowington, Warwickshire	22
The Gaydon Inn	Gaydon, Warwickshire	24
The Great Western	Southam, Warwickshire	25
The Stags Head	Offchurch, Warwickshire	28

NORTHAMPTONSHIRE

The Bull's Head	Clipston, Northamptonshire	42
The Carpenters Arms	Lower Boddington, Northamptonshire	43
The Coach and Horses	Brixworth, Northamptonshire	44
The Eastcote Arms	Eastcote , Northamptonshire	47
The Fox Inn	Wilbarston, Northamptonshire	48
The Lamb Inn	Little Harrowden, Northamptonshire	51
The Montagu Arms	Barnwell, Northamptonshire	52
The Red Lion	Hellidon, Northamptonshire	58
Rose and Crown	Oundle, Northamptonshire	59
Rose and Crown	Yardley Hastings, Northamptonshire	60
The Royal Oak	Naseby, Northamptonshire	61
The Royal Oak	Walgrave, Northamptonshire	62
The Sun Inn	Whitfield, Northamptonshire	63
Tollemache Arms	Harrington, Northamptonshire	65
The Wharf	Welford, Northamptonshire	66
The Windmill	Badby, Northamptonshire	67
The Woolpack Inn	Islip, Northamptonshire	68

LEICESTERSHIRE

The Black Horse	Hose, Leicestershire	79
The Carington Arms	Ashby Folville, Leicestershire	80
The Coach and Horses	Lubenham, Leicestershire	81
The Delisle Arms	Shepstead, Leicestershire	83
The Fox Inn	Hallaton, Leicestershire	84
The Golden Fleece	South Croxton, Leicestershire	86
The Navigation Inn	Barrow upon Soar, Leicestershire	91
The Old Barn Inn	Glooston, Leicestershire	92
The Plough Inn	Diseworth, Leicestershire	94
The Queens Head	Heather, Leicestershire	95
The Red Lion	Great Bowden, Leicestershire	96
The Saddle	Twyford, Leicestershire	97
The Stag and Hounds	Burrough-on-the-Hill, Leicestershire	99
Wheatsheaf Inn	Woodhouse Eaves, Leicestershire	100

RUTLAND

The Fox and Hounds	Kossington, Rutland	107
The Horse and Panniers	North Luffenham, Rutland	109
The Kingfisher	Preston, Rutland	110

350 GARDEN, PATIO OR TERRACE

GARDEN, PATIO OR TERRACE 351

THE PEAK DISTRICT AND DERBYSHIRE DALES

STAFFORDSHIRE

352   _LIVE ENTERTAINMENT_

LIVE ENTERTAINMENT **353**

NORTHEAST DERBYSHIRE & THE AMBER VALLEY

The Apollo Inn	Balborough, Derbyshire	227
Bulls Head	Old Whittington, Derbyshire	230
The Clock Inn	South Normanton, Derbyshire	231
The Greyhound Inn	Pinxton, Derbyshire	237
Hare and Hounds	Stone Gravels , Derbyshire	239
Hearts of Oak	Dronfield Woodhouse, Derbyshire	240
Jolly Farmers	Holmewood, Derbyshire	242
The Pebley Inn	Balborough, Derbyshire	245
The Railway	Belper, Derbyshire	246
The Summit	Shirebrook, Derbyshire	249

THE PEAK DISTRICT AND DERBYSHIRE DALES

Beehive	Glossop, Derbyshire	274
Chinley Lodge	Chinley, Derbyshire	276
The George and Dragon	Ashbourne, Derbyshire	281
The Miners Arms	Carsington, Derbyshire	288
The Oddfellows Arms	Whitehough, Derbyshire	289
The Shepherds Arms	Whaley Bridge, Derbyshire	295
Sir William Hotel	Grindleford, Derbyshire	296
The Sycamore	Birch Vale, Derbyshire	298
The Victoria Inn	Hadfield, Derbyshire	299

STAFFORDSHIRE

Bird In Hand Motel	Sharpley Heath, Staffordshire	320
The Butcher's Arms	Forsbrook, Staffordshire	323
The Hollybush Inn	Denford, Staffordshire	327
The Swan	Draycott-in-the-Clay, Staffordshire	332

354   RESTAURANT/DINING AREA

Hidden Inns Reader Reaction

The *Hidden Inns* research team would like to receive reader's comments on any visitor attractions or places reviewed in the book and also recommendations for suitable entries to be included in the next edition. This will help ensure that the *Hidden Inns* series continues to provide its readers with useful information on the more interesting, unusual or unique features of each attraction or place ensuring that their stay in the local area is an enjoyable and stimulating experience.

To provide your comments or recommendations would you please complete the forms below and overleaf as indicated and send to:

The Research Department, Travel Publishing Ltd,
7a Apollo House, Calleva Park, Aldermaston, Reading, RG7 8TN.

Your Name:

Your Address:

Your Telephone Number:

Please tick as appropriate: Comments ☐   Recommendation ☐

Name of *"Hidden Place"*:

Address:

Telephone Number:

Name of Contact:

Hidden Inns Reader Reaction

Comment or Reason for Recommendation:

....

....

....

....

....

....

....

....

....

....

....

....

....

Hidden Inns Order Form

To order any of our publications just fill in the payment details below and complete the order form *overleaf*. For orders of less than 4 copies please add £1 per book for postage and packing. Orders over 4 copies are P & P free.

Please Complete Either:

I enclose a cheque for £ [   ] made payable to Travel Publishing Ltd

Or:

Card No: [   ]

Expiry Date: [   ]

Signature: [   ]

NAME: [   ]

ADDRESS: [   ]

POSTCODE: [   ]

TEL NO: [   ]

Please either send or telephone your order to:

Travel Publishing Ltd   Tel : 0118 981 7777
7a Apollo House   Fax: 0118 982 0077
Calleva Park
Aldermaston
Berks, RG7 8TN

The Hidden Inns of the Heart of England

	PRICE	QUANTITY	VALUE
Hidden Places Regional Titles			
Cambs & Lincolnshire	£7.99	....	....
Chilterns	£8.99	....	....
Cornwall	£8.99	....	....
Derbyshire	£7.99	....	....
Devon	£8.99	....	....
Dorset, Hants & Isle of Wight	£8.99	....	....
East Anglia	£8.99	....	....
Gloucestershire & Wiltshire	£7.99	....	....
Heart of England	£7.99	....	....
Hereford, Worcs & Shropshire	£7.99	....	....
Highlands & Islands	£7.99	....	....
Kent	£8.99	....	....
Lake District & Cumbria	£7.99	....	....
Lancashire & Cheshire	£8.99	....	....
Lincolnshire	£8.99	....	....
Northumberland & Durham	£8.99	....	....
Somerset	£7.99	....	....
Sussex	£7.99	....	....
Thames Valley	£7.99	....	....
Yorkshire	£7.99	....	....
Hidden Places National Titles			
England	£9.99	....	....
Ireland	£9.99	....	....
Scotland	£9.99	....	....
Wales	£11.99	....	....
Hidden Inns Titles			
Central and Southern Scotland	£5.99	....	....
Heart of England	£5.99	....	....
South East England	£5.99	....	....
South of England	£5.99	....	....
Wales	£5.99	....	....
West Country	£5.99	....	....
WelshBorders	£5.99	....	....
Yorkshire	£5.99	....	....
TOTAL		____	____

For orders of less than 4 copies please add £1 per book for postage & packing. Orders over 4 copies P & P free.